The Life and Death of
ROBERT DEVEREUX
EARL OF ESSEX

By the Same Author

AN ELIZABETHAN JOURNAL, 1591–1594
A SECOND ELIZABETHAN JOURNAL, 1595–1598
A LAST ELIZABETHAN JOURNAL, 1599–1603
SHAKESPEARE UNDER ELIZABETH
SHAKESPEARE'S FELLOWS
JOHN BUNYAN: A STUDY IN PERSONALITY

Editor of:

THE LETTERS OF QUEEN ELIZABETH
THE BODLEY HEAD QUARTOS
THE CHURCH BOOK OF BUNYAN MEETING
THE EARL OF NORTHUMBERLAND'S ADVICE TO HIS SON
THE TRIAL OF THE LANCASTER WITCHES
A COMPANION TO SHAKESPEARE STUDIES (WITH HARLEY GRANVILLE-BARKER)
DE MAISSE'S JOURNAL (WITH R. A. JONES)

ROBERT DEVEREUX, EARL OF ESSEX

Reproduced by courtesy of the Council of Trinity College, Cambridge, England.

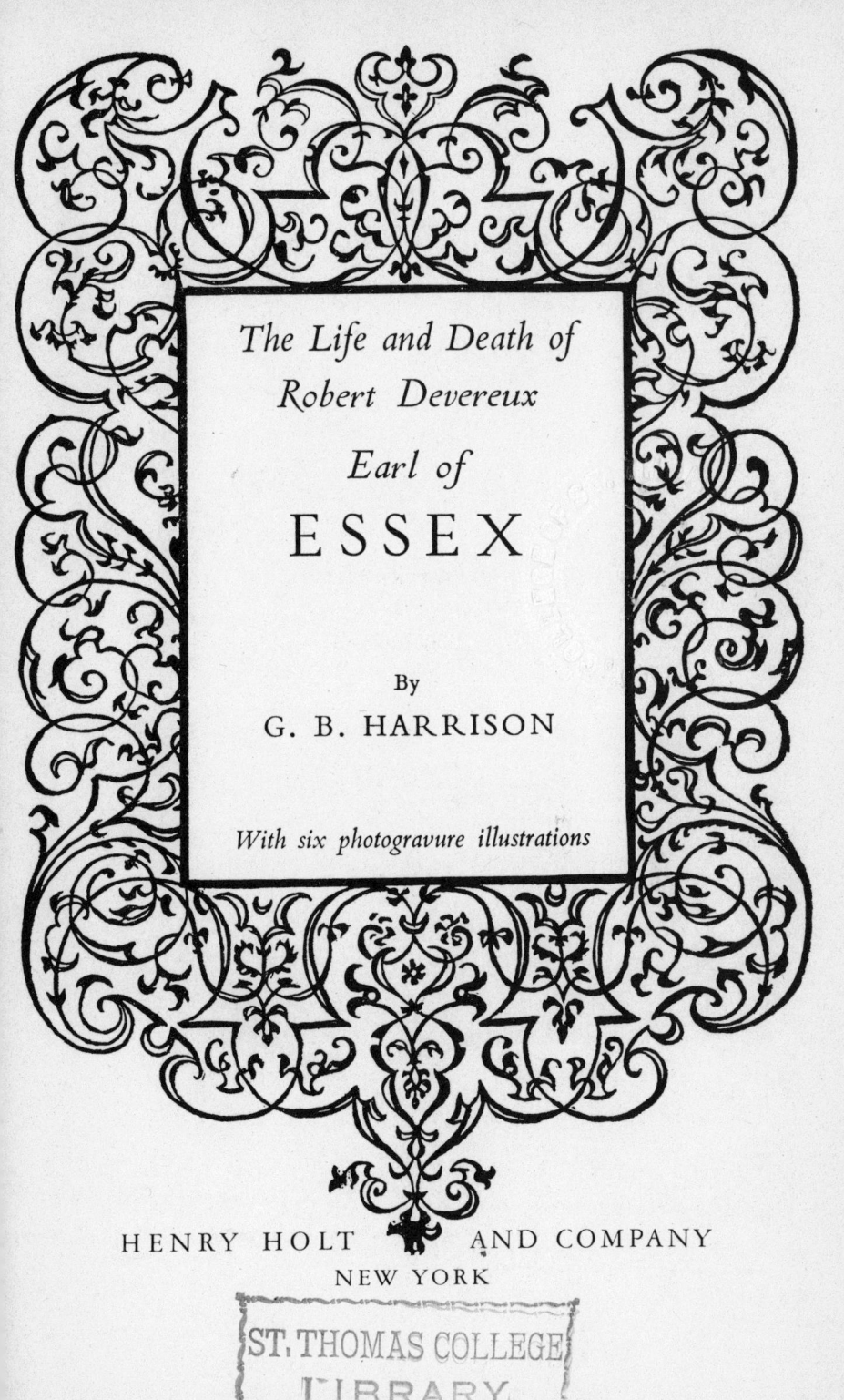

The Life and Death of
Robert Devereux
Earl of
ESSEX

By
G. B. HARRISON

With six photogravure illustrations

HENRY HOLT AND COMPANY
NEW YORK

Copyright, 1937
by
G. B. HARRISON

PRINTED IN THE UNITED STATES OF AMERICA

TO
HELEN WADDELL

PREFACE

DR. JOHN HAYWARD, in the book which brought so much trouble upon his head, observed in his Preface to the Reader: "Among all sort of human writers there is none that have done more profit or deserved greater praise than they who have committed to faithful records of Histories, either the government of mighty States or the lives and acts of famous men; for by describing the order and passages of these two, and what events have followed what counsels, they have set forth unto us not only precepts but lively patterns, both for private direction and for affairs of state."

Although few men made greater stir in their own generation, and in so many ways affected the lives and emotions of their fellow-men in the spectacle of their rise and fall, only two considerable biographies of Robert Devereux, Earl of Essex, have been written in the last ninety years—by Walter Bourchier Devereux in 1853, and by Lytton Strachey in *Elizabeth and Essex* in 1928. The chief source for any biography is the collection of Cecil Papers at Hatfield House; these were not available to Devereux, nor much used by Strachey. There would therefore seem to be room for another attempt to tell again the story of the life and death of Robert Devereux.

I wish to express my thanks and gratitude to those who have in various ways helped me: to the Most Honourable the Marquis of Salisbury for permitting me to consult the Salisbury Papers, and to Mr. J. A. Lyle, the Librarian at Hatfield; to Mr. H. M. Hake, Director of the National Portrait Gallery, and to Mr. S. George West, who spent much labour in comparing the many portraits of Essex; to the Master and Fellows of Trinity College, Cambridge, for permission to reproduce the portrait of Essex used as frontispiece; to Mr. D. C. Collins, Mr. S. H. Atkins, and Miss Hazel Rowe.

CONTENTS

CHAPTER		PAGE
I.	ROBERT DEVEREUX, EARL OF ESSEX	1
II.	FIRST LESSONS IN STATECRAFT	8
III.	THE ROYAL FAVOURITE	23
IV.	THE PORTUGAL VOYAGE	36
V.	FIRST COMMAND	45
VI.	COURTIER AND STATESMAN	69
VII.	WARLIKE PREPARATIONS	93
VIII.	THE CADIZ VOYAGE	108
IX.	AFTER CADIZ	125
X.	THE ISLANDS VOYAGE	142
XI.	A TRIAL OF STRENGTH	168
XII.	DANGEROUS COURSES	183
XIII.	THE IRISH EXPEDITION	211
XIV.	THE ECLIPSE	248
XV.	THE REBELLION	276
XVI.	THE TRIAL	294
XVII.	THE END	315
	THE COMMENTARY	326
	INDEX	351

LIST OF ILLUSTRATIONS

ROBERT DEVEREUX, EARL OF ESSEX . . . *Frontispiece*

TO FACE PAGE

MAP OF CADIZ 112

LETTER WRITTEN TO LORD BURGHLEY AFTER THE SUCCESS AT
    CADIZ 126

MAP OF THE AZORES 160

ESSEX IN 1600 240

MAP OF LONDON IN 1601 . . , . . 288

CHAPTER I

ROBERT DEVEREUX, EARL OF ESSEX

ABOUT noon on Saturday, September 22, 1576, in the Castle of Dublin, died Walter Devereux, Earl of Essex, Earl of Ewe, Viscount Hereford, Lord Ferrers of Chartley, Bourchier and Lovaine, Knight of the Most Honourable Order of the Garter and Earl Marshal of Ireland. He was aged thirty-six. His life had latterly been full of disappointments, and his end was very painful.

This Walter Devereux was the eldest son of Sir Richard Devereux and grandson of Walter Devereux, created Viscount Hereford in 1550. Sir Richard died in 1547, Walter succeeded his grandfather in 1558. Some four years later, he married the Lady Lettice Knollys, daughter of Sir Francis Knollys and his wife Mary, who was the sister of Anne Boleyn. The Lady Lettice was thus cousin to Queen Elizabeth, and one of the first of her maids of honour, a lady of great beauty, courageous personality, and quick, tart speech. After their marriage, the Viscount and his wife lived principally at Chartley, taking small part in the life of the Court. They had four children: Penelope, born in 1563; Dorothy, in 1564; Robert, born on November 10, 1567; and Walter in 1569. A fifth child died in infancy.

In 1569, the Northern Lords raised their rebellion to help Mary, Queen of Scots. Viscount Hereford being called upon to aid the Queen's forces joined the army of the Earl of Warwick, of which he was made Marshal of the Field, and showed such zeal for the Queen's service that in 1572 she made him Knight of the Garter and advanced him to be Earl of Essex. In 1578, he undertook to colonise Ulster as a private speculation, and offered those who would support him great hope of gain. The venture was a disaster. The expedition set out in July, 1573; in May, 1574, those who survived famine and disease took refuge in the English Pale. He achieved a little success in the following autumn, when he persuaded Brian MacPhelim, the Irish chieftain largely responsible for his failing in Ulster, to come to a feast in Dublin. MacPhelim's men were murdered, MacPhelim himself, his wife and his brother were sent to Dublin for more ceremonious extinction. In May, 1575, the Queen ordered that the expedition should be withdrawn. Essex came back to Wales in November. For the next half year he was negotiating with the Queen and Council for compensation and further grants for a renewed attempt in Ulster. He went back to Dublin in July, 1576, but early in September he developed dysentery and died at Dublin Castle.

The Countess of Essex did not accompany her husband to Ireland. She was at Kenilworth for the celebrated revels; the attentions of the Earl of Leicester were conspicuous, and when Essex died scandalmongers said that he had been poisoned. So strong was this belief that the body was opened, but no decisive signs of poison could be discovered. The dead Earl was very popular, and he had certainly been treated shabbily by the Queen and her Council.

THUS on September 22, 1576, Robert Devereux succeeded to the titles, estates, and debts of his father, being then in his ninth year. He was a delicate child, and forward in his studies, for even at this age he could, as was reported to Lord Burghley, "express his mind in Latin and French as well as in English, very courteous and modest in his bearing, disposed rather to hear than to answer, greatly given to learning, weak and tender, but very comely and bashful." He did not follow the funeral of his father at Carmarthen on November 26, for the weather was bitter, and his guardians considered that he was too tender to endure the long journey from Chartley. Lord Burghley, however, sent him some precepts and sage advice in his bereavement, and he wrote, unaided, a proper letter of thanks, very mature for one of his years :

"MY VERY GOOD LORD,
"I have received your Lordship's letters by Mr. Waterhouse, wherefore I think myself bound to your Lordship both for your counsel and precepts. And I hope that my life shall be according to your prescriptions. And since my Lord and father commended me to your Lordship on his deathbed for your Lordship's wisdom, I hope to institute my life according to your Lordship's precepts. Whereas I am appointed of the Queen's Majesty and your Lordship, together with my Lord Chamberlain, to do my Lord and father the last service, I would be willing to do not only this service, but any other in my power, if that my weak body could bear this journey, and that all things were convenient, wherefore I most humbly desire her Majesty and your Lordship to pardon me. And thus wishing your Lordship prosperous health, I bid your Lordship farewell. From Chartley the 18th November, 1576.
" Your Lordship's at commándment as your son,
"R. ESSEX."

After the Christmas holidays the boy came to live in Lord Burghley's house until May, when he went up to Cambridge and became a member of Trinity College, whose Master at this time was Dr. John Whitgift. As a young nobleman he had special privileges, and on arriving at Cambridge he was very well entertained both in the University and the town. Lord Burghley had not caused proper provision to be made for him, so that before he had been at Cambridge for a month his tutor was obliged to write that he was not only threadbare but would soon be ragged, and begged that clothes and plate should be despatched at once, a request which Essex himself accompanied with a brief Latin letter.

" *Tanta tua in me bonitas, optime Domine, hoc tempore mihi animum addit, ut pro illis quae necessaria sunt, ad te scribam, quia placuit dominationi tuae apte essem discessurus hoc mihi mandatum imponere : idcirco te oro, Domine, ut mittas ad me vestes, quoniam quas mihi Londini dedisti, iam tritae sunt. Et sic, sperans, Domine, te velle mihi condonare, quod istis senioribus te reipub. negociis occupatum interpello. Deum precor ut servet te salvum et incolumen. Vale. Cantabrigiae, x. Junii,* 1577.

"R. Essex."

The boy lived very modestly at Cambridge, and little was heard of him. Other members of his family were more conspicuous. On September 21, 1578, his mother married the great Earl of Leicester. Leicester's first wife, the unfortunate Amy Robsart, had been dead for eighteen years. Rumour said she was murdered to leave Leicester free to marry the Queen. The years went on, and the Queen dallied with a succession of suitors, until at last Leicester realised that his ambition was hopeless. He had not, however, lived solitary. About five years before, he went through a form of marriage with Lady Douglas Sheffield, who bore him a son, Robert Dudley. Lady Sheffield in later years claimed that she was indeed Leicester's lawful wife, but Leicester so completely destroyed the evidence that she was never able to prove it. Leicester soon tired of Lady Sheffield, and she thought it safest to accept an offer of marriage from Sir Edward Stafford lest she, too, should go the way of Amy Robsart. Leicester was thus left without an acknowledged heir.

The Countess of Essex was his next choice, and—so the gossip ran—he made another secret marriage. When Sir Francis Knollys, her father, heard of it, he insisted that the marriage should be indubitably confirmed before reputable witnesses. In the presence of the Earls of Warwick and Pembroke, Lord North, and Richard Knollys, the bride's brother, Sir Francis Knollys duly gave his daughter to be married at the hands of Mr. Tindale, Leicester's chaplain. The marriage was kept from the Queen for some months.

By this time she had entered well into negotiations for marriage with the Duke of Anjou who, in January, 1579, sent over as his representative Jehan de Simier, to forward the match. Leicester did his best to obstruct Simier, who retaliated by telling the Queen of the marriage. The Queen was bitterly angry and was for imprisoning Leicester in the Tower, but the Earl of Sussex, though none of his friends, bluntly observed to her that no man was to be troubled for lawful marriage. Leicester was soon forgiven, his new Countess never.

Essex continued at Cambridge until 1581, when he took his Master's degree. He then retired into a quiet privacy, living for the most part at his house at Llanfydd in Pembrokeshire, entirely content with country pursuits and reading. He visited country houses a little, but at this time there was small sign of ambition in the boy, except that he overspent his allowance, which drew down a rebuke from Lord Burghley, to which Essex replied:

"MY VERY GOOD LORD,
"I hope your Lordship in courtesy will pardon my youth, if I have, through want of experience, in some sort passed the bounds of frugality. I cannot but embrace with duty your Lordship's good counsel, whose love I have effectually proved, and of whose care of my well doings I am thoroughly well persuaded. I do beseech your good Lordship, notwithstanding the lapse of my youth, still to continue a loving friend unto me, as I will acknowledge myself in all duty bound unto your Lordship. Thus I humbly commit your Lordship to the tuition of the Almighty. York, this 13th December, 1582.
"Your Lordship's most humbly at commandment,
"R. E."

In the meanwhile, both his sisters were married. It had been the hope of the late Earl that Penelope Devereux would marry Sir Philip Sidney, but Sidney at the time was not much interested in a girl of thirteen. About four years later she was secretly betrothed to Charles Blount, but she was obliged to marry Lord Rich. She had now developed into a court beauty, and Sidney fell passionately in love with her. She became his star, and the emotions of the unhappy months when Sidney realised that he had loved too late were embalmed in *Astrophel and Stella*.

Dorothy Devereux also made a marriage which was sensational, but for different reasons. In July, 1583, she was living in the house of Sir Henry Cock at Broxbourne, where she was wedded to Sir Thomas Perrot, son of Sir John Perrot the boisterous Lord Deputy of Ireland. One morning the vicar of the parish was visited by two strangers, one of whom said that he was a minister and a Bachelor of Divinity. He asked for the key of the church. The vicar refused to give it up. A little later he went down to see if anything was happening. He found that his church was open, and Sir Thomas and Lady Dorothy were about to enter, by which he perceived that a wedding was toward. The vicar tried to persuade the strange minister, who was in his cloak, boots and spurs, unsurpliced, not to proceed further. He read him an injunction against any minister performing a marriage except in his own church. The wedding party refused to listen, and one of them produced a sealed licence. The vicar began to read it, but before he was half-way through Sir Thomas snatched it out of his hand and offered him a *real* to marry them. As the vicar refused, Sir Thomas ordered the strange minister to proceed, whereupon the vicar shut the book. He was pushed aside by Sir Thomas and some bickering followed, but the vicar, being outnumbered, at length held his peace. At this point a gentleman named Lucy, who was one of Sir Henry Cock's household, came in and snatched the book away. The strange minister retrieved the book and hastily finished the service. Dorothy Devereux was seventeen at the time of her marriage.

Essex still preferred a private life, though his stepfather, the

Earl of Leicester, urged him to come to Court. Essex disliked his stepfather, and at first refused, but in the end he yielded to the persuasions of his mother. At last, in 1584, Leicester brought him into the Presence and presented him to Queen Elizabeth. He was now in his seventeenth year.

Leicester's motives were diversely interpreted. Everyone agreed that the great Earl did nothing by chance or for mere affection. Some said that he was growing elderly, and tiring of the strain of constant attendance on the Queen, and so wished a younger man to ease him of part of the burden, and of the envy. Others, remembering that Leicester had also introduced Ralegh to Court and had then found the pupil too great for his master, thought that his real motive was to supplant Ralegh in the Queen's favour, though in fact Ralegh had passed the meridian of his success with the Queen. Whatever his true purpose, Leicester succeeded. From his first coming to Court, Essex was conspicuous. In appearance he was a very towardly youth, with charming, unspoilt manners, and he bore a kind of urbanity and innate courtesy that attracted the Queen's admiration, and, which was dangerous, the notice and applause of the people. Elizabethan noblemen were few. They had many and peculiar privileges, which marked them as different from other men; they seldom troubled to show much courtesy to mere commoners.

CHAPTER II

FIRST LESSONS IN STATECRAFT

AT first Essex was a follower of his stepfather, and in 1585, he had his earliest experiences of statecraft and soldiering.

For some years bitterness with Spain had been growing and there was a strong feeling that Englishmen should aid their fellow Protestants in the Low Countries, who were being harried by the Spaniards. On July 10, 1584, William Prince of Orange was assassinated. With his death all unity and cohesion between the various States was dissipated, and in desperation the States combined to offer the crown to the Queen. She was unwilling to undertake the responsibility, but she agreed to send over troops, which were despatched towards the end of July, under command of Sir John Norris. A few weeks later Leicester was appointed to be her representative. As part of the bargain with the States, Flushing and Brille were to be held as pledges of their debts. Leicester began to make his preparations, and then the Queen hesitated. She heard that the Countess of Leicester had come to London from Kenilworth, and thought that it would be better to send someone else. She relented. Then because she was feeling out of sorts she thought that she was about to die, and so she could not let Leicester go. She recovered her good spirits, and for the next three days Leicester was to go: on the fourth she decided to do nothing. It was now the end of September, and in this continuous vacillation affairs in the Low Countries were steadily deteriorating. The Queen was not quite so irresponsible as she seemed to outside observers, for she had her own notions of the situation, which she did not generally reveal to her advisers. She was averse from war with Spain, and, indeed, secret negotiations with the Duke of Parma were going forward.

Meanwhile there was the perennial problem of Mary, Queen of Scots, who at this time was a prisoner at Tutbury. It was not a convenient place for her following, and it was suggested that she should be removed to Chartley, Essex's house in Staffordshire. The proposal did not please Essex, and was embarrassing, for it was the only house which was freely his own; all his other properties were encumbered with the debts of his father. He wrote to his grandfather, Sir Francis Knollys, to complain of the inconvenience which would follow. He would himself, he said, have to live in borrowed lodgings, his little furniture would be marred, his woods spoiled, and his tenants undone. Moreover, the place was not easy to defend.

Sir Francis forwarded the complaint to Walsingham with the additional argument that it was " no policy for her Majesty to lodge the Queen of Scots in so young a man's house as he is." For the moment the proposal was dropped.

At length Leicester's appointment to the supreme command in the Low Countries was confirmed, and Essex was to go with him as General of the Horse. In spite of his very real poverty, he began to levy a company of private followers, who must be handsomely equipped for nobility's sake, and to this end he added another £1,000 of debt to the burdens of his estate. Sir Francis was annoyed, and wrote indignantly:

" My Lord,
    " If I should not love you, I should be unnatural; again, if I should flatter youthful humors in you, I should be guilty of the ruinous race of your undoing. Wherefore you must give me leave to say unto you, that wasteful prodigality hath devoured and will consume all noble men that be wilful in expenses before they have of their own ordinary living to bear out such wilful and wasteful expenses. You are so far off from being beforehand in land and living left by your father

to you, that by unhappy occasions your father hath not left you sufficient lands for to maintain the state of the poorest Earl in England; and also you are so far from goods and riches left unto you by your father, that you are left more in debt than one quarter of your land, to be sold by you, is able to discharge your debt.

"Now, for you to put yourself to £1,000 charges (as I hear you have done, by borrowing reckonings vainly beforehand), for your journey into the Low Countries, by levying and carrying with you a furnished band of men, needless and causeless; which band of men do also look to be recompensed with the spoil of your leases and livings; now if I should flatter you in this wasteful spoiling of yourself, then I should justly be accounted guilty of your ruinous race. I do like very well your desire to see the wars, for your learning; and do like your desire much the better, that you do take the opportunity of honouring my Lord of Leicester with your service under him; but this might have been done without any wasteful charge to yourself, for my Lord of Leicester doth set much by your company, but he delighteth nothing in your wasteful consumption. I do say no more, but I beseech our Almighty God so to assist you with His heavenly grace, that youthful wilfulness and wasteful youth do not consume you, before experienced wisdom shall have reformed you.

"Your Lordship's assuredly,
"F. KNOLLYS.
"At Richmond, the 14th November, 1585."

By this time the troops promised for the Low Countries had been collected, and throughout November and December detachments were being drafted over. Sir Philip Sidney had already sailed from Gravesend to take up his appointment as Governor of Flushing: Brille was assigned to Sir Thomas Burghley, the Lord Treasurer's elder son by his first marriage.

On December 6, Leicester, having taken his leave of the Court, and accompanied with a great following of noblemen and gentlemen, made for Colchester, where they were all sumptuously and ceremoniously entertained by Sir Thomas Lucas, the bailiffs and aldermen. It was a gallant party and included young Essex, Lord North, Lord Audley, Sir William Russell, Sir Thomas Shirley, Sir Gervase Clifton, and other knights, esquires, and gentlemen to the number of nearly seven hundred, all voluntaries, bravely appointed and well mounted; and in addition there were 1,585 common soldiers. Next day they moved on to Harwich, where a fleet of fifty sail was ready to waft them over. They put out to sea to the sound of trumpets and drums, with the crowds on shore shouting and praying for their good success. On the 8th they landed at Flushing.

The next month was spent in a royal progress. Leicester went from town to town in the Low Countries, and everywhere he was received with ceremony, pageants, and feasting. At Dort, as the ships came to anchor they were saluted with cannonading, and a crowd of small boats put off to land the soldiers. When Leicester came on shore, his own guard of archers, shot, and halberds were drawn up. The gate where he entered was emblazoned with the Queen's arms, his own, and the States'. He passed a guard of honour of Dutch musketeers, escorted by 800 men, and for an hour and more the salutes continued to be shot off.

On December 23, he reached Rotterdam, after a tempestuous passage. Here three barges of pleasure were waiting to escort him, stored with fireworks and rockets, with cressets at the stern, which were lighted as night fell and gleamed bravely on the dark water. On the banks stood ranks of musketeers, and by every fourth man a blazing cresset, and all the way as they passed, the blaring of trumpets. They landed through excited and cheering crowds who escorted Leicester to his lodging through the market-place, where they had set up a lifelike image of Erasmus, in a pulpit as though he were preaching. Thence to Delft, by cresset light, and as the barges passed along the narrow canals rockets and fireworks were let off. Here Leicester was lodged in the house where the Prince of Orange had been murdered. Next day, which was December 25, the Earl was feasted royally, and the day following he entertained the States at a great feast where many ladies were present.

The further he went, the braver was the entertainment. Next day he journeyed to the Hague. There were more cressets, fireworks, and volleys of welcome. As he came nearer on the river bank some fishermen met him, representing the saints Peter, James, and John, and by them Christ walking on the water, who bade them cast in their nets. They drew them in filled with fish which they made show of presenting to Leicester, who returned them great thanks as he passed by on the water. Next Mars and Bellona were waiting, who made him speeches of welcome. They landed and there was a troop of horsemen in antique garb to display feats of horsemanship. In the chief street galleries had been set up, hung with black bays, and upon each stood virgins, clad all in white, with branches of palms or box, bearing wax candles in their hands, who did reverence as he passed. And so through triumphal gates, and streets hung with broadcloth, to a high scaffold, blazoned with the Queen's arms, and at the top seven virgins, one for each Province, and in their midst Minerva armed, wearing the arms of England. And then the Seven Liberal Sciences, who yielded to Leicester by desert. Out of every window hung lanterns, and every street was ablaze with cressets and torches. At the entrance to the court gates of his lodging stood Arthur of Britain, typifying Leicester, and, as they went in, a triumphal salute of hautboys, cornets, and other instruments of music blared out. The night was lit up by rockets, squibs, catherine wheels and balls of fire, and a dragon belching fire continuously for an hour.

Early in the morning of January 1, a solemn deputation of the States came to Leicester's lodging. He was not fully dressed and was not sure of their mission. As soon as he was ready he went into the great chamber and their spokesman began an oration. One of Leicester's staff whispered to him that they were about to offer him the absolute governorship of the whole of the United Provinces. Leicester interrupted the speaker, and asked the deputation to withdraw into the privacy of his bed-chamber. Davison, the Queen's second secretary, was at the Hague, and present in the house. Leicester summoned him and a few others. The speech was then delivered and the offer made. Leicester asked for time to consider his answer. The Queen, he said, had sent him only to serve them, and so he would, faithfully and honestly as she had commanded him.

On January 3, 1586, Leicester, with his retinue, escorted by 300 horsemen, entered Leyden, where the chief burghers met him, in their black velvet gowns. The streets as they passed were hung all over with saye of different colours. Leicester himself was escorted beneath a canopy to his seat, by which a stage was set up whereon two poets presented various shows symbolical of the past misfortunes and present hopes of the town. Thence Leicester went back to the Hague, where, on January 10, he mustered his horse and assigned them to their garrisons; and on this day, too, Essex was appointed to be General of the Horse. The 12th was proclaimed as a solemn feast, and Leicester spent the whole day in listening to sermons, reading of the Scriptures and psalm-singing, and neither he nor any of his people ate anything till night.

Meanwhile the petition that he would accept the Governorship was renewed with increasing fervour, and at length, with the advice of Davison, Sir Philip Sidney, and others, he agreed. He did not, however, inform the Queen either of the petition or of his acceptance, nor did he send Davison back to report.

On January 25, Leicester was solemnly installed at the Hague. At the upper end of the Great Hall a cloth of estate was set up, emblazoned with the arms of England. Here Leicester was seated, and on either side, two steps lower, sat twelve of the representatives of the principal States, and below them again twenty others. On either side of him stood his chief officers,

Don Antonio, Prince of Portugal, Essex, the young Grave Maurice, and a number of others. Then a Dutchman made an oration in Dutch, summarising the events which had led to the present ceremony, and rendering thanks to the Queen and her Lieutenant-General. The covenants between them were read in Latin, and formally exchanged. Leicester held up his hand and swore to observe his part. The representatives of the States took their oaths, and were sworn to the Queen and her Lieutenant-General. The proceedings ended with speeches of thanks and Leicester withdrew to the salutes of trumpets.

The same day a solemn meeting of the States was held, and a publication made of their resolution that they accepted and authorised the Mighty and Honourable Prince, Lord Robert, Earl of Leicester, to be their Governor-General, Captain over all the United Provinces and associate cities, and gave him, besides the authority of the Queen, the highest and supreme commandment and absolute authority in all matters of warfare by sea and by land. Further they committed to him the administration and use of policy and justice to administer the same with such power and authority as had all other Governors of the Low Countries before him.

Strange rumours were reaching the English Court which were as yet unconfirmed by any communication from Leicester. The Queen's anger rose at the thought that Leicester should have so far exceeded his instructions, and especially when she heard that the Countess of Leicester was about to join her husband with a lavish train of ladies and gentlewomen and rich coaches, with litters and side-saddles far more magnificent than her own, and that there would be such a court of ladies at the Hague as would far surpass Whitehall. The report was a malicious exaggeration, but it moved the Queen to declare with great choler that she would have no more courts under her obeisance but her own, and that she would revoke Leicester with all speed.

At length, on February 13, Davison, who had been delayed by contrary winds, arrived at Court. The Queen saw him alone. She was in one of her tempestuous moods. Leicester, she began, had treated her with the utmost contempt, as if her consent was nothing worth and the thing no way concerned her. Then she turned on Davison and abused him for not openly opposing the proposal; he had greatly deceived her opinion and the trust she reposed in him. When the Queen ceased, Davison tried to defend both Leicester and himself. The argument was long, and when Davison at last left the Queen she was calmer but still unsatisfied. She was still in a mood to disavow the whole business and to make Leicester renounce his governorship as ceremoniously as he had assumed it.

Next morning Davison was again admitted into the Presence in some trepidation, for he learned that Sir Thomas Heneage had just been despatched in great haste to go over to Leicester with the Queen's commands. With tears in his eyes, Davison begged the Queen not to impose so great a humiliation on Leicester. He did at least achieve one result: Heneage was ordered to stay the Queen's further pleasure.

Heneage reached Flushing on March 3, with the Queen's orders. She had slightly modified her first demands and allowed Heneage a small margin of discretion. He brought with him a personal letter to Leicester, written in the Queen's most pointed style. Leicester blamed Davison. It was by Davison's advice, he said, that he had been hardly won to accept the offer of the States. Davison, when he heard, could only retire into private life until the Queen's anger subsided, muttering indignant complaints that the Earl was making him a scapegoat: Leicester had shown no reluctance to accept his advice.

Leicester and Davison between them had touched the Queen upon two matters upon which she was most sensitive—her standing in the eyes of her fellow princes, and her own authority. She always felt strongly that princes were not as other men; they were beings apart and bound to observe towards each other the most punctilious rules of conduct. She had publicly declared in print that she had no intention of assuming the Governorship of the Low Countries; indeed, she privately regarded them as rebellious subjects of her Cousin of Spain, and she disliked rebels in any country. By Leicester's action she would appear infamous amongst all princes. Moreover, as she remarked to Sir Thomas Shirley, "I may not endure that any man should alter my commission and the authority that I gave him upon his own fancies and without me."

Meanwhile Heneage, acting on his own discretion, was discreetly inactive at the Hague. When the Queen heard that he was returning to Court and that nothing had been done to modify Leicester's titles, she sent for Burghley and Walsingham and once again her passion rose. Burghley tried to persuade her to moderation; she told him to keep his mouth shut. An official letter was despatched to Heneage bidding him carry out his instructions. At the same time the Queen wrote him with her own hand:

"Jesus: what availeth wit when it fails the owner at greatest need? Do that you are bidden, and leave your considerations for your own affairs: for in some things you had clear commandment, which you did not: and in other none, and did; yea, to the use of those speeches from me that might oblige me to more than I was bound or mind ever to yield."

These distractions considerably upset Leicester and diverted his attention from the campaign. The result was to bring him from his parade of pomp to a sense of realities, and to subject him to the critical observation of the States. The great man found it irksome to be polite to burghers.

Essex, meanwhile, in the troubles of his stepfather received an excellent object lesson in the difficulties of statecraft. The campaign opened with a success at the end of February. Colonel Martin Schenck, usually called "Skink" by the English, captured Werle in Westphalia. This Skink was a magnificent soldier, and a ferocious thruster. He had formerly been in Spanish pay, but having a grievance he deserted to the service of the States and was thereafter a terror to the Spaniards. There was a further success in April, when Count Hohenhoe (whom the English called Hollock) and Sir John Norris relieved Grave, which had been besieged by the enemy since December. The town was reorganised and provisioned for nine months, and left in charge of Hemart, a conceited young man who had insufficient experience of war, and devoted his time to the entertainment of a mistress.

On April 23, Leicester celebrated the feast of St. George at Utrecht. Essex was conspicuous in the festivities. In the procession to the cathedral he rode by the side of the Bishop of Cologne. After the solemnities, he escorted the princes and ladies back to the Court, which was held at the old Hall of the Knights of Rhodes. Here a great feast was held, with all magnificence and ceremony of service. After the feast, the tables were removed and the company fell to dancing, until evensong. Then they returned to supper, and a further abundance of good cheer, and after supper there were barriers between challengers and defendants whereat Essex greatly distinguished himself with his weapons. A sumptuous banquet of sugar-meats for the combatants and ladies followed, and at length, about midnight, the Lieutenant-General rose and, wishing them all good rest, went off to his lodgings.

The proceedings were, however, disturbed by alarming news: Parma was advancing to the assault of Grave. Leicester was not ready to gather sufficient forces to meet Parma in the open, for the other forces of his army were with Hollock and Skink, but, with 3,000 foot and 1,000 horse, he moved to Arnheim and thence to Nimeguen. There was no fear for Grave, which was strong enough to resist for many days, but suddenly Parma attacked the town with all his forces and by a strong bombardment so terrified Hemart that he surrendered on terms, before even the enemy had made a breach or assault.

The unexpected loss of Grave was a great blow. Hemart, after the surrender, came to Leicester's camp at Nimeguen, where he was put under arrest, and a court, which included Count Hollock, Lord North, Essex, and other captains, was commissioned to try him. He and two of his captains were sentenced to death, and, though Norris tried to save him by pointing out that Leicester's powers were doubtful in such a case, all three were publicly beheaded. Parma followed up this victory by attacking Venlo, which surrendered at his arrival.

The general gloom and panic which succeeded these reverses was somewhat lightened at the end of July by the capture of Axel. Sir Philip Sidney had the post of leading the attack on the town, and with him were Count Maurice and Lord Willoughby. After a long march, a small body of thirty or forty swam the ditch, clambered up the wall and opened the gate to the rest. The alarm was given as the main body were rushing through, but most of the garrison were slain and the town was occupied, with considerable booty.

Elsewhere Leicester's difficulties were increasing, for his soldiers were starving for lack of pay, and in two days five hundred ran away, many of them to the enemy. Leicester was sick of the business, and expected general mutiny. His own officers were squabbling amongst themselves and with the Dutch. Another disaster followed. Parma attacked the town of Nuys. The garrison resisted heroically, and, after assaults which lasted continuously from four in the morning to five in the evening, the few survivors were about to parley when Parma's soldiers got out of hand and rushed the defences. The town was sacked, the women raped, the governor, who had been wounded earlier in the action, was dragged out of bed and murdered, and then the houses were burnt.

There was some improvement towards the end of July; Leicester was joined by Sir William Pelham as Marshal of the Army, and reinforced by new men and supplies of money. From Nuys, Parma proceeded to Berck. Here his reception was very different, for the garrison was commanded by the ferocious Skink, with a mixed force of English and Dutch troops.

Essex had little chance of distinguishing himself in these events. Early in August he witnessed an incident which, for a time, seemed likely to have a disastrous sequel. A number of officers were assembled at Gertrudenberg, and at supper there were present the Count Hollock, Sir William Pelham, the Marshal, Lord Willoughby, Sir Philip Sidney, Essex, Sir Roger Williams, and others. The Marshal and the Count, who was a notorious tosspot, began to ply young Edward Norris with healths, which as a soldier he could not refuse. At last Pelham took up a great glass to drink to the health of Lord and Lady Norris, his parents. Norris, alarmed at the size of the cup, asked Pelham to take a smaller, for he did not wish to be drunk. Pelham insisted, so Norris drank, pledging the toast to Essex, who in his turn drank to the Count. The Count was by this time very fuddled, and not understanding who or what was being pledged, asked, whose horse? He wasn't used to pledging horses. Nor could Essex drive any sense into his head. The party grew more drunken, and the Marshal became quarrelsome. At length the Count, taking up the cover of a great wine bowl, sent it spinning at Norris's head. It caught Norris above the temple and cut him to the bone. The Count, now thoroughly roused, drew his dagger, but Sidney and the others took hold of him and led him away to bed. The quarrel fortunately blew over, but for a time it seemed likely to lead to a mutiny.

Berck still held out, and Leicester decided to go to Skink's aid. When the troops had been assembled, the council of war declared that the force was too small for a direct attack on Parma, but that the most promising move would be to attack Doesburg on his northerly flank. Doesburg was captured on September 2. The walls were continuously bombarded by ten cannon until the early afternoon, by which time two breaches had been made. To prevent jealousies, Leicester gave the leading of the assaults on the breaches to Count Hollock with the Dutch and Scotch, and to Norris with the English and Irish. As they advanced to the ditch the town was yielded, on condition that the soldiers should pass out unarmed but safe. As they marched out some women came with them. The victorious troops handled them roughly, and began to ransack their belongings until Essex and some other gentlemen came down to the breach and smote at the soldiers to make them desist. Leicester sent other troops into the town to prevent looting, but instead both captains and soldiers made sad havoc of the place. The casualties had been small, though Roger Williams was hit in the arm, and was lucky to escape with his life. He was in the trench by Leicester's side, wearing a great plume of feathers in his gilt morion, and to Leicester's alarm kept bobbing over the parapet, though the enemy were then within close caliver range.

From Doesburg the army moved off to attack Zutphen. Parma abandoned the siege of Berck and marched to the relief of Zutphen. A report reached Leicester that a large convoy of provisions was expected, and he determined to intercept it. In the evening of September 21, Sir John Norris with 200 foot and 60 horse was sent forward about a mile and a half from the camp to take up a position covering the road by which the convoy would approach. A patrol was sent out and towards morning came in with the report that a large body of the enemy could be heard approaching. Norris withdrew his force to a stronger position in a churchyard, and sent on the information to the camp.

It was a dull morning, with a thick autumn mist. The alarm was given in the camp; the troops armed and paraded. A reinforcement of horse and foot was sent forward to strengthen Norris's position, including Sir Philip Sidney, Essex, Lord Willoughby, Sir William Russell, Sir Thomas Perrot, and a few others, with their troops of horse. They rode on in the mist and joined Norris. Sir William Pelham, the Marshal, rode with them. He had been severely wounded at Doesburg and was unable to wear thigh pieces, whereupon Sidney, with a typical gesture of chivalry, threw away his own that their danger might be equal. The mist cleared, and the English saw drawn up and ready for action before them the Spanish force, 2,200 musketeers, 800 pikes, 1,200 horse.

The Spanish musketeers fired a volley, and then, without waiting for them to reload, Norris led the English horse against them. Essex threw his lance into its rest, and shouting to his men to follow, overthrew his man, and then taking to his curtelaxe laid about the enemy. Forty were overthrown at the first onset. Willoughby unhorsed the leader of the Albanian cavalry and tumbled him into a ditch. Twice they withdrew, re-formed, and charged again. The Spanish cavalry was broken and their losses heavy. It was the bravest fight in living memory; but towards the end Sir Philip Sidney was wounded in the left thigh by a musket ball which shattered the bone. He rode back to headquarters, in great pain and thirsty with loss of blood. They brought him a waterbottle. He was about to drink when a soldier, mortally wounded, was carried by. "Thy necessity is greater than mine," he said.

Meanwhile the convoy rumbled on and was safely housed in Zutphen. In the days following there was hot fighting in the sconces round Zutphen, which were occupied. On October 7, Leicester knighted the officers who had distinguished themselves, amongst them Henry Goodyere, John Wingfield, Robert North, and Robert Sidney (Sir Philip's younger brother). Essex, Lord Willoughby, Lord Audley, and Lord North were made knights bannerets. Thence Leicester went to Arnheim to visit Philip Sidney, for whose recovery there was now small hope. He lingered for twenty-five days after his wound, nursed by his wife, and died in the afternoon of October 17.

A few hours before he died Sidney sent for his will and added a codicil, disposing of certain personal mementoes to his particular friends; amongst them was the bequest, "I give to my beloved and much honoured Lord, the Earl of Essex, my best sword." To one of Essex's temperament, no relic could have been holier or more symbolic.

The campaigning season was now over, and a week later Leicester began to make preparations for his return to England. There was much to be settled, but on November 18, he took ship from Dort, and after further delays from frosts and ice, at length he reached Margate on the 21st. On November 23, bringing Essex with him, he came to the Court at Richmond, where the Queen received him gladly. He was thoroughly disgruntled with the whole business, and once home, as he sat in his own chamber, he clapped his hands on his knees, exclaiming, " If God give me leave, these legs of mine shall never go again into Holland. Let the States get others to serve their mercenary turn if they will make themselves rich, for me they shall not have."

CHAPTER III

THE ROYAL FAVOURITE

WHEN Essex and his stepfather returned to Court towards the end of 1586, the tragedy of Mary, Queen of Scots, had entered upon the last act. About a year before, as soon as Essex went abroad, Mary was removed to Chartley. Here Walsingham carried out a subtle plan by which Mary should entrap herself into treasonable correspondence. In this business his chief agent was a certain young man called Gilbert Gifford, one of the sons of a Catholic recusant, of good Staffordshire family, who had already suffered for his faith. Gifford had two brothers who were both Jesuits in the seminary at Rheims, and one of them had bargained with the Duke of Parma to assassinate the Queen. Gilbert Gifford offered his services to Walsingham, who found him well qualified. Moreover, the Gifford family lived near Chartley; after the close confinement at Tutbury the freedom of the place would encourage Mary to indiscretion; and Gilbert Gifford, as a Catholic, would have every opportunity, and local encouragement, to act as her go-between. Walsingham's plot was elaborate and melodramatic. It was kept a close secret, shared only by four others—Sir Amyas Paulet, Mary's keeper; Thomas Phellippes, Walsingham's secretary, an expert master of cipher who was sent down to Chartley, nominally to assist Paulet; Gifford; and a brewer of ale at Burton who supplied Chartley with beer.

One day a hint was conveyed to Nau, one of Mary's two secretaries, to examine closely the cask of ale which was sent specially for Mary and her ladies. At the bottom of the cask he found a small box. In the box was a letter introducing Gifford as a Catholic gentleman by whose aid she might correspond with her friends, *via* the weekly cask of ale. Gifford would collect letters from the brewer, and pass them on to another Catholic sympathiser, and so from hand to hand they would reach their destinations. The replies returned by the same channel and were fished out of the cask. Unfortunately for herself, it did not occur to Mary that her enemies might be as subtle as she, and that both Gifford and the brewer were betraying her; for, as it happened, as soon as the packets of letters reached the brewer, they were handed to Phellippes, who copied, resealed, and returned them, and then set to work at deciphering them. Gifford drew pay from both sides for his treachery. The brewer was even more successful: not only did he draw a double bribe, he also increased the price of his beer, which Paulet was obliged to pay. Thus Walsingham knew from the first the whole truth of Babington's plot to murder Queen Elizabeth, and possessed the most damning proofs of Mary's complicity.

The conspirators were arrested, and confessed. They were brought to trial on September 10, and executed on the 20th and 21st. Meanwhile Mary's papers had been seized and examined; they revealed not only that she was an accessory to Babington's plot, but that several noblemen were secretly corresponding with her. On October 11, Mary was tried at Fotheringay by a special commission. After two days the commissioners were ready to pronounce sentence, when the Queen sent for Secretary Davison and ordered that they should return to London before publishing their judgment. Parliament met on October 29, and both Houses agreed to beg the Queen that Mary should be executed. The Queen received their deputation on November 12, and was unwilling to grant their request. They came again on the 24th, and again she refused a definite answer; but when Parliament was prorogued, she promised that the sentence should be publicly proclaimed. The proclamation was received with universal joy and expectation. Into such a state of excitement Leicester and Essex returned from the Lowlands.

The Queen hesitated. Much as the Council and the people at large might roar after Mary's blood, the responsibility was hers, and no one knew what might follow, especially as the ambassadors of France and Scotland were pressing for mercy. As the days went by, and no decision was made, the general agitation increased. Many rumours were bandied abroad, as that the Spaniards or Scots or French were already invading the country, and that there was a new rebellion in the North. Then a fresh conspiracy, hatched in the French ambassador's house, was discovered. At last, on February 1, the Queen consented to sign the warrant for Mary's death. It was a terrible decision, though she wished Mary dead, and she tried to persuade others to take the responsibility from her. Davison took up the document, which was in the customary form of a writ for a warrant under the Great Seal to be prepared for Mary's execution. She signed it, after some talk with Davison, and told him to have the warrant prepared. Next day she asked whether the warrant had been sealed. She was still hesitating whether to send it or not, and for the moment her thought was to keep the warrant as a threat to Mary, but not to have it carried out. Davison came out from the Presence and told Hatton, and they went together to Burghley. Next day nine of the Council, with Davison, met secretly to consider what was to be done; amongst them were Burghley, Walsingham, Leicester, and Sir Francis Knollys. The Queen had remarked to Davison that she wished to be troubled no more in the matter; they conspired to take her at her word. Walsingham made notes on the details discussed, including the outline of the speeches to be moved by the Earls of Kent and Shrewsbury at the execution, and the determination that the Lords at Court should give out that there would be no execution. Then they resolved on a letter to be written to the Queen, explaining and justifying their action. Burghley drafted it, but it was not sent.

Meanwhile the Queen, quite ignorant of the events at Fotheringay, was still putting off her final decision, hoping that somehow luck would find a solution. On the morning of February 9, she mounted her horse and went out with her attendants for her morning ride in Greenwich Park. She did not notice the arrival of the messenger who had ridden all night to tell Burghley that Mary was dead: nor did he think it wise to inform her. She came back, and gave an audience to Don Antonio, the pretender to the throne of Portugal. Still no one dared tell her; but as she sat at dinner, she heard the bells pealing from the church towers. She asked the reason for such merry bells; and then, for the first time, she was told. She said nothing for the time, but afterwards she went to her own chamber and broke down into a passion of weeping. It was a great shock. She would have spared Mary if she could. The responsibility for her death was terrible enough, but her own Council, with the connivance of her Secretary, had thrust it upon her unawares.

The tension at Court was relaxed by one momentary distraction. On February 16, Sir Philip Sidney was carried pompously to his burial in Paul's. First came thirty-two poor men in black gowns (one for every year of his age); then the soldiers with fife and drum, and ensigns trailed; sixty of his servants; sixty of his physicians and surgeons, and the squires of his kindred; twelve knights, his kindred and friends; the preacher and chaplains; his pennon; his horse for the field, ridden by a page with a broken lance; the barbed horse, ridden by a page with a battle axe with the head downwards; the heralds and their attendants, carrying his banner, his gilt spurs, his gauntlets, helmet and crest, shield of arms and coat of arms. And then the body itself, covered with a pall of velvet, carried by fourteen yeomen. Sir Robert Sidney followed as chief mourner; and after him the Earls of Huntingdon and Leicester riding together, and then Essex, riding with the Earl of Pembroke. Behind them came Lord Willoughby and Lord North, and then the Lord Mayor and his brethren on horseback; the Grocers' Company in their liveries; the train bands of London, marching three and three with their drums, fifes, and ensign. When the body had been lowered into the grave, they honoured him with a double volley of shot, and so departed.

Essex had matured under the experiences of the last eighteen months, and the Queen began to take more notice of him. Queen Elizabeth was won in her fifty-fourth year and was still a handsome woman, for she was austere in her diet, very energetic, and interested in many things. Life had never been easy for her, and during the closing months of Mary's tragedy she was very much alone. She could not even trust her chief ministers. Burghley, Walsingham, and Leicester showed not only that they were opposed to her policy of peace with Spain; they worked against her; and even after two months she had not forgiven them for the execution of Mary. She was so bitterly angry that for a while she had a mind to dismiss all her Council, and was only dissuaded by Ambrose Dudley, Earl of Warwick, Leicester's brother.

Mary was dead, and the consequences were irrevocable. Her Councillors were as essential to her as she to them, and she had too much sense of reality to send them away, for there were no others competent to take their places, and in her calmer moments she realised their worth. Davison's offence in her eyes was the worst. He had worked against her before, and this time she would not forgive him. He was sent to the Tower. At first she was for having him tried for high treason, but the judges advised that there was no case. He was therefore brought before a special commission in the Star Chamber. Their sentence was that he should be fined ten thousand marks and be imprisoned. Very considerable sympathy was felt for the unfortunate Secretary, whose worst fault was that he had let zeal outrun discretion, and Essex was amongst those who tried to help him. He even wrote a letter to King James of Scotland to intercede for him.

Burghley and Walsingham were, in time, forgiven. As ministers of State they were admirable, but those steady qualities which make men admirable as civil servants are prone to make them duller company in hours of relaxation. With young men, eager, handsome, and dashing, the Queen replenished her vitality. She had a wonderful instinct for men; and being herself great she chose great men to serve her. By instinct and observation she sensed that young Essex was a boy of amazing promise. At the tilt he was dashing and gallant, and he had proved his bravery in real war. He was a wide reader and very intelligent, eager to learn statecraft. He had good looks and a thoroughbred charm fascinating to most men, and all women. He was alive in every mood, very passionate, quick to resent unkindness but in ecstasy at praise, almost a glutton for honour. When time should have tempered him with experience, he promised to become really great.

But the Queen made two mistakes. She tried to bring Essex on too quickly, advancing him to honours and offices before he was mature for their burdens; and she spoilt him, as a rich spinster aunt will spoil a favourite nephew. It was a mistake easy to make, for there was exhilaration in the company of this boy, so adoring and adorable, with his moods and romantic passions, and his admiration for his Queen, so genuine, and yet so very frank. There were flatterers in abundance at her Court, with their hymns and fine phrases, but Essex was different, and his very lack of the glibness of an accomplished courtier was the subtler flattery. He dared to be open with her. When he sulked or tried to bully her to win some favour for himself or his friends, she admired his pluck, and amused herself sometimes by yielding to his whims. Nor was the admiration of Gloriana entirely artificial; Queen Elizabeth was still a divine mistress, and there was glamour in her service.

On both sides it was a genuine affection, for nothing is more gratifying to the middle-aged than the frank admiration of the young, or to a young man than the encouraging friendship of a great woman. It soon developed into a feeling far deeper than friendship or affection, which was not the love of an elderly mistress for her young lover, though it had something of the jealous love of a widow towards her only son. Essex always stirred the Queen emotionally. Towards her ministers and servants she felt annoyance or approval; Essex roused in her passion, of admiration which might rise into ecstasy, or of anger which could soon swell into hate. Moreover, beneath the ceremonies and trappings of royalty, she was a very lonely, childless woman, whom no one loved for her own sake; perhaps Robin might.

And so, at the age of nineteen, Essex became a royal favourite, and this spring he was constantly in her presence. When she went abroad, Essex was at her side; and at night, he would play cards with her, and sit chatting, till dawn appeared, when he would slip back to his own lodgings to an aubade of birdsong.

In these months the clash with the Spaniard became inevitable. The Queen still hoped that somehow war might be avoided, but the news that Philip was preparing an armada for the invasion of England was reliable. The Council proposed that Drake should be allowed to lead a small fleet against the enemy. The Queen consented, on the understanding that if necessary, Drake should be disavowed. In April he set out with a fleet of thirty ships. On the 16th, two ships returning from Cadiz to Middlesborough were encountered, from which it was learnt that Cadiz was full of ships laden with stores. Drake therefore made for Cadiz, and an hour before sunset, in the evening of April 19, the fleet entered the harbour. Six galleys which opposed were beaten back under the protection of the forts, an argosy of 1,000 tons, furnished with thirty brass cannon and richly laden, was sunk. There were sixty ships in the Road; twenty fled to Port Royal; of the others thirty were taken before night, rifled and set on fire, amongst them a carrack of 1,400 tons belonging to the Marquis of Santa Cruz. The English fleet remained off Cadiz for two nights and a day, looting and burning the ships. On the morning of the 21st, they put to sea. Thence they sailed to Cape Sacré and, that their stay might be quieter, landed and took the forts. Then they descended on the fishing-boats, which were destroyed and burnt with their nets, and the tunny fishing spoilt for the year. After this they sailed up to Cascaes, before Lisbon, and here Drake challenged the Marquis of Santa Cruz to come out and fight, but the invitation was declined. Thence they sailed over to the Azores, and some thirty leagues from St. Michael's met and took a great carrack, the *St. Philip*, with a very rich cargo, enough to give every man a sufficient reward for his travel. After this they came home.

In the Low Countries matters had gone badly since Leicester's return. In January, Sir William Stanley, who was in command of Deventer, deserted to the enemy. In the early summer Leicester was again sent over, with instructions to persuade the States to come to terms with the Spaniards; but though Parma was still making a show of negotiating for peace he was also attacking Sluys, which was being magnificently defended by Sir Roger Williams.

On June 18, a week before he sailed, Leicester was made Lord Steward of the Household, and Essex Master of the Queen's Horse. Essex did not accompany Leicester in his second journey to the Low Countries. He stayed in Court in constant attendance on the Queen, and soon experienced some of the crosses and disappointments which perpetually disturbed the peace of her intimates. She was always capricious in her moods, and temperamental, and when annoyed or anxious she would relieve her feelings in bitter outbursts of temper. Essex, too, was moody, and as violent in his hates as in his devotions, and he could not abide Ralegh.

In July, there was almost a quarrel with the Queen. She was on progress, and on the 18th was at Theobald's, staying with Lord Burghley. Thence she purposed to visit the Earl of Warwick at North Hall. Essex was troubled, for his sister was staying with the Countess, and she was not acceptable to the Queen. Essex sent warning to the Queen, who intimated that she would treat his sister well, but when she arrived, she commanded the Countess that Essex's sister should keep her chamber. He was greatly troubled. As soon as the Queen had supped, he went to her and protested. She excused herself for the command, saying that she did not know of his sister's coming, and, besides, the world would say, if she received her, that it was for love of him. Essex was indignant. It was merely to please that knave Ralegh, he exclaimed; to please Ralegh she would disgrace him and his sister, she would grieve his love, and disgrace him in the eyes of the world.

The Queen tried at first to allay his indignation. There was no cause, she said, for him to disdain Ralegh. This defence of his rival only increased Essex's passion. He gave full vent to his jealousy of Ralegh, in a flow of bitter words describing Ralegh's past, what Ralegh had been, what Ralegh was: had he not cause to disdain Ralegh as his competitor for the love of his Mistress? What comfort could he give himself in the service of a Mistress who was in awe of such a man? He spoke loudly, for Ralegh himself was on duty outside the door, and would overhear his own dispraise.

The Queen was irritated by his persistence, and turned the conversation to unkind comment on Essex's mother. Essex retorted that since she was determined to disgrace him and his house—for his sister, she should not stay any longer to disquiet her. Though it was almost midnight he would send her away that night. For himself, he had no joy to be in any place, but loath to be about her when he knew that his affection was so much thrown down, and such a wretch as Ralegh highly esteemed. The Queen was unwilling to continue the conversation, and turned to speak with the Countess of Warwick.

Essex withdrew from her presence. He roused up his sister and sent her away from the house under the escort of his servants to London, whither he followed her soon after. He was angry and hurt, for he believed that the Queen was by this curious behaviour trying to force him into a reconciliation with Ralegh. He resolved forthwith to leave England and go back to the Low Countries, to Flushing; he would be in time for the fall of Sluys, and if he were killed, then a fair death was better than an unquiet life. The Queen heard of his departure and sent Robert Carey post haste in pursuit. Carey found him at Sandwich, just as he was going on board. Essex obeyed the command, and reluctantly came back to London.

Essex had other rivals, amongst them Charles Blount, who had some share of the Queen's favour. Blount first came to Court about the same time, and was the elder by some four years. He was a scion of the ancient nobility, but poor; for his grandfather was extravagant; his father had poured his patrimony into the sink of alchemy, being convinced that he would ultimately find the philosopher's stone; and his elder brother, William, Lord Mountjoy, was a prodigal. When Charles Blount first was introduced into Court the Queen was at dinner, and her glances fell upon this tall neat young man. She asked her carver who he was, but he could not answer, and so the question was passed round until at last the information came back to her that it was the Lord Mountjoy's younger brother. Blount noticed that the Queen was watching him and blushed. She called him and gave him her hand to kiss, with gracious and kindly words, remarking to those around her that she knew there must be in him some noble blood, and so, with promise of her favour, she dismissed him.

Blount was also conspicuous amongst the younger courtiers for those qualities which most of them lacked. He was bashful and modest, a great reader of books of all kinds, but particularly of history and travel, and so economical in his habits that he managed to subsist at Court on a younger brother's meagre portion.

One day at the tilt, Blount so distinguished himself before the Queen that she sent him a gold chessman—a queen, richly enamelled—as a token of her favour. Next day he appeared in the Privy Chamber with the chessman tied to his arm with crimson ribbon, and the better to display it he carried his cloak under his arm. As Essex passed through the Privy Chamber he noticed Blount's unusual decoration and asked Fulke Greville what it was. Greville told him that it was the Queen's favour which she had sent after yesterday's tilting.

Essex, jealous and annoyed that anyone should share her sunshine, remarked contemptuously, "Now I see every fool must have a favour."

The remark was so insulting, and so public, that Blount sent him a challenge. They met by Marylebone Park. Essex was wounded in the thigh and disarmed. The Queen missed the two young men from their usual places, and guessing that something had happened, was very curious to know the truth. When she heard that Essex had been humiliated, she exclaimed, "By God's Death, it is fit that someone or other should take him down, and teach him better manners, otherwise there would be no rule with him." From this time, as so frequently happens in such a case, the two young men became friends.

By the new year Englishmen were reconciled to a war with Spain, and as the spring went on, their enthusiasm grew into fervour. Soldiers were busily trained for home defence, and there was an unusual spirit of idealism abroad which caused Englishmen to open their purses and give generously. The Council sent to ask the citizens of London what they would contribute. The Lord Mayor replied by asking what the Council considered a fitting contribution. Five thousand men and fifteen ships was the demand. The Lord Mayor asked for two days to consider, and then he returned with the request, on behalf of his brethren, that the Council would be pleased to accept ten thousand men and thirty ships.

The Queen was still hoping that her negotiations with Parma would end in peace, but preparations were continued. The Spanish plan was an invasion of England directed against London; and the defence of England by sea was under command of Lord Charles Howard and by land under Leicester, as Lieutenant-General. Essex was chosen General of the Horse. The preparations went on throughout the spring and summer. At last, on July 19, the beacon fires gave the warning that the Spanish fleet was in the Channel, and the troops for the defence of London marched to their rendezvous at Tilbury. Soon there was a force of some 16,000 men assembled, the noblemen in tents, the rest in cabins made of poles and leaves. Essex's own contingent consisted of sixty musketeers, sixty harquebusiers, and two hundred light horse wearing his colours of orange, with facings of white silk.

The Queen herself came down by water to visit them and passed in her coach through the kneeling ranks to her lodging. She had been warned by some of her more cautious advisers that there was a risk; there might be traitors in the camp. But she was never afraid for herself. Next day, mounted on a charger and wearing a breastplate, she rode out to inspect the troops. She refused an escort and, accompanied only by Leicester and the Earl of Ormonde, carrying the Sword of State before her, with a page following with her helmet, she rode down the line, and then when the cheering had died down, she made a speech to the troops. On public occasions the Queen was brilliant, but this was the greatest of all her speeches. After the morning's work she dined with Leicester. A message came that Parma's army was on the way. At such a moment of danger she said that she would stay with her army, and she was still at Tilbury when the true report reached her, on August 8, that the Spanish Armada was utterly routed.

The Queen had always been fond of Leicester, and in these emotional days she felt so grateful to him that she decided to promote him to the extraordinary office of Lieutenant-General of England and Ireland. The patent was made out, but Burghley and Walsingham protested that it was dangerous to grant so much power to one man. A few days later, when the camp was broken up, Leicester set out for Kenilworth. He was taken ill at Cornbury Park in Oxfordshire and died on September 4. He left behind him a long will, written by himself. To " my good son-in-law the Earl of Essex," he left certain lands, and " the best armour I have, one my Lord Chancellor gave me, two my best horses, with a George and Garter, in hope he shall wear it shortly." And indeed he did, for the Queen rewarded his late services at Tilbury by admitting him to the Order.

Essex's mother was thus for the second time a widow, and soon afterwards she married Christopher Blount, Leicester's Master of Horse. Scandalmongers as usual talked of poison. Leicester in his last days, they said, was so jealous of his Master of Horse that he had a poisoned draft prepared for the Countess, which she exchanged for his medicine.

CHAPTER IV

THE PORTUGAL VOYAGE

IN the spring of 1589, it was decided to carry the war into Spanish territory. The proposal was heartily seconded by Don Antonio, the ex-King of Portugal. This unfortunate Prince had been an exile in England since 1581. The year before, Henry, King of Portugal, died leaving no certain heir. The people elected Don Antonio, Prior of Crato, bastard son of the late King's brother; but the Spanish King had a claim to the throne through his mother, the late King's sister. He sent the Duke of Alva into Portugal, and ten weeks later Portugal passed under Spanish rule.

Don Antonio remained hopeful that one day he would win back his kingdom. The Spaniards were not loved by the Portuguese, and after the Spanish disaster he received most encouraging messages from the Portuguese clergy. He declared to the Queen that if she would but have him landed in Portugal, the whole country would rise against the Spaniard.

An expedition was therefore fitted out which Drake was to command by sea and Sir John Norris by land. The main object was loot. The Queen invested £60,000 and loaned six ships. The two generals ventured £50,000, and the City of London and other port towns contributed ships to the total number of one hundred and forty-six, great and small. By their commission the generals were entitled to impress 4,000, but such was the general optimism that they were ready to sail on the day first appointed with 17,000 soldiers and 5,000 sailors.

Most of the experienced professional soldiers were eager to join in another blow at the Spaniard. Essex naturally was on fire to go; he saw not only adventure and honour, and the romance of restoring an exiled Prince to his own, but here was a chance of making some money, which he badly needed. The Queen was unwilling to allow him or any other nobleman to take part, and he knew that if he asked permission it would be refused. He therefore kept his plans very close, confiding only in his brother Walter, Sir Roger Williams, and his particular friends, Sir Philip Butler and Sir Edward Wingfield.

The expedition was almost ready. The main fleet was at anchor in Plymouth Sound, but the Queen's ship *Swiftsure*, with Sir Roger Williams on board, was at Falmouth. For some days Essex had been quietly preparing, and writing farewell letters—more than forty—to the Queen, the Council, his particular friends and servants. To his grandfather he wrote:

"SIR,

"What my courses have been I need not repeat, for no man knoweth them better than yourself. What my state now is, I will tell you: my revenue no greater than when I sued my livery; my debts at the least two or three and twenty thousand pounds; Her Majesty's goodness hath been so great as I could not ask more of her; no way left to repair myself but mine own adventure, which I had much rather undertake than to offend Her Majesty with suits, as I have done heretofore. If I should speed well, I will adventure to be rich; if not, I will never live to see the end of my poverty. And so, wishing that this letter, which I have left for you, may come to your hands, I commit you to God's good protection. From my study some few days before my departure.

"Your assured friend,
"R. ESSEX."

To lull any suspicion that might have arisen, he sent to invite Lord Rich, his brother-in-law, to sup with him in his chamber. He shut the letters in his desk, locked it, and took the key. Between five and six in the evening of April 3, he quietly made his way to St. James's Park. Master Reynolds, his secretary, and a groom were waiting for him with his hunting horses.

They mounted and rode off. For ninety miles he used his own horses. Then he took up post horses, sent back his own with the groom, together with a letter to Lord Rich and the key of his desk. He rode on to Plymouth, which he reached in the early morning of the 5th, having covered nearly 220 miles in thirty-six hours. He had ridden so hard that he was hours ahead of the regular posts and of anyone who might have been sent to recall him.

At Plymouth he avoided Drake and Norris, and went on to Falmouth, where he boarded the *Swiftsure*. Roger Williams was waiting for him, and immediately they put out to sea. They had no certain knowledge of the plan of campaign, and supposed that the expedition would make for Cadiz. Thither they sailed, and for some weeks beat up and down the coast waiting for the fleet. They took some corn ships, and then sailing northwards they reached the Islands of Bayon and made a landing at Cannas, but the garrison fled at their approach. It was not until May 13 that they fell in with the fleet and learnt what had happened.

A short time after their hasty sailing Sir Francis Knollys had arrived at Plymouth and had put out to sea in a pinnace. The Queen was very angry. The Earl of Huntingdon arrived soon after, with peremptory orders for Essex's return, followed by the command that if Roger Williams had not already been put to death for his gross breach of discipline he should be deprived of his command and kept in close restraint.

As for the expedition, Essex had missed some considerable fighting. The fleet had sailed from Plymouth on April 14, and anchored off the Groin on the 20th. They landed in pinnaces and long boats a mile from the town, and drew up the army without opposition. There was some resistance as they advanced, but the enemy withdrew within the walls and that night the army bivouacked in the villages and mills adjoining, though troubled in their passage by the cannon from the great galleon *St. John* and other ships lying in the Road. The following morning Norris reconnoitred the town, which was built on the neck of an island, and decided to attempt an entrance by escalade. Next day, after some sharp fighting, they entered the town, when the inhabitants fled to the upper town. A number of prisoners were taken and some few spared, but about 500 had their throats cut. The soldiers also came on great stores of wine which they pillaged, and soon many were so drunk that they paid no attention to the shot from the upper town, and so perished.

Then followed several days of hard fighting to make a breach through the walls and to assault the town, but because of the failure of the mines there was no entry. On the sixth day news came that the Spaniards were assembling an army, already 8,000 strong, at Puente de Burgos. On May 6, Norris led out nine regiments, and found the enemy in position about half a mile from their camp. They were soon dislodged and retired to the camp, which was approached by a bridge over a creek. The English troops followed resolutely to the bridge, whose defenders fled. There was rather more resistance in the camp, but soon the Spaniards were in complete rout, and for three miles the pursuit and killing went on. The field being thus cleared of the enemy, Norris set his men to pillage and burn, and good plunder was taken, though the upper town of the Groin still held out. The army was therefore re-embarked, and every house in the lower town set on fire. On the 8th, the ships weighed anchor and continued the journey towards Lisbon, which was his main objective, being very much hampered by contrary winds. This was the news which Essex learnt five days later, when the *Swiftsure* met with the fleet.

Essex's arrival was embarrassing to the two generals. The Queen's orders to send him home at once were so definite that they hardly dared disobey, but yet they could ill spare either the *Swiftsure* or Roger Williams. Fortunately the wind was with them; even if he had wished, Essex could not return. So, without further delay the fleet went on its way down the coast of Portugal until the castle of Peniche was sighted. The wind was blowing hard and the sea ran high, but the generals determined to make a landing at once, and the soldiers went down into the boats. One was overset, and twenty-five men were drowned, but the rest were rowed in towards the shore. The men jumped into the sea breast high and struggled ashore.

Essex was the first to land. As the English soldiers clambered up the beach, the garrison made a sally, five companies under the Count de Fuentes, and were seen advancing. Essex and his brother, with Williams, had by this time collected enough men to make two troops. Of these one was left to cover the landing, the other was sent round by the sandhills to take the advancing Spaniards in the flank. As soon as Fuentes perceived this move he changed direction and moved towards the threatened flank. The flank troop charged and the Spaniards made a brief stand, but they soon gave way and retired into the town, whither the English followed them. There was no further fighting.

That night Norris summoned the castle to surrender. The commander, who was a Portuguese, ascertaining that Don Antonio had landed, yielded. Within the castle there were discovered many shot and pikes with which Antonio's Portuguese could be armed. The next day was spent in organising the army, and the horse were brought ashore. While this was being done, the local friars came in, and promised that in two days many more horse and foot would be ready to help Don Antonio.

The two generals now drew up their operation orders. One company of foot was to remain in the castle of Peniche to guard the sick and wounded; the rest of the army under Norris, less six companies left in the ships, to march along the coast to Lisbon; the fleet, under Drake, to sail round and join the army as quickly as the wind would allow. Strict orders were given that there was to be no pillaging.

Next day, the 18th, the army was marshalled. As the column moved forward Drake stood on a hill by the route of march, saluting each commander as he passed. Early in the march the troops received a sharp reminder that discipline was to be maintained. A soldier broke into a house for plunder; he was promptly hanged by the provost marshal. The first night the army bivouacked at Lorinha; the troops were greatly handicapped, for there was no transport and all munition had to be carried. Next day this lack was remedied, and the march was continued to Torres Vedras, which the Spaniards evacuated.

The difficulties of the expedition were now increasing, for food was running short, as the men were obeying the orders not to plunder and Antonio's new subjects were showing no eagerness to supply their King. The fourth day's march brought the army to Lores, and still, except for a small cavalry action, there was no resistance. At night Drake's regiment was billeted in a village a mile in advance of the main body. Next morning a number of the Spaniards drew near with the cry " *Viva El Rey Don Antonio.*" The inexperienced soldiers who were on guard, not suspecting the treachery, allowed them to approach and were overpowered; but the alarm was given and the enemy driven out. Next day the army again moved forward and reached Alvelana, where a number of the soldiers, unadvisedly drinking water from two pools, were poisoned.

The same night Essex and Roger Williams attempted an ambush. About eleven o'clock they led out a thousand men and posted them near the town. Then some men were sent forward to raise an alarm; but the enemy refused to be drawn out and at dawn they rejoined the main body.

On May 25, the army entered the suburbs of Lisbon, where they found the houses shut up and cleared of their movables. Only a few old folk and beggars were left to cry " *Viva* " for Don Antonio. The troops stood to arms all night. No one assailed them, but at midnight the sky was lit up by the flames of the houses on the city walls, which the Spaniards were burning lest the invaders should use them. The next day was spent in billeting the troops and posting musketeers to keep down the fire from the walls.

By this time the men were very weary after six days' hard march and a sleepless night's watch, and they dispersed to their billets to rest. Then suddenly the enemy were upon them. The alarm was given, and Colonel Brett, into whose quarters the first rush was made, rallied his men. For a while there was fierce fighting; Brett was killed, and one of his captains and two more were wounded. But the attack was held, and soon the Spaniards fled in disorder, Essex with his own men pursuing them right into their gates.

Next day Norris called a council of war and they debated the next move. Drake had reached Cascaes with the fleet and supplies, but he would not or could not pass the batteries in the river to join with the army. The situation was not too good. Don Antonio's promised supporters failed to appear. Should they fetch the heavier guns from the fleet and await the Portuguese? If so, then they might be overwhelmed by the Spanish forces which were reported to be on their way. Moreover, the casualties by sickness were daily increasing. Norris's decision was that unless Don Antonio's reinforcements came that night, he would abandon Lisbon in the morning.

When morning came Don Antonio's Portuguese were not sufficient to make a cornet of forty horse. The army was paraded and marched away. Essex and Williams remained to the last with the rearguard to cover the withdrawal. Then Essex walked back to the gates of Lisbon and thrust in his pike demanding if any Spaniard mewed therein durst adventure forth in favour of his mistress. There was no reply.

The army withdrew to Cascaes without engagement, but followed by the Spanish cavalry, who cut down any straggler that could not keep up with the column. Two days later a friar reported that the enemy were in the field and had reached San Julian. It was welcome news to Norris, who desired nothing so much as a fight in the open. To goad the enemy into action he sent off a messenger with a challenge, giving the Spanish general the lie, and daring him to come on next morning with his whole army. Essex joined in the challenge. He offered to fight any of the enemy, if they had amongst them a nobleman of his quality; and if not, then six, eight, ten, as many as they would appoint, should meet as many of theirs between the armies to try the fortune of battle. Norris was so hopeful that he paraded the army at three o'clock in the morning and marched back to San Julian, but the enemy were gone from their camping-ground, which showed all the signs of a hasty retreat.

The castle of Cascaes had so far resisted Drake, but when the army approached the governor surrendered. For the next few days there was better success. The fleet came on a great convoy of sixty ships from the Baltic, laden with corn, masts, cables, copper and wax, and some of them tall ships of great burden intended for the Spanish king's shattered navy.

For Essex the adventure now ended. The supply ships from England arrived, bringing with them a letter from the Queen, dated April 15 and now nearly two months old.

"ESSEX,
"Your sudden and undutiful departure from our presence and your place of attendance, you may easily conceive how offensive it is, and ought to be, unto us. Our great favours bestowed on you without deserts, hath drawn you thus to neglect and forget your duty; for other constructions we cannot make of those your strange actions. Not meaning, therefore, to tolerate this your disordered part, we gave directions to some of our Privy Council to let you know our express pleasure for your immediate repair hither; which you have not performed, as your duty doth bind you, increasing greatly thereby your former offence and undutiful behaviour, in departing in such sort without our privity, having so special office of attendance and charge near our person. We do therefore charge and command you forthwith upon receipt of these our letters, all excuses and delays set apart, to make your present and immediate repair unto us, to understand our

further pleasure. Whereof see you fail not, as you will be loth to incur our indignation, and will answer for the contrary at your uttermost peril."

There could be no argument. On June 6, Essex sailed for home. The Queen was delighted to see him and all was forgiven.

Drake reached Plymouth on June 21, and Norris on July 5. Don Antonio returned to the Court, discredited and despised. The moral effect of the voyage was considerable, for valuable booty was brought home, and the Spaniard's weakness at home amply revealed. In itself the voyage was a disaster; six thousand men were dead of disease, and for some days the disbanded soldiers terrorised London.

CHAPTER V

FIRST COMMAND

ESSEX'S prospects at Court were brightening. The Queen was very generous to him, and amongst other gifts she had granted a lease of the farm of sweet wines, which would give him a princely income, so long as he held it. With such encouragements his ambitions were growing, and he began to take a hand in State affairs.

For the last year and more he had exchanged casual letters with the King of Scots. This autumn he renewed the correspondence, and with his sister, Penelope, and her husband, Lord Rich, he began to sue the King's favour. Richard Douglas, an agent of the Scots King, was in London. When he returned to Edinburgh he took with him one Ottoman, who had been one of Leicester's secretaries. Ottoman was introduced to the King and delivered a letter from Essex, promising his service and fidelity. The King replied, but the most important part of the message was not committed to writing. The correspondence was partly in cipher, at least the proper names were concealed under appropriate pseudonyms which Penelope Rich devised, the King being "Victor," Queen Elizabeth "Venus," Essex "Ernestus," or the "Weary Knight," and Penelope herself "Rialta." But nothing came of it, for the King, who had long been anxiously awaiting his bride from Denmark, suddenly decided to make a romantic journey and fetch her himself.

At Court Essex allied himself with the Secretary, Sir Francis Walsingham. Walsingham's daughter, Frances, was a lady of great beauty. She had married Philip Sidney in 1583, and since Sidney's death lived quietly with her mother. Essex saw much of her in the last days at Arnheim before Sidney died.

He now came to Walsingham saying that he was a suitor to his daughter, not for any wealth or portion, but only that he might be enabled by his good counsel to be fitted to do his prince and country some service. Walsingham agreed, and they were married secretly. Unfortunately the bargain went awry; Walsingham died on April 6, 1590, and by Lord Burghley's orders his papers were impounded. Walsingham died so poor that his body was secretly buried at midnight in St. Paul's, lest his creditors should seize it.

Nothing was said to the Queen until the autumn, when the new Countess was obviously pregnant, and Essex acknowledged the marriage. The Queen, as had been anticipated, was enraged, but less than was expected, and contented herself with threats. She was angry, she said, not only that she had not been told, but because Essex had by this marriage disparaged the dignity of his house. Essex acted tactfully, neither denying the marriage, nor boasting of it, and as he did not bring his wife to Court the Queen's anger was lessened. By the end of November he was again in favour.

The troubles in France were at this time occupying the Queen and the Council. In the previous August, Henri of Navarre became King of France on the assassination of Henri III. The new King was a Protestant, and the French Catholics, who had formed themselves into a Catholic League, rebelled. Henri was in great difficulty, for the Leaguers were too strong for him, and in a few weeks he was driven north to Dieppe and was apparently in a hopeless position. The Queen, however, helped him with a large loan and an army of 4,000, and the Leaguers were defeated at the battle of Arques.

In 1590, the Spanish King sent the Duke of Parma to help the Leaguers. Parma advanced through Picardy; another Spanish force entered Brittany. In October Viscount Turenne arrived in London as ambassador from the French King to ask for a force of English soldiers to be sent over to help him. Amongst other instructions, he was told to visit Essex and to say that his Majesty of France knew of his affection, and prayed him to use his good offices to render the Queen more gracious and favourable to his ambassador. The request was backed by a personal letter from the King.

The Queen was at first more concerned at the threat to Brittany, for if the Spaniards could occupy any of the ports they would be very favourably placed for an invasion of England. An appeal for help came through the French ambassador from the Prince de Dombes, the French King's general. The Queen answered that she was surprised to receive a direct request from a subject of the French King that she should send troops without his knowledge. Nevertheless, at the end of January, 1591, Sir Edmund Yorke was sent over to tell the King that the Queen would aid him in Brittany with two or three thousand men. Two months later Sir Roger Williams with 600 men was despatched to Dieppe to help the Governor there, and in May, Sir John Norris landed a small expeditionary force at Paimpol to join the French in Brittany. Both commanders soon distinguished themselves. On the evening of May 19, Williams set out with the Governor of Dieppe, and a combined force of 700 English and French marched by night against Cinqsen, which they reached about noon next day. They broke through the defences after a two hours' fight, and slaughtered the garrison to a man. Four days later Norris was mainly responsible for the capture of Guingamp.

Henri was still desperate, and needed far greater assistance. Essex begged the Queen to grant it, and to send him in command. She refused three times, though Essex pleaded with her on his knees for two hours at a time. At last she consented, and on June 25, an agreement was signed for the despatch of 3,400 men to Normandy, to be added to the force already there under command of Williams. Essex was very excited, and sent to his tenants to demand that according to the terms of their leases they should provide themselves with horses and accompany him. Requisitions for troops were sent out by the Council to the City of London and twenty counties, who were to be ready to embark on July 20. On the morning of the 15th, the Queen changed her mind, and messages from the Council went out to the Lords Lieutenant to let it be known that her Majesty's will and pleasure was that the soldiers levied should not leave their shires until new warning had been received; but in the afternoon a second set of messengers were sent chasing the first to announce that, upon further consideration, " it is now her Majesty's pleasure that the said companies with their captains and officers shall come and march to the place afore appointed to take shipping, notwithstanding anything written by us in the forenoon."

Four days later the Queen came to Burghley's house in Covent Garden to see Essex's own contingent of horse, made up of his tenants and romantic young gentlemen who volunteered to go with him for the love of adventure, amongst them being his brother Walter.

Essex's instructions as Lord General were drawn up on July 21. Although nominally in command of the expedition, he was provided with three experienced men to be his tutors, Sir Thomas Leighton and Sir Henry Killigrew, as officers in the army, and Sir Henry Unton, the new ambassador to the French King. Unton's instructions, which were signed on July 24, included a clause that he was to have especial regard to the actions of the Earl of Essex, and he was charged on his allegiance to deal plainly with him.

Essex was held up for some days at Dover by contrary winds. He landed at Dieppe on August 3, to find that Sir Roger Williams had gone off to be with the French King, who was besieging Noyon. On the 7th Essex wrote to the Queen:

" MOST DEAR AND MOST GRACIOUS SOVEREIGN,

" We have, since our coming hither, thrice advertised the King of our landing, and desired to have his direction, both for your Majesty's satisfaction for the confirmation, and also how he would have these forces employed. But I do not hear yet that our letters are arrived: the way is dangerous for a single man to pass, and I fear they may be intercepted; but I look every day for answer, and I hope your Majesty shall have present satisfaction. Till I receive the confirmation, or know that it is safely sent unto your Majesty, these troops shall be as well accommodated here about as I can get them. Your Majesty's army is, I dare say, for the number, the finest troop in Christendom. I protest unto your Majesty, the French do more admire them than can be believed. I hope your Majesty shall receive honour by them. But if I could be an instrument of the greatest honour to your Majesty, and the greatest good to my country, and yet another in mine absence should rob me of your gracious and dearest favour, I were in his case, *qui mundum lucratus perdidit animam*. I am jealous of all the world, and have cause, since all other men that have either open eyes or sensible hearts are my competitors. I do conjure you, by your own worth, to be constant to him who will, for your Majesty's favour, forsake himself and all the world besides. I wish your Majesty's joys to be as infinite as your worth, and my fortune to be as everlasting as my affection. Arques, this 7th of August.

"Your Majesty's servant, whose duty and affection is greater than any man's, or than all men's.

"R. Essex."

Six days later Williams appeared. He came from the French King to report the capture of Noyon, and to invite Essex to visit him. The journey would be risky, for it lay through country which swarmed with enemy patrols. Essex immediately decided to go. His lancers and all other voluntary gentlemen were ordered to parade the next day and to carry no baggage but a spare shirt. They started about noon, and riding through the dust and heat, reached Neuchatel at ten o'clock at night. At six the next morning they were on horseback again on the way to Gisors. That day they rode about ten leagues, and were in the saddle for twenty hours, until two in the morning of the 16th. Compiègne was reached on the 18th, and next day Essex invited M. Revience, the Governor of Picardy, and the evening was spent in dancing and music. Thence Essex went on to meet the King, escorted by Monsieur D'O, the Great Treasurer of France, and the Marquis de Pisana. The King had come from Noyon to a castle near Compiègne to meet the party. At the gate, Essex was saluted by the Marshal Biron, a very lively old gentleman, who conducted him into a garden where the King was waiting with many of his noblemen. He received Essex with great demonstration of cordiality, and after long discourse led him into the castle and there feasted him. Afterwards, Essex and his party were escorted to a neighbouring village for the night. The King showed himself very gracious to Essex's followers, riding after them on their way and bidding them welcome in English.

Next day Essex went to the King, and after listening to a sermon they went to dinner together. Then, escorted by a dozen gentlemen, they rode to Noyon. The town was in ruins, the bridges broken, all the suburbs burned out, orchards and gardens utterly destroyed, churches and walls cracked and rent, and the whole town filthy. Essex conferred with the Marshal Biron, and this day, and until the afternoon of the 23rd, the troops rested.

The French King was an affable monarch, and his sense of dignity at times seemed unbecoming to those more used to the formalities of Whitehall. One evening he started a leaping contest with his nobles, and Essex outleaped them all. Essex took his leave of the King after dinner on the 23rd, and all the chief English gentlemen were introduced and kissed his hand. He promised that he would soon be with them, and meanwhile he hoped that they would not be idle.

The outward journey had been risky, for they went through the enemy's country, and were closely followed by enemy scouts. The return was more dangerous, for the Leaguers would be waiting for them. About midnight on August 29/30, Essex reached Pont de l'Arche, having narrowly missed a force of 700 horse, commanded by Villars, the Leaguers'

Governor of Rouen, which lay up for the party. Here he sent for his army to join him.

He now reported at length to the Council:

" Upon my coming to the King, I found him in his estate; his army consisted of some 7,000 foot, whereof 3,000 were Swisses, the rest French, and 2,000 horse, the most French gentlemen, so well mounted and so well armed, as they are able to beat double their number of any entertained horsemen in Christendom. Before the taking of Noyon, both the horse and foot were in great misery for want of money. The inhabitants of Noyon in the composition agreed to give the King 40,000 crowns, which sum hath satisfied his army for a while; but stayed Mareschal Biron's coming into these parts eight days, because the money was not readily paid. But by this time he is marching this way.

" The King, as your Lordships have heard by M. de Reaux, is gone, with 300 gentlemen and as many harquebusiers on horseback, into Champaigny, to join with his Allmayne army; he shall be there strengthened by the Duke of Nevers with 1,000 horse and some foot. Perhaps your Lordships are unsatisfied that the King, both intending and promising the siege of Rouen, doth bend himself to a contrary course. Surely so was I also much troubled when I first heard of this new resolution; but, upon conference with the King and his Council, I understood the reasons of his journey; which, though I dare neither censure nor allow, yet I assure your Lordships I cannot impugn.

" First, his person being there, he is sure to keep them from mutinies or breaking; which, by so poor a King, and of so mercenary a nation, are things to be feared. Secondly, he will draw them to be divided, whereby he shall leave some in Champaigny to go join with Mareschal d'Aumont, to stay the Pope's succour from coming to the Duke de Mayne; and send others into Brittany, to strengthen the Prince de Dombes, and yet bring the greatest part with himself. Lastly, he shall make them pass the river of Seine; and so he hath them engaged to go with him, either to the siege of Rouen, or to fight with the Duke of Parma.

"And yet, to satisfy her Majesty, and to show he hath no intent but the siege of Rouen, he sends Mareschal Biron, with all his army he had before Noyon, to join with us, and hath commanded the Duke of Montpensier to be there also with the forces of the Normans, which are 1,000 horse, and 4 or 5,000 foot. Further, he saith by this means he shall more surely effect that which her Majesty desires; for, drawing his whole force together, he shall be able to fight with the Duke of Parma if he come, and yet keep Rouen besieged.

"If Mareschal Biron keep his word, we will invest Rouen by the 15th of this month, by our computation; and, by the 25th, the King and his whole forces of Allmaynes and all will be with us. We shall make the approaches and trenches before he come; and, after he comes, I hope we shall be in it within eight days. Upon this action the whole state of France depends; for if Rouen be taken, the King is sure to have all Normandy brought into obedience, there being no town able to hold out two days, but Newhaven, and that, being shut up by land, may be by her Majesty's ships starved in two months. Also the King shall have means in Rouen to make wars of himself, I mean by the ransom of the inhabitants, not by the customs, for they are already assured to her Majesty for debt. Noyon gave 40,000 crowns ransom, and Rouen is worth forty of Noyon; and ransomed it will be, for a populace that is fearful and distressed will never endure the danger of a sack.

"But it may be objected that Rouen may be as obstinate as Paris, and that would never hear of any composition. I answer there is great difference between a lingering siege, where there is nothing but famine to constrain the defendants, and a furious battery, the terror whereof is so great, as we see few towns in our days endure an assault, when there is a sufficient breach made, and a royal army ready to enter; and the defences of Rouen must be as well of the burgesses as of the soldiers, by reason of the greatness of the place, which the soldiers in garrison there cannot man.

"To be short, if he take it, he possesseth the wealth of France, for all the merchants, since the decay of Paris, are retired thither; he absolutely commands the Seine, even to Paris, and, all places that stand upon it; he besiegeth Newhaven by land in ruining all the country round about it; and he gets so great reputation to his side, as all between Paris and the sea will in all likelihood revolt to him. Of the other side, if he gets it not, his strength is weakened, his party discouraged, his means clean spent, the enemy coming still stronger upon him, and he every day less able to resist; therefore, *hic labor, hoc opus*.

"It is miraculous that he hath held out all this while, for I assure your Lordships that I find, upon conference with his ministers, that all his certain revenue doth not answer the wages of his garrison soldiers, so as he hath nothing to maintain himself and his army but what he gets with the sword. But God hath raised him with small means to do great things, that all might be ascribed unto Him from Whom all victory comes. And next unto God, her Majesty hath done most for him; for she hath delivered him in his danger, strengthened him in his weakness, and increased him when he grew in strength, that she might be a partner with him in his conquests against the League, and with Nature in making him King of France; for as Nature in his birth gave him a title, so her Majesty by her succours will help him to a possession.

"Your Lordships will pardon my rude and disorderly writing, I having but one company of horse for my guard, and an enemy six times my number, that still these four days hath attended on me; I have passed sometimes within caliver shot of his scouts, and see them when we pass through any champain on both sides; but I thank God I have not yet lost so much as a carriage horse. As soon as I join with our troops, I hope your Lordships shall hear we will not be idle. I humbly take my leave, and commend your Lordships to God's best protection.

"Your Lordships' humbly at command,

"R. Essex.

"Pont de l'Arche, this 2nd September, *stilo novo.*"

For the next few days Essex was afflicted by trouble after trouble. From Pont de l'Arche the army moved to Ravilly, about four miles from Rouen. A sudden and very violent attack of fever came over him, leaving him so weak that he had to be carried between two horses in a litter made of sticks. There was constant fighting between patrols and larger bodies, and on September 8 Essex sent a considerable force to try to draw Villars out of Rouen. Unfortunately they fell into an ambush, and were fired on at close range by musketeers hidden behind a hedge. Walter Devereux, Essex's dear and only brother, was shot in the head and died instantly. His body was saved from the enemy and brought away through the bravery of John Wotton and Sir Conyers Clifford. His companions embalmed it and enclosed it in lead, intending to carry it with them when Rouen was entered.

This grief was followed by angry criticism from the Queen. Everything annoyed her. At first Essex wrote every third day. Then, when he set out for Noyon, the letters suddenly ceased; she neither received news, nor did her letters reach him. As a result, a pretty proposal of hers went awry. This year she made her annual progress in Sussex and Hampshire, and on August 26 she was at Portsmouth. She expressed a wish that Essex should bring the French King with him to pay her a visit. She stayed at Portsmouth for five days, without news and with daily increasing anxiety and irritation, which swelled when she did hear of Essex's foolhardy journey to Noyon. She was angry, too, with the French King. Her troops were sent over for two months with the definite object of assisting him to capture Rouen, and she expected him to undertake the siege at once. A month had passed, nothing was being done, and the expenses were mounting. She wrote that at the end of the two months she would recall her soldiers, and Essex.

Essex was greatly distressed, mentally and physically, by the Queen's bitter complaints, which reached him at Arques on September 10. "I want words to express my just grief," he complained to Sir Robert Cecil. "I was blamed as negligent, undutiful, rash in going, slow in returning, undiscreet in dividing the horse from the foot, faulty in all things, because I was not fortunate to please." On the 12th, he wrote to the Queen to answer her criticisms, especially that he had not written more often. Before going to the King, he said, he had written four times in a fortnight, but afterwards he could not send a letter unless he had an army to convey every messenger. After his return to Pont de l'Arche, he was so ill that for a day he seemed likely to die. He was still very ill.

"I have been sick all day, and yet write at night till my dim eyes and weak hand do fail me. I wish your Majesty's honour, health, and contentment to be infinite, and that you may encourage all those who serve you for hope; as for me, I will not be weary till my last hour, what wrong soever you do me. Your Majesty's servant, miserable by his loss, and afflicted with your unkindness,

"R. Essex."

Next day he wrote to Burghley to report:

"Mareschal Biron is come into these quarters with all the King's army; all his preparations are almost ready, he will be ready to besiege Rouen within ten days, but he is loath to leave Gournay on his back. The reasons are, first, because if the enemy hold Gournay on the one side, and Caudebec on the other, we shall be in greater necessity than they that are besieged; for if the enemy put 4 or 500 horse into either of these two garrisons, there shall not a tittle of bread come to our army without a wonderful great convoy; of the other side, if

Gournay were taken, there is no enemy that can hurt us during the siege, for between Dieppe and Gisors all the country would be the King's. Also, if we take that town, we do put off all succours from Rouen; for, if the Duke of Parma come, his army must be victualled from Abbeville and Amiens, or from Beauvais, which Gournay being won, are both unprofitable to him, for Gournay and Gisors do cover Rouen towards Picardy.

"But your Lordship may think that this protracts time; surely I think not, for I think that since the place is weak, and yet of such use for the siege of Rouen, it is a readier way to take Rouen than if we went straight thither. I do not think that Gournay can hold out six days. If I durst have gone with our English to have joined with the Mareschal when he first wrote for me, I think we should have been almost in it ere this. He hath written to me again to come nearer to him, which my Lord Ambassador and Sir Thomas Leighton think necessary; Mr. Killigrew is not well, but I will go to him anon to know his opinion. I do nothing without a general assent, and yet all the fault is laid upon me.

"We shall do well to draw our men nearer to him, because we are nearer Rouen by much, and we shall have them live upon the country, and so, perhaps, save a week of their sendings: if he be importunate on us to draw our men before the town, I will tell him I have my hands bound. I would be glad to be directed by your Lordship what we should do, for surely this restraint to do nothing but besiege Rouen may hinder the siege of Rouen very much; for a man must first take the port, that will lodge in the market-place. Your Lordship may now be assured that Rouen is besieged, for Gournay would never be attempted for itself, since it is of no importance, but for the siege of Rouen; and in all reason Rouen is sure to be taken, for I assure your Lordship that place is not strong, and the new works are so imperfect as they will disadvantage themselves. I do not think it will hold out a month; I hope not twenty days.

"Her Majesty writes unto me that I shall not make account to stay longer than the 3rd October. I beseech your Lordship put her Majesty in mind how I serve her; good cheap for her, and my preparations were chargeable to myself; also I have lost in this action him, who, next herself, was dearest to me of all the world. If her Majesty would now revoke me with disgrace, when Rouen were to be won, I would humbly beseech her that she would take from me my life, and not my poor reputation, which I cannot lose, the place I hold considered, without some dishonour to her Majesty. I do conjure your Lordship, by the true honour which I assure myself to be in you, that you defend your poor absent friend, who, with his tongue and his sword, will do you all right, and be most ready to do you service.

"Arques, this 13th of September, 1591.

"R. ESSEX."

Marshal Biron continually urged Essex to help him capture Gournay, which lay eight leagues from Rouen and would be a constant embarrassment if left in the enemy's hands. At last Essex led his army thither, and on September 19 the siege began. The town held out for a week. Then the cannon were brought up and battered two breaches. Biron assigned one breach to be assaulted by the French and the other by the English. They marched forward with great resolution, each column striving to be the first in; but as soon as the garrison saw the troops advancing they capitulated. The conditions of surrender were hard. The governor and officers were made prisoners, not *de guerre*, but at the King's mercy; the soldiers were allowed to depart carrying white sticks only in their hands; the citizens became the King's subjects.

At Gournay a letter from the Queen reached Essex to say that he was to return to England and hand over his command to Sir Thomas Leighton. He had no wish to go home, especially as the war was just beginning to be interesting. He therefore sent Sir Francis Darcy to the Queen with a letter to beg that he might stay longer, for the King was at last about to undertake the siege of Rouen and it would be a dishonour to him for ever to come home at such a time.

As soon as Gournay had surrendered Essex sent Robert Carey with a second letter to the Queen to report its capture. Carey reached the Court, which was at Oatlands, in four days, and then learnt that Darcy was already on his way back with a peremptory order that Essex should return at once, or he would answer it to his utmost peril. The Queen was not yet up when Carey arrived. He spoke to some of the Council, who told him that there was no moving her from her resolution, and that he would only bring trouble on himself by trying to persuade her. At ten o'clock the Queen sent for him. He delivered Essex's letter. She broke out in rage against Essex and vowed that she would make him an example to all the world if he did not return at once on receiving Darcy's message.

Carey said nothing while she read the letter. The success at Gournay did not greatly please her. Then Carey began to plead boldly for Essex. He would return as ordered, Carey said, but with such a sense of disgrace that he would never afterwards have anything to do with Court or State affairs. " I know his full resolution," Carey went on, " is to retire to some cell in the country, and to live there, as a man never desirous to look a good man in the face again. And in good faith, Madam, to deal truly with your Majesty, I think you will not have him a long-lived man after his return. The late loss of his brother, whom he loved so dearly, and this heavy doom that you have laid upon him, will in a short time break his heart. Then your Majesty will have sufficient satisfaction for the offence he hath committed against you."

The Queen was still in bad humour and told him to go to his dinner. He had scarcely finished when he was again summoned. The Queen handed him a letter, in her own writing, to be given to Essex, saying that if there was anything in it that pleased him he should give Carey thanks.

Whilst waiting for the reply to his letters, Essex amused himself coursing with his officers. It was a risky amusement, in a country patrolled by the enemy, for one day they were suddenly surprised by a troop of cuirassiers who dashed out at them crying, "*Qui vive, qui vive!*" Fortunately they were troops of the King's party. He was conferring most days with Marshal Biron concerning the opening stages of the investment of Rouen.

Early on October 7, he was asked to be ready with his army for a special enterprise. Essex arrived at the head of his men at Biron's lodgings at Cinqsen, very magnificent with a great plume of feathers in his hat. The old Marshal was in good humour. "What, you young gallant," he exclaimed, "are your come hither to brave me with your white feathers? I think I have white feathers too." Whereupon he sent for a hat set with a mighty plume, and with this, and a horseman's coat of tawny velvet, covered with silver lace, he emerged looking like some swashbuckler from the haunts of Smithfield. He had some reason for feeling gay, for he had received a message that a traitor was ready to betray one of the gates of Rouen. The combined French and English army moved off in good spirit. They marched three leagues towards Rouen, and then halted in a wood. Here another message came that the information was false, and that they were marching into a trap. The troops were much dejected by this news, but Biron gave order that they should move on and occupy Darental, a village neighbouring on Rouen, which they entered so suddenly that the inhabitants were still in their houses.

Sir Francis Darcy now returned from Court, with his orders for Essex's return. Next morning, October 8, Essex rode up a hill and looked over the city of Rouen. Then he came back to his troops who were drawn up on parade. They were far fewer than when he landed two months before. He called the gentlemen to him and made a short speech. He was very sorry, he said, that no opportunity had been offered to him to lead them to a place where they might have gained great honour; but the fault was neither his nor theirs. He had received great goodwill in all and therefore he was determined to give notes of honour to some. Thereupon he bestowed knighthood on twenty-four, amongst them Charles Percy, brother to the Earl of Northumberland, Griffin Markham, Henry Danvers, and Ferdinando Gorges. Then he took leave of the army and of the Marshal Biron and rode straight to Dieppe, where he went on board a little skiff and put out into the tide. Two hours later, Carey landed at Dieppe.

When Essex reached Court, the Queen received him coldly. Whenever Essex came to her after a long absence she usually felt an immediate irritation, and her first words were critical and unkind. He was hurt and bewildered, and wrote a little note of protest.

" I see your Majesty is constant to ruin me; I do humbly and patiently yield to your Majesty's will. I appeal to all men that saw my parting from France, or the manner of my coming hither, whether I deserved such a welcome or not. To be full of words when a man is full of affliction, is for him that is not resolved what to do with himself.
" Your Majesty's humble servant,
" R. ESSEX."

The Queen's mood soon passed, and for the next week Essex stayed at Court spending the time in jollity and feasting. Then, with tears in her eyes, she gave him leave to go back to France. She was not, however, prepared to pay for her army indefinitely. Before Essex's return she had caused to be drawn up a declaration of the causes moving her to revoke her forces in Normandy, which was a long recapitulation of her grievances against the French King. She had changed her mind, but the troops were allowed to remain only on condition that he paid them.

Essex reached Dover on October 16, whence he wrote a letter to the Queen, begging her to be constant in her favour. Next day he landed at Dieppe, where he found the army in a state of disorder. The soldiers were not receiving the pay due from the King, and were robbing the countryside. Many were sick or dead, many had deserted, and most of the gentlemen were gone home. He wrote again to the Queen on the 18th:

"Most fair, most dear, and most excellent Sovereign,

"The first suit I make unto your Majesty on my arrival is, that your Majesty will free me from writing to you of any matter of business; my duty shall be otherwise performed by advertizing my Lords of your Majesty's Council of all things here, and yet my affection not wronged, which tells me, that zealous faith and humble kindness are argument enough for a letter.

"At my departure I had a restless desire honestly to disengage myself from this French action: in my absence I conceived an assured hope to do something which shall make me worthy of the name of your servant: at my return I will humbly beseech your Majesty that no cause but a great action of your own may draw me out of your sight, for the two windows of your privy chamber shall be the poles of my sphere, where, as long as your Majesty will please to have me, I am fixed and unmoveable. When your Majesty thinks that heaven too good for me, I will not fall like a star, but be consumed like a vapour by the same sun that drew me up to such a height. While your Majesty gives me leave to say I love you, my fortune is as my affection, unmatchable. If ever you deny me that liberty, you may end my life, but never shake my constancy, for were the sweetness of your nature turned into the greatest bitterness that could be, it is not in your power, as great a Queen as you are, to make me love you less. Therefore, for the honour of your sex, show yourself constant in kindness, for all your other virtues are confessed to be perfect; and so I beseech your Majesty receive all wishes of perfect happiness, from your Majesty's most humble, faithful, and affectionate servant,

"R. Essex."

The fighting round Rouen was becoming more serious as, the besiegers were closing in. On October 29, the troops were in action all day, and on November 2 the English soldiers began to dig trenches and to fortify strong points. These labours were somewhat relieved by gallantries on both sides. Essex, learning that the Chevalier Picard, whom he had met in the English Court, was within the city, sent him a letter to the effect that, but for the cause he was defending he counted him a friend, and so hoped to meet him again, at the head of his men.

The challenge was taken up by the Marquis of Villars, Governor of Rouen, who sent a reply that if Essex was willing, he would bring Picard into the field with him, armed or in his doublet, and further, if he wished it, he would bring sixteen of his gentlemen to meet the like number of Essex's gentlemen.

To this offer Essex replied in writing:

"As for your offer to make a match for me; I answer that I am in command of an army wherein are many of the quality of Chevalier Picard, and am the Lieutenant of an absolute Sovereign. But if you wish to fight yourself, on horseback or on foot, armed or in your doublet, I will maintain that the King's quarrel is juster than the League's, that I am better than you, and that my Mistress is fairer than yours. If you refuse to come alone, I will bring with me twenty, the worst of whom will be worth a colonel's place, or sixty, the least being a captain."

Villars answered that it was not in his power to accept a private challenge until the arrival of the Duke of Mayne, his superior. Meanwhile, concerning the personal clauses in the challenge, Essex was a liar. Essex retorted, "I have received your letter by my trumpet, wherein I find myself in no sort charged since the means to revenge the lie is not in myself; and, therefore, I return you this answer, that it is a foolish lie that is given upon any such terms and rests upon the giver. If it be given upon equal terms, you shall receive a fit answer."

The letters were passed round the camps and much discussed. On the French side there were many *la-las* on the odd customs of these English who ran about the world to defend the beauty of their middle-aged Mistress.

The siege now began in earnest, but Essex's army was reduced to about a thousand. He sent Sir Roger Williams over to the Queen to beg for reinforcements. The Queen was impressed by his report, and replied that she would despatch a thousand trained soldiers from the Low Countries, and 450 pioneers and miners from England. She was also pleased to send her princely thanks for the good services rendered in the fighting.

Both the French King and the Queen were in great difficulties. The King, in spite of his promises, was unable to pay the English troops. He was so poor at this time that he was himself almost without bread. A lesser man would have abandoned the business as hopeless, but he inspired devoted loyalty, as Unton noticed. "He is a most noble brave King," he wrote, "of great patience and magnanimity, not ceremonious, affable, familiar, and only followed for his true valour, but very much hated for his religion and threatened by the Catholics to forsake him if he convert not." Nor could the Queen desert him, for if she recalled her troops his army would break and he would be forced to leave the field and lose his crown, and the Spaniards would be in Dieppe.

On November 13, Henri reached the army outside Rouen. Essex rode out to meet him with an escort of all his personal company. After conferring with the King and the Marshal Biron, he waited until the King had dined and stood by him, covered, whilst the rest of the company stood bareheaded. Then he went back to prepare his men for an inspection by the King.

The siege was now pressed on more vigorously, and every day there was fighting in one or other of the quarters. Essex was showing such enthusiasm and energy that his personal followers were tired out, and agreed among themselves to take it in turns to escort him. He had a body made of iron, they complained, supporting travail, and passioned with all extremities.

The chief fighting was round a fort called St. Katherine's Castle, which defended Rouen from attacks down the Dieppe road. To mask this fort the English pioneers began to build a strong point. On the night of 18th 19th, about midnight, the King himself came down to see the work started, and because it was more than a night's work, the King's nobles and twenty-five of Essex's principal gentlemen took up a position, armed with pikes, to guard the working party. The King came again early in the morning to encourage the pioneers.

The same day Essex decided that he would go over to England to beg the Queen to send reinforcements and to allow him to continue in the command. He reached Court on November 23, to the Queen's surprise. The news from France was so uncertain that she could not make up her mind whether he should return or not. At last she consented, on the condition that if he found that there was any hope of Rouen being taken he should remain, but otherwise he was to come back to Court. The army also was to be reorganised, and its establishment lessened. Companies were to be reduced in number and captains superfluous to the new establishment dismissed.

Essex returned to Rouen on December 14. By this time the trenches near St. Katherine's Castle had been advanced so near that the English troops were actually in the enemy counterscarp, and the sides could even talk to each other. Essex and his followers were weary after their long journey, but before alighting he insisted on going up to the trenches. Hence he shouted to the enemy sentry to tell Monsieur Villars that he had come back with twenty gentlemen with him, and if he would enterprise anything against the English quarter he must do it that night or never, for 2,000 old soldiers from the Low Countries were arriving.

On December 17 and 18, a muster was taken of the English forces. Less than 200 horse remained, and the foot, who had originally been organised in twenty-five companies of 150 men, were now reduced to eight of 100, and these under strength.

About a month before, Sir Christopher Hatton, the Lord Chancellor, had died. Hatton was also Chancellor of the University of Oxford, and the University wished Essex to succeed him. It was a very honourable office, with much patronage depending, and Essex desired it. The Queen decided otherwise and chose Lord Buckhurst. On December 23, Essex wrote to Sir Robert Cecil:

"I have even now heard that the Queen, in favour of my Lord of Buckhurst, will take from me that which the University of Oxford would bestow, and ere I had read my letters the news of the Duke of Parma his passing of the river of Oise and coming with all speed hither did arrive. The first made me say I had lived too long to be so dealt with by her I held so dear; the last shewed me the fairest tomb that ever unfortunate man was buried in. If I die, pity me not, for I shall die with more pleasure than I live with. If I escape, comfort me not, for the Queen's wrong and her unkindness is too great."

Essex was all for an assault on Rouen. The town walls were weak and a resolute battery would breach them. Henri and the Marshal objected. They thought it better to continue the siege and drive the inhabitants to a composition through surrender than to risk the spoiling of the town by the soldiers, which would inevitably follow a capture by assault. Essex, as it happened, was right, for the town was well supplied and Villars was an energetic commander who gave his besiegers small rest, and plenty of excitement.

On Christmas Eve, Essex led a raid on the enemy defences at St. Katherine's, forced them from their counterscarp, and slew many. Marshal Biron undertook to defend the newly won trenches, but at eleven o'clock next morning the enemy counter-attacked and forced them back. The next night scaling ladders were prepared for an attempt to win the castle by escalade. The raiding party, wearing shirts over their armour, moved forward in the darkness, whilst Essex and the gentlemen of his army waited in support, but the ladders when set against the walls were found to be too short. The counterscarp which the enemy had retaken was again occupied after a counter-attack on the 28th, and henceforward Essex undertook to defend it himself. Every third night he and his principal gentlemen took their turn in the trenches within three pikes' length of the enemy's ground. Sometimes they chatted with the enemy across the narrow strip of no man's land. This custom almost led to a disaster, for during one of these amiable exchanges of courtesy Sir Ferdinando Gorges happened to look through a loophole and spied a party about thirty strong approaching stealthily by a byway with the intention of taking Essex and his party unawares and cutting all their throats. Gorges, though unarmed and having only his rapier, called on the nearest soldiers to follow him, and leapt over the trenches. The enemy retired back into the protection of the fort.

On December 29, when the lost ground had been recovered, Essex wrote a short note to Cecil to report that all was well.

" SIR,
"I write in haste, and with as little ease as ever man wrote: my man that brought me pen and ink doth swear he thinks the place unfit to write in, because his wits are not his own. We have now again all our first lodgings, whereof two of them are in the counterscarp, and one is in the trench which the enemy made to command ours: we will now keep it, or be as well beaten as ever men were. This day I have undertaken to guard it, and ere to-morrow it will be so strong as it will be out of danger. I wish you all good, and rest your most assured friend, " R. ESSEX.

" From the counterscarp of St. Katherine's, this 29th of December."

The Queen's patience was now at an end. She realised that the siege was hopeless. Henri had no money; his control of his own troops was slight; and the Duke of Parma was coming up with Spanish reinforcements to relieve the city. Essex, in spite of his orders, was evidently determined to stay, whatever the prospects. On December 23, she wrote him a letter, outlining her old criticism of the French King.

"We hear besides," (she went on) " to our no small wonder, how little the King regards the hazard of our men, and how you, our General, at all times refuse not to run with them to all service of greatest peril, but even, like the forlorn hope of a battle, to bring them to the slaughter. And therefore in regard that divers gentlemen of good quality, dear to their parents and blood, should not be vainly consumed to the grief of such as were contented to suffer them to go there for our service, we do command you to send them back although yourself should stay; which for our own part, notwithstanding daily entreating to revoke you, we are determined not to do so long as one man is left behind; only this we are content to let you know, that if at last you shall be so well advised as to think how dishonourable it is for you to tarry with so mean a charge, after so many men consumed so little to the purpose they were sent for, with many other absurd defects, which blemish the honour of the place you hold under us as our General, we shall right well allow of your judgment to return as a thing very fit and necessary to be performed, and hereby do authorize you to leave our said companies with the Marshal and Serjeant Major, without putting Sir Thomas Leighton to any further trouble in this hard time of the winter, so great an enemy to his infirmity; of which our pleasure, leaving other particularities to be answered by our Treasurer, we have thought good to acquaint you by our own handwriting."

Next day she signed another letter, repeating much of the former, but adding that she required him " upon the sight hereof to make your speedy return, and bring with you the best sort of the gentlemen there."

Essex himself was tired of the business. Even he realised that the siege could not last much longer, for his soldiers were dying daily, but he felt that he could not honourably return lest his example should lead to desertion in the King's army. The King urged him to go. The Queen had anticipated the difficulty, and to avoid further argument she ordered Cecil to write to Unton, enclosing a private letter to Essex in her own handwriting, which was to be given to him only if he showed reluctance to come home. When the packet of letters reached Unton in his lodging Essex happened to be standing by. Unton opened the package. Essex seeing a letter addressed to himself snatched it away before Unton had read Cecil's letter. The tone of the Queen's letter left no choice but to come home. On January 8, he handed over the command of the eight companies which remained to Sir Roger Williams. As he went on board he drew his sword and kissed the hilt.

CHAPTER VI

COURTIER AND STATESMAN

BY the beginning of 1592, Essex, young as he was, was widely recognised as the coming man. In the last four years three of the elder statesmen had died—Leicester, Walsingham, and Hatton—and no one had taken their places. Ralegh was no longer a serious rival. Burghley was as surely established as ever, and he was insinuating his son Robert Cecil into the Queen's notice as his own successor. It was not likely that the Queen's confidence in Burghley would be disturbed, but her political instinct to keep a balance of opposing interests in her Court was so ingrained that those who had nothing to gain from the Cecils sensed that Essex would be the counterweight in the Queen's Council.

Three very different examples of greatness were immediately before him: Leicester, his stepfather; Walsingham, his father-in-law; and Sidney, whose widow he had married. From each there was a different lesson to be learned. Leicester had long been a favourite, perhaps even the lover of the Queen. His ambition had been boundless; he had only just missed becoming Prince Consort. From Leicester could be perceived the pomp of greatness, and the magnificence. In the Low Countries Essex had seen how Leicester was but little less than the Queen herself; and with such a military greatness there came both power and glamour; to be the sole distributor of awards and knighthoods, and, more practically, the dispenser of commands and office, attended by an obsequious following of military men. Military greatness offered its prizes, immediate, spectacular, and gratifying, and especially to a nobleman, for few of the great soldiers of the time were noble. In his recent experiences in France, Essex had tasted this kind of power, and he was eager for more. When it comes to the push, soldiers, not statesmen, decide the fate of kingdoms.

From Walsingham there was a very different lesson, that another kind of greatness in a State came from being indispensable. With Walsingham universal knowledge was power. He knew what was being said in London taverns and in foreign Courts through the elaborate system of spies, intelligencers, and correspondents which he had built up. It was a less spectacular kind of greatness, but more stable.

The third was not so much an example as an ideal. No one who was admitted to intimacy with Sir Philip Sidney was ever afterwards quite the same. At rare intervals there is born a man who evokes in his fellows a feeling of ecstasy, a consciousness of some unique, indefinable quality which is called genius, beauty, nobility, charm. They seldom live long, and when they are dead, to those who know of them only by hearsay, they are something of a mystery, for what they leave behind seems often too little to account for their glamour. Sidney was such a man, and his life crossed Essex's again and again. Sidney had been the lover of Penelope, Essex's sister; Sidney was his fellow in the great charge at Zutphen, and now he had married Sidney's widow. Here was an example of that greatness of personality which comes neither by military glory, nor by statecraft, but, like the phœnix, is self-born, and will lead a man to leap up to pluck honour from the very horns of the moon. In Sidney its outward qualities were courtesy, courage, charm, and Essex possessed all three.

Essex was thus ready to take what gifts Fortune should offer, when there came into his world the two brothers Francis and Anthony Bacon. They were the sons of Sir Nicholas Bacon, Lord Keeper of the Great Seal of England, by his second wife. This lady was Anne, the second of the four learned daughters of Sir Anthony Cook, of Giddy Hall, in Essex. Her elder sister Mildred married Lord Burghley, as his second wife, and was the mother of Robert Cecil; and Elizabeth, her younger, was married first to Sir Thomas Hoby, by whom she had Sir Thomas Posthumas Hoby, and secondly, to Lord John Russell, son and heir to the Earl of Bedford, whom (to the sempiternal grief of his widow) he predeceased before coming to the title.

Of the two sons of the Lady Bacon, Anthony, the elder, was born in 1558, Francis on January 22, 1561. They were devoted brothers. Together they matriculated at Trinity College, Cambridge, on June 10, 1573. Neither was very strong, and Anthony especially was always something of an invalid. When they had finished their education at Cambridge they returned to London where Francis entered Gray's Inn. Sir Nicholas intended him for high office in the State, and to that end he was sent abroad in the embassy of Sir Amyas Paulet to Paris. Unfortunately for Francis, his father died suddenly in February, 1579, leaving him little portion but his own wits, so that from affairs of State he was obliged to seek a private fortune as best he could.

Anthony was better provided, and in 1579, on the suggestion of his uncle, Lord Burghley, he began to travel. He resided for some time in Paris, and for the next twelve years he lived in various cities of Europe, whence he came to know many persons of influence and importance. He was, in fact, one of the most able of Sir Francis Walsingham's intelligencers, a man with a vast knowledge of the intricacies of European Courts, politics, and personalities. He returned to England at the beginning of February, 1592, to the joy of his brother Francis, who prepared a lodging for him in Gray's Inn. At first Anthony expected much from his uncle Lord Burghley, who had, as he put it, " inned my ten years' harvest into his own barn without any halfpenny charge," but Lord Burghley gave him only fair words, unsupported even by promises, for he had his own son to cherish and saw no reason to encourage possible rivals.

Francis had already discovered that he could expect nothing

from his uncle. His career at the Bar was fairly successful, but his tastes were ample and his income insufficient. He was very ambitious in a queer way, and something of a visionary. He had half formed the far-off dream of the advancement of knowledge, to be himself, as it were, the first discoverer of new lands of the mind, the geographer of science. So persistent was this dream that he even wrote to Lord Burghley to help him in some practical way.

"I confess that I have as vast contemplative ends as I have moderate civil ends; for I have taken all knowledge to be my province, and if I could purge it of two sorts of rovers (whereof the one with frivolous disputations, confutations, and verbosities, the other with blind experiments and auricular traditions and impostures, hath committed so many spoils) I hope I should bring in industrious observations, grounded conclusions, and profitable inventions and discoveries—the best state of that province. This, whether it be curiosity, or vain glory, or nature, or (if one take it favourably) *philanthropia*, is so fixed in my mind as it cannot be removed. And I do easily see that place of any reasonable countenance doth bring commandment of more wits than of a man's own—which is the thing I greatly affect.

"And for your Lordship, perhaps you shall not find more strength or less encounter in any other. And if your Lordship shall find now, or at any time, that I do seek or affect any place whereunto any that is nearer unto your Lordship shall be concurrent, say then that I am a most dishonest man.

"And if your Lordship will not carry me on, I will not do as Anaxagoras did, who reduced himself with contemplation into voluntary poverty. But this I will do. I will sell the inheritance that I have, and purchase some lease of quick revenue, or some office of gain that shall be executed by deputy, and so give over all care of service, and become some sorry book-maker, or a true pioneer in that mine of truth which (he said) lay so deep.

"This which I have written unto your Lordship is rather thoughts than words, being set down without all art, disguising, or reservation. Wherein I have done honour to your Lordship's wisdom in judging that that will be best believed of your Lordship which is truest and to your Lordship's good nature in retaining nothing from you. And even so I wish your Lordship all happiness, and to myself means and occasion to be added to my faithful desire to do you service."

Lord Burghley was a very practical old statesman, and he was not much impressed by the offer. In these difficult and dangerous times, he saw no good reason to encourage large and distant prospects of general philanthropy.

Francis therefore proffered his services to Essex. The two men were attracted to each other. Bacon realised in Essex the touch of idealism, and was charmed by his courteous manners. Bacon's was not a happy generation, and any man who was by temperament or faith unable to conform himself to accepted patterns of thought and conduct felt frustrated and confined. In Essex he found sympathy and understanding which he could not expect from his uncle. For his part, Essex perceived the astonishing breadth and wisdom of Bacon's mind, for he combined rare learning with practical discernment. Both had one quality in common; they were ambitious, and Bacon felt that Essex might help him to secure that practical help which was essential to his hopes: in return he was prepared to devote his mind and labour to Essex's service.

A little later, when Anthony returned from his travels, he also was brought along, and in a short while the two brothers became members of Essex's increasing band of followers; Francis was his wise councillor, Anthony his secretary for foreign affairs. Anthony could render him as valuable services as in former times he had rendered Walsingham. He soon organised an intelligence service, and from all parts news began to accumulate. All the reports from his many correspondents were available for Essex, who was thus able to convince the Queen that he was a serious statesman.

In June, Ralegh fell from grace. He had spent the spring organising a private expedition to raid the Spanish treasure fleet, and in the early summer he put out to sea. A few days later the Queen learnt that he was secretly married to Elizabeth Throckmorton, one of her own ladies-in-waiting. There was the inevitable tempest of indignation. Ralegh was recalled from his command and sent peremptorily to the Tower, whence he wrote extravagant letters of grief which failed to move the Queen to sympathy.

Essex's reputation continued to grow during the year, and Francis Bacon laboured for him in trifles as in more serious matters. At the annual feast of the Queen's Coronation on November 17, Essex was conspicuous as a courtier. In the morning he came into the Presence to salute the Queen, wearing his collar of S's, an innovation in ceremonial attire which pleased her, and in the evening, with the Earl of Cumberland, he appeared fully armed and issued a general challenge that on February 26, following, they would fight all comers to maintain that their Mistress was the fairest and worthiest Amadis of Gaul.

In the following February, a Parliament was summoned, the first since 1589. Its main purpose was to raise money to meet the danger from Spain, for it was well known by various intelligences that King Philip was making even greater preparations than before to invade England. Parliament met on the 19th. Essex took his seat in the Lords, and Bacon sat in the Lower House as Knight of the Shire for Middlesex. The Queen came in person to listen to the Lord Keeper Puckering's charge at the opening of Parliament. He outlined the general situation: the great danger from Spain, and the Queen's need of money. In the past, he said, grants had been made to the Queen, but the money when collected was far short of expectation. The purpose of this Parliament was not oratory or the enacting of new laws, but to consult about the means for defending the country. Three days later the Queen came again to receive the Speaker elected by the Commons. He was Edward Coke, the Solicitor-General.

On February 25, at the beginning of the Parliament, Essex achieved one of his greatest ambitions. The Queen advanced him to be a member of her Privy Council. He took the oath of Privy Councillor, and then, as was customary, he was invited by his new colleagues to sit with them and to sign the letters which lay on the table. The other members of the Council present at the time were the Lord Keeper Puckering; Lord Burghley, the Lord Treasurer; the Earl of Derby; Lord Charles Howard, Lord High Admiral of England; Lord Thomas Buckhurst, Lord High Butler of England; Sir John Wolley, Latin Secretary; and Sir Robert Cecil. The absent members were John Whitgift, Archbishop of Canterbury; Lord Henry Hunsdon, Lord Chamberlain; Lord William Cobham, Lord Warden of the Cinque Ports; Sir Francis Knollys, Treasurer of the Household; Sir Thomas Heneage, Vice Chamberlain; and Sir John Fortescue, Chancellor of the Exchequer.

Privy Councillors were directly responsible to the Queen herself. Individually they were the heads of the various offices and departments of government. As a Cabinet they held the supreme power in the State. They even formed their own court of law when they sat as a judicial body in the Star Chamber, where they dealt with a vast range of cases which could not always be conveniently tried in the ordinary courts of law—riots, disobedience of royal commands, libels, seditions, assaults, and the like. The Councillor's responsibility was heavy and arduous. Though he had the privilege of direct access to the Queen, he had also to attend on her. Essex was only twenty-five, and by including him in this small inner circle the Queen showed that she already thought him a responsible statesman and adviser.

For the first few days of the session the Commons debated the subsidy to be offered to the Queen. A committee was appointed to confer with a committee of the Lords. Then difficulties arose. The Lords demanded more than the Commons had intended to offer. It was proposed that the two committees should meet together to discuss the matter. When this motion was brought forward in the House of Commons Bacon objected. It was customary, he said, for the Commons to take the initiative in making proposals for the offering of a subsidy. To join with the Lords in this business would prejudice the privileges of the Lower House. The objection pleased the members, but not the Queen; and when the Parliament had ended she felt considerable resentment against Bacon, whilst Coke, from her point of view, had been a most successful Speaker. Bacon still further damaged his prospects by refusing to admit that he had committed any error, with the result that the Queen forbade him to come into the Presence.

To the ambitious man access to the Queen was the most valuable of all privileges. Favoured Councillors could seek admission to her private apartments, where they could talk with her privately and intimately. Privileged courtiers might wait in the Presence Chamber until she entered, in the hope that she would notice them and permit them to speak to her. Common men outside this privilege could only petition some Councillor or palace official in the hope that perhaps the Queen might be made aware of them, and access even to a Councillor was difficult and expensive.

Bacon was in great need of money and proper employment, and appealed to Essex to help him to regain the Queen's favour. The office of Attorney-General would shortly be vacant; and the two likeliest candidates were Bacon himself, and Edward Coke, the Solicitor-General. Both men had claims on the office. Coke was brilliant as a lawyer, in his knowledge of law and in practice in the courts. He was now forty-one, and, as he had recently shown as Speaker, he was likely to support the Crown; but he was so bad-tempered that his judgment was not reliable. Bacon was eight years

younger. He had far less legal experience, but he was very cool-headed and the Queen had known him from infancy and trusted his judgment.

Essex backed Bacon's candidature with enthusiasm. For months the Queen would make no decision between the two men. Towards the end of August Essex wrote to Bacon:

" SIR,
"I spake with the Queen yesterday and on Wednesday. On Wednesday she cut me off short; she being come newly home and making haste to her supper. Yesterday I had a full audience, but with little better success than before. The points I pressed were an absolute ἀμνήστια and an access as in former times. Against the first she pleaded that you were in more fault than any of the rest in Parliament; and when she did forgive it and manifest her receiving of them into favour that offended her then, she will do it to many that were less in fault as well as to yourself. Your access, she saith, is as much as you can look for. If it had been in the King her father's time, a less offence than that would have made a man be banished his presence for ever. But you did come to the Court when you would yourself; and she should precipitate too much from being highly displeased with you to give you near access, such as she shows only to those that she favours extraordinarily. I told her that I sought for you was not so much your good, though it were a thing I would seek extremely and please myself in obtaining, as for her honour, that those excellent translations of hers might be known to them who could best judge of them. Besides, my desire was that you should neither be stranger to her person nor to her service; the one for your own satisfaction, the other for her Majesty's own sake, who if she did not employ you should lose the use of the ablest gentleman to do her service of any of your quality whatsoever. Her humour is yet to delay. I am now going to her again: and what I cannot effect at once I will look to do *saepe cadendo*. Excuse my ill writing. I write in haste and have my

chamber full of company that break my head with talking. I commend myself to your brother and to yourself, and rest your assured friend,

"ESSEX."

Other members of the Council were less favourable. The Lord Keeper favoured neither candidate, and Lord Burghley thought that Coke should be promoted and that Bacon should have the Solicitorship. A month later, Essex tried again, but the moment was not opportune, for the Queen was in a wayward mood and annoyed with him. On the evening of October 13, Essex had a long conversation with her. When he detailed Bacon's qualifications for the Attorneyship, she replied there were two arguments against Bacon; Lord Burghley favoured him only for the second place, and Coke was the older man. Essex answered that it was Burghley's habit to prefer men dependent on himself, and, as for age, there was such a difference in the character of the two men that if Coke's head and beard were grown grey with age, it would not counterpoise his other disadvantages. The Queen said that she would continue the conversation later.

When Essex came to her again, she was still stiff in her opinion not to have Bacon. He grew more vehement with her. She said that she would be advised by those who had more judgment in such matters; to which he retorted that so she might be, and yet it would be more for her service to hear him than them, for his speech had truth and zeal to her without respect of private ends. If he lacked judgment to discern between the worth of one man and another, the world would teach it him; and it was not an ill rule to hold him for a wise and honest man whom many wise and honest men held in reputation, but those whom she trusted left out the wisest and worthiest, and praised for affection. Whose name, she asked, had been left out? Thereupon Essex named Morris, Attorney of the Court of Wards. The Queen agreed that he ought to have been considered, but still she would not commit herself to a decision.

By Christmas nothing had been settled about the Attorneyship, which was but one of Essex's many preoccupations. Since he was made a Councillor, he had, in nine months, pushed himself into a chief place. Essex House was becoming a centre for the collection and collation of foreign news, and chambers for the entertainment of travellers and conferences were always ready. The Queen was pleased with his zeal and remarked upon it to the Cecils, who were less pleased. Since Walsingham's death Lord Burghley had known no competitor, and he did not relish the rivalry of Essex, who, though he lacked years, experience, gravity, and discretion, had youth, energy, style, and at times a kind of fanatical persistence; and unfortunately these foolhardy gestures—the challenge to Villars, for instance—were more attractive to a woman who affected gallantries than discretion and more solid achievements. The two Cecils were a great contrast to their rival, —the old man with his grave white beard and rosy cheeks, his gout and deafness, his tidy, methodical ways; and his son Robert Cecil, a little humpback, with delicate features and gentle, patient manner, subtler perhaps than his father nowadays, and certainly more sensitive. Those who were fascinated by Essex's charm, would think of his rivals only as subtle politicians, dark moles who worked underground : the Queen knew better. Of the other councillors John Whitgift, the Archbishop of Canterbury, had always a fondness for Essex since he first knew him as a grave little student of ten years in the days when he was Master of Trinity. He was not too fond of Lord Burghley, for they were at cross purposes over Church discipline; Burghley, to the Archbishop's notion, was too lax with the Puritans.

Those who contributed to Essex's intelligence service were men of varying characters and reputations. One of the most useful was Anthony Standen, whose experiences had been somewhat similar to those of Anthony Bacon. He was a Catholic who went to Scotland early in the reign to avoid persecution. There for two years he was in the service of

Mary, Queen of Scots, but in the time of her troubles he went on to Spain. The Spanish King pensioned him, and he acted as his agent in Scottish intrigues engineered in Paris. Then Walsingham gathered him in. He went on to the Court of Florence. Thence he went again to Spain and spied on Spanish preparations. In 1590, he was in Bordeaux, and there was arrested as a Spanish spy. Walsingham, who might have helped him, was now dead, and he remained in prison until the spring of 1591, when he was luckily able to get in touch with Anthony Bacon. Bacon befriended him and caused him to be set at liberty and advised him to appeal to Lord Burghley. Standen returned to Spain, whence he sent useful letters of news to Bacon. Essex read his letters to the Queen, who was inclined to encourage him. His news, she observed, was useful, but stale. He was allowed to return to England, and on June 13, 1593, he arrived at Gray's Inn and was lodged in Francis Bacon's chamber. Standen had intended to offer his services to Burghley, but when he reported his arrival at Calais Burghley did nothing, whilst Essex provided him with the necessary passports. He immediately waited on Essex, who received him most graciously, and as a token of future favours hung round his neck a gold chain worth a hundred marks. Standen had most useful connections abroad.

For Spanish information Essex consulted Antonio Perez. This Perez, as his father before him, was once Secretary to the Spanish King. The story of his downfall was melodramatic and sinister. In 1577, Philip the Second grew very suspicious of his brother Don John of Austria, and thought that his secretary, John de Escovedo, was feeding his ambition. The following year Escovedo was sent to Spain, and King Philip felt it desirable that he should not return to his master. Perez was told to see to the matter in such a way that no suspicion fell on the King. Escovedo was accordingly murdered, but his family accused the Princess of Eboli, the King's mistress, and Perez, who was very intimate with her. The King, whether moved by jealousy of his Secretary or desire to save his own reputation, imprisoned both. Perez lost all his offices and was treated with great brutality until, in 1590, he managed to break prison and fled to Aragon, his native country, and there took sanctuary. He was hauled thence by Philip's orders and in danger of being tried by the Inquisition. The people of Aragon greatly resented this treatment of their countryman and rescued him by force. The King sent an army against them, but Perez fled to France in November, 1591. There were several attempts to murder him, but he succeeded in reaching England.

He now offered to betray Spanish secrets to the Queen, but she did not encourage him, though Essex was able to persuade her to allow him a pension. Perez was welcomed to the circle, and was soon very intimate with Francis Bacon, to the horror of Lady Bacon, who wrote to Anthony, "though I pity your brother, yet so long as he pities not himself, but keepeth that bloody Perez, yea, as a coach-companion and bed-companion, a proud, profane, costly fellow, whose being about him I verily fear the Lord God doth mislike, and doth less bless your brother in credit, and otherwise in his health, surely I am utterly discouraged, and make conscience farther to undo myself to maintain such wretches as he is, that never loved your brother but for his own credit, living upon him." Essex, however, found Perez attractive in spite of his conceited fantastical Spanish manners, and there was considerable friendship between them.

Another possible source of information for Spanish affairs was Dr. Roderigo Lopez. Lopez was a Portuguese Jew who had fled to England in 1559 and set up as a doctor. He was now an old man. In time he had a large and successful practice amongst the circle of the Court, and in 1586 he was made Physician to the Queen. He had already collected information for Walsingham. Essex approached Lopez, and pointed out that if he were to pretend to be a traitor to the Queen and to feign a desire to go back to Portugal, it was likely that information of great value would come his way.

Lopez asked the Queen's advice, and she told him to use his own judgment. As a result, letters began to pass to and fro and some valuable information came in. As soon as he received it, Lopez would tell the Queen, and then he went on to Essex and drew a second reward. Thus, when Essex came to give his information to the Queen she knew it already. This enraged him, and especially because Lopez was making him look foolish in a matter which most nearly touched his reputation as a statesman. He annoyed Essex still further when he told Don Antonio and Antonio Perez certain secrets of how he had cured Essex, and of what diseases. When Lopez had gone, they told Essex. Such actions were not matters of high treason but they were enough to make Essex bitterly prejudiced against Lopez.

Since the failure of the Portugal voyage Don Antonio had lived on in England in faded gentility, which monthly grew shabbier. His money was gone, and his few servants were forced to live on their wits. Some took to the dangerous trade of peddling information between Spain and England, amongst them Ferrara de Gama, Emanuel Andrada, and Emanuel Louis Tinoco.

Andrada, on his return from Spain in 1591, was arrested on suspicion and then declared that he had been sent over actually to poison Don Antonio but ostensibly to sound the Queen on the proposals for peace. He also gave some useful information of Spanish naval preparations. Lopez was instructed to assist in the examination and ultimately persuaded the Council to let him go back to Spain. In the autumn of 1593 de Gama was suspected of some treason and was arrested in England. His papers were handed over to Essex, and thereafter it was decided to tap the correspondence which was passing through the hands of Don Antonio's followers.

Early in January, 1594, Tinoco turned up at Calais and there asked an English merchant to arrange for him to come over to England, as he had most important secrets to tell the Council. He was sent to London and told Sir Robert Cecil a tale of how he had been in conference with Count de Fuentes and Stephen de Ibarra, the Spanish King's secretary, who ordered him to get in touch with Lopez and to win him over to the King's service, and in general to spy on English affairs.

On January 16, Tinoco was brought before Essex for examination, and on being pressed he faltered in his tale. A week later, he said that Lopez had received a jewel of great value from the King of Spain for service to be rendered. Essex was excited by the extraordinary secrets which were being revealed, and soon concluded that he was on the track of a most sinister and dangerous plot. Lopez clearly was implicated. The Queen was incredulous, as were Burghley and Cecil, who knew more of the comings and goings of Antonio's followers than they had told Essex. Lopez, however, was summoned to Burghley's house and questioned before Burghley, Cecil, and Essex. After the examination they sent Lopez to Essex House, where he was entrusted to the care of Gelly Meyrick, Essex's steward. His house and papers were examined, but nothing incriminating was found.

When Essex next came to the Queen, Sir Robert Cecil had forestalled him with the report that there was nothing at all against Lopez. The Queen was irritated, and rounded on Essex as a rash and temerarious youth to enter into a matter against the poor man which he could not prove, and whose innocence she knew well enough. Malice and nothing else hatched all this matter, which displeased her much, and the more since her own honour was interested.

Essex was furious. He stalked out of her presence and went home to Essex House. He strode through his own chamber, flung the door open for himself, slammed it to, and passed into his private cabinet, where he shut himself in. He was so angry that he did not notice Standen and a groom, who were waiting in the chamber. After about an hour he opened the door and asked who was there. Then, learning from the groom that it was Standen, he ordered him to be brought in. Standen was, and looked, ill. Essex made him sit down and ordered his coach to be prepared. They talked for a little about Francis Bacon's affairs, and then Standen went home.

For two days Essex refused to see anyone but the Lord Admiral, who was kept passing to and from the Court to smooth matters over. Then he returned with greater zeal than ever to justify himself. Scarcely pausing even for his meals, he persisted in examinations and cross examinations. Two days later, January 28, he had, to his own satisfaction, made out a convincing case. He dashed off a note to Anthony Bacon, "I have discovered a most dangerous and desperate treason. The point of conspiracy was her Majesty's death. The executioner should have been Dr. Lopez: the manner poison. This I have so followed, as I will make it appear as clear as the noon day."

Although the Lopez business was occupying so much of his time Essex did not forget Bacon and the Attorneyship, and as soon as he returned to Court, he again asked the Queen to give it to Bacon. As before, she objected that he was too young, and would not commit herself to a decision. This increased Essex's irritation towards the Cecils.

On February 5, the case against Lopez seemed blacker, and he was sent to the Tower. At seven o'clock next morning he was again examined before Essex and Sir Robert Cecil, and confessed enough to convince Cecil that Essex, after all, had very good grounds for his suspicion.

Essex and Cecil returned together in a coach. On the way Cecil remarked innocently, "My Lord, the Queen has resolved, e'er five days pass, without any farther delay to make an Attorney General. I pray your Lordship to let me know whom you will favour?"

Essex was astounded at the question. Cecil could not but be aware, he answered, that he stood for Francis Bacon against all other competitors.

"Good Lord," observed Cecil, "I wonder your Lordship should go about to spend your strength in so unlikely or impossible a matter."

Hereupon the old arguments were repeated backwards and forwards. At length Cecil remarked, "If at least your Lordship had spoken of the Solicitorship, that might be of easier digestion to her Majesty."

Essex lost his temper at this insinuation that the Cecils, and not he, had the Queen's ear. "Digest me no digestions," he said; "for the Attorneyship for Francis is that I must have; and in that will I spend all my power, might, authority, and amity, and with tooth and nail defend and procure the same for him against whomsoever; and that whosoever getteth this office out of my hands for any other, before he have it, it shall cost him the coming by. And this be you assured of, Sir Robert; for now do I fully declare myself. And for your own part, Sir Robert, I think strange both of my Lord Treasurer and you, that can have the mind to seek the preference of a stranger before so near a kinsman. For if you weigh in a balance the parts every way of his competitor and him, only excepting five poor years of admitting to a House of Court before Francis, you shall find in all other respects whatsoever no comparison between them."

Dr. Lopez was brought up for trial at the Guildhall on February 28. An imposing commission was appointed, which included the Lord Mayor, the Lord Admiral, Essex, Sir Robert Cecil, Sir Thomas Heneage, Sir John Fortescue, and other illustrious persons. Coke, as Solicitor-General, opened for the Crown, and tossed off some heavy abuse against the Pope, the King of Spain, and the prisoner, whom he called a perjured murdering traitor and Jewish doctor, worse than Judas himself. He detailed the conspiracy, showing how Lopez had dealt with de Gama and Tinoco who were the agents of Count de Fuentes and de Ibarra. As for Lopez, he had denied with blasphemous oaths and horrible execrations that he had ever had speech or understanding of such a matter, until confronted with the evidence, and then first he confessed, and then withdrew the confession, declaring that he only confessed to avoid the rack. Lopez said little in his own defence. De Gama and Tinoco, he declared, were liars: he admitted that he had received a jewel from the Spanish King, but his sole intention was to deceive him and cheat him of his money. When he was found guilty and condemned, the spectators applauded loudly.

A month later the Queen made up her mind about the Attorneyship; Coke should have it. His patent was made out. The decision being irrevocable, Essex and Bacon now tried for the lesser office, and soon the Queen was again being badgered with the name of Bacon. This time he had most influential support, for Burghley and Cecil favoured him, as well as the Lord Keeper. On March 26, Essex again broached the subject to the Queen. So long as he was calm in his advocacy, she was reserved and showed no hostility, but as Essex grew more vehement, she became more critical. This insistence irked her and at length in passion she told him to go to bed if he would talk of nothing else; and in passion he went, with the remark that while he was with her he could not but solicit for the cause and the man so much affected, and therefore he would retire himself till he might be more graciously heard.

Essex was thus learning the increasing difficulties of dealing with the Queen. To one of the more placid temperament of old Lord Burghley, her whims and delays, and hesitations and changes, her storms and sunshine, were like the English weather, to be endured philosophically and without emotion. From years of experience he knew that however unreasonable she might be, somehow, as things turned out, she was usually right; and her will, when she did make up her mind, was iron. Only a fool would go against her. To Essex, she was maddening. Indeed, he was not a good courtier, for he could never learn to conceal or suppress his feelings. Few others ever dared to show temper in the Queen's presence.

Apart from the Queen, the increasing flattery was satisfying. In April, King James of Scotland, despatching two ambassadors to complain that the Queen was supporting Bothwell, sent them with a personal letter asking Essex to assist her with his good advice, and adding that the ambassadors had been commanded to use his advice in all their proceedings. Bowes, who was the Queen's ambassador in Edinburgh, was now sending him news. In the following spring Thomas Bodley, who had gone out to the Hague as the Queen's agent, was reporting intimate news of the Low Countries; as was Thomas Edmondes, the agent in Paris. These were but signs of Essex's growing power in the State.

Not only was he securing the co-operation of men of state, he was attracting also several of the younger noblemen and gentlemen, particularly Henry Wriothesley, Earl of Southampton, and Roger Manners, Earl of Rutland. Southampton was an early admirer; he was six years younger than Essex. In March, 1591, being then at Dieppe, he wrote to Essex:

" To continue the profession of service which I have heretofore verbally made unto your Lordship; which, howsoever in itself it is of small value, my hope is, seeing it wholly proceeds from a true respect borne to your own worth and from one who hath no better present to make you than the offer of himself to be disposed of by your commandment, your Lordship will be pleased in good part to accept it, and ever afford me your good opinion and favour, of which I shall be exceeding proud, endeavouring myself always with the best means I can think of to deserve it."

Rutland was born in 1576. He had just taken his Master's degree at Cambridge and was about to travel. Essex composed for him some elegant letters of advice for his guidance, in which Francis Bacon had considerable share.

In the early autumn Bacon was again disappointed. The Queen chose Sergeant Fleming as her Solicitor-General. It was a mortifying experience for Essex. He often argued with Bacon about the proper ways of managing the Queen, and always maintained that she should be bullied into a decision; and, from time to time, when she yielded he would triumphantly note the success of his methods. Bacon disagreed, and events again showed that he was right.

Now that he had failed, Essex rode over from Richmond to Twickenham to break the news. "Master Bacon," he said, "the Queen hath denied me yon place for you, and hath placed another; I know you are the least part of your own matter, but you fare ill because you have chosen me for your mean and dependence; you have spent your time and thoughts in my matters: I die if I do not somewhat towards your fortune: you shall not deny to accept a piece of land which I will bestow upon you."

In spite of his disappointment, Bacon realised the truth of Essex's remarks, and was a little afraid of the gift. He had perceived that Essex was inclined to demand personal service from his friends. These constant quarrels and reconciliations with the Queen might, some day, develop into a trial of strength; Essex was rash and impetuous, and underrated the Queen and her strength. Bacon was unwilling to sell himself to become Essex's man, body and soul. He replied cautiously that Essex's offer reminded him of the Duke of Guise, who had turned all his estate into obligations, meaning that by great gifts he had sought to bind men to his service. Essex insisted that he should take the gift. At length he replied, "My Lord, I see I must be your homager and hold land of your gift: but do you know the manner of doing homage in law? Always it is with a saving of his faith to the King and his other Lords: and therefore, my Lord, I can be no more yours than I was, and it must be with the ancient savings: and if I grow to be a rich man, you will give me leave to give it back to some of your unrewarded followers."

A few days later Essex was seriously alarmed. For some weeks gossips had been talking of a very dangerous and seditious book, published on the Continent with the title *A Conference About the Next Succession to the Crown of England*. A few copies had been smuggled over and were being passed round. The author's name was R. Doleman, but this was taken to be but another of the many pseudonyms of Robert Parsons, the Jesuit, the most energetic and implacable of all trouble-makers abroad. The book was long, and divided into two parts. The first part was intended to show that blood descent by itself was not a sufficient claim to a crown. In the second part the author went on to consider the various claimants to the throne of England, which ranged from the King of Scots to the Infanta of Spain abroad, and at home the Earls of Beauchamp, Derby, and Huntingdon, or one of the children of the Earl of Hertford, or the Countess of Derby. No particular claimant was put forward and the argument was entirely objective, very lucid, and almost deliberately arid, but led to the conclusion that in any event civil war seemed inevitable on the Queen's death.

To Essex's embarrassment he learned that the book was dedicated to himself, and in terms which could not but move the Queen's suspicions and anger. Two causes, said the author, move men to dedicate books to a person in authority, private duty and obligation. Some of his friends were obliged to Essex for certain favours received in France, and he himself had received favours from Essex's father, grandfather, and great-grandfather. For " the second point of public utility," the dedication went on, " I thought no man more fit than your Honour to dedicate these two books unto, which treat of the Succession to the Crown of England, for that no man is in more high and eminent place and dignity at this day in our Realm, than yourself, whether we respect your nobility, or calling, or favour with your Prince, or high liking of the people, and consequently no man like to have a greater part or sway in deciding of this great affair (when time shall come for that determination) than your Honour, and those that will assist you and are likeliest to follow your fame and fortune.

" And for that it is not convenient for your Honour to be unskilful in a matter which concerneth your person and the whole realm, so much as this doth, and finding this conference had by two learned lawyers, to handle the question very pithily and exactly, and yet with much modesty and without offence of any, and with particular affection and devotion to her Majesty, and with special care of her safety, I thought not expedient to let it lie unpublished, as also I judged that no hands were fitter to receive the same, nor any protection more secure or plausible than that of your Honour, whom God long preserve in all true honour and felicity, to the comfort of your Lordship's faithful servants and clients, and to the public benefit of your country. From my chamber in Amsterdam, this last of December, 1593.

" Your Honour's most affectionate
" R. DOLEMAN."

At last a copy of the *Conference* was given to the Queen, who showed it to Essex. He was so worried by the business that he fell ill, and took to his bed. Fortunately the Queen did not suspect his loyalty. She visited him, and, when he recovered, to show how much she trusted him, she gave him the letters which had been sent from foreign Courts to answer. So Essex put off his melancholy and busied himself with statecraft, and, with Bacon's assistance, a pretty device for the Accession day celebrations, symbolical of his relations with the Queen and of his own discordant aspirations.

The device was much admired by the courtiers, who were quick to read its allegory. Some little while before he came to the tilt, Essex sent his page to the Queen, who returned with her glove. Then the spectators in the tiltyard beheld a hermit, a secretary of state, and a soldier who came up to one representing a squire (this part being taken by Toby Matthew, prodigal son to the Archbishop of York). Each in turn presented the squire with an argument suitable to his nature, a book of meditations, political discourses, and orations of brave-fought battles. As this little induction was in playing, Essex himself appeared, and while they were all endeavouring to persuade him to their own course of life, in came the ordinary postboy of London, all covered with mud, on a poor lean jade, blowing and galloping. He handed his letters to the secretary, who passed them to Essex.

After supper the charade was continued before the Queen, and the four characters each delivered himself of an elaborate speech. The squire began, briefly offering to the Queen his master's complaint that he was tormented with the importunity of a melancholy dreaming hermit, a mutinous, brainsick soldier, and a busy, tedious secretary, signifying thereby the three ambitions by which Essex was divided. So they delivered in turn their petitions. The hermit would have persuaded him to the service of the Muses, the soldier urged him to seek his fortune in the field, the statesman to let policy and matters of state be the chief and only thing he intended. The squire replied to all three, rebuking them for their several illusions and concluding that his master's resolution was fixed. "For recreation he will confer with his Muse; for her defence and honour, he will sacrifice his life in the wars, hoping to be embalmed in the sweet odours of her remembrance; to her service will he consecrate all his watchful endeavours; and will ever bear in his heart the picture of her beauty, in his actions of her will, and in his fortune of her grace and favour."

When the device was finished the Queen rose, remarking that if she had thought that so much would have been said of her, she would not have come down that night, and so went off to bed. As soon as she had gone the courtiers began to fit names to the characters, identifying the soldier with Sir Roger Williams.

Williams did not long survive to be Essex's military councillor. He fell sick of surfeit, and died at Baynard's Castle at three in the morning of December 13. He died well and very repentant, for Essex succeeded, when all others failed, in making him take a feeling of his end and prepare his soul for its journey. Sir Roger left all his possessions to Essex, including jewels to the value of £1,600. Three days later he was buried in Paul's as a soldier with all martial rites, with Essex as chief mourner.

Directly after the funeral Essex was sent off post haste to the north, for news came from York that Lord Huntingdon, Lord President of the North, was dangerously ill. Essex was despatched to be with him at the end, and to take charge until a successor could be found.

Meanwhile the military men were in the ascendant. Throughout the summer and autumn reports from Spain all showed that the Spaniard was preparing another expedition, though whether for England or Calais no one knew. In July, Penzance in Cornwall was raided and burnt by a party of four hundred Spaniards. At the end of August, Drake and Hawkins, with six of the Queen's ships and a force of 2,500, sailed for South America to raid Porto Rico; both died on the voyage. Policy was debated with the Queen and in the Council, and at last, on December 13, the Council were able to issue orders that the Queen's navy was to be sent out for a spring campaign, with victuals for 12,000 men for five months, to be ready by the end of March. The Lord Admiral went down to Chatham to supervise the preparations. The aldermen of London were sent for to Court and commanded to furnish fifteen of their best ships. Letters went out to all the ports of England to have their ships ready at command.

CHAPTER VII

WARLIKE PREPARATIONS

SINCE the unlucky siege of Rouen, Essex continued his friendship with Henri IV, who was still fighting desperately for his kingdom. In 1593, he had made his peace with the rebels by renouncing Protestantism and accepting the Roman faith, but the Spaniards werestill in France and the war went on interminably. In 1595, they won Cambrai from him. When news of the loss reached England the Queen sent Sir Roger Williams over to France. He returned with an ambassador from the King, who bluntly told the Queen that unless she gave his master greater help he would make his own peace with the Spaniard. At the end of the year she despatched Sir Henry Unton to him.

Unton was also one of Essex's party, and before he went, Essex sent him secret instructions to be conveyed to the French King as to the best way of obtaining help from the Queen. The instruction was partly in cipher, in which A. stood for France, F. for Spain, 100 for Queen Elizabeth, 99 for Henri, 15 for Unton, 19 for Essex, and 93 for Antonio Perez.

" 15 is sent ambassador into A. to discover how 99 standeth affected towards 100 and this state, and partly to excuse our late proceedings, as denying of succours, not taking hold of the treaties, and such-like. If, when he comes there, he discovers 99 alienated from us, and treating openly or underhand F. he is warranted by his instructions to seek by all means to recover him, and upon 15 advertisements new overtures will be made to 99 to please him, as treaty, and offer of good succours. If he find, at his coming over, that 99 is no way looking to F. nor so discontented with our courses, as he pretends, then upon this news we will leave all things as they were, and 99 and his ministers shall be thought to be but men of words; and such councillors in B. as have given credit to the French advertisements, and persuaded 100 to satisfy 99 are utterly discredited. Therefore 99 and his ministers must remember what they have written and spoken, and be constant to themselves for the causes before recited.

"For our excuses, if they in A. do much impugn them, we shall have everlastingly a battle of letters and words, while the opportunity passeth away of impeaching the enemies' designs, and uniting these two crowns. The soundest and surest way then is, to give us jealousy, and to awake us with matter of fact, and not with words and threatenings. So shall 99 be more respected, his friends gain credit on this side, and those, that have traversed him all this while, be convinced and driven to cry *peccavi*. Let him show his means to treat, not as if he would make ostentation of it, but let him devise that it may come to 15 knowledge. Let him not impugn our excuses, but allowing them say he is sorry we are not able to help him, and as sorry that he is not able to make the wars without us. But when he sees that 15 brings nothing but words, he must seem to take this worse than all the rest, as either meant to do him a scorn, or else that he hath cause to think he hath some other secret design than is pretended, for on so idle a message he could not believe that we would have sent him.

"To conclude, he must so use the matter as 15 may send us thundering letters whereby he must drive us to propound and to offer. He must give some public shew of coldness at 15 first coming, and of discontent after he hath heard him, but so as it be without offering him disgrace; and he must welcome him as 15, though he do not as ambassador. He must propound no treaty, nor make no request; for that will make us value him less than we do. He must cast out words, that either 100 is carried to some secret treaty with F., the hope of which makes 100 abandon him; or else that some of her ministers are corrupted to seal her eyes, and gnaw with their envious teeth the cords of amity betwixt B. and A. asunder. But all this without passion, for any show of passion will make us think him destitute of all other remedy to his affairs.

"93 must write to 19 such a letter, as may be shewed, wherein he shall say that the sending of 15 hath made all things worse than ever; and he must expostulate with me, why I, knowing the humours of 99 and the affairs of A. so well, as I do, would not stay his coming since he brought nothing else. He must write also that he fears, ere he shall have leisure to send again, and to treat, 99 will be too far gone to be brought back. But let him put nothing in that letter but that which may be seen, for the ordinary courier shall bring it."

The King acted his part well, and Unton faithfully reported his very real anxieties to the Queen. The Cardinal Archduke Albert of Austria, the King of Spain's Governor in the Netherlands, was in the Low Countries with an army prepared either to invade France or to make peace. Unton, however, was taken sick and died at the end of March. The Queen was not disposed to use the force which was being collected for another profitless campaign in France.

In England the pace of the preparations for the voyage was quickening. The estimates of the cost had been prepared, stores and munitions were fast being assembled, and the organisation of the fleet and army was nearly complete. The fleet was to be divided into four squadrons, under the command of Essex, the Lord Admiral, Lord Thomas Howard, and Sir Walter Ralegh. For the land service, Sir Francis Vere was to come over from the Low Countries to be Marshal. The commanders of regiments were Sir John Wingfield, Sir Thomas Gerrard, Sir Conyers Clifford, and Sir Christopher Blount. The Council were busied in demanding men from the counties, whilst Essex was writing personal letters to his friends.

In the midst of all the haste, the situation was unexpectedly changed. The Cardinal Archduke, who had been threatening the French King's siege of La Fère, suddenly moved northwards, and before anything could be done to forestall him he was investing Calais. The French King urgently appealed to the Queen and to Essex, who pledged himself to bring help.

Essex and the Lord Admiral were ordered to organise a relief expedition. Essex immediately posted down to Dover, leaving the Admiral to collect ships, men, and supplies in London. The situation as yet was obscure. Apparently the Governor was holding out in the Citadel, and it was still possible for ships to make their way in and out of the harbour. On the morning of April 3, Essex despatched Sir Conyers Clifford in a small man-of-war to reconnoitre and report. Meanwhile he sent post after post to urge the Queen and the Council to hasten the troops, for he had all the shipping ready to transport them.

Next day Essex forwarded Clifford's report: the harbour could still be entered, but the enemy's ships lay about on either side to oppose any attempt. Essex wrote again at noon: the Governor was asking for men; if sent at once they would be in time, but the opportunity was fleeting. He wrote again at 10 o'clock at night; he had received a list of the Spanish army; until the enemy took the raveline the harbour could still be entered on the east side. Meanwhile, he had summoned sailors who knew the coast and was studying maps in readiness.

The greatest impediment was, as usual, the Queen herself. Her mind was revolving around various possibilities. She had lent the French King more than £350,000; the results were meagre; and there were no signs of repayment. The succours might be too late; there was a risk of disaster; but to have an English army in Calais once more was worth some risk. She consented to send help.

Very late at night Essex set out from Dover to Court to report and hasten the troops. He was on the road between Canterbury and Sittingbourne when he met the post from London. The post brought a letter from the Admiral that the Queen had consented to aid Calais and referred all things to

Essex's discretion. Essex immediately turned and rode back to Dover. He wrote off to the Council that he proposed to send Sir Francis Vere over as soon as the troops were available. " The honour," he sighed, " will be only theirs and no part ours that shall stand still in one of the Queen's ships, and point them what to do, yet the shame and dishonour will be most ours if they should receive any manner of blow." Unless restrained by instructions, he hoped for good success. The enemy was still battering at the raveline at the east of the harbour, but the Governor hoped to hold out for two days longer.

Next day, at noon, Essex wrote to Sir Robert Cecil to say how greatly he appreciated the Queen's confidence, and to report on his arrangements. He had appointed Sir Thomas Wilford to be colonel of the troops, and had given him the necessary captains. The transport was ready, and the plans for entering the harbour. He hoped to have the troops on board the next day, and in Calais by the 7th.

For the next three days the preparations went on with zest. Essex posted back to London, and attended a meeting of the Council on the 7th. On April 9, which was Good Friday, orders went out to the Commissioners of Musters to have 6,000 furnished with arms at Dover by Sunday night at the latest. In the afternoon the Lord Mayor and his brethren were listening to the sermon at Paul's Cross when they were suddenly called out to receive a command to raise a thousand men forthwith. Such was their zeal that by eight o'clock in the evening the men were all assembled.

The next morning the Queen cancelled her previous orders. She was not satisfied with the securities offered by the French King, and anyhow it appeared that the expedition would be too late, and if so, then the present expenses would be wasted. The Council were disgusted and annoyed. Even Lord Burghley, who at the moment was gripped by one of his periodical attacks of gout, ventured to criticise the Queen in a note to his son. " These so many changes," he observed, " breed hard opinions of counsel."

Next day Monsieur de Sancy, who had been sent over to plead with the Queen, arrived with the latest reports of the situation. It appeared that there was yet time for Calais to be saved. The Queen veered round once more, and the messengers were again sent out to command that the levies should march to Dover at once. The order reached the Lord Mayor in the early morning. It was Easter Sunday and law-abiding citizens were making their Easter communion in their parish churches. The aldermen and the constables went round, each to his own parish church, and shut up the doors till they had collected the men. By noon a thousand men had been assembled, and by night most of them were on the march. Essex rode back to Dover to await their coming.

On April 13, Essex's commission as Lieutenant-General over 6,000 men for the purpose of relieving Calais was drawn out and despatched, together with the special instructions to be observed. He was not to carry over his forces unless the King agreed to the condition that Calais should be delivered to the Queen until she was assured of her great expenses, and he was better able to defend it. He was not to take more than the 6,000 men specified, and they were not to be embarked unless he was likely to be in time to save the town. The soldiers were to be used as auxiliaries only and not to be employed unless the French King had sufficient horse and foot to take his proper share of the burden.

At Dover, Essex and the Admiral were impatiently waiting for their orders. Of the two, Lord Charles Howard was the more disgusted, especially when he learnt that Essex alone was to have the honour of leading over the expedition. He was so angry that he wrote an indignant letter to Sir Robert Cecil, vowing, " by the Lord that made me, I will never serve but as a private man whilst I live, and if her Majesty lay me in the Tower it shall be welcome to me." Let someone else be sent to take his place; the Queen had shown her poor opinion of him; he was but a drudge. " But since I see it is the account of me, I will take care of myself and estate in time. This is far from that which her Majesty made show of to me at my departure; and for the voyage, since my disgrace cannot now be salved, except by my importunate suit, which I will never do having this offered me, and therefore I pray you for the other journey let me not be pressed, for I vow it to God I will not stir in it. And therefore I mean to return with my own two ships, and would be glad that order were sent for someone to take the charge I have. I mean to go presently abroad and not lie in Dover to my shame, and thus I leave for ever farther to deal in martial causes."

He even wrote another letter in the same strain to the Queen herself, which so alarmed Essex that he sent to Cecil, praying him to suppress it, "for it is too passionate and it may break all our actions if she take him at his word."

The next day, April 14, there was still uncertainty at Dover. From over the water the rumble of the cannonading was louder than before. Essex was frantic with impatience, for he could not embark until he received definite orders. Towards evening he wrote again to Cecil, "It is the greatest scorn in the world to lie here, in sight of a French King that stays but to join with us, and of a place that imports us and all our friends in these parts of Christendom so much, and to have moved an expectation of doing somewhat, and yet to have our hands tied."

To Burghley he wrote:

"MY VERY GOOD LORD,
"I remember how much I saw your Lordship afflicted for the alteration of the Queen's former order to succour Calais, and I doubt not but your Lordship is as much grieved that her army should be levied, and we sent down; and yet, by an instruction, our hands bound behind us. I am he whom the Queen commanded by letter to the Count St. Pol, to promise succour directly without condition. I only am called upon

from the French King to keep promise. I am named to the service, and I lie here to be witness that the citadel doth hold out well, and is only lost for our not keeping troth. My letter to the Count St. Pol is sent in to Vedazant by the King, when the last succours did enter; therefore, your Lordship will pardon me if I do passionately importune for a sound resolution. If the first stay had not been, the citadel had been relieved ere this, and what it will do now, upon this second stay, when our first promises are discredited, your Lordship shall see shortly, and I do fear already. I beseech your Lordship to keep in your favour your Lordship's humble poor friend, that will do you all the service he can.

"ESSEX.

"Dover, this 14th April, 1596."

But the Queen had at last consented to let Essex go, and earlier in the day she had written to him with her own hand:

"As distant as I am from your abode, yet my ears serve me too well to hear that terrible battery that methinks sounds for relief at my hands; wherefore, rather than for lack of timely aid it should be wholly lost, go you on, in God's blessed name, as far as that place where you may soonest relieve it, with as much caution as so great a trust requires. But I charge you, without the mere loss of it, do in no wise peril so fair an army for another Prince's town. God cover you under His safest wings, and let all peril go without your compass. Believe Cecil in the rest."

Essex was able to move. All day on April 15 the embarkation of the soldiers went on, Essex supervising them troop by troop. It was a still day, but no sound came from over the water. Essex himself went on board the *Rainbow* in the evening, and was at supper when news came that Calais had fallen.

It was a discreditable affair, and dangerous, for if the

Spanish fleet could again make its way to Calais, it was not likely that the mistakes of 1588 would be repeated. The preparations for the voyage were therefore pushed on. The Admiral was brought to his senses by a tart rebuke from the Queen, conveyed, as so often, in a brief postscript to an official letter. He and Essex put to sea and sailed round to Plymouth where there was considerable muddle, as the ships, stores, and men were daily accumulating with no one to supervise their organisation, and, as might be expected, naval and military officers were quarrelling over their rights and precedences. With Sir Francis Vere to advise him, Essex at once set to work to bring this chaos to order. As there was no treasure to pay the troops, he borrowed coin locally. He caused lists of the officers to be drawn up, assigning to each his duty and place. He organised the army into companies and regiments, allotting to each a proportion of old soldiers to stiffen the discipline of the recruits. Training and drilling went on continuously.

There were many delays. Shipmasters and sailors who had been pressed for service were so slack in reporting for duty that it was necessary to issue a proclamation threatening them with martial law. Ralegh was still in London supervising the despatch of the ships. At this moment Essex was even prepared to be friendly with Ralegh. On May 3 he wrote to him:

"SIR,
"Your pains and travail in bringing all things to that forwardness they are in doth sufficiently assure me of your discontentment to be stayed now by the wind. Therefore I will not entreat you to make haste, though our stay here is very costly, for besides all other expenses, every soldier in the army has his weekly lending out of my purse. But I will wish and pray for a good wind for you. And when you are come, I will make you see I desire to do you as much honour, and give you as great contentment, as I can. For this is the

action and the time in which you and I shall be both taught to know and love one another, and so I wish you all happiness and rest,

"Your very assured friend,

"Essex.

"When you come I will show you the fairest troops for their number that ever were looked upon."

The Queen was still difficult. There were not wanting critics of the expedition and its commanders. The French King, who was sore at the loss of Calais, sent over the Duc de Bouillon and he was trying to persuade the Queen to fight the enemy in France. In her despatches to Essex she was critical, and even unfriendly. He protested with dignity at her unkindness, and with some bitterness he wrote on May 7 to Cecil, "I have undertaken and hitherto proceeded with a greater work than ever any gentleman of my degree and means did undergo. I have asked her Majesty no money to levy, no authority to press, nor no allowance to carry the troops from the places of their levies to this general rendezvous; but here I have our full number and here I keep them without spending our sea victuals or asking allowance or means from her Majesty. I am myself, I protest, engaged more than my state is worth; my friends, servants, and followers have also set up their rests; my care to bring a chaos into order and to govern every man's particular unquiet humours possesseth my time, both of recreation and of rest sometimes. And yet I am so far from receiving thanks as her Majesty keepeth the same form with me as she would do with him that through his fault or misfortune had lost her troops. I receive no one word of comfort or favour by letter, message, or any means whatsoever. When I look out of myself upon all the world I see no man thus dealt withal; and when I look into myself and examine what that capital fault should be that I had committed, I find nothing, except it be a fault to strive to do her Majesty more service than she cares for."

WARLIKE PREPARATIONS

Essex indeed had just cause for complaint, for the whole burden and expense was falling upon him. On May 12, he wrote again to Cecil:

"If I seem impatient, think how many things concur to move my patience. Sir Walter Ralegh, with the rest of our fleet, is not come, and yet he hath had (if the winds be the same there that they are here) all the wished winds he could desire, both to bring him out of the river and after he was in the Channel along to this place. Mr. Ashley is not come with our instructions and yet I hear he was despatched long since. Mr. Dorrell is not at hand, who would help in bestowing the proportions of victual in every ship, and yet he promised to be here a week ago. I have not touched one penny of her Majesty's money, and have spent infinite sums of mine own, and neither here see any short end of my charge, nor find that above there is any feeling had of it. I pray you, therefore, in friendship resolve me whether it be decreed by her Majesty that I only shall be undone and the service fall to the ground to the end that I with it might be ruined; for except her Majesty had given out some words to show her mislike or neglect of our going on, this slackness of all hands could not be used. I pay lendings to above 5,000 soldiers, I maintain all the poor captains and their officers, I have a little world eating upon me in my house, am fain to relieve most of the captains and gentlemen and many of the soldiers that come from the Indies; and yet I complain not of charge, but of want of direction and certainty in your resolutions above. Therefore I do conjure you to deal freely with me in answering this letter, and to let me have answer quickly."

In the middle of May the Queen caused further difficulties. She took it into her head to recall Essex and the Lord Admiral and to entrust the expedition to Lord Thomas Howard, Sir George Carew, and Sir Francis Vere. This would have been disastrous. As the officers concerned pointed out, many of the troops, soldiers as well as gentlemen, had joined out of affection for the Lord Generals; if they were recalled there would be wholesale desertions. The gentlemen who remained would not be disposed to obey inferior commanders. The fleet from the Netherlands would be discouraged. Nor would they, or anyone, willingly take over the command.

In another mood the Queen decided that she would cancel the expedition altogether, or else send the fleet only. On this proposal Essex commented fiercely in a letter to the Council:

"Because my words shall not offend her Majesty, I am resolved never to use argument to persuade or defend our journey, but to leave it to her Majesty's choice, whether she will break it or have us proceed. Yet that your Lordships may see, that I understand both myself and it, I have set down certain questions, for all the idle discoursers and envious crossers of our journey to answer.

"What shall be done with the £30,000 worth of victuals of her Majesty already provided, since it cannot be sold to London nor to the ports, they themselves having provided more than they can utter? What shall come of the preparations of the city and the coasters? and how it may be hoped for, that upon the like summons they will show the like readiness, since they shall see that our alarms are but false and our journeys but dreams?

"The like may be said of them of the Low Countries: what account shall be given of the great sums of money already laid out for impressing and rigging the ships, that shall serve for victuallers and transporters; the most of which money Flemings have received? What my Lord Admiral and I shall do with the victuals we have provided for ourselves and our companions for five months, since it is not such sea-victual as is used in ordinary journeys? What shall be recovered of the money laid out at Flushing, for ships and all things necessary for the transporting of the soldiers, that come out of the Low Countries, since it is ten days since, that we sent one authorised and furnished for that purpose? What shall be answered to the States of the Low Countries, to whom the Queen wrote so earnestly, using this motive, that her intended purpose was as well for their good as her own? And what shall be pretended to the world for this sudden change of counsel, since your Lordships know what censure is given of *haud putaveram*? What shall be done to keep France from making peace with Spain; when we neither assist them against the invasion there, nor prevent invasions of our own countries; but like men that are only strong in suffering, stand still, and bear off all with head and shoulders? How shall we prevent his sending of forces into Ireland, when, if nothing be done against him at home, he will weary us out with charge, and send till we are able to keep our fleet to impeach him no longer at sea? Lastly, what the insolent rebels of Ireland may think, when they both find themselves prosper, and see all our preparations but smoke, and our threatenings prove but wind?

"If it be said, the Queen may seem to do somewhat, and send her fleet, but stay her army, I am persuaded, that though some ignorant soul both of sea-actions and of the wars may by the fireside make such a proposition; yet there cannot any man be found so vain, that will undertake the action. But if there be, I would ask him, where he would save himself; or how he will get a port, if he have not a land-force to command the shore? Next, how he will distress, or burn the maritimes of Spain, if he go not to them where they are? or how he dare go into them, or shall be able to take such forts, as they make for their defences in the harbours? Lastly, when he hath spent his victuals, and must return, after he hath sailed unprofitably up and down some few months, why shall not the Spaniard, that without impeachment prepares all that while, follow him, and when the English ships are laid up, execute any thing upon them, that they list?

"But I have said enough. Thus much my duty to her Majesty and love to my country did challenge of me. Of my own interest I will not speak, since every day I do more and more incline to the Stoics' opinion, and will, if I can attain unto it, bring myself to their temper."

The Queen again relented, and at last it seemed possible that the expedition would sail. On May 21, Ralegh and his ships reached Plymouth. The next day a third part of the army was reviewed. Eight regiments were drawn up on parade, and put through their drill. They marched, advanced, retired, filed and unfiled with great precision and steadiness to the admiration of a large gathering of gentlemen and country folk.

Everything was now ready. On the whole the force was united and enthusiastic, and very gay, for the young gentlemen volunteers had equipped themselves with clothes plastered with gold and silver lace. There had been a few displays of temper, as was inevitable in a force where there were no clear regulations for seniority and precedence. Ralegh, Vere, and Sir Conyers Clifford at one time fell into undignified squabbling. Clifford was a man of far less military experience, but of haughty stomach. Vere proposed that Essex should settle the matter. He therefore directed that Ralegh should be senior by sea, and Vere by land; and further to prevent future disputes the particular duties of each officer in the field were drawn up and circulated. There had also been an outburst of temper from the Lord Admiral. In a joint letter to the Queen, Essex signed above him; he took a penknife and cut out the signature. Amongst the soldiers discipline was strict. An English soldier who murdered a Dutchman was tied to the corpse and thrown into the sea; another was executed for stirring up mutiny; a lieutenant, who took money to substitute inferior men for pressed soldiers, was disgraced and cashiered, and his punishment proclaimed by sound of drum through all the streets of Plymouth. Otherwise there had been few troubles.

At last, on May 24, the Queen's orders for departure were received. The packet of letters included a prayer of her own composing for their good success, and one of those personal letters to Essex which seemed recompense enough for all former troubles:

"I make this humble bill of requests to Him that all makes and does, that with His benign Hand He will shadow you so, as all harm may light beside you, and all that may be best hap to your share; that your return may make you better, and me gladder. Let your companion, my most faithful Charles, be sure that his name is not left out in this petition. God bless you both, as I would be if I were there, which, whether I wish or not, He alone doth know."

CHAPTER VIII

THE CADIZ VOYAGE

ON June 1, the wind blew favourable from the north-west. All were on board, waiting for the signal. At last the warning gun was fired from the *Ark Royal*. At once the anchors were raised, sails hoisted, and the whole fleet began to move. It was a slow business, and while the ships were still making their way out to sea, Essex dictated a long letter to the Council detailing his view of the plans to be adopted, the policy of the present expedition, and his own responsibility.

In general, he wrote, it was better to seek an enemy in his own country than to wait for him at home. For the English a protracted war was a disadvantage, but the moment was opportune, when the Spaniard was likely to receive most hurt. His treasure would be intercepted, " whereby we shall cut his sinews, and make war upon him with his own money, and to beat him, or at least discontinue him by sea, whereby her Majesty shall be both secured from his invasions, and become mistress of the sea, which is the greatness that the Queen of an island should most aspire unto." Moreover, more carracks were due home this year than ever, and this was the time to give him a blow by sea.

But, Essex continued, he was not responsible for the project; it had been devised and presented by the Lord Admiral, and had the Queen's approval with the assent of the Council. He did, however, acknowledge that he had urged, at times forgetting the reverend formalities, that once the troops were assembled the expedition should go forward. He trusted that they would expect neither too much nor too little; lest they should seem to accomplish either nothing or by chance.

There was another proposal. Let the Queen have, as it were, a thorn sticking in the foot of Spain, that is, let her seize and maintain a port in Spain which would be a continual annoyance. The hazard and charge would not be great; the hazard was confined to the garrison, and the charge would be amply recovered, for in short time the golden Indian stream might be turned from Spain to England. As to the place—he would discuss it in his next letter. If their Lordships thought the suggestion good, he begged them to move it to the Queen, on the understanding that the plan was first approved by the Council of War.

He concluded by asking that his own actions should not be condemned until he had had a chance of answering criticism, " for as the nature of my place is subject to envy and detraction, so a little body full of sharp humours is hardliest kept in temper, and all the discontented humours of an army do make their greatest quarrel to him that commands the army, not so much for his faults, as because he bridles theirs."

The wind held until the fleet was by Dodman's Head in Cornwall, and then veered, so that they were obliged to turn back and anchor once more in Plymouth Sound. The Lord Admiral, therefore, called a council, and it was ordered that until Cadiz was reached, the fleet should sail well out of sight of land, and that no attempt to land should be made. The destination of the expedition was still kept secret from all but the select council. Sealed orders were sent out to the ships' commanders with the superscription, " If you be separated from the fleet by foul weather or otherwise, you shall herein find to what place you shall repair, till when you shall not open the enclosed upon pain of death." The directions were that the rendezvous was to be Cape St. Vincent (called the South Cape); if the fleet was not then encountered, the next rendezvous was Cadiz.

Next day the wind blew favourable; anchors were raised once more, and the Lord Admiral led his fleet out to sea. The fleet was in five squadrons. The Lord Admiral led the first in the *Ark Royal*; the second was in the command of Essex in the *Due Repulse*, a fine new ship; Lord Thomas Howard in the *Mere Honour*, and Ralegh in the *Warspite*, commanded the third and fourth; the fifth was the Dutch squadron of twenty-four ships, commanded by Jan van Duyvenvoord in the *Neptune*. In all there were some 150 ships of all kinds, manned by about 5,000 sailors, and carrying some 6,500 soldiers.

For the land service, the chief officers of the army were Sir Francis Vere, Lord Marshal; Sir John Wingfield, Camp-master-General; Sir Conyers Clifford, Sergeant Major; Sir George Carew, Master of the Ordnance; and Anthony Ashley, Secretary to the Council of War. The regiments were commanded by the Earl of Sussex, Sir Christopher Blount, Sir Thomas Gerrard, Sir Richard Wingfield, Sir Edward Wingfield, Sir Matthew Morgan, and Sir William Woodhouse, and in addition there were the Dutch troops.

The daily routine of the voyage was for the ships to draw together with their squadrons at dusk when the watch was set and they ceremoniously saluted each other with trumpet calls, and cheers. All night the ships followed the Admirals' lanterns, but when light returned they again extended over a wide area. In this way the sea was swept clear of ships which might give an alarm. A few were taken which yielded some booty and valuable information.

On June 11, a select council was summoned, for which the signal was to hang out the flag of the arms of England, and to shoot off a warning piece. The members of this council were the squadron commanders, Vere, Carew, Clifford, and Ashley. At the meeting the first plans were considered for the attack on Cadiz, but after a lengthy discussion nothing was decided, except that a further council should be held when the place had been viewed. Then the flag for a general council was shown, which was the flag of St. George. When the ships' masters and captains had come on board, they were asked to give an opinion of the present position of the fleet: a variety of opinions was expressed, but the general conclusion was that they were 42 degrees to the southward, and 30 leagues from the coast.

Another select council was held on June 15, and instructions were drawn up to ensure an orderly landing. Where it was necessary for regiments to be landed in several journeys, then equal detachments of the best men of each regiment should be landed simultaneously. The boats were to keep rank and order, no one stirring to get ahead of his leaders or neighbour; rowing should be directed by beat of drum, and the pace was to be that of the slowest boat. As the first boat landed, the men were to be led to a convenient place to make a stand to cover the landing of the rest.

The ships moved on slowly in calm weather. In the night of the 18th/19th a strange ship was discovered to be sailing in the fleet, which tried to make off as soon as she discovered her unwelcome company, but was soon summoned to surrender. It was an Irish barque, two days out of Cadiz, and homeward bound for Waterford. The captain gave the exciting news that the town of Cadiz had not yet received any alarm and was but weakly garrisoned; and, moreover, that in the Road lay a rich fleet of merchant ships, outward bound for the Indies, with the King of Spain's ships waiting to escort them.

A select council was immediately called to consider the plan for the assault. There was considerable difference of opinion whether town or fleet, or both simultaneously, should be attacked; but at length it was agreed that Essex should land the army and assault the town where it appeared best after view of the landing places; the Lord Admiral should either attack the Spanish ships or confine them within the bay, whilst Captain Alexander Clifford, with four ships and three hoys, should prevent the galleys from annoying the fleet or the landing.

The wind freshened, and early in the morning of Sunday, June 20, Cadiz was in sight. A little later the fleet was concentrated at anchor half a league off St. Sebastian, a friary at the west end of Cadiz.

The town of Cadiz lies at the end of a narrow spit of land, about six miles long. To the west is the open sea, but on the east the shore curves away in a great bay, on the north-east of which lies Port Royal. At the extreme east of this bay there is a narrow channel which winds away to the south-west and opens into the sea about ten miles south of the town, so that, in fact, Cadiz stands on an island, though it was connected to the mainland by a bridge called the Suazo Bridge.

As soon as the ships had anchored, Essex at once ordered the soldiers to embark in the barges and long boats. By this time the wind was rising and the waves were running high. Two boats were tossed over and sunk, and fifteen men drowned. The landing would be a risky operation, especially as the garrison was coming down to resist them. Ralegh now came on board the *Due Repulse*, and pointed out the dangers ahead, which Essex already sufficiently realised, but he was not willing to abandon the attempt unless ordered by the Lord Admiral. Ralegh went off to the *Ark Royal*, and persuaded the Lord Admiral not only to cancel the landing but to agree instead to an attack on the Spanish fleet. Ralegh came back with the good news to Essex, who thereupon ordered the men to be re-embarked.

When the English ships first came to anchor, the Spanish fleet, which consisted of four of the great galleons named after the Apostles, and the galleys, was at anchor at the north-east of the point. These now drew into the shore and took up a position to the east of the town, covered by the guns of the fort St. Philip.

It took some time before the soldiers could all be fetched back, and then towards the late afternoon the English fleet took up a new anchorage near to the station which the Spanish fleet had abandoned earlier in the day. Another select council was held on the *Due Repulse* and the plan for the attack on the Spanish fleet was discussed. The Lord Admiral was so anxious

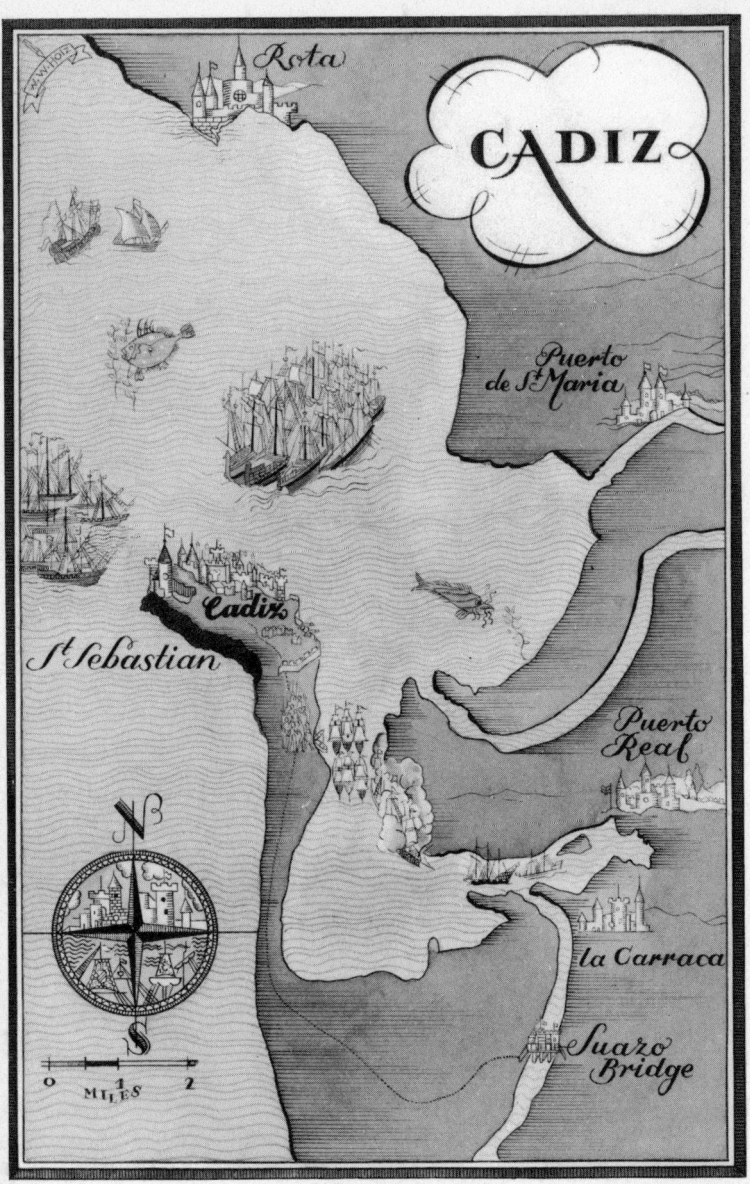

MAP OF CADIZ

for the safety of the three flagships—the *Ark Royal*, the *Due Repulse*, and the *Mere Honour*—that he would not allow them to take part in the action. Essex claimed the honour of leading the attack, but the Lord Admiral refused, partly because a disaster to Essex's ship would have hazarded the whole action, and not less because he had been strictly ordered by the Queen that Essex was not to expose himself to danger unnecessarily.

After much argument it was finally agreed that Lord Thomas Howard on the *Nonpareil*, Ralegh in the *Warspite*, Vere in the *Rainbow*, Sir George Carew in the *Mary Rose*, Sir R. Southwell in the *Lion*, Captain Cross in the *Swiftsure*, and the Dutch Admiral with some Dutch men-of-war, should attack the Spanish ships, whilst Sir John Wingfield in the *Vanguard* should deal with the galleys. The main fleet was to be in readiness to come up to their support if needed.

Next morning, before the English ships had weighed anchor, the Spanish fleet left their anchorage and moved further into the bay, to take up a new position in the narrow strait between Fort Puntal and the mainland. Here the strait was so narrow that not more than ten ships abreast could pass through. Meanwhile the merchant ships of the West India fleet, which lay in Cadiz harbour ready laden for their western voyage, crept out, and along the coast and so beyond into the bay and thence to Port Royal, where they took refuge.

The English ships were now ready for attack. Before them in the strait the four great galleons were anchored athwart the passage so that they could use their full broadsides; in the intervals were posted the galleys. Ralegh led, but dropped anchor too soon and found himself out of effective range. Vere passed him and to shoreward, and neglecting those galleys which lay in the shallow water, anchored within culverin shot of the galleons. Ralegh weighed anchor and moved up higher beyond Vere, and masking his fire. Then he also anchored athwart the strait and used his whole broadship. The rest of the ships anchored with their bows towards the enemy.

The fight developed. The two guns in the Puntal Fort were fired off, but the effort was too much for them; one burst, the other collapsed. From the galleons the shooting was more successful, but the gunnery was bad and the powder less effective than in the English ships, for whilst the shot from the galleons only bruised and shook the English, the English cannon balls tore through the sides of the galleons and smashed into the ranks of soldiers behind. In a while blood could be seen dribbling from the scuppers.

As soon as he heard the noise of the cannon ahead of him, Essex forgot his promise to the Lord Admiral, and listening to the persuasions of Monson, his captain, weighed anchor and crept up into the channel and joined the cannonade. It was some time before the Lord Admiral knew of this move. Then he, too, must have a share in the adventure. The *Ark Royal* was at anchor in the midst of the main fleet and unable to approach nearer. He ordered his barge to row him aboard the *Mere Honour*, and thence he took part in the fight.

The cannonade went on for three hours, and it was now getting on for midday. By this time Ralegh, fearing for the safety of the *Warspite* on which the galleons were concentrating their fire, rowed round to the *Due Repulse* to consult with Essex and ask him that the Dutch boats which had been detailed for boarding should be brought up. They drew near but fell foul of each other. Then Essex gave order that Ralegh might board with the *Warspite*.

The Spaniards were badly shaken. As soon as they saw that Ralegh's ship was moving towards them, the four galleons cut their cables, intending to cross the bay and to take shelter with the merchant fleet at Port Royal. But such was the confusion and panic that with the incoming tide all four galleons drifted on the shore of the mainland. As the ships grounded the soldiers poured out from the portholes like coals from a sack. Many were drowned, others embedded in the mud. Sir Robert Southwell in his pinnace tried to board the *St. Philip*, but she was blazing and soon afterwards blew up, with many of her crew. The *St. Thomas* was set on fire; but Ralegh and his men were too quick for those on the *St. Matthew* and *St. Andrew*, which yielded intact. It was a horrible scene while it lasted, with great roaring flames licking the masts and sails of the *St. Philip* and the cannon bursting as the fire reached them, whilst the men in the water, some wounded, some blackened and scorched, clung to the ropes or struggled to drag themselves ashore, so that, as Ralegh observed, if " any man had a desire to see Hell itself, it was then most lively figured." To add to the carnage, the Dutch put out in their boats to kill without mercy, until driven off by Ralegh and the Lord Admiral.

The sea fight was now over and the way clear for an attack either on the town of Cadiz or the merchant fleet in Port Royal, or both simultaneously. Essex, Vere, and the army officers were for the land fight. The soldiers had been for some time waiting ready in the boats. Without stopping to consult with the Lord Admiral, which would have meant yet another council of war, Essex gave the order for the boats to move. Essex himself, with Vere and some picked men, led in the first boat. The rest followed, keeping perfect distance and interval, the oars dipping together to the sound of Essex's drum. There was no opposition from the land, and almost as soon as they came ashore the soldiers were drawn up in formation on the sandy shore north of Fort Puntal. About 2,000 men were ready for the advance.

The first intention of Essex and Vere was to bivouac for the night until the whole army and the cannon had been landed, and then to advance on Cadiz in the morning, when the cannon would bombard the walls to make breaches for the assault. They would therefore lead the men forward to seek a suitable bivouac. As they went, bodies of Spaniards, horse and foot, could be seen hurrying along the outer edge of the isthmus to the town. At this point the isthmus was only about half a mile wide. It was resolved to send three regiments with Conyers Clifford, Christopher Blount, and Thomas Gerrard to occupy the Suazo Bridge to prevent any reinforcements from the mainland, and there to remain until they received further orders.

Then Essex, with the rest of his force, which was reduced to less than 1,000 including the company of gentlemen adventurers, continued to advance towards the town. Cadiz lay about three miles off, and the going over deep loose sand on a hot midsummer afternoon was bad and very exhausting. Nevertheless, they pushed on at a rapid pace, almost a double. As they came nearer, the Spaniards could be seen drawn up outside the walls, about five hundred in all, mostly horse, with a screen of skirmishers in front.

Vere soon realised that, if pushed, the Spaniards were not likely to put up much fight. He suggested to Essex that if the Spaniards could be drawn on to fight at some distance from the walls, they might be thrown back into confusion and then destroyed in the ditch, and perhaps even followed into the town in the rout. Essex approved and left it to Vere. He chose an approach by which the main body could advance on the town concealed by dead ground. Then he ordered Sir John Wingfield to attack the enemy and drive in the skirmishers; if the main battle counter-attacked, he was to retreat as if in panic until he reached the support, and then to turn short and charge with fury. The support was under Sir Matthew Morgan and consisted of 300 men; they were to follow Wingfield by a concealed way, and then when they charged the enemy to pursue them pell-mell into the town. The rest of the column with Essex and Vere were to follow in reserve.

The plan succeeded beyond hope or expectation. The Spaniards were thrown into confusion when Wingfield's men suddenly turned, and they fled in panic. Most of them crowded through the gates, but those within were so eager to have them shut that forty of the horse found themselves barred out. They jumped off their horses and clambered over the half-finished walls, for by ill chance to the Spaniards their defences were in process of reconstruction. The English followed hard after them, Essex among the first. There was some fighting on the walls, but soon many of them were on and over the top. They pushed on without waiting to reform, Essex leading. Vere, realising that such a disorderly advance might easily be repulsed, collected as many as he could and with much ado broke open the gates. When he reached the market-place, Essex was already there with about fifty men, who were for the moment held up. At the approach of Vere, the Spaniards who were resisting Essex fled into the Town House, which overlooked the market-place. Vere broke in and cleared the upper rooms of Spaniards. Then he asked Essex to hold the Town House whilst he made good the neighbouring streets. The rest of the Spaniards, together with most of the inhabitants, had already taken refuge in the Castle which overlooked the market-place.

By this the Lord Admiral had landed with Lord Thomas Howard. As he went down into his boat, Ashley and Monson had rowed up to him with a message from Essex that it would be as well for him to see to the capture of the merchant fleet at Port Royal. But the Admiral, knowing that Essex's force was far too small for an attempt on the city, decided to follow him. In spite of his age, the heat and the sand, he led his men so resolutely that he entered the city and had come up to Essex in the market-place. Vere had now cleared the city. The few remaining Spaniards fled, either into Fort St. Philip or the abbey of St. Francis. The abbey surrendered at once. Those in the fort promised that they would yield in the morning. Then Vere went back to report to Essex. By 8 o'clock at night the whole city was in English hands, except for the castle.

Darkness was now coming on. The two generals made the Town House their headquarters for the night, and here, after returning suitable thanks to God for the victory, they waited for daylight. All night there were constant alarms and shooting, for the Dutch were merciless.

The casualties had not been heavy, about a hundred in all,

including the sea fight. A few had been killed by shots from the loopholes in the castle, amongst them Sir John Wingfield, who was wounded at the assault on the walls and had entered the city riding a captured horse. He was struck in the head by a musket ball and killed instantly

A message was sent to the castle that unless the defenders surrendered unconditionally before morning every man would be put to the sword without mercy. When daylight appeared, the flag of truce was hanging out. Essex took the surrender of the castle, and the Lord Admiral of the Fort; and soon the red ensign was flying over each.

Much reorganisation was necessary. The first business of the generals was to settle the terms of surrender. The conditions imposed on the Corregidor and chief men of the town were that they should be allowed to leave the town alive, and in the clothes they were wearing; all goods should remain as a spoil for the soldiers. For the privilege of their lives they should pay a ransom of 120,000 ducats, for which forty of the chief men should remain as pledges and be sent to England until the money was paid.

These terms having been perforce accepted, the generals next drew up a Proclamation to the troops that all killing and violence should cease forthwith, and that upon pain of death no violence of any kind should be done to women or children, or any Spanish subject. Then the soldiers were turned loose to plunder, and soon the streets were cluttered with furniture, broken jars of wine and olive oil, baskets of almonds, olives, raisins, and spices, thrown out in heaps and trampled under foot in the zeal for more valuable and portable wealth.

In all this confusion nothing had been settled about the merchant ships, some forty in number, which were huddled together in the harbour of Port Royal, across the bay. Being a naval matter, the decision lay with the Lord Admiral. He ordered Lord Thomas Howard to take some of the Queen's ships and others of light draught, and to arrest the merchant ships; if they resisted, they were to be sunk or burnt. The sailors, however, were too busy in Cadiz to be recalled quickly. Captain Conway offered to lead soldiers over in the long boats. Ralegh objected that it was a seaman's business. To the Spanish merchants the cargoes were as valuable as the ships, and during the day a deputation came to Essex with the petition that both should be ransomed for 2,000,000 ducats. Essex consulted the Lord Admiral, who refused the offer. He was not going to allow the Spaniards to keep a ship, though he could consider an offer for the merchandise. The matter was hotly argued, but nothing was concluded for the night.

Next morning the controversy was settled by the Duke of Medina Sidonia. He had observed the battle from Port St. Mary, and he realised that though nothing could now be done to save the merchant fleet, at least it need not fall into the enemy's hands. Early on the morning of Wednesday, the 23rd, great columns of smoke could be seen rising from the harbour of Port Royal. The English ships put out and raced across the bay. They were too late to save any of the ships, but they made some plunder and took off a few cannon. The loss to the Spaniards was enormous. The galleys, however, escaped. In the afternoon of the day of the action they were apparently trapped in the narrow passage leading to the Suazo Bridge; but Clifford and the rest of his troops left the bridge in the morning, and hurried off to the town to be in time for the sack. When they had gone the men from the galleys broke down an arch of the bridge. The galleys slipped past, made their way round into the open sea, and safely reached Rota.

There were still many matters to be arranged, and the Council of War sat continuously during Wednesday, Thursday, and Friday. The first problem was to evacuate the civil population. All women and religious persons of both sexes were allowed to go. Sir Amyas Preston was detailed to transport to Port St. Mary a hundred and more of the richer gentlewomen, who were permitted to wear their jewellery and as many clothes as they cared to put on, and, lest the rude soldiery might be tempted to rifle such rich land prizes, Essex and the Lord Admiral stood at the water gate to supervise their embarkation. The rest of the inhabitants were escorted in parties to the Suazo Bridge and turned loose on the mainland.

Amongst the prisoners was the Bishop of Cuzco, who was to have sailed in the West Indian fleet. When he was brought before the generals they observed that he should be released without ransom, for they came not to deal with churchmen or men of peace, or women, and children, nor had they made this voyage for gold or silver or riches, but to revenge the dishonourable practices of their enemy and to defend the true honour of England.

As to the next move, the council was divided. At first it was thought best to hold the town, and orders were given for the cannon and munitions to be brought ashore. At the same time Ashley was to be sent to England to know the Queen's wishes. Edward Hoby was also to be despatched to ask help of the King of Morocco. Next morning these resolutions were cancelled.

On Saturday, June 26, Sir John Wingfield was buried with military honours in the church of Santa Cruz. The body was carried by six knights, with the drums and trumpets sounding dolefully, and the shot bearing their pieces with the muzzles downwards and pikes trailed. The generals cast their handkerchiefs, wet with their tears, into the open grave, and the ships of the fleet fired off a funeral volley.

On the Sunday there was a service of thanksgiving at the church of San Francisco, attended by the generals and the principal officers and gentlemen, and followed by a banquet; after which honours were awarded. More than sixty gentlemen were knighted by the generals, amongst them being Charles Blount and Gelly Meyrick, Essex's steward.

On the Monday the Lord Admiral, who was suffering a reaction after his great exertions, went on board the *Ark* to take physic, and to have some leisure to consider the further movements of the fleet. He caused a letter to be written to the Duke of Medina Sidonia, proposing that the English prisoners who were serving as slaves in the galleys should be exchanged for Spaniards from Cadiz. The Duke agreed, and orders were accordingly sent to the Adelantado of the galleys at Rota.

The same evening there was another council. Upon a survey of the provisions it was reported that, with the victuals on board and in the town, there was enough to keep 3,000 to 4,000 men for four months, by which time further supplies from England, the Low Countries, and Barbary might be expected. It was then agreed that the flagships and weaker vessels should return to England, and that Lord Thomas Howard, with Ralegh and a sufficient fleet, should go to the Islands to wait for the treasure fleet.

These resolutions were upset by Essex, for he nominated himself as Governor of Cadiz, and refused to listen to any other proposal. The Lord Admiral, on the other hand, refused to go home without him. Absolute deadlock was reached and the whole plan abandoned in favour of a return home.

Essex made one more attempt to win glory. He learnt that a number of Spanish troops had made their way across the Suazo Bridge and were occupying a castle called Herod's House, which defended the bridge. He led a column of twenty-nine companies and his own cornet of horse there one evening, hoping to draw the enemy out into the open. The plan was not successful, and they returned to the city.

Thereafter Essex stayed in the town to supervise the destruction of the defences. The cannon were collected and stowed in the fleet. The castle and forts were demolished by the pioneers, and on July 1, the tower of the Town House was battered down. On July 4, the town of Cadiz was systematically set on fire, except for the churches and religious houses. The ships were loaded with provisions and all that could be stowed aboard, and then the soldiers were re-embarked, Essex himself coming away with the last boatload.

Next morning the fleet once more put out to sea. As they

were passing out of the bay, a galley bearing the white flag of truce met them. It was bringing the English prisoners from Rota. Unfortunately the captain of a small English vessel in his zeal fired at her, killing one and wounding two. The Lord Admiral, as soon as he realised the purpose of the galley, caused her to be saluted with trumpets, and then summoned the officers on board the *Ark Royal* and feasted them. He was at first for hanging the zealous captain who had fired on the flag of truce, but by persuasion of the galley's captain, who told him that no English had been hit, he refrained. Then he called for his barge and conducted the Spanish officers to Essex's ship, where they were again entertained and handed over their prisoners, twenty-nine in all.

As soon as the fleet was at sea, the council assembled on the *Ark Royal* to consider the next enterprise, and it was resolved to land at Ayamonte and march thence to Tarilla and Faro, where the fleet would meet them; but on the next day, as the wind was uncertain and there was some risk that the fleet might be completely becalmed, the plan was abandoned in favour of a direct attack on Faro. At this point Sir Anthony Ashley (who had received his knighthood with the rest) was sent to England to report to the Queen, and with him went the Earl of Sussex, who was sick, and the other casualties. Ashley carried many letters.

The galleys scored a small success, for they captured a hoy of Lord Thomas Howard, with six men and horses on board, and towed her into Villa Nueva, the fleet being immobile in the calm and unable to rescue her.

On July 13, the fleet anchored on the west of Cape St. Mary and the army was again disembarked. The Lord Admiral claimed that it was his turn to lead. The privilege was granted, but when he realised that there would be a ten-mile march in extreme heat he yielded to the request that he should stay with the fleet and leave the command to Essex.

Essex bivouacked for the night on shore. Next morning the army was divided into sixteen battalions and marched forward. The advanced guard was under command of Sir Christopher Blount, to whom all the principal knights and gentlemen adventurers resorted. When Essex heard that so brave a troop was ahead, he left the main body and took command of the advanced guard.

No enemy opposed them as they marched forward, and when they entered Faro they found the town deserted. The inhabitants had taken their goods and fled to the mountains. A force of 800 men was sent in pursuit, but nothing was taken except some oxen and sheep, which were distributed amongst the fleet. In Faro itself a few cannon and brass culverin were found, and to Essex's share fell a library of books belonging to the bishop. The town was set on fire and the army marched back to the fleet and re-embarked.

Another council was now held, and the question of attacking Lagos was propounded. The Lord Admiral opposed it, for he was anxious to get back to England as soon as possible. The intelligence showed, he said, that the place was well walled and mounted fifty cannon: the attempt would cause much delay and many casualties. The resolution of the council was that the fleet should double Cape St. Vincent and go for the Rock, and having taken in water should then look for the return of the carracks. On arrival at the Cape the wind was favourable for a dash to the Azores. Essex was emphatic that the attempt should be made, if not with the whole then with a selected fleet. Vere supported him, but the seamen in the fleet opposed.

The wind, however, soon changed, and another council was held at which it was decided that the fleet was not in a fit state, either in general condition or supplies, to wait for the carracks. They resolved to make for the Groin to see if any Spanish ships lay there.

The Groin was reached on August 1, but the port was empty. The council assembled for the last time, and it was agreed that the fleet should return to Plymouth. Sir Edward Conway was sent on to report to the Queen and to learn her pleasure, whether the army was to be kept together or dismissed on arrival. The council ended, the two generals, holding one sword, knighted the Dutch General Sir Jan van Duyvenvoord. Then each commander returned to his ship and ran for home. The fastest reached Plymouth on August 6.

CHAPTER IX

AFTER CADIZ

WHEN Sir Anthony Ashley sailed for England, Essex sent Henry Cuffe, one of his secretaries, with him bearing his letters. To Lord Burghley he wrote:

"My very good Lord,

"I shall not need to tell your Lordship that Cales is won, and the King of Spain's great fleet at Cales defeated and destroyed. I shall less need to relate the particular circumstances of either: for as Fame itself will bring the first, so this gentleman that carries my letter will perform the second. This is to crave of your Lordship that I may be continued in your Lordship's good favour, and to pray you that you will plead for me till my return; that before I be heard I be not, upon report or misconceit, brought into Her Majesty's displeasure, for I doubt not but your Lordship and such honourable judges shall think I do acquit myself like an honest man. I wish your Lordship all honour, health, and happiness, and rest at your Lordship's commandment,

"Essex.

"Cales, the first of July."

Cuffe also took a letter to Reynolds, Essex's senior secretary:

"Reynolds,

"You shall receive from Cuffe a relation of that is passed here. It is particular and most true. Keep it to yourself; only give M. la Fontaine a sight of it, and let him draw out of it an abstract to send into France. Do the like to Mr. Bodley. Mr. Ashley knows of it; and if you confer with him, the effect of this or the like may be printed, which he is to procure, and you to solicit, and to compare that, which is to be printed, with this that you have. Deliver all the letters I send you safely, especially those to my Lord Burgh and to Mr. Fulke Greville.

"From Cales the 1st July,
"Your loving master,
"ESSEX.

"Commend me humbly to my Lord's Grace of Canterbury; and if he will procure a public thanksgiving for this great victory, he shall do an act worthy of him. Commend my service to my Lord of Shrewsbury and my Lady."

Ashley reached London on July 30, but Cuffe was unfortunately taken ill on the journey after leaving Portsmouth. He therefore sent off Essex's letters in post to Reynolds, and enclosed the account of the Cadiz action with particular instructions that Reynolds should have a fair transcript made, and cause it to be given to a good printer. In order to hide the true author, Sir Anthony Ashley should be the agent of delivery. The whole was to be made up in the form of a letter and published as *A true relation of the action at Cadiz the 21st June, under the Earl of Essex and the Lord Admiral, sent to a gentleman in Court from one that served there in good place.* To the Preface, perhaps Fulke Greville would append his initials, or else D.T. or R.B. would serve.

The Lord Admiral, with the greater part of the fleet and army, dropped anchor in Plymouth Sound on August 8. Essex did not land until the 10th, for he had waited to bring the great galleon *St. Andrew* in his squadron. The news on his arrival was disturbing. Burghley had taken advantage of his absence to persuade the Queen to promote Sir Robert Cecil to be Secretary; Essex's candidate was Thomas Bodley. Ashley had proved treacherous. In spite of his promise of secrecy to Reynolds, he told both the Queen and the Council of Essex's account of the action, with the result that when it was taken to the printers they had already been strictly com-

**LETTER WRITTEN TO LORD BURGHLEY AFTER THE
SUCCESS AT CADIZ**

Reproduced from a manuscript in the British Museum, London.

manded through the Archbishop of Canterbury not to print any discourse of the action without special order from the Council. Further, Cuffe received a message from the Queen that on pain of death he was not to publish any discourse without her knowledge.

Anthony Bacon did what he could to persuade the Archbishop and the printers, but, though sympathetic, they dared not disobey the order. He had, therefore, caused written copies to be made which he sent to the Earl's friends to copy and pass on: by this means a copy had been sent to Scotland, Bodley was sending a copy to the Low Countries, and M. de la Fontaine a copy in French for the French Court.

Most disturbing of all, the Queen herself, far from expressing gratitude for the victory, was wholly discontented. Essex's enemies at Court had used every argument to move her anger and to diminish his reputation in the action. They attributed the greater part of the success to Ralegh and the sailors, and hinted that the Queen had been grossly abused in the division of the spoil. As one great man put it, there were many knights made, and the Queen would not hereafter be troubled with beggars, all were become so rich by Cadiz; but what did she gain by it? She had ships and ordnance enough, but where was the £50,000 which she had laid out for the voyage? She was reported to have said that hitherto, to her great damage, she had been contented to follow Essex's humours and he had had his desire, but henceforth she would please herself and serve her own.

On the other hand, the Archbishop had been his friend. He obtained leave for a general thanksgiving for the victory throughout the Kingdom, though the Queen afterwards confined it to London; and in the sermon at Paul's Cross, which was preached on August 8 by Dr. William Barlow, the Archbishop's chaplain, Essex had been highly commended for his noble behaviour and compared with the greatest of generals, and, moreover, those who minimised the victory had been severely criticised. The sermon was loudly applauded. There was no doubt that in the opinion of the people at large Essex was the hero of Cadiz.

Essex reached Court at noon on August 12. He immediately urged that the fleet and army should not be dispersed but used for some further venture against the enemy. He spent some days in hopeful bustle, but there was no answering enthusiasm. The Lord Admiral, Ralegh, and Conyers Clifford opposed his suggestion, and the sailors helped to settle the matter, for many of them made for their homes to stow the plunder.

There was also some trouble in Essex's own household. He was not satisfied with the way in which Reynolds had managed his affairs and purposed to take a fifth secretary, in addition to Cuffe, Henry Wotton, and Temple. Reynolds felt hurt, put his papers in order, and wrote pathetically to Anthony Bacon to explain his sad case to Essex. Bacon, however, persuaded him to patience and Reynolds's injured pride was gradually healed.

The Queen's annoyance was not unreasonable. It was obvious that the spoils of Cadiz were enormous. Officers and men had helped themselves liberally, but it was soon clear that her own share would be very small. When the customs officials went on board the ships they were shown boxes and bundles of miscellaneous plunder, but the money and jewels had mostly been conveyed away. Some private ships had followed the fleet expectantly, and the loot was bought up from the captains far below its value. Inquiries were held, and there were many tales of how someone had been seen making off with bags of ducats, priceless jewelled hatbands, and the like, but little fell into the customs' hands. Nor was it possible to make out any definite case of peculation, though Sir Anthony Ashley, being particularly charged by Sir Gelly Meyrick, was sent to the Fleet Prison, where he made loud complaints and lame excuses.

Essex had anticipated trouble, and whilst still at the Groin he drew up a criticism of his fellow commanders. Had his advice been followed, he noted, the Indian fleet would have been seized before the Spaniards had time to set it alight. His advice to hold Cadiz had been overruled. His proposal to wait for the treasure fleet at Lisbon had been rejected, especially by the Lord Admiral and Ralegh. He had urged further raids, but again he had been outvoted. As for the advantages of the voyage, they were incalculable; two galleons taken and brought home to be added to the Royal Navy; English captives restored; thirteen of the best ships of war lost to the enemy; forty merchantmen, fully laden, worth 12,000,000 ducats to the merchants, destroyed; infinite naval provisions destroyed; English sailors and soldiers made rich and eager for any action; the Spanish King's weakness and bankruptcy revealed to all the world.

In the first week of September Essex was dramatically vindicated. News reached Court that the Indian fleet, laden with treasure worth 20,000,000 ducats, had anchored safely in Lisbon two days after the English fleet had left. The Queen's anger turned against those who had voted against Essex's proposals, and Ralegh especially received a full share of blame. Nevertheless, in spite of the zeal of the commissioners, little was coming into the Treasury.

Matters reached a crisis towards the end of September. The Queen, realising by this time that her share of plunder would be slender, and that the expedition would leave her with a large debit balance, declared that she would take from Essex the ransoms of such prisoners as had fallen to his share. Lord Buckhurst, Sir John Fortescue, and Lord Burghley were present. Burghley tactfully suggested that it would be as well if she first inquired upon what conditions Essex had received the surrender of his prisoners. This increased the Queen's annoyance, and she rated Burghley soundly as a coward and a miscreant, who for fear or favour regarded Essex more than herself. Burghley was greatly troubled. Essex, as he knew, considered him as his enemy, and to be taunted by the Queen was a double burden. As soon as he reached Theobalds he wrote a very humble letter to Essex explaining his troubles. Essex replied kindly and soberly that his own annoyance had been greatly exaggerated. His friends, however, were exultant, and a few days later Anthony Bacon wrote to Dr. Hawkins in Italy that Essex was now in the full sunshine of the Queen's favour, " which hath made the old Fox to crouch and whine, and to insinuate himself by a very submissive letter to my Lord of Essex, subscribed in these terms, ' Your Lordship's, if you will, at commandment.' " Burghley's letter and Essex's answer were freely shown to Essex's friends.

Essex's fortunes at this moment were at their height. He was immensely popular in the country; he had the Queen's favour; his enemies were under a cloud; his conduct at Cadiz had been magnificent, and his judgment as a commander was completely vindicated. His greatness in every way had increased. From all parts his agents were gathering news of foreign affairs, which were passed through the capable hands of Anthony Bacon. In France, the King regarded him as his chief friend at the English Court. In Venice, Dr. Henry Hawkins, his own agent, sent off every few days reports of Italian affairs. He had his own spies in Spain. From the Low Countries, Sir Francis Vere, George Gilpin, the Queen's agent, and Sir Robert Sidney, when they wrote their despatches to the Council, reported simultaneously to Essex. Essex House was almost a European Court in miniature, and diplomats from foreign rulers were careful to pay as much respect to him as to Lord Burghley.

On his return to Court Essex set a new fashion. He had grown a beard full and square, and for a time the Cadiz beard was affected by young Benedicks who wished to be in the mode. In other respects he ceased to trouble about his appearance. Indeed, it was an anxiety to his followers that he cared so little for dress that he hardly knew what he wore when he went up to the Queen, and she was particular about such matters. Of a morning his chamber was thronged with friends and suitors, and whilst the barber trimmed him and his servants were dressing him he would read his letters and listen to his petitioners. Then his gentlemen of the robes would throw a cloak over his shoulders, as he passed into his closet, where he said a short prayer, and was gone.

Essex lacked another courtly accomplishment. He was a poor dancer, and indeed not graceful in his movements, for he was tall and walked with his head thrust forward. In manner he was thoughtful, and especially at dinner, for after he had taken a few morsels of food, he would sit silent and contemplative. At times he would lapse into brooding and black melancholy, sometimes even into religious melancholia. As he grew older these fits of depression increased, and he became more and more self-centred as he brooded over his own troubles, until he lost all sense of proportion and even of loyalty.

For many weeks Essex had seen nothing of Francis Bacon. Early in October, Francis came back. He had been watching Essex's ascent, and he alone saw that his patron was gliding into danger. He went to Essex to utter a warning. Essex was in no mood for criticism, and Bacon's intended appeal was interrupted. He therefore set down in writing his own view of Essex's position, begging him to realise how the Queen in her unfriendly moments must, of necessity, regard him.

Essex was always making the mistake of underrating the Queen, for he did not understand that beneath her peevishness and her infuriating vacillations and obstinacies there was the keenest political mind in Europe, vast experience of statecraft, and an uncanny power of estimating character. Elizabeth was a woman who thwarted Nature, and Nature, as always, took vengeance. At times she was still half in love with Essex, and nothing would be too good for him; and then again, with a change of mood, love would turn to jealousy. When he was ill, or in misfortune, she was all sympathy; but when he was prosperous and triumphant, her love soured and she hated him because she was a little frightened of him, and when frightened Elizabeth could be cruel. The relationship between the two had indeed changed since the early days when Essex sat up half the night chatting happily with her. He no longer felt her charm, and as he grew older he took less trouble to keep up the pretence of the adoring slave. The goddess had become a tiresome woman, impossible to please. The greatest danger, however, was in Essex's popularity. For nearly forty years Queen Elizabeth had lived on the public applause of her people, and her favourites hitherto had been generally hated. Essex was the best-loved man in England, and the old actress would not tamely yield her popularity to the young star.

Bacon was one of the very few who perceived the changes in this curious relationship. He began his letter by saying that the prejudices which the Queen naturally formed against Essex were fourfold. He was of a nature not to be ruled; his estate was not equal to his greatness; he was popular; and he was a soldier. "I demand," wrote Bacon, "whether there can be a more dangerous image than this, represented to any monarch living, much more to a lady, and of her Majesty's apprehension? And is it not more evident than demonstration itself, that whilst this impression continueth in her Majesty's breast, you can find no other condition than inventions to keep your estate bare and low; crossing and disgracing your actions; extenuating and blasting of your merit; carping with contempt at your nature and fashion; breeding, nourishing, and fortifying such instruments as are most factious against you; repulses and scorns of your friends, and dependants that are true and steadfast; winning and inveigling away from you such as are flexible and wavering; thrusting you into odious employments and offices to supplant your reputation; abusing you and feeding you with dalliances and demonstrations, to divert you from descending into the serious consideration of your own case; yea, and percase venturing you in perilous and desperate enterprises?

"Herein it may please your Lordship to understand me; for

I mean nothing less than that these things should be plotted and intended as in her Majesty's royal mind towards you; I know the excellency of her nature too well. But I say, wheresoever the formerly described impression is taken in any King's breast towards a subject, these other recited inconveniences must, of necessity of politic consequence, follow; in respect of such instruments as are never failing about Princes: which spy into their humours and conceits and second them; and not only second them, but in seconding increase them; yea, and many times without their knowledge, pursue them further than themselves would."

Thence Bacon proceeded to some practical advice. First, for what was past and irrevocable, let Essex pretend to be satisfied. Then let him declare that he was taking Leicester and Hatton as his models. He must avoid an offhand manner with the Queen, his compliments must seem genuine, and not mere formality. Then he should take care always to have some projects in hand which could be ostentatiously dropped when the Queen showed disapproval, such as to propose someone for a vacant office of whom the Queen was likely to disapprove and then to withdraw the proposal. Or, perhaps, to propose a journey to Wales to view his estates there, and to abandon it at the Queen's request. And not to neglect the lightest sort of particulars, apparel, gestures and the like.

The next greatest prejudice in the Queen's mind was Essex's military dependence. Let Essex keep it in substance, but conceal it outwardly, for the Queen loved peace, and loved not change, and that kind of dependence made a suspected greatness. Essex should therefore relinquish his aim at the place of Earl Marshal or Master of the Ordnance and seek rather to become Lord Privy Seal—it was a fine honour, quiet place, and worth £1,000 by the year—anything to divert the Queen from her impression that he was seeking martial greatness. It would be an advantage if he were diligent in the Star Chamber, continued such intelligences as were worth cherishing, and pretended to be as bookish and as contemplative as ever.

Then there was the matter of popularity, good in itself, but to be handled tenderly. Let Essex take all occasions to speak about popularity in the Queen's ears, vehemently condemning all those who sought it; but he need not to seek real unpopularity by dealing in monopolies. Yet in Parliament he might be forward in demanding treasure for the wars, and if the Queen should accuse him of seeking popularity, then his answer would be that "the next Parliament will show," which would feed her with expectation.

The next apprehension to be removed was the matter of the inequality of his means and his ambitions. Until the Queen saw that he was careful of his own estate, she would not only think him likely to continue chargeable to her, but suspect him of higher imaginations. To be plain, nothing would sooner make the Queen or the world believe that he was becoming provident than to alter some of his officers, who might be true, but the world did not believe it.

And lastly, to be a favourite with this reputation could only make the Queen more apprehensive. "The only way to remedy this," Bacon concluded, "is to give way to some other favourite, as in particular you shall find her Majesty inclined; so as the subject hath no ill nor dangerous aspect towards yourself. For otherwise, whosoever shall tell me that you may not have singular use of a favourite at your devotion, I will say he understandeth not the Queen's affection, nor your Lordship's condition."

Such was the gist of Bacon's advice. Essex might seriously have considered it, but events soon showed that the direction of his fate was no longer in his own hands. Three weeks later there was an alarm that the Spaniards were coming. Reports that King Philip intended to avenge Cadiz had been constant and reliable, and the danger seemed imminent when two English ships brought in Portuguese prisoners who declared that the Adelantado had set out from Lisbon three weeks before with twenty of the King's ships and seventy transports full of soldiers, and that many other ships were to join him.

Defence measures were immediately taken in hand. From Plymouth three carvels were sent out to watch for the enemy, and to give timely warning. Knights and gentlemen residing in London posted down to their counties to take command of their neighbours and tenants. The beacons along the south coast were made ready and beacon watches set nightly. Lords Lieutenant of counties were warned to organise their men into companies of a hundred, with ten pioneers to each, equipped with entrenching tools. Munitions and supplies were to be collected. In all, a force of nearly 70,000 men was to be ready to meet the invader.

Intelligence of the Spanish preparations continued to come in, and in this crisis the Queen turned to Essex as her chief military adviser. On November 2, she ordered him to assemble a council of war to advise her, as had been done in 1588. Essex consulted with Lord Burgh, as a soldier of great experience, and sent him a list of questions on which he desired an opinion. Burgh's advice was sensible and to the point. He thought it likely that the enemy would attempt a landing; the season being so far advanced it would be intended as a surprise, for the English ships were out of trim, the dearth (which had been very serious this summer) would make it difficult to keep troops in the field, and the harbours in the Low Countries would be convenient bases. The enemy could not be prevented from landing; if he did, then he must be kept away from all victuals, and the country should be deserted before him. There should be incessant skirmishing but no battle, and he should be worried by several armies at different points. Beyond general preparations nothing further could be done, for there was no indication where the enemy would strike, if he came. Four points seemed likely, the Isle of Wight, Portsmouth, Southampton, or else an attack on London itself up the Thames.

The alarm gradually died away, and just before Christmas the troops who had been sent for the defence of the Isle of Wight were dismissed to their homes. A month later it was generally known that the reports were trustworthy. The Spanish fleet had been caught in a great storm and forty ships destroyed, with great loss of life.

Other members of the Bacon family were watching Essex closely. Old Lady Bacon had for a long time been shocked by his amours. Indeed, what she expressed in writing as his "καρναλ κονκυπισσενς" had been the subject of her prayers. Gossips were again busy with scandals of his familiarities with a certain nobleman's wife, and on December 1, she wrote to him a very frank and religious letter. For the erring lady herself Lady Bacon had no excuses. She was a " foul impudent," an " unchaste gaze and common by-word in respect of her place and husband." " But you, my good Lord," she went on, " have not so learned Christ and heard His holy word in the 3rd, 4th, and 5th verses of the fourth chapter to the first Epistle of the *Thessalonians*. It is written, ' This is the will of God, that ye should be holy and abstain from fornication, and every one know how to keep his own vessel in holiness and honour; and not in the lust of concupiscence, as do the Gentiles, which know not God.' And more, if it pleases you to read and mark well, it is a heavy threat, ' That fornicators and adulterers God will judge,' and that they shall be shut out: for such things, saith the Apostle, commonly cometh the wrath of God upon us. Good Lord, remember and consider your great danger hereby both of soul and body. Grieve not the Holy Spirit of God, but honour God, that honoured you, and reward Him not with such evil for His great kindness towards you. Good my Lord, sin not against your own soul."

As it happened, the gossips were wrong. The alarms and disturbances of the autumn, varied by bad colds and touches of fever, kept Essex too busy for much distraction, and he was able to assure her Ladyship that her anxiety was unnecessary.

" I protest before the Majesty of God, and my protestation is voluntary and advised, that this charge, which is newly laid upon me, is false and unjust; and that since my departure from England towards Spain, I have been free from taxation of incontinency with any woman that lives. I never saw or spoke with the lady you mean but in public places, and others being seers and hearers, who, if they would do me right, could justify my behaviour. But I live in a place, where I am hourly conspired against, and practised upon. What they cannot make the world believe, that they persuade themselves unto; and what they cannot make probable to the Queen, that they give out to the world. They have almost all the house to serve them for instruments. Yea the very oracles (I mean those, that are accounted to be plain and sincere) do φιλιππίζειν, do speak the largest language of the strongest faction. Plutarch taught me long since to make profit of my enemies; but God teacheth it me much better now. Worthy Lady, think me a weak man, full of imperfections: but be assured I do endeavour to be good, and had rather mend my faults than cover them. I wish your Ladyship all true happiness, and rest,

"At your ladyship's commandment,

"Essex.

" 1 of December, 1596. Burn I pray you."

Details of the Spanish disaster continued to come in during January, and when all the different accounts had been collated it appeared that the Spanish objective was not England but Ireland. Though nothing further was to be expected for the present, the Spaniard had not given up his intention of attacking England, and was already assembling troops and supplies at Ferrol. In the circumstances it was agreed in the Council that a further attempt should be made on the enemy. Both the Earl of Cumberland and Essex put forward plans. Cumberland asked for two of the Queen's ships, twenty Hollanders, and with some of his own he would sail in and burn the ships at Ferrol. Essex's plan was more ambitious. He wanted ten or twelve of the Queen's ships, twenty Hollanders and 5,000 soldiers. Lord Burghley, after his manner, wrote down both proposals, the objections to them, and the steps to be taken if they were to be adopted.

The usual disquiets followed. The Queen refused to let Essex have his way; whereupon, remembering a little of Bacon's advice, he gave out that he would leave Court and go on a journey to Wales to view his estates. Then he took to his chamber for a fortnight, which kept the Court gossips busy, for it was clear that he and the Queen had fallen out again, and yet each day he went up to see her privately. Then there was a reconciliation, and the Queen announced with grudging admiration that she had resolved to break him of his will and push down his proud heart, but found it impossible, for he inherited it from his mother. Two days later all was trouble again; Essex was back in his room and renewing his proposals for the Welsh journey, which he would make for his health's sake. The pretext was not entirely fictitious, for his health was never good, and this winter he was constantly, though not seriously, ill.

Early in March there were further crosses. Lord Cobham, who was Lord Warden of the Cinque Ports and Lord Chamberlain, had been ailing for some time, and his death was daily expected. The event, as was customary, was eagerly anticipated, and various interested parties sued for his office. His son, Henry Brooke, desired the Wardenship; but Essex disliked the young man and promised to support the claims of Sir Robert Sidney; other claimants were Lord Buckhurst, Lord Hunsdon, and Sir Edward Wotton. Meanwhile Ralegh, who had his own private hopes at the time, and was for once friendly both with Essex and Cecil, laboured to reconcile them to each other, and there was some hope that, if only the two Court factions could be united, public affairs would progress more smoothly.

Essex obtained leave from Court for his Welsh journey for twenty days, but he put off his departure on the death of Lord Cobham. The question of his successor in the Wardenship immediately became acute. Essex moved the Queen for Robert Sidney. She replied that he was too young. He answered that he was older than some that sought it. She observed that Sidney was Governor of Flushing and could not attend to the affairs of the Ports. Later in the day, Essex again approached her, and more insistently. She replied that Sidney should not have it, nor would she wrong the new Lord Cobham by bestowing it upon anyone who was inferior to him. The Council sat in the afternoon. At the meeting Essex said that he had just cause to hate Lord Cobham for his villainous dealing and abuse; there was no worth in him; if the Queen should grace him with honour he would have right cause to think himself little regarded by her. Moreover, he gave out that he was himself a candidate for the Cinque Ports. This was on Monday, March 7.

On the 9th, the Queen told Essex definitely that Lord Cobham should have the Cinque Ports. He left the Court in anger and gave orders for his horses to be ready for the Welsh journey in the morning. He had actually started, and was riding past Somerset House, when a messenger from the Queen met him with the command that he should come back to Court. She talked to him in private for some time, and then she told him that she had decided to make him Master of the Ordnance. So the journey was put off and once more the two were reconciled.

Then the Queen dallied for a week and refused to sign the patent. Sir John Fortescue twice offered it to her and each time she made objections. Essex took it and presented it himself, but again she put it off, and all his old irritation returned; but meanwhile Cobham also was kept waiting and his rivals were still hopeful. The patent was at last signed on the 18th.

There were other troubles. The effect of Lady Bacon's good advice had now worn off, and Essex was indulging in an intrigue with Mistress Bridges, one of the Queen's maids of honour. The Queen had some inkling of the affair, for she banished the lady, and her companion Mistress Russell, from Court for three days for taking physic without leave, and for going privately through the privy galleries to watch the tennis, at which Essex had so over-exerted himself that he had to retire to bed for three days.

The Spanish preparations, meantime, continued, and early in April were reported to be well in hand. So orders were at last given for the English Fleet to be made ready and all was bustle once more. The reconciliation with Cecil and Ralegh was complete. On April 18, the three dined privately together at Essex House, and conversed for two hours, when it was resolved to make up all the old differences. All three had something to gain from the others. Ralegh undertook to find the victuals for the voyage, at 9*d*. a head a day for 6,000 men for three months, which was reckoned to be a fair bargain for him, and he desired to be restored to his place as Captain of the Guard from which he had been banished since his marriage five years before; Cecil wanted the Chancellorship of the Duchy of Lancaster; and Essex needed all the help he could get to push forward with his preparations.

Throughout April and May progress was continuous and satisfactory, but on May 20, there was a scene in the Council Chamber. The Queen took it into her head to cancel the expedition. When the Lords urged that her safety demanded that the preparations should go forward, she retorted that no danger appeared anywhere, and that she would not make wars, but arm for defence. Then she asked how much these preparations were costing her, and rounded on Burghley for allowing it, and the others for so much haste seeing there was no greater occasion. No argument or persuasion would move her. She commanded that all preparations should cease, and that Lord Thomas Howard was not to go to sea. The storm was soon over, and two days later the Court news was that Essex was to be in command, and that he was to be well supplied with cannon and battering pieces from the Tower. As yet, however, the destination of the fleet was secret, and it was generally supposed that it would be Ireland, or perhaps Calais.

The goodwill between Essex, Ralegh, and Cecil continued.

On June 1, Ralegh had his wish. Cecil brought him to the Queen, who greeted him kindly, and gave him full authority to return to his place as Captain of the Guard. In the evening he rode with her, and talked to her in private, and henceforward resumed his old post in the Privy Chamber. Three days later the Queen definitely promised Cobham the Wardenship, whereupon he complained that Essex's anger with him grew and he knew she would protect him.

CHAPTER X

THE ISLANDS VOYAGE

ON June 15, Essex's instructions as commander of the expedition were signed. They began by setting out the cause of the expedition, which was that, before the beginning of the year the King of Spain had prepared a great army and navy to assist the rebellion in Ireland or to attempt some great act of hostility towards England. Essex was to proceed to Ferrol, where, if the Spanish fleet and army yet remained, they should destroy the enemy's fleet, but with the least danger and loss of men. If the fleet and army had left Ferrol for Ireland or England, he should follow them at his discretion. Having frustrated and ruined the enemy and his ships, he should consider how to intercept his carracks from the Indies by making course for the Azores. If he should intercept the Indian fleet, wherein there was treasure of gold, silver, jewels or spices, then he should exactly determine the boarding lest through greedy zeal his men should perish, and moreover he should send prizes home under guard, with an inventory in writing, noting those men who deserved reward. The ships of the Low Countries should also be notified that for any good service, they should be rewarded on their return.

As his assistants in this voyage there were appointed Lord Thomas Howard, Vice-Admiral; Charles Blount, now (since the death of his brother) Lord Mountjoy, Lieutenant of the land forces; Sir Walter Ralegh, Rear Admiral; Sir Francis Vere, Marshal; Sir George Carew, Master of the Ordnance; and Sir Ferdinando Gorges, Sergeant Major. These five were appointed as councillors. If there should be any diversity of opinion, to avoid lack of resolution he might follow his own opinion with the consent of any three or four of them; in all cases of importance he would do well to commit resolutions to writing, adding the names of those giving the advice. He was especially instructed to be merciful. There was to be no slaughter of any that did not resist, nor of women, children, aged or sick persons. Churches and hospitals should not be spoiled or destroyed upon pain of death. Finally, if " by sickness or death (which the Lord prevent with His Holy Hand) you should do otherwise than well, to our no small grief and loss," then Lord Thomas Howard should be General by sea, and Lord Mountjoy by land.

A few days later Essex was with this fleet at the Downs, waiting for a favourable wind to take them round to the rendezvous at Plymouth. Here Sir Francis Vere, with a thousand old soldiers from the Low Countries, joined him, together with the squadron of ships of the United Provinces. Vere was chagrined when he learnt that Mountjoy was to command the land forces, nor would he accept Essex's explanation that Mountjoy owed his appointment to the Queen's whim. He asked therefore that in actions where Essex himself was present he would be pleased not to use his services.

At Court, for the moment, all was harmony and friendliness. Essex wrote off almost daily to the Queen in a tone of reverent affection. On June 23, his letter ran:

" Your spirit I do invoke, my most dear and most admired Sovereign, to assist me, that I may express that humblest and most due thankfulness, and that high and true joy which upon the reading of your Majesty's letter my poor heart hath conceived. Upon your spirit, I say, I call, as only powerful over me, and by his infinite virtue only able to express infinite things. Or if I be too weak an instrument to be inspired with such a gift, or that words be not able to interpret for me, then to your royal dear heart I appeal, which, without my words, can fully and justly understand me. Heavens and earth shall witness for me. I will strive to be worthy of so high a grace and so blessed a happiness. Be pleased therefore, most dear

Queen, to be ever thus gracious, if not for my merit, yet for your own constancy. And so you shall bestow all those happinesses, which in the end of your letter you are pleased to wish; and then, if I may hear your Majesty is well and well pleased, nothing can be ill with your Majesty's humblest and most affectionate vassal,

"ESSEX."

Essex was on equally good terms with the Cecils and the Lord Admiral, and the friendliest letters passed between them. But the wind still blew from the west. On June 25, an attempt was made to sail, and the fleet by tacking got as far as Beachy Head, but the wind grew stronger and the fleet was obliged to take refuge under Dungeness. Conditions were more favourable two days later, and on July 6, Essex anchored off Portland.

Next day the fleet again moved westward, but that night, when they were within three leagues of Plymouth, a storm of extraordinary violence broke over them. The night was pitch dark, except for the flashes of lightning, and the gale blew them towards the lee shore. Next morning, however, all but one of the ships were anchored off Plymouth, and the Council of War at once despatched a letter to the Council to notify the Queen, that, unlike their enemy, they had safely ridden the storm. At the same time there were some unpleasant surprises. The press masters committed monstrous abuses, pressing men of all trades, some of whom had never handled a rope before or even been to sea, whilst the good men had been released for 20s. a piece. No men were available in Dorset. At Plymouth they learnt that an order had come from the Lord Admiral to discharge the soldiers who were held in readiness. Moreover, by the delay a month's provisions were already consumed. As a result the fleet was held up for three days whilst the deficiencies were made good.

On Sunday, July 10, the fleet was again under sail, and kept good company together till the evening of the 11th, when the wind increased to a great gale. When day broke the ships were scattered over the grey sea and the squadrons had lost touch. Next day the storm increased, and for four days the gale was so fierce that all hope of safety was lost. In Ralegh's ship the company commended themselves to God, for the men were utterly exhausted after their labours, the timbers strained, the bulkhead rent, and the brick cookroom shaken to powder. One by one the ships made for home and crawled for safety into Plymouth or Falmouth. By the 19th most of the captains had reported their arrival. Essex was at Falmouth, Ralegh at Plymouth, only the squadron of Lord Thomas Howard was missing, but a message reached Court, reporting that he had parted company from Essex during the night of the 15th/16th and was making for the Groin. On the 20th, Essex, with thirty ships, reached Plymouth and joined Ralegh, who was so sympathetic at his disappointment that he wrote to Cecil:

" I beseech you to work from her Majesty some comfort to my Lord General, who, I know, is dismayed by these mischances even to death although there could not be more done by any man upon the earth, God having turned the heavens with the fury against us, a matter beyond the power or valour or wit of man to resist, such accidents as the war draweth with itself. This much I thought myself abound to let your Honour understand of."

The Queen, when her anxiety for Essex's safety had been relieved, was not dismayed, and on July 23, the post left the Court at Greenwich with a comforting letter signed by the Lord Admiral, Burghley, and Cecil:

" On the first return of her Majesty's ships, there was great uneasiness about your safety. Since the news most welcome to her Majesty and all of your arrival, she has considered whether you could in good time reunite the army, separated in so many places, and the ships impaired by storms. She understands by your letters that your resolution, derived from a noble mind, is to pursue your voyage. You know the state of your army, and the forces you will have to encounter, but we give you some later informations which may influence your councils. The Queen's chief end in this action was to divert the Spanish forces from her kingdoms, especially Ireland; and also to make some profit. As to the first, they have been so long expecting the attack that they had time to prepare a defence; your victuals must be nearly consumed if the winds detain you long in Plymouth; also it will take time to supply the boats you have lost, and to know what has become of the ships with soldiers. You should therefore, having failed only by God's pleasure, consult those of the council with you before you go on. The Queen wishes you well, and has spared no expense in satisfying your demands. She will send you the *Lion*, and have three months' victuals more put into her, though she stuck at that at first."

With this letter came a pious note from Burghley, apologising for its brevity " by reason of a flux fallen into my left eye," and continuing :

" My Lord,
"I trust you will with your company refer all your accidents to God's will, thanking Him for all your favourable accidents, and acknowledging the contrary to come for the punishment of you and us all that have interest in your actions.
"And in the time now of this disaster, I did, by common usage of my morning prayer, on the 22 day of this month, in the 107th Psalm of David, read these nine verses, very proper for your Lordship to be repeated, but specially the six of these which verses your Lordship shall find often repeated and so I wish your Lordship would follow that example. This my writing savoureth of divinity; as for humanity, I refer myself to a joint letter sent from my Lord Admiral, myself and my son."

Other letters followed the next day. It was Sunday morning. As the Queen sat in her private pew her thoughts were not on divine service. She sent for Cecil and told him to write to Essex in her name to tell him that from her information it was probable that the Spanish fleet was at Lisbon. Essex once said that he could have taken Lisbon if he had been let alone. He must not attempt the town, for it would mean great loss, but if he and his council of war thought that the fleet could be attempted, she did not disallow it, and she left everything to his own judgment.

The Queen was indeed in a very good humour, for the day before she had scored the most satisfactory public triumph that had come her way for years. An ambassador had arrived from Poland, and it was reported to her that he was a very handsome man and his mission was a proposal for peace. She resolved, therefore, to receive him herself in public audience. He approached and kissed her hand. Then, retiring ten yards from her, with threatening countenance he broke into a Latin speech, violently complaining of the way the Queen treated his master; she allowed his merchants to be spoiled without restitution, not for lack of knowledge but from sheer injustice. Her action in forbidding his master to trade with the Spaniards claimed a superiority over other princes which was intolerable, and if she would not reform it, he would.

The Queen was at first astonished, and then furious at such an unexpected attack. When the ambassador finished she launched without any preparation into a Latin reply: "*Expectavi legationem, mihi vero querelam adduxisti,*" she began, and then, as her fury swelled, she overwhelmed the wretched Pole with her eloquence. It was a magnificent effort, properly appreciated by her admiring courtiers, and it put her in a good humour for days. Cecil wrote a long account of the incident to Essex, adding in his covering note, "The Queen is so disposed now to have us all love you, as she and I do every night talk like angels of you: she hath also said somewhat to the Earl of Worcester of Sir Walter Ralegh's true description of your valour, and judgment, and of his protestation of the loss the Queen should have of you. It is true, by the mercy of God, that he did write so passionately and rightfully of your worth for her as, if I could have forborne to show it for other things, by Jesus, I would not have showed it, for you know that in all these cases *omne nimium vertitur in vitium*."

At Plymouth, Essex was stirring up everyone to put the fleet in repair. The council of war met daily to consider what was now best to be done, for the season was far advanced. Several changes were made in the establishment of the expedition. A number of gentlemen volunteers were so distressed by sea sickness and the late tossing that their appetite for glory was altogether gone. They crept home without any ceremonious farewell. Others were quite incapable of continuing, amongst them Gorges, who was succeeded as Sergeant Major by Sir Anthony Shirley. All the damaged ships except the *Mere Honour* were now repaired. They decided to diminish the fleet by discharging some of the ships which had proved unserviceable, as well as the worst of the sailors and soldiers. With this smaller but more efficient fleet they proposed to make for the Groin, where they hoped to join with Lord Thomas Howard's squadron, and, if they could, to entice the enemy out to battle in the open sea. Then they would seek the carracks and the fleet from the Indies. On July 29, it seemed that they were ready for a start in the morning; but the weather again turned against them, and they were stormbound in harbour.

Two days later, Lord Thomas Howard's squadron came to anchor in Plymouth Sound. After parting company with the main fleet they had gone to the rendezvous at the North Cape, whence they cruised in sight of the enemy to tempt them out until, on the 28th, they fell in with the ships which Essex had sent to find them. The ships which needed repairs were immediately made ready for sea.

But the wind still blew from the west, day after day, and the chance of any sudden departure seemed so remote that Essex even posted to Court to consult with the Queen. She was so greedy of his presence that Cecil had no opportunity for any long talk. Everyone at Court was in good humour, vying who could give the kinder compliment.

At last the wind changed, and on August 14, the ships made their way out of harbour into Plymouth Sound. At midnight Essex wrote two letters with his own hand, the one a report to the Council, and the other a little note to Cecil. The letter to the Council ran:

"Though only my hand be to this letter yet write I in my associates' names as well as mine own. This busy day, in which we had the whole fleet to get out of the harbour, and many men and much victuals to ship, hath almost tired us all. I have taken this despatch upon me and sent them to rest, that I may have more help of them in the morning. And if in this hasty letter, I do not give your Lordships a full account of all things to your satisfaction, I beseech you to consider what a confused mind I am like to have, being straighted with time and oppressed with business.

"When I sent my cousin Shirley to inform her Majesty and your Lordships of the state of this fleet and army, we saw no hope of a wind to carry us hence, and therefore sought for direction what to do. But the wind coming fair this day, which is now past, I, being aboard, got my ship first and then the rest out into the Sound, and then went ashore to confer with all my associates. They agreeing with me that we ought not by any means to lose this fair wind, urged me to dismiss the land army, saving the 1,000 old soldiers of the Low Countries, and did all so strongly concur in that opinion, as I durst not contradict it, though I would have been glad that her Majesty's commandment had directed us, and we not driven to presume that her Majesty will believe our poor judgments in that point.

"This being resolved on, I sent as many as might by sea go near the place where they were levied, in the ships that were discharged. The others I sent from hence by land, giving to those that went by sea both conduct money from the sea side home, and victuals while they were upon the sea for a large proportion, and those that went by land after 8*d*. a day and fifteen miles daily march. I also sent into every county a captain or some other sufficient officer to conduct them, and have left the arms of the whole army with Sir Ferdinando Gorges.

"The reasons which moved us to do so were, first, that we put them into a safe hand whence either the county might have them restored, and her Majesty have the ready use of them, as also because we feared that the soldiers having them would embezzle and make most of them away. To discharge this army I have been driven to take up of Mr. G. Carew, of Cockington, the other £1,000 for which your Lordship, my Lord Treasurer, gave me warrant. And I do assure your Lordships faithfully that though I have been a thrifty servant to her Majesty, yet I have been an ill master of mine own purse, for so long lying in so dear a place with so poor a company hath made me lay myself to gage.

"The particulars of my account of her Majesty's money shall be sent to your Lordship, my Lord Treasurer, if I can have but one hour's leisure in the morning. But if your Lordship find any faults with it, I pray you suspend till I may justify it, for I am almost blind and dizzy, and therefore may commit errors. I will conclude in the name of all my fellows, beseeching your good Lordships to censure favourably our poor endeavours."

It was not, however, until August 17, that the fleet was away, for the wind was so scant that they were obliged to use the tow boats to pull the ships into the open sea.

Once more the ships made for Ferrol. It was Essex's intention to smoke the Spanish ships out; and to this end he proposed to send into the harbour the fireships, backed by the two great galleons captured at Cadiz—the *St. Andrew* and the *St. Matthew*—and some merchant ships, while the main fleet lay outside to keep the way of retreat open. Again the plan was defeated by tempest, for on August 24, a fierce storm scattered the fleet. The *St. Matthew* was dismasted and for a time in great peril. She would have been lost but for the resolution of Sir George Carew, her commander, who was obliged to make for home.

Next morning, when the storm subsided, Essex found that his fleet was greatly diminished. Ralegh's ship and thirty more were nowhere to be seen. Upon this there ran a rumour that Ralegh had deserted and was gone off on his own devices. An attack on Ferrol was now hopeless, especially as the wind was blowing from the east. The next rendezvous, according to previous plans, was the Rock. Essex, therefore, with the main fleet, sailed down the coast of Spain.

As the original plan had failed, Essex thought it advisable to report to the Queen. On August 28, he therefore despatched Robert Knollys with a letter to the Queen, and with instructions written in his own hand.

"You shall upon your landing in England make what possible speed you can to the Court and there you shall address yourself to Master Secretary and tell him you are sent by me to inform her Majesty and my Lords of the state of the fleet and army under my charge, and that you have a letter to deliver to her Majesty when you are admitted into her royal and sweetest presence. You shall in all humility present my letter unto her Majesty and then inform her as follows :

"Setting sail from the Sound of Plymouth the 17th of this month of August, having sometimes calms, but for the most part calms and west-north-west winds, we fell on Thursday the 25th of this month with the land that is to the east of Cape Ortingall, which land we made in the morning about ten o'clock, and stood in with the shore till three in the afternoon. Then, finding the wind slant so nigh to the southwestward, stood off all night into the sea, and the next morning in again to the land, by which boards, by reason of the head sea and the bare wind, we got nothing. On Friday night I stood off again to the sea, and about midnight, the wind coming all northerly, we got a good slant to lie all along the coast. On Saturday in the morning I discovered the *St. Andrew*, whom we had lost sight of two or three days before. I bore with her and had no sooner got her up, but Sir Walter Ralegh shot off a piece, and gave us warning of his being in distress. I presently bore with him and found he had broken his main yard. Whereupon I willed him to keep along the coast that berth that he was, till he got in the height of the North Cape, and, myself having a desperate leak as ever ship swum withal, I was fain to lie by the lee, and seek to stop it (which how it held us you can relate) and, God be thanked! that night we overcame it and stopped it. The next morning we all came to Cape Finisterre, saving the *St. Matthew*, who, upon the breaking of her foremast, went home, and the *Warspite* with the *Dreadnought*, who went without stop to the South Cape. This is all that is happened to us.

" If her Majesty ask you why there was no attempt upon the fleet at Ferrol, you may say—I neither had the *St. Matthew*, which was the principal ship, for that execution, nor the *St. Andrew* till mine own ship was almost sunk, and I not able to make sail till Sir W. Ralegh with his own ship the *Dreadnought*, and very near twenty sails, were gone. We are now gone to lie for the Indian fleets, for, by Spaniards we have taken, we find the Adelantado is not to put to sea this year. Of our successes her Majesty shall from time to time be advertised. You shall acquaint Mr. Secretary with this instruction."

A few days later, a small man-of-war joined the fleet with a message from Ralegh, who reported that, according to information given by an English ship returning homeward, the Adelantado and his fleet had gone off to the Azores to escort the Spanish treasure fleet home. Essex at once called a council of war and it was resolved to go for the Azores in the hope of catching the Spanish fleet there. The man-of-war was sent back to Ralegh with letters rebuking him for failing to give information and bidding him follow to the Azores.

Essex and his fleet made first for the island of Tercera, passing it by on the south. There were no signs of the Spanish fleet. Passing between Gratiosa and St. George, he continued the voyage to Flores. Here the ships anchored to take in water and supplies, and to wait for Ralegh.

At his landing a deputation of the islanders came to Essex with a present of fruit, hens, and fresh victuals, to ask him to grant them favour and to protect from the spoil of his soldiers. Essex treated them kindly, and told them that he had not come to afflict poor men but was sent by the Queen, his mistress, to chastise the intolerable pride of the Spanish. He made close inquiry about the usual times and seasons when the Indian fleets passed that way, and in the end dismissed them with presents and a protection under his own hand and seal from all violence from his men, commanding that nothing, not even a hen, should be taken from the islanders without payment.

At last, on September 14, Ralegh's squadron was sighted. Ralegh immediately came off in his barge to report to Essex, who received him joyfully, and invited him to dinner. Essex now apologised handsomely for having misjudged Ralegh's intentions, and told him what guesses had been made of the cause of his disappearance. He even named those who had been most forward with their uncharitable surmises, not, he added, that he ever believed them, but had thereby the better observed some men's scandalous and cantankered dispositions. He also promised to send a despatch to England to mitigate any scandal which might have followed the arrival of Knollys.

The council was summoned, and it was concluded to make separate landings on each of the islands. Essex and Ralegh were to attack Fayal; Lord Thomas Howard and Vere to attack Gratiosa; Mountjoy and Christopher Blount to attack St. Michael's; whilst the Netherland squadron was detailed for the attack on Pico, as that island was richest in wine.

Two days later Essex wrote to Robert Cecil :

"The sudden extreme sickness of the Admiral of the Low Country squadron hath made me send him back with his own ship only and two other fly-boats of transportation, of whom I have no use. I pray you inform her sacred Majesty, that now all the whole fleet is together; yesterday Sir Walter Ralegh came to me, and the *Dreadnought* the day before; the *St. Matthew* we only miss, who went for England before we came to the North Cape. By my uncle, Robert Knollys, and by Osborn, I have advertized all that happened to me before our coming to these islands, and of our purpose in coming thither, and the cause of it; we have missed of the Adelantado, who will not leave Ferrol this year, and, as yet, the wind has been contrary for all Indian fleets, but now it is good, and I hope if they come for Spain or Portugal, they shall not escape us; besides we will, by God's grace, both relieve ourselves, and sack all the islands but Tercera, which I have very well discovered, and perceive to be too hard a work for me, our land forces being so small, and our provision for battery and other great works being gone in the *St. Matthew*. You must excuse my followers for not writing, for this despatch was sudden, and they knew not of it; they are all well, and have these two days eaten me more good meat than their skins are worth. Sir Walter Ralegh with the *Warspite*, the *Bonadventure*, the *Dreadnought*, and the *Swiftsure*, is watering and taking in victuals under the island of Flores; with the rest I keep the sea like a high constable to arrest all in the Queen's name that pass by in thirty leagues space. I pray let my dear Sovereign know I do spiritually kiss her fair royal hands, and think of them as a man should think of so fair flesh. And so I commend you to God's will and protection, and rest your very affectionate and assured friend,

"Essex.

"From aboard the *Due Repulse*, the 16th of September."

The ships in Ralegh's squadron were preparing to take in water. It was always a long and tedious operation, for the casks had to be carried ashore, filled, manhandled into the boats, and slung on board. Essex received news that the Adelantado and the treasure fleet were approaching the islands. He ordered the other squadrons to put out to sea at once and follow him. Then he sent a message to Ralegh to recall his men and to follow him to Fayal, where he could take in water and supplies; he did not, however, inform Ralegh that he was intending to look for the treasure fleet on the way. For three days Essex and the fleet cruised about the islands, finding nothing. Then he abandoned the search and made for Fayal, which was sighted on the morning of September 22.

There in the Road lay five or six English ships. A boat put out, and Sir Gelly Meyrick, who had been left behind at Flores with Ralegh's squadron, came on board, with a long indignant tale of how Ralegh had deliberately disobeyed his orders, and, solely in order to deprive Essex of the honour of taking Fayal, had landed and engaged the enemy; the soldiers were in the town, and at that moment about to assault the high fort which lay behind it. The rest of Ralegh's squadron lay at the other side of the island. Meyrick's account was partial and coloured; and his attempt to breed ill-feeling between Essex and Ralegh was well seconded by Anthony Shirley, Christopher Blount, and Essex's other particular friends.

Essex was peculiarly susceptible to any suggestion that his honour was being touched, and ready at all times to believe the worst of Ralegh. Meyrick and the others continued to incense him. Ralegh's offence in landing forces without the General's leave could not be pardoned—they insisted—without the severe censure of a court martial. Some even said that he ought to lose his head.

Essex sent for the military captains and officers from the town, and when they came on board the morning was spent in censuring some and cashiering others. Ralegh was summoned to the flagship, but, quite ignorant of what was happening, he had already gone back to his own ship and put off in his barge to report the situation to Essex, and to guide him to the front line. He was unaware that Essex had sent for the military captains, and he came on board expecting thanks; but he soon saw from the sullen looks around him that something was wrong.

When Ralegh entered the cabin, Essex, who was surrounded by his officers, gave him a faint welcome, and at once accused him of a breach of order and articles. Ralegh replied that he knew of no breach. There was an article, Essex said, that none should land any of the troops without the General's presence or his order.

Ralegh then begged leave to defend himself by those laws which he himself as well as others had devised, and Essex with the council of war had authorised, and then it would appear that no fault had been committed. It was true, he said, that no captain of a ship or company should land without direction.

" But," he went on, " I take myself to be a principal commander under your Lordship, and therefore not subject to that article, nor under the power of the law martial, because a successive commander of the whole fleet in her Majesty's Letters Patents, your Lordship and my Lord Thomas Howard failing. And besides, your Lordship agreed that I should land at this island, with your Lordship, whom I attended these four days and finding that your Lordship came not, being in your way thitherwards half a dozen leagues before I weighed anchor, I could not but think that you thought me strong enough to take this island, and that your Lordship was gone with some of the rest to some of the other islands; and I stayed so long from landing at Sir Gelly Meyrick's intreaty as I heard mine own company, even at my back, murmur and say that I durst not adventure it. And to tell your Lordship a plain truth, my intent at first was only to water, until I saw them follow me in that brave manner which with our reputation we could not then shun, and give over, being then in our boats for that purpose; for if I had intended the taking of the town, I would never have retired so far off from our first road that lay right before it."

After about half an hour's argument Essex said that he was satisfied, for, indeed, whatever fault could reasonably be found with Ralegh, he had himself committed an elementary blunder in military procedure by omitting to inform his second in command of the change of plan. Essex and Ralegh went ashore together to Ralegh's lodging, and Sir Christopher Blount again tried to stir up ill-feeling. By this time Lord Thomas Howard had heard rumours of the dispute. He went immediately to Essex to find out for himself. Ralegh meanwhile was apprehensive and indignant, and determined that if Essex still purposed to bring him to trial he would go back to his own squadron and resist arrest, or else make off. The whole day was wasted in this profitless bickering.

Meanwhile the Spaniards in the fort, seeing the whole English fleet at anchor in the Road, were more alarmed, for they expected an assault in force to be made at any moment. About midnight they loaded as much as they could on their transport, abandoned the fort, and made off for the wooded hills in the interior of the island.

Next morning Lord Thomas Howard came to Ralegh and said that if he would admit himself to have committed an error in attacking without Essex's instructions, Essex would be satisfied with the apology. Both men had great respect for Howard, and when he further guaranteed that Ralegh by this action should suffer no wrong or violence, Ralegh agreed. He went to Essex; the apology was made and accepted.

Essex was now in the mood to resume the attack on the fort. A column was despatched to cut off any escape, and a message was sent to demand instant surrender. There was no reply, for the fort was empty. The Spaniards left behind them six pieces of great artillery, and the corpses of two prisoners, whose throats were cut. Once more ill-feeling and recrimination broke out between the officers of Ralegh and Essex. Essex's officers sneered at Ralegh for not setting a guard to keep the Spaniards from escaping, to which Ralegh's party muttered that if Essex had been less interested in his own reputation a day would not have been wasted, and the army would not have lost the ransoms of so many Spanish prisoners and the spoil which had been carried off.

However, nothing could be done. The Spaniards were pursued but never brought to action. Tempers subsided, and in a calmer mood Essex heard the full details of what had happened before his arrival at Fayal.

After he had received Essex's message that he was sailing, Ralegh recalled his men and put to sea so quickly that next morning he reached Fayal Road and there anchored before the town, greatly surprised to find no trace of Essex's ships. The town was fair and large, and promised good spoil. It was defended by two forts, one of which was on a high mountain, difficult of access and strengthened with rampiers and a ditch. The cannon fired a few shots at the squadron and then six companies were marched out of the town and began to dig trenches on the shore to hinder a landing. Ralegh went down with his barge and was rowed along the shore by the fort towards the town to see where a landing could be made when Essex arrived. The musketeers from the shore fired at him, but no one was hit, though the shooting was close enough for those in the barge to regret that they had not put on their armour before leaving the ship.

Ralegh returned to the *Warspite* to wait for Essex. For two days he did nothing, and all the time the inhabitants of the town could be seen making off with their goods towards the hills. This was too much for the patience of the sailors and soldiers, who began to show signs of mutiny. Then a council of officers was called. Opinions were divided. Some, particularly Sir Gelly Meyrick, would not agree to a landing without Essex's knowledge. Others, siding with Ralegh, replied that their General would think them a pack of idle cowards to sit so tamely before a rich town. Nevertheless Meyrick's arguments were urged so strongly that it was decided to wait one more day, and then if Essex's ships did not appear, Meyrick and his party agreed to take part in the assault.

Next morning there was still no sign of Essex. As the wind was shifting somewhat, Ralegh ordered his squadron to coast round the point to a new anchorage north-west of the island, and four miles farther from the town. Meyrick refused to budge, and five or six of the other ships remained with him.

From their new anchorage the country appeared pleasant and fertile, with villages and fruitful fields. The ships were now very short of water, for no new supply had been taken in since they had left Plymouth. A landing party, with a guard of sixty muskets and forty pikes, was detailed to go ashore, but before the boats had set off, a detachment of the enemy could be seen coming down to occupy the trenches on the shore and to dispute the landing. Ralegh, seeing that the covering party would be too small to overcome the enemy, ordered another 160 men into the boats to support them. The captains of Essex's own Low Country troops cried out to be allowed to go with them. Ralegh at first was unwilling, and was moreover short of boats, for many had been lost in the storm. He agreed to send back the boats to bring them ashore.

As the boats pulled ashore, the shot soon began to kick up the water around them, at which the sailors, who were eager enough before, slackened their efforts and ceased rowing. Ralegh shouted abuse at them and commanded his own men to row hard for the shore, and let those who were not afraid follow him. They dashed ashore and there was a sharp fight on the rocks. The Spaniards put up a short resistance and then fled. The landing was dangerous, for there was a considerable swell, so that two of the boats were crashed on the rocks and overset. The others were sent back for the rest of the soldiers and soon there was a force of 460 ashore.

Then Ralegh determined to march on the town. He went himself with the advanced guard. At first there was no resistance and they moved forward through fields of melons and potatoes until they came near the high fort. Here the enemy opened fire. The advanced guard moved slowly, about four hundred yards ahead of the main body, and passed the outer trenches; but the men in the main body, as soon as they came under fire, broke into a disorderly double and crowded upon the rear of the advanced guard.

The way into the town was covered by the guns of the fort, and was fenced on either side by low walls of loose stone which flew about dangerously when hit by the cannon balls. Before any further advance was possible, this route must be reconnoitred. As no one showed any zeal for the duty, Ralegh himself undertook it, and went on with two or three of his officers, being hotly sniped by the musketeers of the fort. As soon as he had passed beyond the range of the musketeers in the fort, he sent for the men to follow him, and all advanced through the fire and beyond. They reached the town without further opposition, and marched in to find that the inhabitants had fled, taking with them their valuables. They bivouacked that night in the town, with the intention of assaulting the high fort in the morning. Such had been the situation when Essex himself and his fleet arrived.

When Essex learnt the whole story, he forgot his indignation with Ralegh. All was kindness again, and the cashiered captains were restored to their places. On the 24th the troops were re-embarked; the cannon from the high fort were fetched off, and the town was set on fire in revenge for the two murdered prisoners.

On the 26th, the fleet made for Gratiosa. Here the chief men of the island, who were Portuguese, came on board and submitted themselves. Essex demanded wine, fruit, and fresh victuals for the ship, but no ransom was exacted. After a day's stay they sailed on to St. Michael's, which was reached early in the morning of the 29th. The fleet was drawing towards the shore when two of the sternmost ships were seen to be coming up with all sails set. They brought news that they had sighted the Indian fleet coming directly from the Road of Gratiosa. Then all was excitement aboard the *Due Repulse*. A warning piece was fired, and there was great cheering and throwing up of hats as she cast about. The cheers passed from ship to ship

MAP OF THE AZORES

as the intelligence was shouted across. Three hours later, three Spanish ships from Havannah were chased and caught, the greatest being about 400 tons. She struck to the *Warspite*, but Essex hastened after and would allow only his own boat to go aboard. She was found to be full of good prisoners and booty, besides the cargo, which was principally cochineal. Essex also learnt that there were forty more ships on their way, freighted with the King's treasure.

Meanwhile sixteen other ships of the richest of the Indian fleet fell in with another part of the English fleet. One was sunk, but the English sailors were so busy saving the plunder that the others escaped them and made for Tercera. Thither Essex directed his fleet, but the Spaniards had six hours' start, and when the English fleet reached Tercera the ships had anchored in the Road at the south end of the island. Here they were well protected by a peninsula that flings an embracing arm round the Road. The entrance to the inlet was guarded and commanded by a strong fort.

Essex summoned a council and there was a great debate. The officers of the army were for a landing to capture the fort and island. The seamen replied that the project was altogether too dangerous; the landing of men and munitions on that coast was difficult, the garrison of the fort was strengthened with the new arrivals, and the season of storms was approaching. The colonels made light of the difficulties, and Essex was inclined to favour them. Hereupon Lord Thomas Howard, realising that if the navy refused the army would thereafter boast of what might have happened, offered that he and Ralegh should provide 3,000 men from the fleet. The colonels were sobered by this offer and took more particular note of the difficulties. They finally concluded that, seeing the forces available, and the danger of attempting to land in boats, the project was not feasible. Tercera was therefore abandoned and the fleet turned about and made once more for St. Michael's.

As soon as the ships had dropped anchor in the Road of St. Michael's, Essex went on board the *Warspite*, Ralegh's ship, and the flag for council was hung out. The town lay before them, and promised good plunder. Essex ordered the companies to be ready to take to the boats, but Ralegh asked that he might first reconnoitre the landing places, for the waves sometimes rolled high and made landing dangerous for boats, as he had recently learnt at Fayal. Essex agreed; but Ralegh's boat had only pulled out a few yards when Essex, standing on the gallery, shouted him to come back; he would go himself.

Ralegh therefore returned, and Essex climbed down into the boat. He was unarmed but for his collar and sword, and none of the men in the boat with him carried either pike or musket. Ralegh called out to him to take his helmet and breastplate if he intended to go near the shore; there were many musketeers waiting, with their pieces ready in the rest. Essex shouted back that he would not, for he disdained to take any advantage of the watermen that rowed him.

After a while he came back to the *Warspite* and declared that a landing was inadvisable, as the enemy had too many men entrenched and ready to resist a landing. The council was therefore resumed, and it was decided that Ralegh with all the fleet should remain off St. Michael's to create a diversion, whilst Essex and the army officers took 2,000 men in the pinnaces and small barques by night, and landed about six miles round the point at the town of Villa Franca. Here, according to the reliable information of three English guides who were familiar with the islands, the landing was easy. Once landed, they would march on St. Michael's and take the town in the rear. Ralegh, meanwhile, was to keep up a continuous alarm to persuade the garrison of St. Michael's that a direct landing was about to be made.

This plan was carried out, and next day the army was safely on shore. There was no resistance from Villa Franca, for the town was abandoned. Once in the town the soldiers and their officers showed no desire to leave it. The inhabitants had left too hastily to carry away much with them, and the houses were well stocked with wine, fresh fruit, and corn, and the cellars were full of wool which was worth carrying away. This change from the hard life of the last six weeks was so pleasant that no one was anxious to stir up trouble in St. Michael's.

The town of Villa Franca was occupied and the troops quartered in the empty houses. Then Essex held a council to consider whether it was better to march on St. Michael's and water the fleet there, or to send for the fleet to Villa Franca. The military officers pointed out that the way was rough and uneven, and a few men could hold up the advance, nor was there much hope of taking St. Michael's, for the people, and their goods, would have been concentrated in the castle, which was garrisoned and not be forced without a lengthy bombardment. Water was urgently needed. The decision was that the fleet should be summoned to Villa Franca.

Again Essex neglected to inform Ralegh of his change of plan. The real weaknesses in Essex's character were now revealing themselves. He was too sensitive. Had he won his greatness by experience, he would have learnt that a great commander must always be lonely and often hated. This was his first independent command. Hitherto, though nominally the General, he had been backed by abler and more experienced men. At Rouen, Roger Williams stood behind him. At Cadiz the old Lord Admiral was the senior partner, and even in the assault on the city Vere was with him and was indeed responsible for the success of the land fight.

Moreover, his position as General was difficult, for under Queen Elizabeth commanders of expeditions were not independent; they were bound by their instructions to submit all major decisions to the approval of the council of war. A leader of dominating character—as Drake had been—would impose his will on the council. Essex lacked the essential hardness of character which is insensitive to the criticism of his subordinates. He liked to feel that the others were with him. At this moment Ralegh was absent; and whatever the fundamental differences between the two men, Essex knew that

Ralegh's advice was usually sound, and once accepted would be effected fearlessly. Nor was Vere much help. He was the greatest English soldier of his time, but he was now on his dignity and deliberately refrained from prompting his General. As a result, Essex leaned more on those who were wholeheartedly with him, such as Southampton, who was his devoted admirer, and Blount and Meyrick, both reckless men who were ready to push him into situations whither they might follow him to their own advantage.

Ralegh meantime carried out his instructions. All night the boats plied up and down the coast, keeping up a continual alarm with shots, the roll of drums and trumpet calls, while the Spaniards on shore were shifting about from place to place where they imagined the landing was being made. Next morning Ralegh's lookouts watched the hills, expecting to see the land army appear over the skyline in its march on St. Michael's; but there was no sign or message from Essex, and those in the fleet made cynical guesses about the movements of the army which were not far from the truth.

Soon they had their own excitements. A little Brazil ship was sighted. All unsuspecting she came into the fleet and anchored. It was an easy mistake, for the Spanish King hired many of his ships from foreign countries, and the English fleet was itself mixed; not only were there Dutch ships, but also the great galleon *St. Andrew*.

A richer prize was reported. A great carrack, with all sails set, was bearing straight towards the Road. Ralegh sent round a command that all flags should be taken in and that no one should weigh anchor, shoot off a piece, or put off a boat without order. Nearer and nearer came the carrack, all unsuspecting, and soon she would have rounded the point and fallen into the arms ready to welcome her, when one of the Dutch captains, disobeying the order, weighed anchor and made out towards her. As he came near he opened fire. The carrack at once changed direction, and the wind veering round at that moment she made straight for the shore and ran herself aground between the town and the fort at a point three miles from Ralegh's flagship. Immediately the boats swarmed out from the town to unload her and take off the crew.

There were very few boats left with Ralegh's fleet. Into these men descended and with such eagerness that they were dangerously overcrowded. They pulled over the three miles of tossing sea, regardless of the risk, but by the time that they came to the carrack she was on fire from bow to stern and too hot to be approached, much less entered. She was a fine ship, a great ship of 1,800 tons. She burnt all that night and the next day; and even when the hull had gone under, the smoke still rose out of the sea for many hours from the cargo of spice and sugar still molten between the decks. If only Essex had kept to his plan and had entered St. Michael's from the land, the seamen grumbled, the carrack could not have escaped. As it was, for the sake of the wine and melons in Villa Franca, he had lost the richest prize of all.

Ralegh still waited. Some of his captains were less patient, and without orders they hoisted the anchors and sailed round the point to find out for themselves whether there was any plunder left for late comers. Ralegh himself, after the trouble at Fayal, dared not shift; but in the end, when he had waited without news for six days, he resolved to follow. Before anything had been done, Essex, having heard of the disaster to the carrack, had gone aboard a pinnace, and was seen approaching. Ralegh put out in his barge and went on board. Then a message was sent to the rest of the fleet to weigh anchor and to move round to Villa Franca. The sailors obeyed reluctantly, with growing contempt for the army officers who said so much and achieved so little. As they left St. Michael's their last impression of the place was to see the inhabitants waving their flags and shooting off their guns in derision.

The fleet anchored off Villa Franca, and the ships watered. This took four days, for the sea was so rough that the boats could not be brought too close in shore, and the men were obliged to roll the heavy barrels through the splashing waves. The weather was breaking and the season of autumn gales was at hand, so that it would very soon be dangerous for the ships to ride at anchor in the open road. It was now all haste to get the soldiers on board. In the high seas there was only one place where they could be embarked. Essex himself supervised their embarkation, sending into the town for more men as each boatload drew off.

About 5 o'clock in the afternoon, the lookout on the church tower in Villa Franca reported the movement of troops. Vere was still in the town with about five hundred men. He staged an ambush. Sixty men were sent out; of these thirty were to go to a chapel, distant musket range from the town; the other thirty were to take up a position midway. Having fired their volleys, each body was to run as if in panic to draw the enemy on to the town where Vere was waiting for them.

These movements were in progress when Essex, Southampton, and some other gentlemen came to Vere in the market-place. Essex, who was mounted, did not believe the report, and began to take tobacco while Vere explained what he had ordered. After a while there was a volley from the direction of the chapel. Essex threw away his pipe and listened. Vere suggested that he should advance towards the sound of the firing; but the party which had been sent out, instead of retiring as ordered, kept where they were. The enemy, suspecting an ambush, held back.

The situation was not without danger, for the Spaniards, if they came out in force, could muster three thousand fighting men, well armed and equipped, besides the garrison. Vere therefore proposed that they should remain where they were and complete the embarkation in the dark. This was done. Essex stayed till all were embarked except the rearguard under Sir Christopher Blount, who came away with Vere. It was a skilful withdrawal and gave Essex an excuse to knight a few of the noblemen and young gentlemen. Villa Franca was left intact, and not even its defences were destroyed.

The fleet was now ready to sail. Before the ships separated, Essex drew up a report of the voyage, which was signed by the council of war. It made the most of the difficulties, and discreetly glozed over any errors of judgment of the General.

On October 9, the ships put out to sea. Some were in a bad way. In Ralegh's squadron was great lack of fresh water, and in Essex's squadron many of the men were suffering from their surfeits in Villa Franca. In a short time the weather, which had been rough, degenerated into a storm. The ships were so scattered that all order was lost and the swiftest made for home without waiting for their General.

CHAPTER XI

A TRIAL OF STRENGTH

AS he neared England Essex grew apprehensive. The *Due Repulse* was making slow progress; others would be before him with their tales at Court. This time he determined that some at least of the difficulties that followed the return from Cadiz should be avoided. He therefore gave order that immediately they reached land Sir Thomas Jermyn should post off to Court to give the Queen and the Council an account of the expedition. On October 21, he drew up in his own hand a long and detailed instruction of what Sir Thomas should say. There was no account or criticism of Ralegh's action at Fayal; moreover, he entirely exonerated Ralegh from any blame for the firing of the carrack, a disaster which was likely to move the Queen's wrath. He thanked the Queen for so greatly honouring him by entrusting him with this command, and asked for instructions for the disposal of the Low Country troops, the prizes and the ships of the royal navy. On October 26, Essex reached Plymouth and Sir Thomas was despatched to the Court.

When he landed, Essex found the port in a state of the greatest excitement. A few days before a gentleman had ridden off to Court with the alarming news that the Spanish fleet was at sea and nearing England. One ship lagging behind had been captured, and her captain, master, and purser taken off. From an examination of her papers it was apparent that the rendezvous was Falmouth. The news reached Court on the 23rd, and the Council immediately sent out orders for the defence forces in the counties all along the south coast to be mobilised. Victuals and munitions were to be collected at Plymouth to replenish Essex's fleet. The soldiers from

Picardy were summoned home. Money to the amount of £3,000 was sent off to the west.

Essex immediately took command of the situation. At ten o'clock in the morning he wrote off to Cecil to say that most of his ships had returned. "The news we find is that the Spaniards are upon the coast; upon which, if we do not bestir ourselves as never men did, let us be counted not worthy to serve such a Queen. For the country, by the grace of God, I will take order, and I will instantly out with as many ships as I can, but at this hour the wind blows full up into the harbour, and we were all in ere we had this news. But we do set ashore our sick men, take in fresh, and water, for though we eat ropes' ends and drink nothing but rain water, we will out that we may be partly th' instruments to make a final end of this proud nation that is destined to destruction. They are already in distress, and if we can get out, I hope none of them shall escape. From your true friend, ESSEX."

A few hours later, being more fully informed, he wrote again to Cecil to give him an appreciation of the situation. The Spanish fleet and army were, he believed, making for Ireland. If they were followed and fought with at sea, not a man or boat of them would escape unless by a miracle. But if they should once land, then the troops should be in readiness to fight with them, and a commander appointed; shipping and provisions should be ready. The commission for the commander was the first thing to be prepared, for want of authority would breed delays. For his own part, if his late commission had stirred any envy, he would serve under whomsoever the Queen appointed. He had already despatched experienced officers to West Cornwall, Bristol, and Milford Haven with letters to the Deputy Lieutenants to take their advice in all occasions of these wars.

The next day, the 27th, Essex reported to the Council, apologising for not writing sooner and more fully. "But to supply a fleet that hath been out four months and felt much ill weather, and to draw out mariners that had so lately surfeited of the sea, is so tiring a task as yet in my life I never had; and yet the falling of some of her Majesty's fleet with other places, and the sending out every way to enquire both of them and of the Spanish fleet, as also the sending out such experimented commanders as I could spare from the army to all places where I could suspect the enemy would go, these things, I say, have increased my business." All the Queen's ships but the *Hope*, the *Warspite*, and the *St. Andrew* had come in to Plymouth, but in poor condition. Some were leaky, others had their masts spoiled, and all wanted men; but he hoped to have all ready in three days. Meanwhile, he outlined the various alternatives open to the enemy and the necessary action to be taken against them.

On the 28th, the Queen wrote confirming Essex's appointment as Commander of the Forces. He was authorised to draw out all the available forces to go against the Spaniard. If he should find that the enemy had made for Ireland and that the English coast was free from danger, then he should follow them with such force as he found necessary, with full authority of command. In Ireland he should take precedence of the Earl of Ormonde, who had been appointed to succeed the late Lord Deputy. She repeated the warning that he should not leave England unprotected upon any light advertisement, " but that you do proceed in this great affair according to the rules of advised deliberation as well as affections of zeal and diligence. For treasure, for victual, and what may be fit for us to send, you shall find that you serve a Prince neither void of care nor judgment what to do that is fit in cases of this consequence. Of all which particulars we do advertise you by the hands of our ministers, to which we further refer you."

By this time detailed information of the Spanish fleet had been brought in by a certain Captain Bowden, a Plymouth man. In a little ship, manned only by twenty-eight men and boys, he came upon a flyboat which was separated from the main fleet. Although the flyboat carried forty soldiers, as well as the crew, he boarded and took her. The prisoners, being questioned in the presence of Ralegh, Lord Mountjoy, Lord Thomas Howard, and other officers, declared that there were five squadrons, in all a hundred and ten to a hundred and sixty sail; 10,000 to 12,000 infantry, 500 horse, with a further supply of 5,000 more foot to follow. There were twenty boats, each made to hold 100 soldiers, specially constructed for the landing; the landing was to be at Falmouth.

There was no further news. The wind was now blowing in the face of the enemy, and in the night of October 31, it rose to such a tempest that no Spanish fleet could have ridden against it. The danger was over and there was nothing more to be done.

Essex had reached Court, which was now at Whitehall, on October 29, weary and fordone with the labours of the last fortnight, and, after the long ride from the west, in no mood to meet criticism. The old bitterness against the Cecils and their friends flared up. As he had anticipated, Ralegh's friends had forestalled him, and the Queen was angry. She blamed him for the ill success of the expedition, the failure to burn the fleet at Ferrol, or to take the Indian fleet, and for the treatment of Ralegh. Essex in his turn had his grievances. Only a few days before, Sir Robert Cecil had been made Chancellor of the Duchy of Lancaster, and, which touched him more deeply, on October 23, the old Lord Admiral had been created Earl of Nottingham. Moreover, the words of the patent rankled, for it set out the Admiral's great services not only in 1588, but at Cadiz this last year, as if his was the greatest share of that glorious adventure. To make matters worse, the new Earl was also Lord Steward of the new Parliament, and by virtue of his offices he would take precedence, and Essex would have to walk behind him. This was intolerable.

Essex remained at Court for a week, and then, finding that his complaints were unsatisfied, he retired to Wanstead dejected and feverish, with the excuse that he had to set his own affairs in order. For some days he suffered from ague, being so acutely sensitive to cold that he sat in his chamber with his head muffled in cloaks, unwilling even to move into another room to hear a sermon. The Queen was disturbed, and remarked to the Lord Chamberlain Hunsdon that she wondered at Essex's absence, for the enemy would take it to be a greater reflection on his actions than he deserved. Hunsdon replied tactfully, pleading Essex's indisposition and adding that he was ready to attend if the Queen pleased to command his service. To this she answered, more tartly, that his duty and place were sufficient to command him; a prince was not to be contested by a subject. Public affairs should come before private, which could wait for some quieter time. Nevertheless, she bore him no ill-will; if he would come back there was comfort and kindness waiting for him.

Essex was in no mood to take the first step towards a reconciliation. He had been wronged, and until righted he would stay where he was. He certainly succeeded in making himself conspicuous by his absence, which would inevitably be much observed on the Accession Day celebrations, on November 17, but it was short-sighted policy which greatly disturbed his friends. One of them ventured to write to him an anonymous letter, franker even than Bacon had written a year before.

"Most worthy Lord,

"I have lately heard the several and different censures of many, much admiring thy absence in this High Court of Parliament, some (even now earnestly expecting the wellworthy advancement of thy most noble unspotted house and hopeful posterity) do in love and duty unfeignedly wish their service might ransom thy contentment, others, yea some of them, (who by an interchangeable brokerage with men great and little in the state of stature make daily use of thy absence as well in this as in other thy deserving services, and infinite love to thy queen and country) do with their tongue confess thy worthiness, and in words only wish with the rest, so that some, yea, the greater, some truly honouring thee, and others with their tongue only confessing thee, all in conclusion say th' Earl of Essex is a most noble gentleman. But hear me great Lord, and with patience pardon me that am and ever will be ready prest in all offices to thy service. Thou art full of wisdom, bounty and valour, and dost perform all things with much honour; and yet methinks thou art least perfect in securely working thy own good, which in this age and time of uncertainty is most needful to be cared for. But by the way let me tell thee; thy own patience, I say, thy patience, hath continually from the beginning given way to thy crosses, practised by a double faction very strong against thee, the proof hereof lest I seem too tedious I purposely omit, and thus to thy present state as it is upon every cross or discontentment, as we by supposition term it, thou absentest thyself from the court and sometimes as now makest a show of going to live in the country."

Admittedly, the writer continued, he had bitter injuries, but his absence from Court always benefited his adversaries. The greatest subject, that is, or ever was, greatest in the Prince's favour, in his absence is not missed. "Let neither occasion, cross, discontentment, nor any other cause whatsoever move or draw thee from the Court. But here, lest I be mistaken, I thus distinguish from the Council table. Sit in every council, yea, so sit that there may nothing be concluded in the settling of our quiet at home or our general good abroad, but with thy good liking and privity; make stay and further, as in thy private conceit thou shalt think most fit, and in that place above all other show the peremptory resolution. Thou hast a hundred thousand true hearts in this small isle, that daily expect and wish thy settled contentment, and the utter fall of them that love thee not. And albeit I say depart not from the Court, I presume not to speak of thy private duties, and services, to the Queen, or the coming into her presence; these and suchlike as a true subject to her Most Excellent Majesty and a dutiful servant to thee, I leave to thy own will, for thou mayest stay in the Court, sit in every council, and perform other thy own occasions in thy private bearing with a greater show of discontentment than in thy absence, for that thy enemies wish, make use of, and rejoice in. What dignity is done to them, or what indignity to thee, but in thy absence? In conclusion I say thy enemies are thereby made strong and thou becomest weak, and whereas thou retainest many in thy Lordship's favour as thy true and secret friends, take heed and remember that Christ had but twelve and one proved a devil."

Essex remained at Wanstead for a fortnight. Then he came back home to Essex House. He went from time to time to Court, but refused to take his seat in the Council, or to attend the meetings of the Parliament. For a while the Queen was willing to believe that the excuse of sickness was genuine, but as his absence continued and it was quite clear that he was determined to defy her, she grew angry, for he was holding up an important negotiation.

In the middle of November there arrived from the French King a special ambassador, M. Hurault de Maisse. The French King was anxious for peace. He had recently recaptured Amiens from the Spaniards, and was in a favourable condition for a conference. At the same time he was bound by a treaty with the Queen, made but a year before, not to negotiate a separate peace. De Maisse was entrusted with the very delicate mission of discovering whether the Queen would welcome peace.

De Maisse kept a careful journal of his mission, and soon after he had settled in London he noted his impressions of the situation at Court. The Queen herself was inclined to peace, but she was unwilling to seek it unless the States would join with her. Burghley naturally favoured it. Essex was against peace, but hardly dared to advocate war openly: but he was ambitious and knew that once peace should be made his reputation and popularity would fade. Meanwhile the Queen was unwilling to proceed to a definite conclusion until Essex delivered his opinion in Council. De Maisse was therefore kept waiting until the English Court could compose its differences.

Essex still held out, demanding that he should be righted. Various proposals were made. He was offered the place of the Lord Admiral, and he could have what words he wished inserted in his patent: he was offered the Keepership of the Privy Seal. He replied that he would be content, but he would not come back to Court until the grants had been confirmed. His friends urged him, but he remained obstinate. The Queen was equally determined that he should return without conditions. Essex was playing with fire, for it was making the affair into a trial of strength. If the Queen commanded his return he could not very well refuse, and then, if he came, he would look foolish and lose all that had been offered. As yet, however, she was not inclined to accept the challenge. Nor would she listen to any advice, and would-be peacemakers were sharply told to mind their own business.

At the beginning of December the Queen relented, for she unexpectedly learnt a very different version of the Islands Voyage. Sir Francis Vere had been in London for some three weeks, but he caught a bad chill and was unable to stir out. At last he came to Court and waited in the garden until the Queen passed by. As soon as she saw him, she called him to her and began to question him concerning the conduct of the expedition, for which she greatly blamed Essex. Vere justified Essex's conduct so vehemently and loudly that all the bystanders overheard his words. The Queen was surprised and interested, and called for some of Essex's critics to answer him, which they could not. The Queen was not ill pleased. She led Vere to the end of the garden and continued the conversation, passing on to Essex's moods and ambitions, and ending by very gracious praise.

On December 2, Essex was summoned to Court and for the moment all was well. But the Queen was, as always, slow to make up her mind to do anything, and Essex was still unwilling to attend the Council unless the Queen was present. He gave out that he wished to withdraw from Court, with the vague but threatening observation that he had with him many gentlemen who had been very ill recompensed. If they stayed there with him, seeing their enemies and those who were the cause of their ill treatment, some accident might chance that would displease the Queen, and he would be considered responsible.

He still held to his refusal to attend the Council which was to meet de Maisse, protesting that Burghley, Nottingham, Cecil, and their friends would be the greater party at the meeting. The Queen offered to send him seven or eight out of the Council, omitting the others. He refused. De Maisse was growing more and more impatient, and on December 16, learning that Essex was again proposing to retire into the country, he observed, " if it be so, the Earl errs greatly, for he gives occasion to his enemies to calumniate him, and to make him suspected by the Queen, as if he wished to make a separate party and withdraw himself, favoured by the nobility and the people. The judgment of the whole Court is that he is illadvised, for this woman might become peevish and in the end grow suspicious, and if once that came to pass he has no means of restoring himself."

De Maisse was fascinated by the Queen, who gave him several personal interviews, and he made many notes of her dress, behaviour, and conversation. At first he was critical and somewhat hostile, but after a while he was won over by her charm and political sagacity; she was, he declared, *une grande Princesse qui n'ignore rien.*

At the first interview the Queen " was strangely attired in a dress of silver cloth, white and crimson, or silver ' gauze,' as they call it. This dress had slashed sleeves lined with red taffeta, and was girt about with other little sleeves that hung down to the ground, which she was for ever twisting and untwisting. She kept the front of her dress open, and one could see the whole of her bosom, and passing low, and often

she would open the front of this robe with her hands as if she was too hot. The collar of the robe was very high, and the lining of the inner part all adorned with little pendants of rubies and pearls, very many, but quite small. She had also a chain of rubies and pearls about her neck. On her head she wore a garland of the same material and beneath it a great reddish-coloured wig, with a great number of spangles of gold and silver, and hanging down over her forehead some pearls, but of no great worth. On either side of her ears hung two great curls of hair, almost down to her shoulders and within the collar of her robe, spangled as the top of her head. Her bosom is somewhat wrinkled, as well as one can see for the collar that she wears round her neck, but lower down her flesh is exceedingly white and delicate—so far as one could see.

" As for her face, it is and appears to be very aged. It is long and thin, and her teeth are very yellow and unequal, compared with what they were formerly, so they say, and on the left side less than on the right. Many of them are missing, so that one cannot understand her easily when she speaks quickly. Her figure is fair and tall and graceful in whatever she does; so far as may be she keeps her dignity, yet humbly and graciously withal.

" All the time she spoke she would often rise from her chair, and appear to be very impatient with what I was saying. She would complain that the fire was hurting her eyes, though there was a great screen before it and she six or seven feet away; yet did she give orders to have it extinguished, making them bring water to pour upon it. She told me that she was well pleased to stand up and that she used to speak thus with the ambassadors who came to seek her, and used sometimes to tire them, of which they would on occasion complain. I begged her not to overtire herself in any way, and I rose when she did; and then she sat down again, and so did I. At my departure she rose and conducted me to that same place where she had come to receive me, and again began to say that she was grieved that all the gentlemen I had brought should see her in that condition, and she called to see them. They made their reverence before her, one after the other, and she embraced them all with great charm and smiling countenance."

The next day, December 17, Essex left Court and returned to Essex House, but he was back again at night, and the old argument continued. Nothing was resolved, though Essex was beginning to hint threats even to the Queen herself, observing that he dared not take his place in public or Council with the Lord Admiral lest something regrettable might happen. He still demanded that right should be done, either by a commission to examine the dispute, or by combat against Nottingham or one of his sons or kinsmen. The whole Court was disturbed by the quarrel. Ralegh was told by the Queen to mediate, but Essex refused to yield a jot unless Nottingham's patent was altered. Nottingham was so indignant with the proposal, and especially when he heard that the Queen was growing more favourable to Essex, that he resigned his white staff as Lord Steward, and went off to his house in Chelsea for a fit of politic sickness.

Four days later, December 21, Essex again went home and swore not to return. He was summoned back to Court. The Queen was all kindness. She had found the solution to the difficulty. Essex should be Earl Marshal of England: it was the most honourable of offices. Henceforward he would take precedence over Nottingham on every occasion. Cecil at once set to work on a draft of the patent, larded with suitable terms of pomp and ancientry. When he had finished he sent it to Essex, who returned it next day with a short note:

" SIR,
" I send you back this paper in which I have been bold to make a note or two, and especially have underlined some lines where I am praised for too innocent virtues, where they are active virtues and not negative that should draw on a

Prince to bestow a Marshal's office. Expedition in this is all, for now the Queen's times of signing and the shortness of time betwixt this and Christmas. And so hoping to meet you above after supper, I rest your affectionate and assured friend,
" Essex.

" The conclusion also is merely impertinent and may, I think, be well left out."

Although Essex stood stiffly on his honour in this affair, his annoyance was rather with the Queen herself than with the Admiral and his friends, for in Court it was very generally believed, and said, that she was deliberately keeping the quarrel alive, even to the extent of discouraging those who would have mediated. This was Essex's own feeling, and now that she promised him proper satisfaction, he immediately sought an interview with the Admiral and soon reached accord. The Queen was not pleased, and kept Essex waiting, with the result that when de Maisse attended the Council on the 27th, he was still absent. Next day she yielded, and in the evening the patent was publicly read out in the Presence Chamber.

Essex and his friends were jubilant. He had defeated the Cecils, the Admiral and their party. He had, for the first time, directly challenged the Queen herself, and she had in the end yielded. It gave him a fatal sense of superiority that he had only to bully her and she would always yield. He entirely misjudged her, for he took her vacillations for weakness, failing to realise that being a woman she acted on the instinct of the moment, and therefore was incalculable. Although his feeling for her was no longer affection or even admiration, she still felt a kind of love for him. Indeed, Essex had kept that charm which evokes faithful service, and those who were closest to him would still follow him blindly and romantically. Others, who could observe him with detachment and impartiality, saw the changes in his character which Bacon had noticed more than a year ago. The greed for honour, so admirable in a young soldier, was degenerating into a greedy and intolerant vanity. His ambition to be the greatest of the Queen's servants was now a mere lust for power. As one who regarded himself as a soldier, he wished the war to continue, but he had no thought of what might happen when the enemy should at last be defeated. With the people at large he was more popular than ever, especially in the City, but it was becoming noticeable that his intimates were soldiers of doubtful reputation, hot-headed gallants, bankrupts, men with a grievance, dangerous and desperate.

As soon as the patent creating him Earl Marshal was confirmed, Essex ostentatiously returned to public life. The first business to be concluded was the despatch of the French ambassador. On December 31, M. de Maisse was invited to confer with the Council. When he reached the Council Chamber only Lord Burghley was present. After a while the others came in and took their places. De Maisse sat in a chair at the end of the table. Burghley, the Lord Admiral, and Buckhurst were benched on his right, on his left Essex, the Lord Chamberlain Hunsdon, and Secretary Cecil. Burghley requested Essex to declare the Queen's decision. Essex refused and sat silent. Burghley therefore continued. Three parties, he observed, were interested in the proposed negotiations for peace: the King, the Queen, and the States. Since all should have an opportunity to give their opinions, the Queen had decided to send commissioners into France to consult with the King; and the States also had agreed to send their commissioners.

Some general discussion followed. Essex made only one remark: that there would be some difficulty over those of the Reformed Religion in France. Burghley added that peace would cause difficulties. De Maisse retorted that after keeping him waiting for six weeks the answer was hardly satisfactory, but since this was the Queen's decision he trusted that there would be no delay in sending the commissioners and that they should come with full instructions.

At this point the Lord Chamberlain withdrew to consult with the Queen. When he had gone Burghley remarked that the Council were not agreed. Some desired peace, but my Lord of Essex, being young, desired war. Essex said nothing. De Maisse replied that Essex being eager to win reputation and nourished to arms might well desire war, for it was his occupation, but they were talking easily of a war that was not in their own country. After some further conversation the Lord Chamberlain returned to conduct the ambassador to the Queen.

At this last interview the Queen spoke very frankly of her own difficulties. De Maisse asked if she had a private message for the King. She bade him come nearer out of the hearing of the councillors who were present. There was no one dearer to her than the French King, she said, but he must consider her point of view; she was an old woman who could do nothing by herself; she had to deal with nobles of divers humours, and peoples who, though they made great demonstration of love towards her, nevertheless were fickle and inconstant, and she had everything to fear; even in this last Parliament they complained that English treasure and English lives were being squandered in France; in the last three or four years more than twenty thousand had died; upon which she commented sorrowfully, *Quidquid delirant Reges plectuntur Achivi*.

Two days later de Maisse paid his farewells to the chief members of the Council. First he visited Burghley. Then he came to Essex, who spoke a little of his own troubles, and then went on to discuss the Queen's resolution to send commissioners to France. He was invited to go himself, but excused himself, for he knew that if the final resolution should be for war, he would be thought responsible, and also because his private affairs were in such a state that if he did not put them in order he could serve neither himself nor the realm. There were, Essex added, in England as in France contrary parties, some for peace, some for war, and they laboured under two disadvantages, delay and inconstancy, which proceeded chiefly from the sex of the Queen. They stayed talking for some time. When he went back to his lodging de Maisse noted of Essex in his Journal, "He is a man who in nowise contents himself with a petty fortune and aspires to greatness."

De Maisse left London on January 5, with the news that Secretary Cecil would lead the English commissioners.

CHAPTER XII

DANGEROUS COURSES

MUCH as Burghley and Cecil desired peace they realised that it would create many new problems. The advantages were obvious; the expenses of the Spanish war would be at an end, and the Irish rebels could be reduced at leisure; trade in the Mediterranean, and with Poland, Denmark, and Germany, could be resumed, to the great increase of customs and the revival of the decaying port towns. On the other hand, all hope of regaining Calais would be gone, and the repayment of the French King's war debts was very doubtful; the States would be at the mercy of Spain, and then, whatever promises might be made by the Spanish King, religious wars would be renewed, and the Queen's debts from the Low Countries would be unpaid. There was also the problem of discharged soldiers, who were always a nuisance and often a menace.

With the return of favour Essex was full of friendliness for his rivals, and was constantly to be seen in the company of Cecil and Ralegh. On January 11, Parliament, which had adjourned for the Christmas holidays, reassembled, and Essex, in the right of his new dignity, took his place before the Lord Admiral. He was added to the various committees of the House of Lords to consider Bills sent up from the Lower House, and for the rest of the Parliament, which was dissolved on February 9, he took an active part in the work of the House.

The preparations for the departure of Cecil's mission were completed. Cecil was anxious, for he was afraid that Essex in his turn might take advantage of his absence to urge the Queen to make Court preferments which would be embarrassing to him. Essex, however, promised that nothing should be done which he might find disagreeable, for Cecil had persuaded the Queen to treat him very handsomely in the matter of the cochineal and indigo taken at the Islands. Essex was allowed to purchase the whole booty for £50,000, at the rate of 18s. a pound when the market price was 30s., and to prevent a fall in the price the importation and sale of cochineal was forbidden for two years. A few days later the Queen granted Essex a free gift of £7,000 from the proceeds.

Essex was not without the usual irritations. He was pressing the Queen to give the vacant office of Vice Chamberlain to Sir Robert Sidney, and she refused. Moreover, his friend the Earl of Southampton was in trouble. He was preparing to go to France with Cecil's mission, to the great distress of Mistress Elizabeth Vernon, who was in secret his mistress. Love affairs with the Queen's maids of honour always caused trouble. In the middle of January Southampton was in disgrace in the Court. He was playing cards with Sir Walter Ralegh and Mr. Parker in the Presence Chamber after the Queen had gone to bed. Ambrose Willoughby, being Squire of the Body, asked them to stop their game. Southampton, who was a desperate gambler, was losing; he took no notice. Willoughby again approached and said that if they did not leave the Chamber he would call in the Guard. Ralegh pocketed his winnings and went. Next day Southampton meeting Willoughby between the tennis courts and the garden struck him. Willoughby retaliated by pulling out some of Southampton's long hair. When the Queen heard of the affair she publicly thanked Willoughby and said that he would have done better if he had sent Southampton to the Porter's Lodge to see who durst fetch him out. Essex also was renewing his intrigue with Mistress Bridges, to the distress of his wife and the apprehension of his friends, who feared that the Queen must inevitably hear of it, and then all his troubles would start again.

Cecil's chief assistants in his mission were Dr. John Herbert, Master of Requests, and Sir Thomas Wilkes. They left Court on February 11. Essex sent one of his men with the party with a note to Cecil, "I send this bearer to see your safe passage and to bring me news of it. I am thus curious of all whom either I value in judgment or love with affection, and therefore I must be doubly careful of yourself. These glustering tempestuous days that are past do awaken and increase my care, which ever shall be constant though it be superfluous." There was some added anxiety for Cecil's safety, for there was a report that Spanish warships were out in the Channel. He crossed safely and reached Dieppe on the 19th, whence he wrote to Essex, commenting frankly on their past differences and present reconciliation.

"Although in good manners I should have returned this gentleman from Dover, yet I confess to you I do not only conceive inward contentment in the knowledge of your care and affection, but am apt to let it appear externally, here to my company, how much I am valued by you. For myself I hope, now that God hath disposed our minds to love and kindness, and that the state of her Majesty's affairs must have a good portion of their distribution by us in our several qualities, I hope we shall overcome all petty doubts what the world can judge of our correspondency, to whom our souls are witnesses that nothing is so dear unto us as her Majesty's service which heretofore hath prospered the worse by our misfortunes of pleasing our followers' appetites by contrariety in ourselves. Shortly, my Lord, I am rich in my own mind by this purchase of your noble favour and protection, and I shall labour nothing more (next God and my Sovereign's service) than the conservation and requital of your true friendship from which nothing shall divide me but separation of body and soul and so I remain."

Around the letter in the margins he added certain intimate postscripts.

"I thank God I passed very well, and yet the *Vanguard* will roll. I could come no nearer in her than within four leagues, which gave us a great row. Young Norris was very sick, and in the *Crane* and *Quittance* Ch. Blount, Vane, Tufton, Cope, Wotton, and divers extremely sick.

"I have no fear but lest Sir Thomas Wilkes should prove worse; but he shall ride in my coach, and have all ease to Paris; he is better than he was, but hath an ill body. The copy of my letter to the King, and all else will appear to your Lordship in this dispatch.

"I pray you be good to London, and if some idle errand can send over Sir Walter, let us have him.

"I touch it in my joint letter that your man came over voluntarily, for haply the Queen would otherwise understand it."

Essex was now acting as Secretary, in diligent attendance on the Queen. He had long wished to have his mother restored to her favour, and the time seemed opportune. He asked that she might be brought into the Presence. Lady Leicester came to Court and waited in the privy gallery for the Queen to pass; but the Queen found reason which prevented her coming out. This happened several times. At length, on March 1, the Queen promised to visit the Controller. A great dinner was prepared; Lady Leicester was standing ready, with a jewel worth £300. The Queen's coach was brought out, and then, when everyone was waiting in expectation, she sent word that she had decided not to go. Essex himself was unwell and keeping to his room. As soon as he heard, he put on his night-gown and went up to the Queen by the private way, but she refused to move.

Next day she consented. Lady Leicester came again to Court and was brought to the Queen. The two women embraced and kissed each other, and all was happiness, for the moment. A week later, however, when Lady Leicester again wished to kiss the Queen's hand in public, permission was refused, and she expressed her irritation in one of her usual tart remarks.

Irish affairs were once more a chief anxiety of the English Court. Serious trouble had been brewing for several years. In the summer of 1594, Sir William Fitzwilliam was succeeded as Lord Deputy by Sir William Russell. Hugh O'Neill, Earl of Tyrone, was in rebellion, but on the arrival of Russell, he came in under safe conduct and asked for pardon. Sir Henry Bagnal, the Marshal of the Army, objected; and there was some discussion whether he should be detained. The Council of Ireland persuaded the Lord Deputy, against his inclination, to let him go; for this he was severely rebuked by the Privy Council. Russell then took the field against the other rebels. Early in 1595, Sir John Norris was sent over with the troops that had served in the Brittany campaign in 1594. Tyrone rebelled and captured the fort at the Blackwater which commanded the passage into Ulster. In July, he was proclaimed traitor, and the fort was recaptured. Russell and Norris quarrelled, as Norris was unwilling to serve under a man who had so much less military reputation than himself, and for the rest of the year they pursued different policies and consequently effected nothing; Russell was for strong military action, Norris for listening to Tyrone's grievances. Tyrone again proposed to submit, and the Queen, though angry at his rebellion, was disposed to admit him to a conference. His submission was accepted, and for the rest of 1596 his country was undisturbed.

In January, 1597, Sir Conyers Clifford was sent over as Governor of Connaught, where he suppressed the rebels with vigour and severity. Another commission was held and Tyrone was called to answer a number of charges. He admitted to correspondence with Spain, and other offences, but countered these charges with a list of his own grievances: and he swore that he would be loyal to the Queen if he should be pardoned. Negotiations dragged on till the end of April, when Sir William Russell was superseded by Lord Burgh as Lord Deputy. Burgh also quarrelled with Norris and told him to go to his own headquarters in Munster, where shortly afterwards he died. Tyrone was playing fast and loose and Burgh decided to go against him. He defeated Tyrone's forces, recaptured the Blackwater Fort and garrisoned it. Tyrone was once more in open rebellion, and to regain his reputation with his own people tried to recover the fort. Lord Burgh again went out against him and drove his forces back, but was soon after taken suddenly sick and died on October 13, to the joy of the rebels.

The Queen's real difficulty in Ireland was not so much the valour of the rebels as the appalling corruption of the English officials, civil and military. Captains and commissioners stole the pay of the soldiers, who were hungry, penniless, and in rags. The soldiers in their turn seized the cattle and food of the inhabitants, who were reduced to starvation. So insanely corrupt were the captains that when the muster masters came round to check their rolls they hired men from the rebels to fill up the ranks. When the muster masters had gone the rebels as often as not made off with their borrowed arms. Lord Burgh was one of the few honest and competent commanders that had appeared, and it was said, with some likelihood of truth, that the English officials had him poisoned to prevent the disclosure of their own rascality.

Pending the appointment of a new Lord Deputy, the Earl of Ormonde was appointed to command the army. Tyrone once more submitted and asked for a truce.

Of late Francis Bacon had been a rare visitor to Essex House. Essex had neglected Bacon's advice and now found that Bacon's prophecies had a habit of coming true. True prophets, whose warnings have been neglected, seldom reap gratitude. Nevertheless Bacon deemed the moment opportune for a further approach. He came to Essex and suggested that he should turn his particular attention to Irish affairs. After the conversation he ordered his thoughts in a letter. "That it is one of the aptest particulars for your lordship to purchase honour upon, I am moved to think for three reasons. Because it is ingenerate in your house, in respect of my Lord your father's noble attempts; because of all the actions of state on foot at this time, the labour resteth most in that particular; and because the world will make a kind of comparison between those that have set it out of frame and those that shall bring it into frame; which kind of honour giveth the quickest kind of reflexion. The transferring of this honour upon yourself consisteth in two points: the one, if the principal persons employed come in by you and depend upon you; the other, if your Lordship declare yourself and profess to have a care of that kingdom."

He went on to suggest some particulars and persons who should be consulted, and added, "for the points of apposing them I am too much a stranger to the business to deduce them. But in a general topic, methinks the pertinent interrogations must be, either of the possibility and means of accord, or of the nature of the war, or of the reformation of abuses, or of the joining of practice with force in the disunion of the rebels. If your Lordship doubt to put your sickle into another's harvest; first, time brings it to you in Mr. Secretary's absence; next, being mixt with matter of war, it is fittest for you: and lastly, I know your Lordship will carry it with that modesty and respect towards aged dignity, and that good correspondence towards my dear kinsman and your good friend now abroad, as no inconvenience may grow that way.

"Thus have I played the ignorant statesman; which I do to nobody but your Lordship; except to the Queen sometimes when she trains me on. But your Lordship will accept my duty and good meaning, and secure me touching the privateness of that I write."

The negotiations with Tyrone drew to an end, and in the middle of April he was granted a pardon under the Great Seal of Ireland.

Cecil's mission in France was brief and fruitless. They travelled more than three hundred miles over France endeavouring to find the French King, and on March 17 reached Angers. The King arrived two days later, and gave them three audiences. On the 24th, the Commissioners from the States arrived. On the 26th, Cecil received a letter from the Queen giving him private information that a packet of letters from the Cardinal to the King of Spain had been fished up from the sea, from which it appeared that the French King had already agreed to make a separate peace. On the 31st, the King moved to Nantes, whither the Commissioners followed him. Negotiations dragged on until April 13, when it was clear to the Commissioners that the King had deluded them. They therefore asked for permission to return home, and parted from the French Council highly discontented.

The news had not reached London by April 23, when the Garter Feast was celebrated very magnificently at Whitehall. The Earl of Shrewsbury was Lord President of the Order for the day, and the other knights present were the Lord Admiral, Essex, Lord Buckhurst, Lord Thomas Howard, the Earl of Worcester, Lord Hunsdon, Lord Mountjoy, and old Sir Henry Lee. In the afternoon, about 3 o'clock, the knights were attired in their robes of purple velvet trailing on the ground, lined with white taffeta. They wore their ordinary hose and doublet, with a side cassock beneath the calf of the leg of scarlet velvet, with a hood of the same material turned on the right shoulder, with the red cross embroidered on the outer robe on their left arms. Each wore a velvet cap and feather, except Lord Buckhurst. So attired they passed through the Presence Chamber to wait on the Queen and to escort her to the Chapel; but as the Queen chose to remain in her own apartments, the knights went on to the Chapel by themselves, preceded by the heralds, two and two, with the youngest leading and the Lord President coming by himself alone. The service followed, being read by the Bishop of Winchester, who was Prelate of the Order, and by the Dean of Windsor. Two psalms and two anthems were sung by the choir of the Chapel Royal, accompanied by organs, sackbuts, and other instruments. Thence they returned to the Presence Chamber for the Feast, which was of forty dishes. The Lord President was served on plate of double gilt, the others on plate of silver, and to each knight was appointed a gentleman pensioner and another gentleman to serve. They sat supping for two hours and a half, and at ten o'clock they rose and departed to their lodgings. Next day the Queen attended chapel in procession, walking under a canopy borne by six knights, and on the following day Essex with three hundred followers and Mountjoy with two hundred paid a visit of ceremony to the Lord Mayor.

Six days later, Essex received a secret letter from Sir Robert Cecil, which ran:

" I am now arrived at Portsmouth, having had a very hard passage from Caen, where I took shipping on Thursday and landed at Sandham Castle Bay about 12 o'clock, this day; from whence overland in the Wight to the passage over against this place I am come. My desire is to advertise your Lordship hereof first as him to whom I have professed entirely love and service, next with desire to be beholding for a coach at Staines, with as much expediency as it may be, for I will be there, God willing, by tomorrow two of clock; and yet, because I would have no expectancy of my coming nor know not whether my addled head will away with such expedition after so hard a passage as I have had and so vile a journey through Brittany to Caen, where I rested but one night, I do humbly beseech your Lordship in no wise to take notice of my arrival, for I protest to the living God I have neither directly nor indirectly written to any creature living, no, not so much as my own dear father, of whom I will steal a sight in my way to Court, though nobody else shall know it.

" P.S.—I beseech you to let him that brings the coach bring in it four horses, and command him precisely to speak no more of it than if you were to send for London to Greenwich.

" I mean not London the city, but Sir W. Ralegh's London. I thought to send this letter to the Lord Mountjoy for you, because my hand should not be on the back with any letter to you that shall pass the posts now, but I do now pass it under the authority of his lieutenant."

Cecil's hasty return was partly due to his zeal to report to the Queen, but more because he had received a letter from one of his servants that the health of his old father was causing anxiety, and wishing for his speedy return for fear of the worst. He reached Court very late in the night of April 30, and went straight to the Queen. After a brief audience he went on to his house in the Strand. For the moment Lord Burghley was rather better in health.

With Cecil's return two problems had to be settled: the war with Spain and the growing rebellion in Ireland. Now that the French had withdrawn from the war, the whole burden fell on England and the States. The French King had stipulated that the Queen should have an opportunity of joining in the treaty. The arguments in favour of peace were stronger even than before, and Essex as champion of the war party was severely criticised.

Lord Burghley was eager for peace, and the question was very hotly disputed. To Burghley's arguments Essex retorted that no peace could be made with Spain but one that was dishonourable and fraudulent on their side. Burghley replied that he breathed forth nothing but war, slaughter, and blood, and taking out his prayer book he opened it and pointed silently to the 23rd verse of Psalm lv—" bloodthirsty and deceitful men shall not live out half their days."

Some of Essex's critics admitted that he was sincere, though mistaken. Others distrusted him and said openly that he was serving his own ambition and the benefit of his followers, and that his courteous behaviour in public was deliberately assumed to win the favour of the mob. So much impressed was one young satirist by this thought that he even made pointed reference to Essex in a satire on hypocrisy:

" This vizard-fac'd pole-head dissimulation,
   This paraqueet, this guide to reprobation,

This squint-ey'd slave, which looks two ways at once,
This fork'd Dilemma, oil of passions,
Hath so beray'd the world with his foul mire
That naked Truth may be suspect a liar.
For when great *Felix* passing through the street,
Vaileth his cap to each one he doth meet,
And when no broom-man that will pray for him,
Shall have less truage than his bonnet's brim,
Who would not think him perfect courtesy ?
Or the honeysuckle of humility ?
The devil he is as soon: he is the devil,
Brightly accoustred to be-mist his evil:
Like a swartrutter's hose his puff thoughts swell,
With yeasty ambition: *Signor Machiavel*
Taught him this mumming trick, with courtesy
To entrench himself with popularity,
And for a writhen face, and body's move,
Be barracadoed in the people's love."

Essex composed a reply to his critics. It was an Apology written in the form of a letter to Anthony Bacon. He would answer, he observed, the charge that he preferred war to peace, and that all his counsels, actions, and endeavours tended to keep the State of England in continual wars, and especially now when peace could be had. Then he ran briefly through his own life. He had got little benefit from war, " in which I have impaired my state, lost my dear and only brother the half arch of my house, buried many of my nearest and dearest friends, and subjected myself to the rage of seas, violence, general plagues, famine and all kind of wants, discontentment of undisciplined and unruly multitudes, and acceptation of all events, in which I did not only leave my known enemies elbow room to see their own and their friends' advancement, but was fain sometimes upon trust in their protestations, after new reconcilements, to make them the receivers, censurers and answerers of all my despatches."

In general he agreed that peace was to be preferred before war, and especially for a trading nation like England. His objection to these peace negotiations was that they would bring no peace; for the Spaniard was not seriously seeking peace, which would give him many advantages but would not be kept. The Spaniard could not be trusted; all he wanted was a breathing space. It was a rhetorical but telling argument.

Anthony Bacon allowed copies to be made and circulated them in secret, but one was divulged and soon the *Apology* was being widely read. Essex was much criticised for allowing such a document to become public. He protested that it was never his intention to have published it either in print or copy. Indeed, he charged his servant not even to allow any of his friends to see it, except in his hands or at least in his presence. He could only suppose that it had got abroad by corruption amongst some of his servants that had access to his chamber who might have copied the loose sheets which lay under his bed's head till he had finished the whole.

The appointment of an able man for Ireland was now urgent, for the rebellion had not been checked by Tyrone's latest submission. On July 1, the choice was discussed. There were present with the Queen Essex, the Lord Admiral, Cecil, and Windebank, Clerk to the Signet. The Queen proposed Sir William Knollys. Essex put forward Sir George Carew; he was an abler man, but—an argument which weighed more heavily—he was also a close personal friend of Cecil and could advantageously be sent away. The Queen treated Essex's arguments lightly, and the discussion became heated. Suddenly Essex lost his temper, looked scornfully at the Queen, and then turned his back on her. The next moment she flared up, gave him a box on the ear and told him to go and be hanged. As Essex laid his hand on his sword, the Lord Admiral stepped between them. In great passion Essex swore that he would not and could not endure such an insult, he would not have endured it even at King Henry the Eighth's hands. And with that he strode out of the Chamber and away from Court.

It was a desperate situation, though but a culmination of an anxious and trying summer when everyone's nerves were on edge. Both parties were in the wrong, which was the more difficult to right because it was so crude and personal. Essex, as subject, should have yielded, but to one of his nature an apology after such an insult was impossible, and the more because, being in the wrong, he was so obstinately certain that he must be right. He went off into the country to nurse his injured pride, and to await events. Day followed day, and neither made any move. The courtiers were troubled, for at such times the Queen was intolerable, and so prodigious a portent might lead to incalculable calamities.

The Queen relented first. She was anxious for a reconciliation, but in so delicate a matter much perplexed. She instructed Mr. Killigrew, a gentleman of the Chamber, to visit Essex, as if of his own accord; but then, she reflected, if one of her own servants came, it would be thought that she had sent him. She remarked, darkly, that she had observed those who followed her, and those who accompanied such as were in her displeasure, and they should know of it before long.

Sir William Knollys, who understood her moods, interpreted them as implying that if Essex cared to yield she was ready to make peace. He therefore wrote to Essex to prepare him for a reconciliation.

"Between her Majesty's running into her princely power, and your Lordship's persisting in your settled resolution, I am so confounded as I know not how nor what to persuade. I will therefore leave it to God's work, to Whom I heartily pray to settle your heart in a right course; your Sovereign, your country, and God's cause, never having more need of you than now; wishing you rather to depart from yourself, than not to be what you ought." After this tactful beginning, he concluded by the plea that "if in substance you may have a good peace, I beseech your Lordship not to stand upon the form of treaty."

Essex did not act upon the hint. A few days later the Lord Keeper Egerton wrote more positively to warn him of the danger of his behaviour.

"My very good Lord,

"It is often seen that he that is a stander-by seeth more than he that playeth the game; and, for the most part, any man in his own cause standeth in his own light, and seeth not so clearly as he should. Your Lordship hath dealt in other men's causes and in great and weighty affairs with great wisdom and judgment. Now your own is in hand, you are not to condemn and refuse the advice of any that love you how simple soever. In this order I rank myself, among others that love you; none more simple, and none that loves you with more true and honest affection, which shall plead my excuse if you shall either mistake or misconstrue my words or meaning: yet in your Lordship's honourable wisdom I neither doubt nor suspect the one nor the other. I will not presume to advise you, but shoot my bolt as near the mark as I can, and tell you what I think.

"The beginning and long continuance of this so unseasonable discontentment you have seen and proved, by which you may aim at the end. If you hold still your course, which hitherto you find worse and worse, (and the longer you tread this path, the farther you are still out of the way) there is little hope or likelihood that the end will be better than the beginning. You are not so far gone but you may well return. The return is safe, but the progress dangerous and desperate in this course you hold. If you have any enemies, you do that for them which they could never do for themselves; whilst you leave your friends to open shame and contempt, forsake yourself, overthrow your fortunes, and ruinate your honour and reputation, giving that comfort to our foreign foes, as greater they cannot have. For what can be more welcome and pleasing news to them than to hear that her Majesty and the Realm are maimed of so worthy a member, who hath so often and so valiantly quailed and daunted them? You forsake your country when it hath most need of your help and counsel: and lastly, you fail in your indissoluble duty, which you owe to your most gracious Sovereign; a duty not imposed upon you by nature and policy only, but by the religious and sacred bond, in which the Divine Majesty of God hath by the rule of Christianity obliged and bound you.

"For the four first, your constant resolution may perhaps move you to esteem them as light, but, being well weighed, they are not lightly to be regarded; and for the two last, it may be your private conscience may strive to content yourself; but it is enough. These duties stand not alone in contemplation and inward meditation; their effects are external, and cannot be performed but by external actions; and where that faileth, the substance itself faileth.

"Now this being your present state and condition, what is the best to be done herein? And what is the best remedy for the same? My good Lord, I want wisdom and lack judgment to advise you; but I will never want an honest and true heart to will and wish you well; nor, being warranted by a good conscience, forbear to speak what I think. I have begun plainly. I hope your Lordship will not be offended, if I proceed still after the same fashion. *Bene cedit, qui tempori cedit.* And Seneca saith, *Lex si nocentem punit, cedendum est justitiæ; si innocentem, cedendum est fortunæ.* The best remedy is not to contend and strive, but humbly to submit. Have you given cause, and yet take scandal to yourself? Why, then all you can do is too little to make satisfaction. Is cause of scandal given to you? Yet policy, duty, and religion inforce you to sue, yield, and submit to your Sovereign, between whom and you there can be no proportion of duty. And God Himself requireth it as a principal bond of service to Himself. When it is evident that great good may ensue of it to your friends, your country, and Sovereign, and extreme harm by the contrary, there can be no dishonour or hurt to yield; but in not doing it, is dishonour and impiety. The difficulty, my good Lord, is to conquer yourself, which is the height of all true valour and fortitude, whereunto all your honourable actions have tended. Do it in this, and God will be pleased, her Majesty well satisfied, your country will take good, and your friends comfort by it: yourself (I mention you last, for I know of all these you esteem yourself least) shall receive honour, and your enemies (if you have any) shall be disappointed of their bitter sweet hope.

" Thus have I uttered what I think, simply and truly, and leave you to determine. If I have erred, it is *error amoris*, and not *amor erroris*. Construe, I beseech you, and accept it, as I mean it, not as an advice, but as an opinion to be allowed or cancelled at your pleasure. If I might conveniently have conferred with you myself in person, I would not then have troubled you with so many idle blots. Yet whatsoever you shall judge of this mine opinion, be you well assured, my desire is to further all good means, that may tend to your good. And so wishing you all honourable happiness, I rest

" Your Lordship's most ready and faithful
" (although of many most unable)
" poor friend,
"Tho. Egerton, C.S."

Three days later Essex replied:

" My very good Lord,
" Although there is not a man this day living, whom I would sooner make a judge of any question that did concern me than yourself, yet must you give me leave to tell you, that in such a case I must appeal from all earthly judges; and if in any, then surely in this, where the highest judge on earth has imposed on me, without trial or hearing, the most heavy judgment that ever hath been known; but since I must either answer your Lordship's arguments, or forsake my just defence,

I will force mine aching head to do me some service for a small hour or two, although against my will.

"I must, then, first deny my discontentment, which was forced, to be any humorous discontentment, and that it was unseasonable, or of too long continuance. Your Lordship should rather condole with me than expostulate about the same: natural seasons are expected here below, but violent and unseasonable storms come from above. There is no tempest comparable to the passionate indignation of a Prince; nor yet at any time is it so unseasonable as when it lighteth upon those who might expect a harvest of their careful and painful labours. He that is once wounded must feel smart while his hurt be cured, or that the part be senseless; but no cure I expect, her Majesty's heart being obdurate against me; and to be without sense I cannot, being made of flesh and blood.

"But, say you, I may aim at the end. I do more than aim, for I see an end of all my good fortunes, and have set an end to my desires. In this course do I any thing for mine enemies? When I was in the Court, I found them absolute; and, therefore, I had rather they should triumph alone, than that they should have me attendant on their chariots. Do I leave my friends? When I was a courtier, I could yield them no fruits of my love unto them. Now I am become an hermit, they shall bear no envy for their love towards me. Do I forsake myself, because I do enjoy myself? Or do I overthrow my fortune, for that I build not a fortune of paper walls, which every puff of wind bloweth down? Do I ruinate mine honour, because I leave following the pursuit, or wearing the false badge or mark of the shadow of honour? Do I give courage and comfort to the foreign foe, because I reserve myself to encounter with him, or because I keep my heart from baseness, although I cannot keep my fortune from declining?

"No, my good Lord, I give every one of these considerations its due right, and the more I weigh them, the more I feel myself justified from offending in any of them. As for the last two objections, that I forsake my country when it hath most need of me, and fail in my indissoluble duty which I owe unto my Sovereign, I answer, that if my country had at this time any need of my public service, her Majesty, that governs the same, would not have driven me into a private kind of life. I am tied unto my country by two bands; in public place, to discharge faithfully, carefully, and industriously, the trust which is committed unto me; and the other private, to sacrifice for it my life and carcase which hath been nourished in it. Of the first I am freed, being dismissed, discharged, and disabled by her Majesty. Of the other nothing can free me but death, and therefore no occasion of my performance shall offer itself, but I will meet it half-way. The indissoluble duty which I owe to her Majesty is only the duty of allegiance, which I never will, nor never can, fail in. The duty of attendance is no indissoluble duty. I owe to her Majesty the duty of an Earl and Lord Marshal of England. I have been content to do her Majesty the service of a clerk, but can never serve her as a villein or slave.

"But yet, you say, I must give way unto the time. So I do; for now I see the storm come, I put myself into the harbour. Seneca saith, we must give place unto Fortune; I know that Fortune is both blind and strong, and therefore I go as far out of her way as I can. You say the remedy is not to strive; I neither strive, nor seek for remedy. But, say you, I must yield and submit; I can neither yield myself to be guilty, or this imputation laid upon me to be just. I owe so much to the Author of all Truth, as I can never yield falsehood to be truth, nor truth falsehood. Have I given cause, ask you, and take scandal when I have done? No, I give no cause to take so much as Fimbria's complaint against me, for I did *totum telum corpore recipere*. I patiently bear all, and sensibly feel all, that I then received when this scandal was given me. Nay more, when the vilest of all indignities are done unto me, doth religion enforce me to sue? Doth God require it? Is it impiety not to do it? What, cannot Princes err? Cannot subjects receive wrong? Is an earthly power or authority infinite? Pardon me, pardon me, my good Lord, I can never subscribe to these principles. Let Solomon's fool laugh when he is stricken; let those who mean to make their profit of Princes show to have no sense of Prince's injuries; let them acknowledge an infinite absoluteness on earth, that do not believe in an absolute infiniteness in heaven.

"As for me I have received wrong, and feel it. My cause is good, I know it; and whatsoever come, all the powers on earth can never show more strength and constancy in oppressing, than I can show in suffering whatsoever can or shall be imposed on me.

"Your Lordship in the beginning made yourself a looker on, and me a player of my own game, so you can see more than I can; yet must you give me leave to tell you in the end of my answer, that since you do but see, and I suffer, I must of necessity feel more than you do. I must crave your Lordship's patience to give him that hath a crabbed fortune, licence to use a crabbed style; and yet whatsoever my style is, there is no heart more humble to his superiors, nor any more affected to your Lordship, than that of your honour's poor friend,

"ESSEX."

To the Queen herself he wrote:

"MADAM,

"When I think how I have preferred your beauty above all things, and received no pleasure in life but by the increase of your favour towards me, I wonder at myself what cause there could be to make me absent myself one day from you. But when I remember that your Majesty hath, by the intolerable wrong you have done both me and yourself, not only broken all laws of affection, but done against the honour of your sex, I think all places better than that where I am, and all dangers well undertaken, so I might retire myself from the memory of my false, inconstant, and beguiling pleasures. I am sorry to write thus much, for I cannot think your mind so dishonourable but that you punish yourself for it, how little soever you care for me. But I desire whatsoever falls out, that your Majesty should be without excuse, you knowing yourself to be the cause, and all the world wondering at the effect. I was never proud, till your Majesty sought to make me too base. And now since my destiny is no better, my despair shall be as my love was, without repentance. I will as a subject and an humble servant owe my life, my fortune, and all that is in me; but this place is not fit for me, for she which governs this world is weary of me, and I of the world. I must commend my faith to be judged by Him who judgeth all hearts, since on earth I find no right. Wishing your Majesty all comforts and joys in the world, and no greater punishment for your wrongs to me, than to know the faith of him you have lost, and the baseness of those you shall keep,

"Your Majesty's most humble servant,

"R. Essex."

Whilst the older statesmen were studying to preserve an impartiality, others were not so successful. Essex learnt that Lord Grey was being very favourably used by the Queen. He spoke to Grey, and told him that he must declare himself whether he was his only, or friend to the Secretary and so his enemy; there could be no neutrality. Grey replied that he would not regulate his loves and hates by Essex's passions; as for the Secretary, he had tasted of his favour and would never be dishonest or ungrateful. Essex answered that though he affected some parts in him, he loved not his person, neither should Grey be welcome to him or expect advancement under him. Grey had been one of the knights of Essex's own creating, and Essex was claiming that he was therefore bound to himself and not to the Queen. It was a dangerous doctrine, and not unnoticed, for Grey complained bitterly to Lord Cobham, who had likewise no cause to love Essex.

For the next few days Essex's affairs were no longer the chief topic of conversation at Court. Old Lord Burghley was dying. On July 15, he attended a Council meeting, but ten days later he was too weak to sit up, and his strength was daily growing less. On the evening of August 4, knowing that his end was come, he began to prepare for death in the same methodical way as he had lived. He blessed his children, and prayed for the Queen. He called for his steward and delivered to him his will. Then the chaplains were summoned to pray for him. At four o'clock in the morning he lapsed into unconsciousness, and died very peacefully four hours later. The news was brought to the Queen in the afternoon, and she went to her private apartment to weep for him alone. For forty years he had served her faithfully and patiently as her right hand, and none of her younger Councillors could ever fill that gap. It was the more unfortunate that Essex should be absent from the Court at such a time, and for such a reason.

Sir William Knollys considered the moment opportune for another appeal. The same evening he wrote to Essex to tell him of the Queen's grief, adding—"Your Lordship's being from Court at this time, is, in my opinion, very unseasonable both for the common good, (many weighty causes now depending) and your Lordship's own private; wishing, that there be no disposing of office or place without your Lordship's allowance. My arguments to persuade your Lordship's presence I leave to be weighed by your own judicial part, knowing how wisely you are able to advise another in so great a cause, praying you to lay down sound and sure positions of your resolution, the cause of religion, the good of your country, yourself and your friends depending thereon, and humbly desiring your Lordship, that opinion do not overrule you, as in regard of your own will you will neglect those great causes formerly by me remembered.

"Remember, I beseech you, that there is no contesting between sovereignty and obedience; and I fear the longer your Lordship doth persist in this careless humour of her Majesty, the more her heart will be hardened; and I pray God your contending with her in this manner do not breed such a hatred in her, as will never be reclaimed. Which passion if she fall into, your Lordship must needs be guilty thereof; and though by necessity she may be forced to use your service, yet shall you be sure, by not having her Majesty's love, to be subject to their tongues, who will practise against you. Pardon, I beseech your Lordship, if I pass my bounds, my love being the guide of my pen."

Four days later Essex was summoned to attend a meeting of the Council at the Lord Keeper's. He came, but would take no part in the discussions until first he had been heard by the Queen herself. As this was refused, he went away, and the deadlock continued. His absence was increasingly embarrassing to the Council, for as Master of the Ordnance his advice and co-operation in equipping the reinforcements for Ireland were essential, and State business was greatly hampered. Moreover, for the Council to be deprived of its most important source of foreign news at this critical time was dangerous.

A fortnight later there was another crisis at Court. News came of a great disaster in Ireland, the greatest which English arms had received in the reign. On August 14, Sir Henry Bagnal, Marshal of the Army, marched out of Armagh with all the available troops, amounting to 3,500 foot and 500 horse, to relieve the fort at the Blackwater. The army was completely routed by Tyrone, with the loss of Bagnal himself, 15 captains, and about 2,000 men. The remainder fled to Armagh, where Tyrone had them at his mercy. It seemed that Ireland would be lost.

When Essex heard the ill news he came again to Court and attended the meeting of the Council on August 22. He asked to be admitted to the Queen, and when she refused to see him, he gave his advice in a letter which was rejected. To be excluded at such a time was disturbing, and for the moment he was more disposed to parley. He therefore composed a letter to the Queen which might, without yielding dignity or sense of grievance, prepare for a reconciliation.

" As I had not gone into exile of myself if your Majesty had not chased me from you as you did, so was I ever ready to have taken hold of any warrant that your Majesty could have given me for my return. But when your Majesty could neither endure that my friends should plead for me to you, nor by their visitations give comfort unto me, and that I heard your indignation did take hold of all things that might feed it, and that you did willingliest hear those that did kindle it, then I said to myself:

> Mene evertere tantus
> Diis superis labor est, parva quem puppe sedentem
> Tam magno petiere mari ?
> Intrepidus quamcunque datis mihi numina mortem
> Accipiam.

Yet when the unhappy news came from yonder cursed country of Ireland, and that I apprehended how much your Majesty would be grieved to have your armies beaten and your kingdom like to be conquered by the son of a smith, duty was strong enough to rouse me out of my deadest melancholy; I posted up and first offered my attendance, and after my poor advice in writing, to your Majesty. But your Majesty rejected both me and my letter. The cause, as I hear, was that I refused to give counsel when I was last called to my Lord Keeper's. But if your Majesty had not already judged this cause, or that I might appeal from your indignation to your justice, I then should think your Majesty, if you had once heard me, would clear me from all undutifulness.

" First, I did nothing but that which the greatest, gravest and most esteemed Councillor that ever your Majesty had did when himself bare less discomfort and the cause was less dangerous. Secondly, I did not refuse utterly to give counsel, but desired to be first heard by your Majesty yourself ; and lastly, as I am sworn to give counsel to your Majesty and not to your Council, so that which I was and, if it please you, am to deliver, is fit to be heard only by yourself. Some general heads my last letter contained, and so might this, but your Majesty would not be satisfied with them if I do not expound them and lay open every one of their parts. If your Majesty will hear me, I stay in this place for no other purpose but to attend your commandment. If this answer be agreeable to the last, then *quid nisi vota supersunt* from your Majesty's servant, in whom you would fain discourage better endeavours than ever you shall find elsewhere.

"ESSEX."

This letter was written on the 26th. On the 29th the first part of the funeral of Lord Burghley was celebrated in London. A procession of more than five hundred persons followed the hearse. Essex himself, hooded and shrouded in his black mourning cloak, was conspicuous. His manifest grief was much noted by the spectators, who cynically wondered whether he was lamenting the illustrious dead or his own troubles. Directly after dinner he retired to Wanstead, where it was reported he meant to remain, as he could not be received at Court. As for the Queen, she said that he had played long enough upon her and she meant to play a while upon him, and to stand as much upon her greatness as he did upon indignation. In a day or two Essex was back at Essex House.

Essex's friends were also in trouble. Southampton had remained in Paris after Cecil's return in the early spring, whither news reached him that his mistress was now pregnant. He came over to London secretly, married her, and went back to Paris, leaving his new Countess with Essex's household, at Essex House. The Queen heard the news and ordered Cecil to have him fetched back.

"I am not a little grieved," Cecil wrote, "that I must use the style of a Councillor to you, by laying her Majesty's command upon you to whom I have ever rather wished to be the messenger of honour and favour; but I must now put this gall into mine ink, that her Majesty knoweth that you came over very lately, and returned again very contemptuously; that you have also married one of her Maids of Honour, without her privity, for which, with other circumstances informed against you, I find her grievously offended; and therefore it hath pleased her to command me in her name to charge you expressly (all excuses set apart) to repair hither to London, and from thence to advertise us your arrival, without coming to the Court, until her pleasure be known."

Essex's quarrel with the Queen had now lasted two months. Whatever his enemies might say or feel, he was so important in the State that nothing could be effected without him, and at last the Queen herself was disposed to receive him. Essex's friends made yet another effort to persuade him to moderate his attitude, and old Sir Harry Lee, perceiving a change in the Queen's feelings, wrote to him that Cecil had won him the Queen's sympathy, and she had said he could do better for others than for himself. Cecil thought all things would go well. The Queen denied the ground of difference, and would probably meet Essex half-way. If he upset her further he would have more reason for grief than if he lost her favour. What he sought could be of no benefit to him, for if he forced the Queen against her will she would never forget it; while in yielding he would do nothing unworthy, and would make a surer peace. His wrongs might be greater than he could well digest, but let him consider how great she was, and how unwilling to be conquered; the disadvantages of defying her; how strong he would make his enemies, how weak his friends; how the State could benefit himself and his friends, yet how offended the world would be if he neglected her. Only, whatever peace he made, let him use no means but himself, for the sake of his honour and the Queen's approval.

The Queen herself was utterly distracted. She would gladly have Essex back, but as a suppliant. She sent Killigrew again with the message that she looked for a better answer from him than his last letter; he must submit or she would not admit him to her presence. As Killigrew was on his way Sir

William Knollys met him and took him back to Court. He had heard that Essex's old fever had returned. He told Killigrew to go back to the Queen and say that Essex was ill, and that he thought it best to know her pleasure before delivering an unpleasing message. She blamed him for not obeying her order. He replied that had he gone Essex's fever might have been imputed to her message. She admitted that it was so. The news that Essex was ill brought a revulsion of feeling. She forgot her indignation and sent him word that he should come back. The message reached him at Wanstead, whither he had been carried in a litter. On September 5, he wrote to her:

"What can be written by a weak hand or indited by a distempered head fit to be presented to your Majesty? Nothing but humble thanks, thanks poorly paid but faithfully owed. I will presume with them to send two humble advertisements. The first, that there is this difference between the favours you now bestow and the afflictions you have lately laid upon me. These are your own that cost you nothing; the other were borrowed and unnatural to you. These ever fruitful: the other best when they are barrenest. These increase my obligation to you: the other add to my merit of you. My other advertisement is, that since your Majesty's will is the law, and your power is the cause by which I am longer kept in this world, if you repent you of it hereafter, you must charge yourself and not

"Your Majesty's humblest servant,
"ESSEX."

Next day the Queen sent her own physician to attend him, and by her orders he was visited by Killigrew, Fulke Greville, and Lord Henry Howard.

On September 10, Essex had recovered sufficiently to return to Court, and once more he took his place at the Council. Outwardly the reconciliation was complete. Essex had again challenged the Queen and again she yielded. It increased his sense of his own power, and lessened his respect for his ageing Mistress. He was growing less and less patient of her whims and more bitter with those who would not give him unquestioned support.

By Burghley's death several important offices were vacant, principally those of Lord Treasurer and Master of the Wards. Essex was a candidate for the last office and asked for it. The Queen was in no hurry to make any appointment and for a time contemplated taking the office into her own hands. Essex made the refusal a personal matter, petitioning her to reconsider her refusal on the ground that if she did not appoint a successor, " the world may judge, and I must believe, that you overthrow the office because I should not be the officer. If you give it to any other of what quality soever I must say: O ! *infelix virtus, quam tu levis umbra et nudum tantum nomen es: Nam cum ego te semper coluerim, tu fortune servieras.*

" Therefore if your Majesty value me as you would do any man that had done you half that service, think again of the suit of your Majesty's humblest servant."

The Queen, however, was unmoved.

On the Continent there was some chance of an improvement. After a long and repulsive illness Philip of Spain at last was dead, and it was believed that his son, a young man of twenty years, would be more disposed for peace. In Ireland the rebellion was quite out of all control. Everywhere Englishmen were being murdered by their tenants and servants; Sir Thomas Norris, Governor of Munster, could do nothing, and was forced to abandon his own house. Even within the English Pale there was no safety, and a plot to surprise the Castle at Dublin and massacre the English was only discovered just in time.

The appointment of a Lord Deputy was now imperative. The Queen and most of the Council favoured Lord Mountjoy. Essex objected that he was hardly suitable; he had small experience in the wars, his estate was mean, his followers few, and he was too bookish. The settlement of Ireland required some great nobleman, respected by the soldiers, and one who had already commanded an army. He was so emphatic in Council in expressing his own views on the proper methods of settling Ireland, that the Queen chose him. He protested that some other man should be sent, but he was so critical of all other nominees that he found himself in the awkward position that he could neither refuse the office nor relinquish it to another. The appointment was discussed all through the autumn, and Essex found it more and more difficult to decline. By the beginning of November word had gone round amongst the unemployed captains that Essex would be appointed, and at once he was besieged by eager applicants. On the 24th, the Lord Admiral was already drawing up the establishment of the fleet necessary to transport Essex and his men.

During these weeks Essex was also busied with Southampton's affairs. In spite of the Queen's command, he was in no hurry to leave Paris. The new Countess gave birth to a daughter on November 8. The Earl returned to London about the same time and was committed to the Fleet Prison. To add to his troubles, his mother, the Dowager Countess, was proposing to marry Sir William Harvey. Essex endeavoured to straighten out these complications. Southampton was soon released, but the Queen was not pacified; and when Essex proposed that he should be his Master of Horse in Ireland she refused.

CHAPTER XIII

THE IRISH EXPEDITION

BY the beginning of 1599 it was definite that Essex would be appointed to go to Ireland, and he began to prepare with all diligence for the campaign. He was crowded with offers of service from professional captains and the younger noblemen and gentlemen who particularly favoured his party. Southampton was eager to go, and the young Earl of Rutland, and the two Danvers brothers, Henry and Charles, and a host of others including Essex's stepfather, Sir Christopher Blount.

Others were sceptical of the expedition and Essex's motives. Some believed that he was going not to serve the Realm but to humour his own revenge. If he performed in the field what he had promised in the Council all would be well. Outwardly the Queen had pardoned him for his contempt of six months ago, and was trusting a man who deserved very different treatment—outwardly; who but God knew her inward thoughts? Certainly Essex had made many enemies, and many of those who pretended to be his friends were moved more by policy than affection. Some were openly alarmed and warned him not to go. He asked Francis Bacon. Bacon saw that circumstances had entirely changed in the last year, and by every possible argument emphatically advised him not to go. Essex's absence, he said, would exulcerate the Queen's mind, whereby it would not be possible for him to carry himself so as to give her sufficient contentment, nor for her to carry herself so as to give him sufficient countenance, which would be ill for her, ill for him, and ill for the State.

Essex's own emotions were in a turmoil. At times he regarded himself as his country's saviour, a willing sacrifice for an ungracious Sovereign who would never realise his worth until he was no more. In this mood he wrote on January 1, to Fulke Greville, "if I might with my death either quench the great fire of rebellion in Ireland, or divert these dangers which from foreign enemies are threatened, I should joy to be such a sacrifice. But how much soever her Majesty despiseth me she shall know she hath lost him who for her sake would have thought danger a sport and death a feast; yea, I know I leave behind me such a company as were fitter to watch by a sick body than to recover a sick State. And all the world shall witness that it is not the breath of me, which is but wind, or the love of the multitude, which burns as tinder, that I hunt after, but either to be valued by her above them that are of no value or to forget the world and to be forgotten by it."

Three days later he had occasion to write to Lord Willoughby concerning the troops at Berwick. He went on to speak of his own difficulties. "Now for myself. Into Ireland I go. The Queen hath irrevocably decreed it; the Council do passionately urge it; and I am tied in mine own reputation to use no tergiversation. And as it were *indecorum* to slip collar now, so would it also be *minime tutum*, for Ireland would be lost, and though it perished by destiny, yet I should only be accused for it, because I saw the fire burn, was called to quench it, and yet gave no help. I am not ignorant what are the disadvantages of absence; the opportunities of practising enemies when they are neither encountered nor overlooked; the constructions of Princes under whom *magna fama* is more dangerous than *mala* and *successus minus quam nullus* : the difficulties of a war where the rebel that hath been hitherto ever victorious is the least enemy that I shall have against me; for without an enemy, the disease of that country consumes our armies, and if they live, yet famine and nakedness makes them lose both heart and strength. And if victuals be sent over, yet there will be no means to carry it.

"And yet all these were better endured than to have a

Hanno at Carthage or a Cato at Rome, barking at him that is every day venturing his life for his country abroad. All those things, which I am like to see, I do now foresee. For the war is hard; *pulchra que difficilia*: the rebel successful; that only makes him worthy to be undertaken: the supplies uncertain; it is safer for me to perform as much as shall lie in me or depend upon me, and to show the world that my endeavours were more than ordinary, when the State that set me out must conspire with the enemy against me. Too ill success will be dangerous; let them fear that who allow excuses, or can be content to overlive their honour. Too good will be envious; I will never forswear virtue for fear of ostracism. The Court is the centre; but methinks it is the fairer choice to command armies than humours. In the meantime enemies may be advanced; so I show who should be, let fortune show who be. These are my private problems and nightly disputations, which from your Lordship, whom I account another myself, I cannot hide. Use them according to their nature and their author's purpose, that is, to commit them to no other eyes than your own."

Essex's position was certainly unenviable, but he had brought his difficulties on his own head. They were the inevitable sequel to the follies of the last eighteen months. He had claimed to be the second in the Kingdom, the only man capable of cleansing the Irish stable, and now he was taken at his word. Moreover, he was granted what he asked, which made the position more difficult, for if he should fail he would have no one to blame but himself.

As the days of his departure came nearer, he became more arrogant, and those who were not his blind followers found his claims intolerable. He argued the terms of his appointment, clause by clause. He threatened to resign, but then he was unwilling that anyone else should go. Bickerings and quarrels were constant. There was trouble with Sir Francis Vere, who was back at his post in the Low Countries. From him 2,000 trained men were demanded, in whose place Sir

William Knollys took over 2,000 men newly levied. Vere sent his worst men and kept the best officers.

At the end of February there was a sensational scandal. A young doctor of the law, named John Hayward, brought out a book called *The First Part of the Life and Reign of King Henry IV, Extending to the End of the First Year of His Reign*. The book itself was an elegant composition rather than serious history, and the speeches, of which there were a number, were pretty exercises of wit. But it was dedicated to Essex in a Latin Epistle which uttered some curious sentiments:

"Ἀρίστῳ καὶ γενναιοτάτῳ, *optimo et Nobilissimo (inquit* Euripides) *ex qua sententia tu primus ac solus fere occurebas (illustrissime comes) cuius nomen si Henrici nostri fronte radiaret, ipse et lætior et tuitior in vulgus prodiret. Magnus siquidem es, et presenti iudicio, et futuri temporis expectatione; in quo, veluti recuperasse nunc oculos, cæca prius fortuna videri potest: Dum cumulare honoribus eum gestit, qui omnibus virtutibus est insignitus. Hunc igitur si læta fronte excipere digneris, sub nominis tui vmbra (tanquam sub* Aiacis *clipio* Teucer *ille* Homericus) *tutissime latebit. Deus optimus maximus, celsitudinem tuam nobis reique publicæ diu seruet incolumem; quo nos videlicet tam fide quam armis potenti tua dextra defensi, vltique, diutina, cum securitate tum gloria perfruamur.*"

After the Dedication came a Preface to the Reader, which was signed " A. P." and began:

" Among all sort of human writers there is none that have done more profit or deserved greater praise than they who have committed to faithful records of Histories, either the government of mighty States or the lives and acts of famous men; for by describing the order and passages of these two, and what events have followed what counsels, they have set forth unto us not only precepts but lively patterns, both for private direction and for affairs of state."

Eighteen months before, when Essex's discontented followers came back from the Islands Voyage, there had been some half-serious joking about the historical parallel between the times of Richard the Second and the present, with Essex as a second Bolingbroke. Whether by accident or design, the behaviour of Bolingbroke in the play of *Richard the Second* which the Lord Chamberlain's players were acting in the Theatre seemed to be modelled on Essex's public manners:

" Ourself and Bushy, Bagot here and Green
Observ'd his courtship to the common people,
How he did seem to dive into their hearts
With humble and familiar courtesy,
What reverence he did throw away on slaves,
Wooing poor craftsmen with the craft of smiles
And patient underbearing of his fortune,
As 'twere to banish their affects with him.
Off goes his bonnet to an oyster-wench;
A brace of draymen bid God speed him well,
And had the tribute of his supple knee,
With ' Thanks, my countrymen, my loving friends ';
As were our England in reversion his,
And he our subjects' next degree in hope."

Moreover, Essex himself used to go to watch the play, and applauded it greatly. As a result, when *The Tragedy of King Richard the Second* was printed in the late summer of 1597, albeit with the Deposition Scene judiciously omitted, it was surprisingly popular, and quickly went into three editions. Much had happened since then to make the historical parallel more significant, and the appearance of Hayward's book at such time seemed to be portentous. What did the Dedication mean ? And who was this A. P. ?

On March 25, Essex's instructions as Lieutenant and Governor-General of Ireland were signed at Richmond. They began by setting forth that any person appointed to manage an affair of this nature could not but have a great sense and feeling of the honour and its responsibilities, for he was chosen after comparison with all the Queen's servants out of former experience of his faith, valour, wisdom, and extraordinary merit. He would need no instruction, yet it was not amiss to prescribe certain things to be observed. He should assemble the Council of Ireland and learn the state of the country. Religion, justice, dishonest finance, economy of military stores and treasure, all must be carefully watched. He might order extraordinary payments by *concordatum*, but the power should be used economically and within the limit laid down. Knighthood should not be conferred upon any who did not deserve it by some notorious service, or who had not an income suitable to the degree. As for Tyrone, he was to be received only on terms of simple submission, and if pardoned, he was to find good security against further disloyalty.

Two days later, at Essex's own request, the Queen signed a licence that he might return to her presence at such times as he should find cause, leaving two Lords Justices there as deputies in his absence.

At 2 o'clock in the afternoon of March 27, Essex took horse at Essex House and set out for Chester. It was a triumphal departure. Many noblemen and gentlemen rode with him as he passed through the streets of the City, and everywhere the citizens flocked out to cheer as he went. For four miles the crowds followed, crying out, " God save your Lordship ! " " God preserve your Honour ! " Some even followed until the evening for the very joy of looking at him. The afternoon was calm and clear as he started, but when the cavalcade reached Islington a sudden spring storm gathered and broke over them with a great downpour of rain and hail, which seemed to the more superstitious a bad omen at his departure.

Essex himself had no great enthusiasm for his journey. He appreciated the difficulties too well, and from the first there were irritations and crosses. At Bromley, where he rested the night of April 1/2, he received a report delivered by Sir Calisthenes Brooke of the wretched state of the army in Ireland, which he forwarded to the Council. He was annoyed with the Queen. He desired that Sir Christopher

Blount, his stepfather, whom he had appointed Marshal of the Army, should be made a member of the Council of Ireland, and the Queen refused. Nor was his health good. He sent Blount back to Court and wrote woefully to the Council:

"I did only move her Majesty for her service to have given me one strong assistant, but it is not her will. What my body and mind will suffice to, I will by God's grace discharge with industry and faith. But neither can a rheumatic body promise itself that health in a moist, rotten country, nor a sad mind vigour and quietness in a discomfortable voyage. But I sit down and cease my suit, now I know her Majesty's resolute pleasure. Only I must desire to be freed from all imputation, if the body of the army prove unwieldy, that is so ill furnished, or so unfurnished, of joints; or of any maim in the service, when I am sent out maimed beforehand. I have returned Sir Christopher Blount, whom I hoped to have carried over; for I shall have no such necessary use of his hand, as, being barred the use of his head, I would carry him to his own disadvantage, and the disgrace of the place he should serve in."

The letter was delivered at Court the next day, and a reply promptly sent that the Queen wished Sir Christopher to go; she very well allowed of his sufficiency for the place of Marshal, but he was to blame in desiring the place of a Councillor.

Essex and his company reached Chester on April 4, and the next day he again wrote to the Council, protesting against the Queen's decision, and lamenting that she would not support him in his undertaking. "But, my Lords, it must be all our devout prayers to God, and our humble suit to her Majesty, that she will be as well served by her vassals as obeyed; and that, when she grants not the ability, she will not expect nor exact great performance. For myself, if things succeed ill in my charge, I am like to be a martyr for her. But, as your Lordships have many times heard me say, it had been far better for her service to have sent a man favoured by her, who should not have had these crosses and discouragements, which I shall ever suffer. Of your Lordships I do entreat that you will forget my person, and the circumstances of it; but remember that I am her Majesty's minister in the greatest cause that ever she had; that though to keep myself from scorn and misery, it shall be in mine own power, yet to enable me to reduce that rebellious kingdom of Ireland to obedience, lies in her Majesty; for, if I have not inward comfort, and outward demonstration of her Majesty's favour, I am defeated in England."

Next day he went on board the *Popinjay* at Hillbree, waiting for a favourable wind, and once more, in a personal letter to Cecil, he complained, " As for Sir Christopher Blount's ill success, or rather mine for him, I fear it will be suitable to all my speed, when I sue or move for anything. I sued to her Majesty to grant it out of favour, but I spake a language that was not understood, or to a goddess not at leisure to hear prayers. I since, not for my sake, but for her service' sake, desired to have it granted, but I see, let me plead in any form, it is in vain. I must save myself by protestation that it is not Tyrone and the Irish rebellion that amazeth me, but to see myself sent on such an errand, at such a time, with so little comfort or ability from the Court of England to effect that I go about. But *video, taceo*." It was self-delusion, for Essex never learnt to keep silent, and from the first he was obsessed with the thought that all his actions were being deliberately crossed by the Queen and his enemies at Court.

The weather continued contrary, with fog and mist. Essex was so eager to get over, and so uncomfortable on board the crowded ship, that he landed again, took post horses over the Welsh hills, and arrived at Beaumaris at midnight on the 10th-11th, wet through. Meanwhile the army had been shipped over from Chester and was lying at Dublin in great discomfort, and already there were many sick.

Essex reached Dublin on the 14th, after a rough and dangerous passage, and immediately went on shore. Soon afterwards there was almost an alarming accident, for the *Popinjay* and *Charell*, which contained the Queen's treasure, both bearing full sail, narrowly missed ramming each other.

The next day Essex received the Sword of State and was formally admitted to his office as Lord Lieutenant. His first official action was to demand of the Council a report on the state of Ireland. This was delivered to him on the 17th, and it was estimated, with a nice exactness, that the forces of the rebels numbered in all 17,997, of whom 8,922 were in Ulster. Then, explaining that his powers as Lieutenant-General allowed it, Essex defied the Queen and appointed Southampton his General of Horse.

The first week was spent in consultations with the Council. Essex first proposed, according to the plan often discussed with the Queen and the Privy Council, to attack Tyrone in Ulster. The Council unanimously opposed the plan. They pointed out that there were various practical objections, principally connected with supplies and transport. To feed the army requisite for a distant expedition cattle were necessary. These were not only scarce, but in such poor condition at this time of the year that they could not be driven with the army nor were they worth eating. Nor, if the army was to be fed on dry rations, was local transport available, and, owing to the contrariety of the wind, the transport horses from England had not yet arrived. The best time to attack Ulster would be mid-June or early July, when the rebels' cows and corn could most effectively be destroyed. They advised, therefore, that an immediate invasion of Leinster should be undertaken.

Essex agreed to their proposal and reported his intention to the Privy Council. At the same time he asked that 2,000 men should be sent as reinforcements by June 1, with 200 additional transport horses, and all necessary supplies and stores. The Council wrote back, some days later, that the Queen approved the plan of invading Leinster, but the reinforcements were not convenient. They were not due until the end of July, and to send them earlier would increase the Queen's charges. They suggested that casualties might be replaced by volunteers from the English who had been driven out from Munster.

Essex set out from Dublin on May 9. Just before he went, he signed a despatch to the Privy Council in reply to their letter, again urging that men and supplies should be sent. As for local voluntaries, they were useless; they had forsaken their own homes and lost strong castles without striking a blow; it would be a waste of weapons to arm them, and, besides, they had fled. For munitions, though he had a sufficient supply of powder and lead, the real need was swords and long targets, for most of the fighting would be in woods and passes. They would need 12,000 suits of clothing, and victuals for that number, for they could not live upon a country so spoiled.

The force taken upon the expedition numbered about 3,000 foot with 260 horse, of which about a hundred were Irish. The foot had been sent ahead the day before, whilst Essex himself stayed behind to supervise the transport of the stores and munitions, for the baggage animals were so few that they had to make a double journey. The first halt was at Naas, where Essex joined the army in the evening. Three days later his force was increased by 700 foot and 200 Irish horse under the command of the Earl of Ormonde.

The first objective was to provision and garrison the fort at Maryborough. On May 14, there was a cavalry skirmish. About 200 rebels were seen in the neighbourhood of Castle Reban. Southampton in command of a small body of foot and cavalry advanced towards them and they retired to the woods, where they were pursued by Lord Grey and his cavalry well beyond the limits ordered, with the result that Southampton severely reprimanded Grey and put him under arrest for the night.

The first serious resistance was made by the rebels about two days later when the army was nearing Ballyknockan, which was about two miles south of Maryborough. The Irish were seen in great numbers towards evening and the next morning, and clearly intended to attack the army as it made its way through the pass called Cashel. This pass could have been avoided by taking a detour round the mountains, but it was resolved as a matter of principle that the rebels should be taught that the Queen's armies could go where they please, and that the pass should be forced. A reconnaissance showed that the pass was about a quarter of a mile long, wooded on both sides, and behind the woods a high hill on the one side and a bog on the other. At the farther end was a ford where the rebels had dug trenches. The intention of the rebels was to wait until the convoy had entered the pass, which would be choked with men and beasts, and then to set on. This plan was neatly foiled.

Essex sent forward an advanced guard of 100 men, in the proportion of three ranks musketeers to two ranks short weapons, with a body of pioneers. Before the advanced guard marched the forlorn hope, consisting of forty shot and twenty short weapons with the order that the shot were not to fire until they presented their pieces to the rebels' breasts in their trenches. They were supported by two bodies each of 300–400. On either side of the pass a flank-guard was posted, which was increased as the enemy were seen to be massing. The advanced guard reached the ford without opposition and soon prepared a way through the trenches. Then the cavalry rode down through the flank-guards and beyond into the open country. The way was now open for the convoy to enter the pass. The rebels began to attack, but were held back for two hours until the convoy was safely through, but the rear-guard came in for stiff fighting. The total losses in the day's fighting were two officers and three other ranks killed, and two officers and six other ranks wounded. Essex himself showed great energy and bravery, dashing from one end of the pass to the other, directing in turn the vanguard, the battle, and the rear-guard.

From Maryborough Essex marched to Kilkenny, where the inhabitants received him with orations and strewed the streets with herbs and rushes. From Kilkenny Essex wrote to the Privy Council, enclosing a journal of his journey, and commenting on his first experiences of the enemy:

"This people against whom we fight hath able bodies, good use of the arms they carry, boldness enough to attempt, and quickness in apprehending any advantage they see offered them. Whereas our new and common sort of men have neither bodies, spirits, nor practice of arms, like the others. The advantage we have is more horse, which will command all champaigns; in our order, which these savages have not; and in the extraordinary courage and spirit of our men of quality. But, to meet with these our helps, the rebels fight in woods and bogs, where horse are utterly unserviceable; they use the advantage of lightness and swiftness in going off, when they find our order too strong for them to encounter; and, as for the last advantage, I protest to your Lordships it doth as much trouble me as help me. For my remembering how unequal a wager it is to adventure the lives of noblemen and gentlemen against rogues and naked beggars, makes me take more care to contain our best men than to use their courages against the rebels. And, had I not in the last day's fight tethered them, and assigned not only their places, but their very limits of going on, doubtless many of them would have been too far engaged. For I assure your Lordships, greater forwardness and contempt of danger could not be showed by any man, than was by the Lords and other principal men of quality in the army; which proves them to be such a treasure to her Majesty as I must husband with all the care and industry I have."

On May 21, Essex returned to his camp, and by the 25th he reached Waterford. His next objective was the Castle of Cahir, which belonged to Thomas Butler, Lord of Cahir, but was now held by the rebels. It was very strongly situated on a rocky island in the river, and elaborately fortified. Lord Cahir promised that the Castle would surrender as soon as

Essex approached, but the rebels within defied them. Essex determined to force a surrender. From Waterford a cannon and a culverin were laboriously manhandled, and at night the cannon was set up within fifty paces of the Castle on a platform, and protected with gabions. The culverin was set up farther off at a flank.

On the morning of May 27, both pieces were discharged. At the second shot the cannon broke its undercarriage and was out of action for a day and a half. The culverin also jammed for a time, but was eventually cleared and fired fifty rounds in all during the day. As evening came on Essex sent Captain Brett and Captain Chamberlain with 300 men to take possession of the orchard, which was effected with some loss. Next day the culverin was drawn nearer, and after a day's bombardment by both pieces large breaches were torn in the walls. The engineers were ordered to prepare ladders, scaffolds, and sows to protect the assaulting infantry, whilst the chief petarryer prepared his petards. In the night the enemy attempted a sally, but they were so roughly handled by the troops of Sir Charles Percy and Sir Christopher St. Lawrence that the few survivors escaped by swimming. Thereupon the Castle was entered.

Elsewhere there was a regrettable reverse. Shortly after his arrival Essex despatched Sir Henry Harington with some 500 foot and 50 horse to garrison Wicklow. On May 28, learning that a large force of rebels was assembled near the Ranelagh river, Harington led his men out to meet with the enemy. The enemy fired volleys into the camp at night. Next morning Harington, realising that the rebels were too numerous for him to attack, decided to retire to Wicklow. The rebels came on, and though the rear-guard put up a resistance, the enemy worked round the flanks and fell on the main battle. The English shot immediately discharged their pieces, threw them away, and ran for their lives. The pikes were seized with panic and joined in the rout, being led by Lieutenant Peter Walshe, who mounted a horse and galloped for Wicklow.

The horse fought bravely, but could not stem the rebels, who went on with their killing until they were within half a mile of Wicklow. When the roll was called 250 were missing.

On June 4, Essex reached Limerick, where he was joined by the Lord President of Munster, Sir George Carew. On the 11th he continued the march forward, having learnt that a considerable force of the enemy meant to oppose him. Lord Grey, who was in command of the vanguard, soon discovered the advanced troops of the enemy and drove them in, pursuing them, as usual, too far. When the infantry of the vanguard came up, the rebels from a great wood on their right began to open fire. Essex called off his vanguard, which retired to draw the enemy after them, when a charge by the cavalry drove them back with heavy loss. There was no further opposition, and the army encamped the night by Crumme Castle.

Next day Essex and Carew met at Killmalough and then conferred how the army might be victualled, for by this time the available money had been spent and there was no victual left in store, and only two days' supply of cows. On the 13th the army resumed the march, and on the 18th a council of war was held in Essex's tent at a little village two miles from Dungarvan. Here he discussed with Carew the forces necessary to keep Munster. After the council had broken up, Essex drew up Carew's instructions, which were, in general, that by spoiling and burning he should make the country unendurable either for its inhabitants or for any reinforcements from overseas. On the 21st Essex lodged in Waterford.

On June 22, the army crossed the river between Waterford and Wexford at the Passage. It was a slow business, because the troops were accompanied by excessive transport, with the result that when Essex rejoined the army from Waterford he found that his horse had not yet crossed. The march was continued along the sea coast and Essex lodged for the night at Ballingar, and marched thence to Enniscorthy. Here a council of war was held, and it was decided to go to Ferns and then to Arklow, because the route through the Duffrey was defended, and the rebels were assembled in force, against whom Essex could now only assemble 1,200, apart from the sick and wounded. The column was considerably hampered by at least three times as many camp followers, who had to be guarded.

So far there had not been any resistance since leaving Waterford, but as the army neared Arklow it was reported that the rebels would dispute the passage on the next day. On the 30th the army marched ready for battle, and to annoy the enemy the more, everything within reach on the line of march was burnt. Four miles from Arklow the enemy's forces had been drawn down to the side of a river, which was parallel with the highway and within musket range. The army crossed by a ford and kept along the sea side, but the enemy made small resistance and an attempt to draw them after the rear-guard into an ambush failed. For the next two miles there was open country, out of which rose a steep ascent, and at the top two high hills on either side.

Essex rode up to view the position and saw that a most dangerous situation was developing. The vanguard had already reached Arklow, but having been led by their guides along the sea side, where they could neither see nor be seen by the rest of the army, they had lost touch with the convoy. Hither about 800 foot and 40 horse of the enemy were hastening to cut off the convoy and a flank-guard of some 50 to 60 foot. Essex sent to the Sergeant Major, then leading the rear-guard, for 300 of the lightest foot and all the horse, and meanwhile galloped with Southampton and his troop to rescue the flank-guard.

The rebels made a stand in a bog behind which was a shrubby wood connecting it to the sandhills. Essex sent all the gentlemen who were mounted with Southampton to the plain on the right hand while he drew down to the wings. The rebels seeing this force to be but small, came on shouting, but Southampton immediately charged and drove them back into the wood so far as the bog would allow. Indeed, three of the gentlemen were badly bogged and obliged to quit their horses.

On the other flank Essex sent down Lieutenant Bushell to lead a wing at the same instant as Southampton charged, and to succour these he sent Ensign Constable with some foot. The men were fearful, but the Ensign was able to make them stand firm and keep order and to refrain from uttering noises of fear and amazement just in time for them to put up a show of resistance. Fortunately the oncoming rebels halted for their main body to arrive, which enabled Essex to reinforce Southampton. There was some sharp fighting in the wood, but reinforcements, both from the vanguard and rearguard, were at hand, and the enemy at length fled in disorder. Many threw away their arms and some were bogged in trying to escape. Except for the pursuit, the fight was over, and the army moved to Arklow, having lost one gentleman and two common soldiers.

After the fight, Phelim McFeaghe, one of the chief rebel leaders, called to an Irish soldier and asked him to tell the Lord General that he craved leave to come to him on condition that he might have safe return. Essex replied to the messenger that if he was asking for a passport as a repentant rebel to tender absolute submission, he might come, but if otherwise the messenger would be executed, for he would not suffer his commission to be dishonoured by treating or parleying with rebels. The night was spent at Arklow. Next day the army moved towards Wicklow and encamped on the scene of the disaster to Sir Henry Harington.

On July 1, Essex forwarded the usual journal of the campaign with a brief covering letter to the Privy Council, in which, after noting that his health had been affected by the continual labour of the last two months, he added:

"The only gloss I can make upon the plain and true text I send, is this, that if so much hath not been here performed, as is there by her Majesty expected, either it hath been because she made choice of an insufficient minister, or else because it hath pleased her to match him with a weak and insufficient Council. For I may boldly protest that I have not failed to execute that which either myself could conceive, or what was remonstrated to me by my fellows, to be for the advancement of her Majesty's service. But, as I ever said, I ever must say; I provided for this service a plastron and not a curate; that is, I am armed on the breast, but not on the back."

Essex returned to Dublin on the 11th. Here he met the Council, and having set affairs in order, he retired for three days to purge. On the 15th, a court-martial was held on the survivors of the Wicklow disaster. Lieutenant Peter Walshe, who had been the first to show cowardice in the face of the enemy, was condemned to death and executed. The other officers, though they did not forsake their posts but were deserted by their men, were cashiered because they did nothing extraordinary in such a crisis. The private soldiers were all condemned to be hanged, but Essex pardoned most of them, ordering that only one in ten should be executed for example's sake. Sir Henry Harington himself, because he was a member of the Council in Ireland, was committed to the Provost Marshal until the Queen's pleasure was known.

Essex then wrote a long despatch to the Privy Council on the general situation. The establishment of his army was 1,300 horse and 16,000 foot; the rebels were far more numerous, and were much increased because they had recently received a supply of arms and munitions from Spain. His own force was decreasing daily by sickness. Allowing for the necessary forces to deal with the enemy in Munster, Leinster, and Connaught, there would remain less than 6,000 foot and 500 horse for the campaign in Ulster. These were not sufficient, for if the proposal to establish a strong garrison at Lough Foyle and to advance simultaneously by Armagh were to be carried out, then either force might be overwhelmed separately. Moreover, very heavy casualties were to be expected.

Unless, therefore, he received considerable reinforcements, the full plan for the Ulster campaign could not be attempted.

There was also the problem of supply. Much of the victual sent over from England was so unsavoury and unserviceable that it would poison the soldiers. Ample supplies for the garrisons were essential, or a large part of the remaining troops would be constantly taken up in convoy duty. Clothing would also be necessary. Essex recommended that the troops should be allowed to buy their clothes in Ireland. He also asked that he might increase his army by a further 2,000 which he would draw from the rebels.

The next day a letter from the Privy Council answering his letter of July 1 was received, in which they congratulated him on his safe return and expressed their great contentment at the success of his journey.

Essex thanked them for their favourable letters, but he went on to repeat more forcibly than before his old complaint that he was being calumniated at home, " in telling your Lordships I came provided of a plastron, or fore-part of an armour, I understood all provisions for the war of Ireland, and resolution to encounter both the Irish rebel and foreign invader; and in professing myself unarmed on my back, I meant that I lay open to the malice and practice of mine enemies in England, who first procured a cloud of disgrace to overshadow me, and now in the dark give me wound upon wound. I know that those who are guilty of them will confidently deny, and cunningly distinguish to excuse themselves. And they are at better leisure than I to study their shifts, and give themselves more liberty to save themselves, they having now compassed their own ends. But England and Ireland, subjects and rebels, do not only familiarly speak of the power they have had in this my absence to supplant me in the favour of my Sovereign, and the insolent liberty they take to scoff and jest at me and my services; but also make collections of every circumstance, wherein I have been offered, since my coming over, disgraces and discomforts.

"The particulars I beseech your Lordships not to press me to recite; for I shall *infandum renovare dolorem*. Your Lordships' own memories, and the Council book, wherein all your despatches are recorded, will make up some part of this account. And as reason of state doth teach that a difficult war cannot be successfully managed by a disgraced minister, so experience, even in this short time, hath proved that a combination of proud, malicious, and successful rebels will not be subdued or daunted, nor an army that serves in a miserable, wretched country will be kept in strength and vigour, by any man that is not countenanced and enabled by all the circumstances of favour that can be; which ere long will more plainly appear. For as, before my time, the Irish subjects, seeing the prosperous proceeding of traitors, did ordinarily and familiarly ask leave to make their peace with them; so now I doubt not but our English voluntaries and persons of quality will ask passport of me (who am utterly unable either to advance or to defend them) to go make their own compositions with such as they have offended by following me thus long. But no more, neither now nor hereafter, of this argument."

Essex was far from happy at the results of his first three months in Ireland, and was thus endeavouring to anticipate the criticisms which he knew would be made that, after all his talk at Court, he had himself achieved nothing very striking. His worst apprehensions were soon confirmed. A few days later he received a letter from the Queen herself, dated July 19. It contained a full, accurate, and very unkind survey of his actions and her own difficulties, which Essex seldom if ever appreciated.

"We have perceived by your letters to our Council, brought by Henry Carey, that you are arrived at Dublin after your journey into Munster; where, though it seemeth, by the words of your letter, that you have spent divers days in taking an account of all things that have passed since you left that place, yet have you in this despatch given us small light either when, or in what order, you intend particularly to proceed to the northern action. Wherein, if you compare the time that is run on, and the excessive charges that is spent, with the effects of anything wrought by this voyage (howsoever we may remain satisfied with your own particular cares and travails of body and mind), yet you must needs think that we, that have the eyes of foreign Princes upon our actions, and have the hearts of people to comfort and cherish, who groan under the burden of continual levies and impositions, which are occasioned by these late actions, can little please ourselves hitherto with anything that hath been effected. For what can be more true (if things be rightly examined) than that your two months' journey hath brought in never a capital rebel, against whom it had been worthy to have adventured one thousand men. For of their two comings in, that were brought unto you by Ormonde (namely, Mountgarrett and Cahir), whereupon ensued the taking of Cahir Castle, full well do we know that you would long since have scorned to have allowed it for any great matter in others, to have taken an Irish hold from a rabble of rogues, with such force as you had, and with the help of the cannon, which was always able in Ireland to make his passage where it pleased. And, therefore, more than that, you have now learned, upon our expenses, by knowledge of the country, that those things are true, which we have heretofore told you, if you would have believed us, how far different things would prove from your expectation.

" There is little public benefit made to us of any things happened in this action, which the President, with any convenient addition to his numbers by you, might not have affected, either now or hereafter, in a time more seasonable, when it should less have hindered the other enterprise, on which depends our greatest expectation. Whereunto we will add this one thing, that doth more displease us than any charge or expense that happens, which is, that it must be the Queen of England's fortune (who hath held down the greatest enemy she had), to make a base bush kern to be accounted so famous a rebel, as to be a person against whom so many thousands of foot and horse, besides the force of all the nobility of that kingdom, must be thought too little to be employed.

"For we must now remember unto you, that our cousin of Ormonde, by his own relation when you arrived, assured us that he had delivered you a charge of a kingdom, without either town of ours maritime, or inland, or hold, possessed by the traitors. But we did ever think that Tyrone would please himself to see such a portion of our fair army, and led by the person of our General, to be harassed out and adventured in encountering those base rogues, who were no way strengthened by foreign armies, but only by such of his offal, as he was content to spare and let slip from himself; whiles he hath lived at his pleasure, hath spoiled all where our army should come, and preserved for himself what he thought necessary.

"Little do you know how he hath blazed in foreign parts the defeats of regiments, the death of Captains, and loss of men of quality in every corner; and how little he seemeth to value their power, who use it so as it is likely to spend itself. It is, therefore, apparent that all places require not one and the selfsame knowledge, and that drafts and surprises would have found better success than public and notorious marches; though, where the rebel attends you with greater forces, it is necessary that you carry our army in the form you use.

"But it doth sound hardly in the ears of the world, that in a time when there is a question to save a kingdom, and in a country where experience giveth so great advantage to all enterprises, regiments should be committed to young gentlemen that rather desire to do well than know how to perform it. A matter wherein we must note that you have made both us and our Council so great strangers, as to this day (but by reports) we know not who they be that spend our treasure and carry places of note in our army. Wherein you know we did by our instructions direct you as soon as you should be arrived, seeing you used reasons why it could not be done so conveniently beforehand.

"These things we would pass over, but that we see your pen flatters you with phrases, that here you are defeated, that you are disgraced from hence in your friends' fortune, that poor Ireland suffers in you; still exclaiming against the effects of your own causes. For if it be not enough that you have all, and more than, that which was agreed on before you went, concerning public service, but that you must, by your voluntary actions there in particular things (which you know full well are contrary to our will and liking), raise an opinion that there is any person that dare displease us, either by experience of our former tolerations, or with a conceit to avoid blame by distinctions; then must we not hide from you (how much soever we do esteem you, for those good things which are in you), but that our honour hath dwelt too long with us, to leave that point now uncleared, that whosoever it be that you do clad with any honours or places wherein the world may read the least suspicion of neglect or contempt of our commandments, we will never make dainty to set on such shadows as shall quickly eclipse any of those lustres.

"And, therefore, although by your letter we found your purpose to go northward, on which depends the main good of our service, and which we expected long since should have been performed, yet because we do hear it bruited (besides the words of your letter, written with your own hand, which carries some such sense), that you who allege such weakness in our army by being travailed with you, and find so great and important affairs to digest at Dublin, will yet engage yourself personally into Offaly (being our Lieutenant), when you have there so many inferiors able enough to victual a fort, or seek revenge of those that have lately prospered against our forces; and when we call to mind how far the sun hath run his course, what dependeth upon the timely plantation of our garrisons in the north, and how great a scandal it would be to our honour to leave that proud rebel unassailed, when we have, with so great an expectation of our enemies, engaged ourself so far in the action, so as without that be done, all these former courses will prove like *via navis in mari*; besides that our power, which hitherto hath been dreaded by potent enemies, will now be even held contemptible amongst our rebels; we must now plainly charge you, according to the duty you owe us, so to unite soundness of judgment to the zeal you have to do us service, and with all speed to pass thither in such order, as the axe may be put to the root of that tree, which hath been the treasonable stock from whence so many poisoned plants and grafts have been derived. By which proceeding of yours, we may neither have cause to repent our employment of yourself for omitting these opportunities to shorten the war, nor receive (in the eye of the world) imputation of too much weakness in ourself to begin a work without better foresight. What would be the end of our excessive charge, the adventure of our peoples' lives, and the holding up of our own greatness, against a wretch whom we have raised from the dust, and who could never prosper, if the charges we have been put to were orderly employed?

" For the matter of Southampton, it is strange to us that his continuance or displacing should work so great an alteration, either in yourself (valuing our commandments as you ought), or in the disposition of our army, where all the commanders cannot be ignorant that we not only not allowed of your desire for him, but did expressly forbid it; and being such a one whose counsel can be of little use, and experience of no great use; yea, such a one as, were he not lately fastened to yourself by an accident, wherein, for our usage of yours, we deserve thanks, you would have used many of your old lively arguments against him for any such ability or commandment. It is, therefore, strange to us that, knowing his worth by your report, and your own disposition from yourself in that point, you will dare thus to value your own pleasing in things unnecessary, and think by your private arguments to carry for your own glory a matter wherein our pleasure to the contrary is made notorious. And where you say further that divers, or the most, of the voluntary gentlemen are so discouraged thereby, as they begin to desire passports, and prepare to return, we cannot as yet be persuaded but that the love of our service, and the duty which they owe us, have been as strong motives to these their travails and hazards as any affection to the Earl of Southampton, or any other. If it prove otherwise (which we will not so much wrong ourself as to suspect), we shall have the less cause, either to acknowledge or reward it."

The Queen, indeed, showed such great indignation that the Council ventured to follow with a letter of their own, corroborating some points of her letter and ending with the regret that it should " bring your Lordship in some things no better contentment."

Essex's letter of July 18 had not been received when the Queen wrote. It was delivered at Court on the 28th. After her severe censure of his proceedings nothing could have been less opportune. The whole purpose of Essex's expedition, prepared with such enormous cost, was to attack Tyrone in his own country and to plant garrisons which would keep him quiet. Essex had wasted three months, and was now declaring that he would not go against the principal traitor unless he received vast increases of men and supplies. The request for reinforcements was most unseasonable because every man at the moment was needed at home. Intelligence seemed to show that the Spanish fleet was again at sea and that an invasion was imminent. As in 1588, a camp was prepared at Tilbury, and the trained men in the home counties were mobilised. There was such alarm that on August 7 general panic broke out in London; gates were shut, chains set across the streets, and everywhere wild rumours and the shrieks of terrified women. The reports, as was afterwards seen, were false, but the alarm persisted for a month.

The Queen wrote again on July 30, peremptorily demanding that Essex should do what he had been told.

" First, you know right well, when we yielded to this excessive charge it was laid upon no other foundation than that to which yourself did ever advise us as much as any, which was, to assail the Northern Traitor, and to plant garrisons in his country, it being ever your firm opinion, amongst others of our Council, to conclude that all that was done in other kind in Ireland, was but waste and consumption.

"If then you consider what month we are in, and what a charge we have ever been at, since the first hour of your arrival, even to the greatest proportion that was intended, when the general prosecution should be made, and what is done of effect in any other place (seeing every Province must require so great numbers as by your letters is set down), you may easily judge that it is far beyond our expectation to find you make new doubts of further proceeding into Ulster, without further increase of numbers, when no cause can be conceived by us, that you should hold the traitor's strength at higher rate than when you departed, except it be that by your unseasonable journey into Munster, and by the small effects thereof (in comparison of that we hoped this great charge should have effected), you have broken the heart of our best troops, and weakened your strength upon inferior rebels, and run out the glass of time which can hardly be recovered.

"For the present, therefore, we do hereby let you know, that the state of things standing as they do, and all the circumstances weighed, both of our honour and of the state of that kingdom, we must expect at your hands, without delay, the passing into the North, for accomplishment of those counsels which were resolved on at your departure, to the intent that all these six months' charges prove not fruitless, and all future attempts there as little successful; especially when these base rebels shall see their Golden Calf preserve himself without taint or loss, as safe as in his sanctuary, and our treasure, time, and honour, spent and engaged in other enterprises, which were always concluded to be of no difficulty, till the capital Rebel had been attempted."

At this point a doubt crossed the Queen's mind that Essex

might be goaded into some desperation. To his original instructions had been added a permission that he might return to England for consultation if he thought necessary. She did not wish to see him, and particularly in the present crisis. It might cause all kinds of disasters if Ireland should be left without a leader at this time.

She therefore added a paragraph, formally and explicitly commanding him not to return without leave; "in which respect, because we know that on your continuance there doth now depend the order and conduct of this important affair, and by your return suddenly (till the northern action be tried), many and great confusions may follow; our will and pleasure is, and so we do upon your duty command you, that, notwithstanding our former licence provisionally given, whereby you have liberty to return, and constitute some temporary Governor in your absence, that you do now in no wise take that liberty, nor adventure to leave that State in any person's government, but with our allowance first had of him, and our pleasure first known unto you what order you shall leave with him. After you shall have certified to us to what form you have reduced things in the north, what hath been the success, and whom you and the Council could wish to leave with that charge behind, that being done, you shall with all speed receive our warrant, without which we do charge you (as you tender our pleasure) that you adventure not to come out of that kingdom, by virtue of any former licence whatsoever."

Much as the Queen disliked the expenses of the Irish war, she was persuaded by the Privy Council to listen to Essex's arguments for reinforcements, and less than a week later the Privy Council wrote that Essex's request to increase his establishment by 2,000 had been allowed. They concluded their letter with the dignified protest " that those imputations of any indisposition towards you are so improper to us, as we will neither do your Lordship that wrong to take them so intended, nor ourselves that injury to go about to excuse them, knowing you too wise to apply those descriptions to any of us, and ourselves too honest to deserve any such exception; and therefore, as your Lordship pleased to say, that you will touch that point no more hereafter, so we desire to give you no occasion by our writing to revive it, nor any other of like nature."

Before this letter reached Essex, another lamentable disaster occurred. On Sunday, August 5, Sir Conyers Clifford, who was Governor of Connaught, set out from Athlone to rescue O'Connor Sligo, an Irish captain who was besieged by rebels in a castle five miles from Sligo, and thereby to create a diversion for a march into Ulster. The column consisted of 1,400 foot and 100 horse. When they reached the mountains called the Curlews, Clifford left the baggage and ammunition under guard of the cavalry, whilst with the foot he went forward to reconnoitre and make good the pass. They had not gone far when from the woods and bogs the rebels assailed them. The troops fought well till their ammunition failed, and then, being weary with the long march, they faltered, broke, and fled. The Irish pursued and made great slaughter. Conyers Clifford himself was killed, with Sir Alexander Ratcliffe, colonel of one of the three regiments. In all 10 officers and 231 men were killed, and 12 officers and 196 men wounded. The fugitives ran back to the transport, where fortunately the horse stood firm and beat back the rebels. The foot retired to Athlone by night; in the morning the cavalry who guarded the retirement also withdrew. It was reported after the action that most of the English casualties were caused by their own officers in trying to rally them. The enemy, so it was said, were only 200 strong.

Essex had written again on August 3 declaring that the Council of Ireland now unanimously voted against the invasion of Ulster, but that he himself, in spite of his misgivings, would obey the Queen's orders. This, coming so soon after the demand for reinforcements to undertake the invasion, still further increased the Queen's annoyance and the Privy Council's difficulties, who were the more disturbed because they had, in spite of the Queen's displeasure, supported Essex's request for reinforcements.

To add to his difficulties, Essex committed a further cause of offence to the Queen. Contrary to the express orders of his Instructions, he sought popularity with the gentlemen of his army by a lavish distribution of knighthoods. Knighthood was an honour which the Queen would keep select, and she was offended by Essex's generosity both at Rouen and after the taking of Cadiz. In Ireland he knighted fifty-nine gentlemen, and it was much noted as a strange thing that a subject in the space of eight years, who had not been six months continuously in any one campaign, should upon so little service and small desert make more knights than were in all the realm besides.

Essex was now in a state of utter perplexity and worry. He was nettled by the Queen's stinging letters, but he had no enthusiasm for an incursion into Ulster. On August 21, he summoned a general council of war at Dublin, and asked the opinion of his senior officers. When they had expressed their views he caused the resolution to be recorded in writing, to which everyone signed his name.

"AT H.M. CASTLE OF DUBLIN

" We the Lords, Colonels, and Knights of the army, being called to a council of war the day and year above written, at what time the Lord Lieutenant exponing to us his purpose of invading Ulster, as well in regard of her Majesty's express commandment, as also to pull down the pride of the arch traitor Tyrone, to redeem the late scorn of the Curlews, and lastly to hold up the reputation of the army, required us to deliver our opinions in what sort a present journey thither might be made; we who were then present, being thoroughly acquainted with the state of her Majesty's forces, as having particular charge of them, some as colonels over regiments, and some as captains over companies, after long debating, every one of us having spoken in order, at last by common consent resolved; that seeing the army so unwilling to be carried thither, that some secretly run into England, others revolt to the rebels, a third sort partly hide themselves in the country, and partly feign themselves sick; and seeing that there could be no planting this year at Lough Foyle, nor assailing of the North but one way, the Connaught army consisting of a great part of old companies being lately defeated, and that our army, which passeth not the number 3,500, or 4,000 at the most, of strong and serviceable men, should be far over-matched when all the forces of the North should encounter them; and sithence that it was a course full of danger, and of little or no hope, to carry the army into their strengths, where the rebels should be first lodged, and were able to bring 6,000 shot to entertain fight with less than 2,000; in which places also our horse should never be able to serve or succour our foot; and further, forasmuch as we could place no garrisons in the north, but such as consisted of very great numbers, and great numbers we could not spare from so small an army, with any likelihood of making a good retreat with the rest; to say nothing of the want of shipping, and especially of victualling, caused by the great decay thereof, and, lastly, sithence if we could spare a sufficient number and could lodge them at Armagh and the Blackwater, it would but tie the army to be ever busied in victualling them, consequently more incommodate us than trouble the rebels, as it appeareth in the former plantations there in the times of the Lord Burgh, Sir William Russell, and Sir John Norris. In regard of the premises we all were of opinion, that we could not with duty to her Majesty, and safety to this kingdom, advise or assent to the undertaking of any journey far north. In which resolution, if any man suspect it proceeded of weakness or baseness, we will not only in all likely and profitable service disprove him, but will every one of us seal with his life, that we dissuaded this undertaking with more duty than any man could persuade unto it."

This is signed by the Earls of Southampton and Kildare, Lord Castle Connell, Edward Wingfield, Oliver Lambert, Henry Power, Matthew Morgan, Henry Docwra, Thomas Jermyn, Henry Danvers, Francis Darcy, Samuel Bagnal, Arthur Champernowne, Robert Drury, Richard Wilmot, Edward Herbert, and John Bolle.

Then Essex changed his mind and, in spite of all advice to the contrary, he decided to risk the northern journey. On August 27, he despatched Cuffe, his secretary, to the Court with a letter enclosing the opinion of the Council of War. Next day, he sent off, with Sir William Lovelace, a brief note, written with his own hand to the Privy Council—

" I am even now putting my foot into the stirrup, to go to the rendezvous at the Navan; and from thence I will draw the army as far, and to do as much, as duty will warrant me, and God enable me."

Essex arranged to meet his army, which consisted of only 2,500 foot and 300 horse, near Kells, and a camp was made at Castlekeran. Here they awaited the arrival of supplies for four days whilst Essex reconnoitred the country round, and debated with his council the best winter quarters for a garrison to keep Tyrone out of the Pale. On September 2, the force moved towards Ferney and encamped for the night between Robertstown and Newcastle. Next day Essex rode to Ardolph where, for the first time, he saw the forces of Tyrone himself, in position on a hill a mile and a half away, but between the two armies lay a river and a wood. Essex drew up his army in battle formation and halted it on the hill by the burnt castle of Ardolph. The troops were without fuel for their fires. He therefore ordered that a foraging party from each company should go down to fetch wood, covered by a force of 500 foot and two companies of horse. Tyrone sent down some men to oppose their passage over the ford of the river, but with orders not to become engaged, and apart

ESSEX IN 1600

From an engraving in the British Museum, London.

from some skirmishing across the river each side left the other unmolested.

On the 5th, Essex marched his army through the open country to the mill of Louth, and encamped across the river towards Ferney. Tyrone followed, and bivouacked for the night in a neighbouring wood, keeping a screen of cavalry scouts between the two armies. Essex summoned his council of war and they debated whether to attack Tyrone. It was unanimously agreed that, with their army half the size of the rebel's, it would be folly to attack him in his trenches, but that the army should be drawn up to tempt him to attack if he would. The same day, however, Henry Hagan, Constable of Dungannon, came in as a messenger from Tyrone desiring a parley. Essex refused, but added that he would be at the head of his troops the next day on the hill between the two camps.

When morning came, leaving 500 foot and 20 horse to guard the camp, Essex led out the rest of his force and drew them up in battle formation on the nearest hill where Tyrone could see them. Then he marched forward to the next hill where Tyrone's guard of horse were posted. These withdrew, and Essex's force occupied the hill and proceeded to make it good. There was some skirmishing with the light horse, but little damage on either side. After a while one of the rebels cried out that Tyrone would not fight but desired to speak with the Lord Lieutenant, but not between the two armies. About three in the afternoon Essex withdrew to his camp.

Next morning the army was again on the march towards Drumconragh. After about a mile Hagan again appeared, and going up to Essex, who was riding with Southampton and other gentlemen of his staff, delivered the message that Tyrone desired the Queen's mercy, and that the Lord Lieutenant would hear him; and if he agreed to this, he would gallop about and meet his Lordship at the ford of Bellaclynthe, which was on the right hand by the way to Drumconragh.

On receipt of the message Essex sent two of his gentlemen forward to view the ford. They found Tyrone waiting, but the water was so far out that they thought it no fit place for a parley. At this Tyrone cried out, " Then I shall despair ever to speak with him "; but at last he showed a place where he could stand with his horse up to the belly in water and be heard by Essex from the hard ground.

As soon as he received the report of his gentlemen, Essex drew out a troop of horse and halted them on the hill overlooking the ford. Then seeing that Tyrone was still waiting for him, he rode forward alone. As he came nearer Tyrone saluted with great reverence. For the next half-hour they conversed together; then each rode back to his own people. A short while after, Con O'Niell, Tyrone's base-born son came down to the water to desire, from his father, that he might bring down some of his principal men and that his Lordship would send some of his to confer. Essex agreed that six should come. When they reached the ford Essex again rode down accompanied by Southampton, Sir Henry Danvers, Sir William Constable, and three other of his officers. At this second meeting Tyrone and his party halted as before in the water with bared heads whilst Essex and his stood on the hard ground. They conferred for half an hour, and it was then concluded that the next morning commissioners from either side should meet to conclude a truce. Essex returned to the army and marched to Drumconragh.

In the morning, as arranged, the English commissioners, who were Sir Warham Sentleger, Sir William Constable, and Henry Wotton, met Tyrone's commissioners, and thereupon it was agreed that there should be a cessation of arms for six weeks, to be renewed for periods of six weeks until May Day, or to be broken upon fourteen days' warning on either side. It was also agreed that such of Tyrone's confederates as should not assent to the cessation should be prosecuted by the Lord Lieutenant, and that restitution should be made for all spoils within twenty days after notice had been given. For performance of the covenants Essex was to give his word, and Tyrone his oath. The next day, which was September 9, the army began to march back to Dublin; Essex himself rode to Drogheda.

A few days later Cuffe delivered his letters, together with the signed opinion of the council of war, at the Court which was then at Nonsuch. Lovelace arrived on September 5, but no news of the Ulster venture had yet reached the Queen. The Council presented Cuffe's letters to the Queen. The Queen was bitterly angry, and on September 14 she wrote yet again.

"Having sufficiently declared unto you before this time how little the manner of your proceedings hath answered either our direction or the world's expectation, and finding now by your letters by Cuffe a course more strange, if strange may be, we are doubtful what to prescribe you at any time, or what to build upon your writing unto us in anything. For we have clearly discerned of late, what you have ever to this hour possessed us with expectation, that you would proceed as we have directed you; but your action always shows the contrary, though carried in such sort, as we were sure to have no time to countermand them. Before your departure, no man's counsel was held sound, which persuaded not presently the main prosecution in Ulster; all was nothing without that; and nothing was too much for that.

"This drew on the sudden transportation of so many thousands, to be carried over with you; and, when you arrived, we were charged with more than the list on which we resolved, by the number of 300 horsemen above the thousand, which was assented to, which were only to be in pay during service in Ulster. We have been also put in charge ever since the first journey, the pretence of which voyage, as appeared by your letters, was to do some present service in the interim, whiles that grew more commodious the main prosecution. For which purpose you did importune with great earnestness that all manner of provisions might be hastened to Dublin against your return. Of this resolution to defer your going into Ulster you may well think that we would have made stay, if you had given us more time by warning, or if we could have imagined, by the contents of your own writing, that you would have spent nine weeks abroad, and your return when the third part of July was spent; and that you had understood our mislike of your former course, and made your excuse of undertaking it, only in respect of your conformity to the Council's opinions, with great protestations, of haste to the north.

" Then we received another letter of new reasons to suspend that journey yet awhile, and to draw the army into Offaly, the fruit whereof at your homecoming was nothing else but new relations of further missing of our army, and greater difficulties to perform the Ulster wars.

" Then followed from you and the Council a new demand of two thousand men, to which, if we would assent, you would speedily undertake what we had so often commanded. When that was granted and your going onward promised by divers letters, we received by this bearer new fresh advertisement, that all you can do is to go to the frontiers, and that you have provided only twenty days' victuals.

" In which kind of proceeding we must deal plain with you and that Council that it were more proper for them to leave troubling themselves with instructing us by what rules our power and their obedience are limited, and bethink them of the courses that have been only derived from their counsel, and how to answer this part of theirs, to train us into a new expense for one end, and to employ it to another, to which we never would have assented, if we could have suspected it should have been undertaken before we heard it was in action; and therefore we do wonder how it can be answered, seeing your attempt is not in the capital traitor's country, that you have increased our list.

" But it is true, and we have often said, that we were ever

won to expense by little and little, and by protestation of great resolutions in generalities, till they come to particular execution, of all which causes whosoever shall examine any of the arguments used for excuse, shall find your own proceedings beget the difficulties, and that no just causes do breed the alterations of lack of numbers.

"If sickness of the army be the reason, why was there not the action undertaken when the army was in better state? If winter's approach, why were the summer months of July and August lost? If the spring were too soon, and the summer that followed otherwise spent, if the harvest that succeeded were so neglected as nothing hath been done, then surely we must conclude that none of the four quarters of the year will be in season for you and that Council to agree of Tyrone's persecution, for which all our charge is intended.

"Further we require you to consider whether we have not a great cause to think that your purpose is not to end the war, when you yourself have often told us that all the petty undertakings in Leix, Munster and Connaught, are but loss of time, consumption of treasure, and, most of all, our people, until Tyrone himself be first beaten, on whom all the rest depend. Do you not see that if this course be in all parts by his sinister seconding all places where any attempt may be offered, who do not see that if this course be continued, that it is like to spend us and our kingdom beyond all moderation, as well as the report of their success in all parts hath blemished our honour, and encouraged others to no small presumption? We know you cannot so much fail in judgment, as not to understand that all the world seeth how time is delayed, though you think that the allowance of that Council.

"How often have you told us that others, that preceded you, had no judgment to end the war, who often resolved us, until Lough Foyle and Ballyshannon were planted, there could be no hope of doing service upon the capital rebels? We must therefore let you know, as it cannot be ignorance, so it cannot be want of means; for you had our asking, you had choice of times, you had power and authority more ample than ever any had, or ever shall have. It may well be judged with how little contentment we seek this and other errors. But how should that be hid which is so palpable ?

"And therefore to leave that which is past, and that you may prepare to remedy matters of weight hereafter, rather than to fill your papers with impertinent arguments, being in your general letters savouring still in many points of humours that concern the private of you, our Lord Lieutenant, we do tell you plainly, and you that are of our Council, that we wonder at your indiscretion to subscribe to letters which concern our public service, and directed to our Council table, which is not wont to handle things of such small importance."

Still the Queen went on. Everything that Essex did was wrong, but what particularly annoyed her was the declaration of the Captains. That her General and Deputy should shelter behind the opinion of subordinates, many of them men of no standing, showed an intolerable weakness and lack of dignity. She continued:

"We have seen a writing, in a manner of a catalogue full of challenges, that are impertinent, and of comparisons, that are needless, such as hath not been before this time presented to a State, except it be done more with a hope to terrify all men from censuring your proceedings. Had it not been enough to send us the testimony of the Council, but that you must call so many of those, that are of so slender judgment and none of our Council, to such a form of subscription ? Surely, howsoever you may have warranted them, we doubted not but to let them know what belongs to us, to you, and them. And thus, expecting your answer, we end, at our Manor of Nonsuch, the 14th of September, 1599."

Essex returned to Dublin, where the Queen's letter reached him about a week later. This was too much. There was a limit even to his endurance of the Queen's temper. In his first anger, he conferred secretly with Southampton and Sir Christopher Blount, in Southampton's chamber in Dublin Castle. The two Earls were for armed rebellion. They would take two or three thousand of their best men and march on London, gathering reinforcements as they went. Blount was horrified; it would ruin Essex, and all who followed him. It was a foul plan, he cried, and would irrevocably blot his good name. Essex was persuaded to abandon the plan, but he resolved to go back to England at once, in spite of the Queen's direct prohibition, and to take with him sufficient picked men to secure him from arrest.

On September 24, he caused a commission to be drawn up constituting the Lord Chancellor Loftus and Sir George Carew Lords Justices of Ireland to act as his deputies, and with a party of his closest followers embarked secretly and put out to sea.

CHAPTER XIV

THE ECLIPSE

EARLY in the morning of Friday, September 28, Essex and his party cantered through Westminster and down to the River, where they left their horses and were rowed over to Lambeth. Here they found other horses waiting for the return of their riders over the ferry. Essex took them, and they rode on towards Nonsuch. Sir Thomas Gerrard, meanwhile, had brought Essex's own horses over by the ferry and rode after him with the news that Lord Grey was on the road ahead. Sir Thomas spurred his horse into a gallop, overtook Grey, and told him that the Earl of Essex was behind, if he would speak with him.

"No," replied Grey, "I have business at Court."

"Then I pray you," said Gerrard, "let my Lord of Essex ride before, that he may bring the first news of his return himself."

"Doth he desire it?" asked Grey.

"No," replied Gerrard insolently, "nor I think will desire nothing at your hands."

"Then," Grey said, "I have business." And with that he made off even faster, leaving Essex's party well behind. Sir Christopher St. Laurence, who was in the party, offered to overtake Grey and kill him, and then to murder the Secretary in Court; but Essex refused. As soon as he reached Court, Lord Grey went up to the Secretary to tell him the news; but no word was carried into the private apartments.

A quarter of an hour later—it was then about ten o'clock—Essex and his party reached the Court gate at Nonsuch. He dismounted, and without pausing even to wash his face of the mud of travel, he hastened up through the Presence

Chamber to the Privy Chamber, and passed right through to the Queen's bedchamber. No one had warned the Queen of his approach, and he found her newly up and still unadorned, with her hair about her face. No living man had ever seen her undressed before. He kneeled and kissed her hands. The Queen, completely taken by surprise, greeted him kindly. After a few words he withdrew to change his muddy clothes. The plan had succeeded so far, and he came away relieved and elated, remarking to those standing without that though he had suffered much trouble and storms abroad he found a sweet calm at home.

By eleven o'clock he was ready for a more formal audience, and for an hour and a half he talked to the Queen of his Irish affairs. She was still amicable, and very gracious. Then he came down to dinner, where his friends joined him, the Earls of Worcester and Rutland, Mountjoy, Lord Rich, Lord Henry Howard, and many others. The courtiers and the ladies flocked round eagerly as he talked of his travels, and the goodness of Ireland, and the entertainment which the loyal nobles had shown him. The Secretary and his party, the Earl of Shrewsbury, the Lord Admiral, Lord Thomas Howard, Lord Cobham, Grey, and Sir Walter Ralegh dined apart and aloof. Essex saluted them coldly, but on the rest of the excited courtiers he bestowed gracious words here and there.

Then for the third time he went back to the Queen. But her mood was changed. She asked him coldly why he had returned, and was very dissatisfied when she heard how he had come away leaving affairs in Ireland at such great hazard. She dismissed him to confer with the Council, and for an hour he sat with four of them, the Lord Chamberlain, Lord North, Secretary Cecil, and the Controller. Meanwhile the messengers were sent out to summon the rest of the Council to Court. That night, between ten and eleven o'clock, word came from the Queen that he should keep his chamber.

Amongst others, Francis Bacon came to visit him, and they

had a brief conversation. Essex asked Bacon what he thought of the Queen's action. He replied that it was a mist which would pass quickly, but he urged Essex to " take away by all means all umbrages and distastes from the Queen." Let him not pretend that the truce with Tyrone was in any way a glorious service, but a shuffling up of a prosecution that was not very fortunate. Nor should he in any way suggest to the Queen that she was obliged to send him back to Ireland. And, above all things, he must seek access to her, " *importune, opportune*, seriously, sportingly, every way." Essex said little in reply, but shook his head. It was a repetition of the old argument with Bacon on how best to manage the Queen, and he was still unconvinced.

The Council sat all the next morning; Essex was not summoned to the Council Chamber until two in the afternoon. As he entered, all the Councillors rose and saluted him, but when they sat down again he remained standing at the end of the table with bared head. Then the clerks were ordered to withdraw and the Secretary began to read out the list of his offences against the Queen. He had contemptuously disobeyed the Queen's letters and will in returning; he had written presumptuous letters; his proceedings in Ireland had been contrary to what was resolved before he went; his manner of coming away from Ireland was rash; his going to her Majesty's presence to her bedchamber yesterday was over bold; he had made over many idle knights. To all these charges Essex, keeping his temper, answered gravely and discreetly, for three hours. He came out of the Council Chamber and went to his chamber. The Lords sat for a quarter of an hour longer, and then they went in to the Queen and delivered their report. She answered that she would pause and consider.

The *coup* had failed. Without opposition, Essex had succeeded in breaking through to the Queen, and alone with her, face to face, he had felt, as often before, that his strength was greater than hers. She had heard him patiently and kindly, and would have taken his side. But as soon as she was decked out in her wig, and ruff, and her other personal defences, and her mind had been poisoned by the little Secretary with his suave, official subservience, all her old resentments flared up. Essex had simply put himself in her power as never before. He was a prisoner, and likely to face charges of contempt which might, in the hands of his enemies, be made very ugly. Moreover, after the turmoils and excitements of the last weeks he was suddenly quiet and alone. Had his entry into the Court been resisted, his followers would have fought for him. As it was they had dispersed, and any attempt would now be hopeless.

Essex remained in his chamber all Sunday. On Monday morning the Queen sent for the Lord Keeper, the Lord Treasurer, the Lord Admiral, and the Secretary to deliver her wishes. After some while they went together to consult, and then returned to her with the results of their conference. Thence they went to the Lord Keeper's Chamber and sent for Essex. As he came into their presence he made a low reverence and stood still. They desired him to come nearer. He moved forward and again bowed. Then he was told that it was the Queen's pleasure that he should leave the Court and be committed to the Lord Keeper's charge in York House. That afternoon the Earl of Worcester's coach was made ready in the stable yard, and Essex with his keeper journeyed to London. Only two of his servants were allowed to attend him, and few of his friends accompanied him, though by this time London was full of knights, captains, and soldiers from Ireland who were unwilling to continue in their commands when their General had left them. Their presence increased the Queen's anger. The next day the Court moved to Richmond.

Now that Essex was quite alone, reaction followed excitement. He lapsed into a blank and hopeless melancholy. There was no spirit or resolution left in him. His letters from Ireland were brought to York House; he sent them away unopened. He would receive no one unless sent by the Queen, saying that he had resolved to continue a true prisoner. Cecil visited him officially, declaring that he would do anything to further his good. Days passed, and the Queen still refused to declare her intentions. The mental worry of these lonely days was too much for him. He was suffering from dysentery when he left Ireland; he grew rapidly worse. His own doctors were anxious and wished to call Dr. Brown from the Court into consultation; he dared not go without the Queen's leave, and she was unwilling to grant more than that that he might confer with his colleagues.

Essex had now been a prisoner for three weeks and was daily growing weaker; he was eating little and sleeping less. Every day Court gossips knew for certain that the Queen was about to make up her mind. The Lords of the Council spoke for him, asking her to set him at liberty. She retorted angrily that so great a contempt should be publicly punished. To which they replied that by her sovereign power and the severity of the law he might be punished, but it stood not with her honour or her clemency to do it. Her answer was to command a summary of his offences to be prepared.

Meanwhile his friends were doing what they could. An attempt was even made to bring about a reconciliation with the Secretary, but Cecil was cautious and foresaw difficulties. Essex, he said, was inconstant in his love, and too violent in his passions. Besides, his estate was so broken that he would petition the Queen for help, and then if he should be denied, the old jealousies would break out again. Cecil did, however, go so far as to promise that he would show no malice, though he had every cause, seeing what bitter things Essex had spoken and written about him to the Queen.

The Queen herself was in a great difficulty, which was aggravated by the foolish gossip of Essex's friends. If she released him without any public trial or inquiry, then the world would say that he had been wrongly imprisoned. But she hesitated to order any inquiry, sensing that general sympathy was against her and with the lonely prisoner. She relented so far as to allow him to use the garden at York House.

Essex's friends were anxious. They, and he, feared that he would be committed to the Tower. Mountjoy had already been very active. Some weeks before, in the summer, he had sent through Henry Lee a message to the King of Scots to declare his own attachment to the King's right of succession, and at the same time to deny the slanders that were being put about by Essex's enemies that he was himself aiming at the Crown. Mountjoy, Southampton, and Sir Charles Danvers now met to consider plans of rescue, and several were discussed. Means might be found for him to escape to France, or to Wales, or else by filling the Court with his friends he might again make a way into the Queen's presence. Nothing definite was resolved, but a message was conveyed to Essex that if he would flee, then Southampton and Sir Charles Danvers would go with him and venture their lives to save him. Essex replied that if they could think of no better course for him than flight, he would rather run into any danger than live the life of a poor fugitive.

Essex grew worse. Still no news came from Court. The Countess of Essex was in the greatest distress, but though she was eager to join him, Essex refused, saying that he would see no one unless sent by the Queen. On Sunday, November 25, she came to Court, very meanly dressed in black, begging to see the Countess of Huntingdon, who sent out to know what she wanted. Her petition was that she might be permitted to go to her Lord who was now in extremity. The messenger returned with the reply that she must await the Queen's pleasure as signified by the Council, and must come no more to Court. The next night, the Court rumour was that Essex was to be sent to the Tower.

At last, on November 29, the long-expected pronouncement was made in the Star Chamber. It was the last meeting of the Court for the term, when it was customary for the

Lord Keeper to give his charge to the justices. Most of the Council and the judges were present, and many others of great account stood by. The Chamber was crowded. The Lord Keeper spoke first. There were many seditious people, he said, spread abroad to breed rebellion, who not only uttered false and slanderous speeches against the Queen and her Council, but had also thrown abroad many scandalous libels in the Court, city, and country. They were no better than traitors. He therefore charged all her Majesty's officers to make diligent inquiry after them and to bring them to punishment. Then he went on to enlarge on Irish affairs, detailing the forces which were supplied for the expedition, and its great cost, and how Essex was given everything that he demanded. And then how he had disobeyed his instructions, and finally, contrary to express command, returned to England.

The Lord Treasurer Buckhurst followed, giving particular details of the Irish army and its huge cost. The Lord Admiral spoke of the cost of transporting the army, declaring that with such an army he could have gone through all Spain. He spoke at length of the conference with Tyrone and the articles of his demand, which were not fit to be harkened unto. Other Councillors followed with their censures, Cecil enlarging on Essex's disobedience to the Queen's express command that he should stay in his place until she had appointed a successor.

This public declaration gave general satisfaction that the Queen had good reasons for her displeasure. Four days later Essex's household was dispersed. His servants, a hundred and sixty in number, were bidden to seek new masters, except for the few that were retained for his immediate attendance. Wiseacres shook their heads at the greatest downfall of a great man in living memory.

On Sunday, December 10, Essex was so ill that he prepared for death. He received Communion. Then he sent his patents as Master of the Horse and Master of the Ordnance to the Queen. She sent them back. Two days later the

Countess was at last allowed to visit him. There seemed little hope of his recovery, for he was so weak that to make his bed, he had to be lifted out in the sheets.

He had few visitors but divines, and amongst them Dr. John Overall, his old tutor at Cambridge, who found him very low spirited and in a state of melancholic piety. All his troubles, he said, were God's just judgments for his sins, and nothing, he thought, had offended God so much as his failure to observe the Sabbath duty. Might a man use any lawful recreation upon the Sabbath after evening prayer? he asked. Dr. Overall thought that he might, and quoted instances and arguments. "Well," sighed Essex, "if it may be so, yet it is safer to forbear; and hereafter I will forbear."

The depression lifted and Essex passed into an ecstasy of confession. If the sinner repented he would be forgiven. This good news must be passed on. He wrote a farewell to Southampton. Let him also repent and make his peace with God before it was too late. His appeal was not the mere vapour of melancholy or the style of a prisoner, but a necessary duty laid on him. "Think, therefore, dear Earl, that I have staked and bounded all the ways of pleasure to you, and left them as seamarks for you to keep the channel of religious ventures; for shut your eyes never so long, they must be opened at last, and then you must say with me, ' There is no peace to the wicked and ungodly; I will make a covenant with my soul,' nor suffer mine eyes to sleep in the night, nor my thoughts to attend the first business of the day, till I have prayed to my God that your Lordship may believe, and may profit by the plain but faithful admonition. And then I know your country and kind shall be happy, and you successful in all you undertake."

The Queen relented somewhat, when she heard of Essex's desperate sickness, and ordered that eight of the most experienced physicians should confer on the best means to effect his recovery. They replied that there was not much hope. Certain conditions were essential, a mind quieted, rest, recreation and a change of air, but he was beyond their physicking, except for gentle glisters to keep him clean within.

When this report was brought to the Queen, she was very grieved, and there were tears in her eyes. She sent Doctor James to him with some broth, and the message that, if she might with her honour, she would visit him. She also ordered that he should be removed to the Lord Keeper's own chamber.

Essex's danger was causing great sorrow in London. Divines prayed for him publicly—to the Queen's annoyance—and on December 10, on the report that he was dead, the bell was tolled. Both his sisters were graciously received by the Queen, and his wife was now with him from morning to night. His hopes revived and he took a turn for the better. By Christmas he was definitely on the mend, and on New Year's Day he even ventured to send a rich present to the Queen, which was neither accepted nor refused. As Essex's health rapidly improved, the Queen's irritation returned, and his gift was sent back. There was still no news of his release, and the Lord Keeper Egerton was tiring of his prisoner, who had now been with him for seventeen weeks; and, to add to other troubles, Lady Egerton died in the house on January 21, which he took so hardly that the Queen sent to remind him of his public duties.

In February it seemed that at last Essex was to be brought to trial before the Court of the Star Chamber, insomuch that a rail was set up to keep back the crowd from the place where he should stand. The trial was fixed for the 7th, but at the last moment Cecil prevailed on Essex to write a very submissive letter which he carried off to the Queen, and for the moment persuaded her to cancel the trial. As the Queen's decision was not made till nine at night, the crowd was not warned, and a great multitude assembled, to be disappointed of their spectacle. Cecil was much praised for this action, for it showed publicly that his malice towards Essex was far less than was usually supposed.

Amongst other preparations for the trial, Dr. Hayward's book about Henry the Fourth was closely examined. The author professed complete innocence that there was any topical or seditious significance in the text or prefaces, but he was not believed. The book was far too popular, and although suppressed, a surreptitious edition had been printed and many copies were abroad. The Lord Chief Justice himself drew up a list of pertinent questions. Who wrote the preface ? What made him conceive that the book might be " not only precepts but patterns for private direction, and for matters of state "? What was the true cause of his setting forth this story, omitting every principal point that told against the rebels ? Who had encouraged him ? When did he begin it ? How did he come by the records of those times ? Coke studied the book carefully, and made notes to prove that it was intended as an attack upon the Government. The prosecution had hoped to prove that Essex himself was responsible for it. The Queen even consulted Bacon, who replied that Hayward was guilty not of treason but of felony—he had stolen from so many authors.

The weary stay at York House still dragged on, and even Court rumours faded away. There was some irritation at the end of the month when it was known that Southampton and other of Essex's friends had entered a house overlooking the gardens of York House whence they saluted Essex below.

By the end of 1599 the state of Ireland was even worse than before Essex had set out. The rebels were so bold that they raided the English Pale almost nightly, even to the very gates of Dublin, and the division of sympathy in England between Essex and the Court party encouraged them to think slightingly of the Queen and whomsoever she should send over as the new Lord Deputy.

The Queen chose Lord Mountjoy. When he knew that he was for Ireland he was very anxious for Essex. He again consulted with Southampton and Sir Charles Danvers. First he made them swear on oath to defend the Queen and her

Government so long as she lived. Then he revealed his proposals. He would send Henry Lee once more to Edinburgh with an offer to the King of Scots. If the King would openly demand a declaration of his right of succession by assembling an army on the Borders and by sending an ambassador to London to publish his demands, then from Ireland he would bring over four or five thousand men; and these, with such friends as Essex would muster, would be enough to enforce the demand. Lee was sent, and remained for some weeks in Edinburgh, where his movements were closely reported to Cecil.

The establishment of Mountjoy's army was fixed at 12,000— a quarter less than Essex had been allowed. He reached Dublin on February 26, and at once the whole situation changed. Away from the intrigues of the Court, Mountjoy took up his duties with enthusiasm. Hitherto he had been overshadowed, and without any opportunity of distinguishing himself. In command, he revealed all those qualities which Essex lacked: talkers and popular men he disliked, he listened and said little; but the incompetents at Dublin soon realised that this quiet and modest man was iron-willed and deadly efficient. After a generation of muddle the change was exhilarating.

Early in March the hopes of Essex's friends rose, and his mother and sisters and the Countess of Southampton met at Essex House to welcome him on his release, which once more caused the Queen to delay it. A week later they were ordered to leave Essex House. At last, on Maundy Thursday, March 20, Essex was allowed to go back to his own house as a prisoner in the charge of Sir Richard Berkley, who kept all the keys of the house, appointing his own servant to be porter. Only the servants necessary for his food and attendance were allowed to remain, and even the Countess was still permitted only to visit him by day.

So affairs continued for the next five weeks. When St. George's Day and the Garter Feast approached, Essex sent to ask what he should do. By the statutes of the Order he was bound to wear his robes. Should he wear them publicly in his dining chamber, or privately in his bed-chamber, or should he be given dispensation not to wear them at all? The reply came back that he should celebrate the feast privately.

About the same time Henry Lee returned from Scotland. The King's answer to Mountjoy's proposals was vague and guarded. Lee was arrested as soon as he reached London and sent to the Gatehouse prison. A few days later Southampton left London and went back to Ireland, in great anxiety lest Lee should say too much of his northern journey. Essex sent a letter with Southampton to Mountjoy calling on him to fulfil the plan. When he reached Ireland Southampton found that Mountjoy had changed his mind. He was too much occupied with the Irish to trouble about Essex, and now that his life was no longer in danger he was not prepared to turn rebel to save Essex's fortunes or to support his ambitions.

There had lately been some relaxation in Essex's confinement, and Cuffe his secretary was now with him. He played an occasional game of tennis and walked in the garden or on the leads, but life was still monotonous and uncertain. Early in May, however, new trouble threatened. Essex learnt that one of the printers had obtained a copy of the unhappy *Apology* and was setting it up. Cuffe was therefore sent to the Archbishop to give warning, and the Master and Wardens of the Stationers' Company tracked it down to Dawson the printer. Over 200 copies were seized, but eighty or more had got abroad.

Henry Cuffe was in many ways Essex's evil genius. Outwardly he was one of those malcontents whom dramatists of the time were so fond of portraying, a man who affected learning, and would utter his mind with such candid frankness that he passed for honest. Inwardly he was overweeningly ambitious, and hoped by following his master to insinuate himself into great place.

Essex also sent Cuffe to tell Sir Charles Danvers that he wished to see him. Danvers was anxious to come, for it had been given out that Essex was grieved that his friends had not done more for him, and complained that they were slack and cold. Danvers told him what had been done by Mountjoy and Southampton, and Essex was touched. Then he went on to speak of his own hopes and fears. At Michaelmas, he said, his lease of the tax on sweet wines came to an end: it was the greatest part of his estate, and by the Queen's renewing it or taking it away from him he would know what was meant for him. He expected that a Parliament would be called in the autumn, and then if he were not restored to his place and offices, which he greatly doubted, for his own part he would give over hope.

Danvers intended to go over to Ireland. Essex encouraged him to go, and there to consult with his friends for the good of England, and for their common good and safety. He talked of the proposal that Mountjoy should bring over the army. Danvers answered that it was hopeless: Mountjoy would never consent. He mentioned the old plan of forcing an entry at Court, and of some project to be carried out in Parliament, which he did not explain.

A day or two later Essex again sent Cuffe to Danvers, desiring that he would go to Ireland and there communicate with his friends. If they agreed, then Southampton should return to England, and Mountjoy should write a letter to Essex complaining of the misgovernment of the State and calling upon him to do something to redress it. Before he was ready to go, Danvers heard that Southampton had left Ireland and sailed for the Low Countries. There seemed no point in the journey. Nevertheless Essex insisted, and he set out.

Essex now made another bid for the Queen's favour. He wrote a letter which ran:

"Before all letters written in this hand be banished, or he that sends this enjoins himself eternal silence, be pleased, I humbly beseech your Majesty, to read over these humble lines. At sundry times I received these words as your own, 'that you meant to correct and not to ruin,' since which time, when I languished in four months' sickness, forfeited almost all that I was able to engage, felt the very pangs of death upon me, and saw my poor reputation not suffered to die with me, but buried and I alive, I yet kissed your fair correcting hand, and was confident in your royal word; for I said to myself, ' Between my ruin and my Sovereign's favour there is no mean, and if she bestow favour again, she gives it with all things that in this world I either need or desire.' But now that the length of my troubles and the increase of your indignation have made all men so afraid of me as my own poor state is ruined, and my friends and servants like to die in prison, because I cannot help myself with my own, I not only feel the weight of your indignation, and am subject to their malicious informations that first envied me your favour, and now hate me out of custom; but, as if I were thrown into a corner like a dead carcase, I am gnawed on and torn by the basest creatures upon earth. The prating tavern haunter speaks of me what he lists; they print me and make me speak to the world, and shortly they will play me upon the stage.

" The least of these is worse than death, but this is not the worst of my destiny; for you, who have protected from scorn and infamy all to whom you once avowed favour but Essex, and never repented of any gracious assurance you had given till now, have now, in this eighth month of my close imprisonment, rejected my letters, and refused to hear of me, which to traitors you never did. What remains is only to beseech you to conclude my punishment, my misery and my life, altogether, that I may go to my Saviour, who has paid Himself a ransom for me, and whom (me thinks) I still hear calling me out of this unkind world, in which I have lived too long, and once thought myself too happy."

The Queen was moved and was heard to speak kindly of him, saying that her purpose was to make him know himself and his duty towards her, but that she would again use his service.

On June 5, Essex was summoned to York House to receive his official censure. At eight in the morning the eighteen special commissioners, most being Councillors or Judges, took their seats at one long table. Essex came before them. None moved his cap or gave any sign of courtesy. He knelt at the upper end of the table on the bare floor, until the Archbishop whispered to his neighbour the Treasurer, and then across the table to the Lord Keeper and Admiral, that a cushion might be allowed.

The Lord Keeper opened the proceedings by showing the cause of their assembly. Then he called on the Queen's four Counsel at Law to inform against the accused. The Sergeant briefly touched on the Queen's princely care, shown in the way she had discharged Essex of £10,000 of debt before he went to Ireland, and had given him almost as much more to buy horses and provide himself; and especially how that although she had received so great cause of offence, yet notwithstanding she was content to be merciful towards him, not proceeding in any of her Courts of Justice but only in this private sort.

At this point Essex was allowed to stand, and shortly after, at the motion of the Archbishop, to sit on a stool.

Then Coke began. With his usual rhetorical bluster he made the most of his case, bitterly aggravating every detail to the full. He divided his speech into three heads: *quomodo ingressus; quomodo progressus; quomodo regressus.* He dealt first with Essex's commission, the largest ever given to a subject, including authority to pardon even treason against the Queen's own person. Next he detailed the five special crimes with which Essex was charged: his making Southampton General of the Horse; his going to Leinster and Munster when he should have gone to Ulster; his making so many knights; his conference with Tyrone; his return from Ireland contrary to the Queen's command.

All these points were amplified in Coke's yeasty style to the conclusion that " the ingress was proud and ambitious, the progress disobedient and contemptuous, the regress notorious and dangerous." He ended the speech with insulting words calculated to touch Essex on his tenderest spot. " Now," he concluded, "nothing remaineth but that we inquire *quo animo* all this was done. Before my Lord went into Ireland he vaunted and boasted that he would fight with none but Tyrone himself; he would pull him by the ears out of his den; he would make the Earl tremble under him; *et cetera*. But when he came thither, then no such matter, for he goes another way; it appeareth plainly he meant nothing less than to *fight* with Tyrone ! "

The Solicitor-General followed: he dealt especially with the state of Ireland since Essex's departure, which showed that he had done so little good that the traitor Tyrone was more insolent than ever.

Francis Bacon rose last to complete the case for the Crown. He hoped, by way of preface, that Essex and all present would remember that any bond of duty which he had always owed to the Earl was laid aside. He reminded the commissioners of the Queen's particular mercy that she had granted Essex's suit not to be brought before the Court of the Star Chamber, and allowed him to be heard in a private place. Then, with considerable eloquence he outlined Essex's actions in Ireland, and thence proceeded to charge him with two points not hitherto mentioned. The first was the angry letter which he wrote to the Lord Keeper nearly two years before. Bacon quoted and stressed some of the more damning passages . . . " no tempest to the passionate indignation of a Prince——" as if her Majesty were devoid of reason, carried away with passion, the only thing that joineth man and beast; and then, " Cannot Princes err ? Cannot subjects suffer wrong ? "— as if her Majesty had lost her virtues of judgment and justice. " Far be it from me," Bacon added, " to attribute divine qualities to mortal Princes, yet this I must truly say, that by the common law of England, a Prince can do no wrong."

The second point of Bacon's accusation was the matter of Hayward's *History of Henry the Fourth*, wherein he observed, " who was thought fit to be patron of that book, but my Lord of Essex, who after the book had been out a week wrote a cold formal letter to my Lord of Canterbury to call it in again, knowing belike that forbidden things are most sought after."

When Bacon ended, the Clerk to the Council was called upon to prove the accusations by reading the documents in the case—the letters which had passed between Essex and the Queen and the Council, and letters from the Earl of Ormonde and the Council of Ireland.

Essex was now asked what he wished to say in his own defence. He knelt down, and began with deep emotion. Since the Queen was pleased to spare him trial before the Star Chamber he laid aside all thought of justifying himself. The inward sorrow and afflictions which he had laid upon his soul privately, betwixt God and his conscience, for the great offence towards her Majesty were more than any outward cross or affliction that could possibly befall him. He would never excuse himself from whatsoever crimes of error, negligence, or inconsiderate rashness which his youth, folly, or manifold infirmities might lead him into, only he must ever profess a loyal, faithful, unspotted heart, unfeigned affection and desire ever to do her Majesty the best service he could, which rather than he would lose, he would, if Christianity and Charity did permit, first tear his heart out of his breast with his own hands.

These sentiments, uttered with passion and sincerity, moved many of the spectators to tears at the spectacle of so great a man so abjectly reduced; but the effect was spoiled when he went on to answer point by point the charges which were made by his accusers, especially those of the Attorney-General. Indeed, he moved the Court to such impatience that the Lord

Keeper interrupted him, observing that he had no need to clear himself of the suspicion of disloyalty, for he was not charged with it, but with contempt and disobedience.

Essex being thus cleared of that charge had little more to say, but to ask them to make a just, honourable, and favourable report of the disordered speeches which were the best that an aching head and weakened body could utter.

The commission then proceeded to its censure. The Lord Keeper was the first speaker, and having given his judgments amply and eloquently he declared that if the case had been heard in the Star Chamber his sentence would have been as great a fine as was ever set upon any man's head in that Court and perpetual imprisonment in the Tower; but, as it was, his censure was that Essex should not execute any of his offices but should return to his own house and continue a prisoner until it pleased the Queen to release him.

One after another the commissioners rose, dilated on the Queen's clemency, and uttered their censures. The afternoon passed, and the June evening drew in before all had ended. At last, when it was nearly nine o'clock at night, eloquence was exhausted, and Essex, weak and very weary, came back to Essex House to await the Queen's sentence.

The Law Term came to an end and the Lord Keeper, in delivering his usual charge in the Star Chamber, enlarged on Essex's faults and bade the justices and the country gentlemen to relate the truth of the matter in their counties. At length the Queen gave an order that Essex's keeper should be removed, and at once cancelled it. Her emotions, indeed, were mixed and tempestuous; she was anxious to appear before the world as unquestionably right in her treatment of Essex, but by his behaviour at York House he had raised certain difficulties. His humble demeanour roused very great sympathy, and by such arguments as he had used against Coke's charges he stirred certain doubts in her mind, especially on two points: the making of the Irish knights, and a plea that Leicester had been pardoned when he had returned contrary to her command.

The second point was soon settled. She sent for her caskets of private papers, and searching through the copies of her letters she found that Essex was wrong: there was a letter giving Leicester permission. But she could not find a copy of the letter which she had written to Essex forbidding him to make knights. A message was sent to Essex commanding him to return her the original. He replied humbly yet regretfully that the letter was either lost or mislaid, for it could not be found.

These Irish knights were a perpetual irritation to the Queen, and she determined on the drastic measure of degrading them all by proclamation. There would be a wail of resentment, for it affected not only the gentlemen themselves, but their wives also, who would by no means amiably submit to the loss of a ladyship. It was so unprecedented and risky a proposal that the Council begged her to abandon it. She yielded, and the proclamation, although signed, was suppressed.

Then she took up another point in the charge: the matter of Dr. Hayward's book on Henry the Fourth. On July 11, Dr. Hayward was summoned to Court and examined before the Lord Keeper, the Lord Admiral, the Secretary, and the Controller. He admitted tampering with the facts of history. The stories mentioned in the Archbishop's oration, tending to prove that deposers of kings and princes have had good success, were his own invention; but, he added, later in the narrative they were confuted by the Bishop of Carlisle. Coke drew up some notes for their Lordships, to prove that in selecting this old story Hayward intended the application of it for the present times—a king taxed for misgovernment, and his council for corrupt and covetous dealings for private ends; the king censured for conferring benefits on hated favourites, the nobles discontented, and the commons groaning under continual taxation, whereupon the king is deposed, and in the end murdered. Their Lordships were convinced of the treasonable intent, and two days later Dr. Hayward was sent to the Tower.

On the same day, John Wolfe, the printer, was questioned by Coke. Dr. Hayward, he said, asked him to print the book, which he did in February, 1599. It had then no Epistle, either dedicatory or to the reader. After some conversation between them, they decided to dedicate it to the Earl of Essex, he being a martial man, and about to go to Ireland, and the book treating of Irish causes. As Dr. Hayward was sick when the book was finished, he took it himself to my Lord at Whitehall. Three weeks afterwards the Wardens of the Stationers Company were ordered by the Archbishop of Canterbury that the Epistle to the Earl of Essex should be cut out. Before this, five or six hundred copies had been sold; no book ever sold better. The Epistle was omitted, and the rest of the edition sold out. About Easter time there was such demand for the book that he obtained a new edition from the Doctor, with a new Epistle Apologetical, to explain that the book was quite innocent in intention. Of this second edition 1,500 copies were printed, but they were all seized and burnt in the Bishop of London's house. For himself, he tried three or four times to see the Earl of Essex and to ask him what he thought of the book, but he was always told that my Lord was too busy to see him. He had made nothing out of the business, and was a very hardly used man, for he lost the whole of the second edition and besides had been in prison for a fortnight.

The Council were still unsatisfied, and next the Attorney turned on the Rev. Samuel Harsnett, Chaplain to the Bishop of London, for Hayward had defended himself by saying that Harsnett officially allowed the book. Harsnett acted for the Bishop, who was partly responsible for the censorship of the press, and had been slack in his duty, for the book was brought to him rather casually without its prefatory matter and he passed it without troubling to read it. The wretched chaplain was greatly distressed.

For the present the matter was allowed to drop, though Hayward remained in the Tower.

Although he had taken so conspicuous a part in the censure

at York House, Bacon was still anxious to serve Essex, and on July 20 he wrote:

"My Lord,

"No man can better expound my doings than your Lordship, which maketh me need to say the less. Only I humbly pray you to believe that I aspire to the conscience and commendation first of *bonus civis*, which with us is a good and true servant to the Queen, and next of *bonus vir*, that is an honest man. I desire your Lordship also to think that though I confess I love some things much better than I love your Lordship, as the Queen's service, her quiet and contentment, her honour, her favour, the good of my country, and the like, yet I love few persons better than yourself, both for gratitude's sake, and for your own virtues, which cannot hurt but by accident or abuse. Of which my good affection I was ever and am ready to yield testimony by any good offices but with such reservations as yourself cannot but allow: for as I was ever sorry that your Lordship should fly with waxen wings, doubting Icarus' fortune, so far the growing up of your own feathers, specially ostrich's, or any other save of a bird of prey, no man shall be more glad. And this is the axletree whereupon I have turned and shall turn; which to signify to you, though I think you are of yourself persuaded as much, is the cause of my writing; and so I commend your Lordship to God's goodness."

To this letter Essex replied:

"Mr. Bacon,

"I can neither expound nor censure your late actions, being ignorant of all of them save one; and having directed my sight inward only, to examine myself. You do pray me to believe that you only aspire to the conscience and commendations of *bonus civis* and *bonus vir*; and I do faithfully assure you, that while that is your ambition (though your course be active and mind contemplative) yet we shall both *convenire in eodem tertio;* and *convenire inter nosipsos*. Your profession of affection, and offer of good offices, are welcome to me. For answer to them I will say but this; that you have believed I have been kind to you, and you may believe that I cannot be other, either upon humour or mine own election. I am a stranger to all poetical conceits, or else I should say somewhat of your poetical example. But this I must say, that I never flew with other wings than desire to merit, and confidence in my Sovereign's favour; and when one of these wings failed me, I would light nowhere but at my Sovereign's feet, though she suffered me to be bruised with my fall. And till her Majesty, that knows I was never bird of prey, finds it to agree with her will and her service that my wings should be imped again, I have committed myself to the mew. No power but my God's, and my Sovereign's can alter this resolution of

"Your retired friend,
Essex."

Nor was Bacon's protestation mere formality. He forthwith devised a plan by which Essex might by indirect means make a personal appeal to the Queen. He concocted a correspondence, which was supposed to pass between Anthony Bacon and Essex. These letters were, on a favourable occasion, to be shown to the Queen, who should thus, as it were, overhear a private conversation about herself. The gist of Anthony Bacon's letter was that the Queen did not intend to ruin him or bar him for ever from her service; he had therefore no cause of dry and peremptory despair. To this Essex was made to answer that he was indeed anxious to amend his errors, but how could the Queen be persuaded of his sincerity when his enemies continued to bar him from all access to her. In both letters Francis insinuated a pretty testimony to his own honesty.

At last, in the afternoon of August 26, Essex was summoned once more to York House. The Lord Keeper, the Lord Treasurer, and Mr. Secretary Cecil received him and announced that it was the Queen's pleasure for him to be set at liberty, except that he was not to come to Court. He thanked them for their message and replied that it was his intention to lead a retired life at Gray's, in Oxfordshire, in the house of his uncle the Controller, Sir William Knollys. He added that he besought their Lordships to be his mediators to the Queen that he might once more come into her presence and kiss her hands that with some contentment he might betake himself to his solitary life. Then he withdrew and went back to Essex House.

When Essex came back, Cuffe renewed his sneers. He said that Essex had shown himself low-spirited and faint-hearted, and those who had persuaded him to humble himself were men of slender and weak judgment. Essex was so angered by these taunts that he dismissed Cuffe from his service and ordered Meyrick to strike his name out of the list of his household. Meyrick disobeyed the order, partly because he shared Cuffe's opinion, but more because he knew Cuffe's bitter nature and realised that if he joined Essex's enemies he could be dangerous; he knew far too many of the secrets of Essex House.

A few days later Essex left London. The crisis was at hand. If the farm of sweet wines was renewed, all would be well. If not, he was ruined, for he owed more than £16,000, of which £5,000 was immediately due. He wrote again to the Queen:

" Haste paper to that unhappy presence, whence only un-happy I am banished. Kiss that fair correcting hand which lays new plasters to my lighter hurts, but to my greatest wound applieth nothing. Say thou comest from shaming, languish-ing, despairing, sx."

The Queen received the letter from the hands of Lady Scrope, read it and re-read it. She seemed pleased, but she gave no definite reply beyond thanks for his care to know of her health. Lady Scrope ventured to remark that Essex's punishment had now lasted almost a year; she hoped that her Majesty would restore her favour to one that with so much true sorrow did desire it. The Queen made no answer, except to sigh and say, "Indeed, it is so"; and with that she rose and went into the privy chamber.

But September was passing and still no decision was made. The Lord Treasurer promised his help. Essex wrote again, and this time a direct appeal:

"If conscience did not tell me, that, without imploring your Majesty's goodness at this time, most dear and most admired Sovereign, I should not only lose the present support of my poor estate, but the hope of any ability to do your Majesty future service, and not that alone, but the means of satisfying a great number of hungry and annoying creditors, which suffer me in my retired life to have no rest, I would appear still before your Majesty as a mute person. But since this day se'night, the lease which I hold by your Majesty's beneficence expireth, and that farm is both my chiefest maintenance and mine only means of compounding with the merchants to whom I am indebted, give me leave, I humbly beseech your Majesty, to suit that canon to yourself which I received from yourself, your Majesty's courses tend *ad correctionem, non ad ruinam*. If my creditors will take for payment many ounces of my blood, or the taking away of this farm would only for want finish my body, your Majesty should never hear of this suit. For in myself I find no boldness to importune, and from myself I can draw no argument to solicit. The only suit which I can make willingly, and must make continually unto your Majesty is, that you will once again look with gracious eyes upon your Majesty's humblest, faithfullest, and more than most devoted vassal,
"Essex."

The Queen read the letter. It was a confession that Essex was beaten to his knees, and she was not displeased. A few days later she noticed Bacon in the Presence. She called him aside and remarked that my Lord of Essex had written her some very dutiful letters, and she had been moved by them; but when she took them to be the abundance of his heart, she found that it was but a preparation for a suit for the renewing of his farm of sweet wines. Bacon, so he reported afterwards, warmly begged her not utterly to extinguish his Lord's desire to do her service. But she kept her counsel and made no immediate decision.

Essex came back to Essex House on October 2, and lived very privately. The gates were kept shut by day and night. Southampton also had returned from the Low Countries. Cuffe sought him out, explained his own position and asked Southampton to intercede for him, with the result that he was soon back at his table in Essex House.

Charles Danvers, too, was back from Ireland. When he communicated Essex's requests to Mountjoy, the response was discouraging. Mountjoy did not approve the projects. He wished Essex to have patience and to recover by ordinary means the Queen's ordinary favour, and though he would not have it in such measure as heretofore, let him content himself. When he came home, he would do for Essex like a friend, but meanwhile he hoped that Essex would do nothing but what should be justifiable in honour and honesty.

Still there was no word of the Queen's decision, and on October 18, Essex tried by one more letter to move her sympathy.

"If I should as often present your Majesty, most dear and most admired Sovereign, with mine humble lines, as mine oppressed spirit would disburthen itself, I should be presumptuous and importunate; if I should as seldom write as your Majesty gives me encouragement, I should be dumb and desperate; and I am confident that your Majesty's inseparable justice in both kinds pleadeth for me. When you say, 'Why is Essex silent?' your Majesty answers yourself, 'His infinitely affectionate heart is overawed with duty.' When your

Majesty saith, 'How dare he write now?' you likewise answer, 'His present fear is overcome by passion.' By passion I say, tyrannous to me, but reverent to your Majesty. Out of that passion my soul cries out unto your Majesty for grace, for access, and for an end of this exile. If your Majesty grant this suit, you are most gracious, whatsoever else you deny or take away. If this cannot be obtained, I must doubt whether that the means to preserve life, and the granted liberty, have been favours or punishments; for till I may appear in your gracious presence, and kiss your Majesty's fair correcting hand, time itself is a perpetual night, and the whole world but a sepulchre unto your Majesty's humblest vassal,

" Essex."

It was now more than a year since Essex had taken any part in affairs of State, and the legend that he was indispensable either in the field or the Council could no longer be maintained. In Flanders, a great victory was won at Nieuport, at the end of June. In Ireland, there was a continuous succession of good news. Within two months Mountjoy so restored the morale of his troops that they forgot how to run away when they met the enemy, were even eager for battle. Great destruction was made of the rebels' corn in the autumn. In September he invaded Tyrone's own territory, and on October 2, a skirmish with Tyrone's men unexpectedly developed into a four-hours' battle in which the English troops drove the rebels from their trenches, and with the loss of twenty killed, slew more than 300 of the enemy. At Court the discretion and good direction of the Lord Deputy were greatly praised on all sides, for his army was now well disciplined, and even when the odds were against them they beat the rebels from their bogs. In less than nine months, it seemed, the end was at last in sight. In other ways there was some return of prosperity. Prospects of trade in the Baltic were improving, and in the City the merchants were becoming so enterprising that they petitioned the Queen to grant a licence for an ambitious voyage of trade in the East Indies. Essex had taken no part in any of these affairs, nor was there any valid reason why his services to the State should continue to be so exorbitantly rewarded.

On October 30, the Queen announced her decision. The grant of the farm of sweet wines would not be renewed; she would for the present keep it in her own hands. Essex and his friends interpreted the omen; it spelt ruin.

Essex's rise and decline was not merely the personal fortune of one man and his immediate followers; it affected the nation more deeply than any event since the Armada. As the reign was drawing to its close the general feeling amongst Englishmen was that the Queen's greatest days were past. In herself she was as great as she had ever been, but the end could not be far off. A long and indecisive war, with its inevitable burdens of taxation and service, brought disillusion and reaction, which appeared in various forms, according to men's different humours. Men of property grumbled at the Queen's ministers: the burden of taxes was heaviest, they said, on those who could bear it least; corruption, they muttered, in high quarters; patents and monopolies, even of essential goods, granted to favourites, forced loans to the Queen who might, or might not, repay them.

With religious men the grievances were as bitter. The Puritans, distilling a form of democracy from Holy Writ, cried out against the corruption of the Anglican clergy, and especially the powers of the Bishops and their Courts of Law, protesting against a forced conformity of doctrine and worship, and demanding liberty of opinion and teaching.

Catholics, with even greater cause, lamented the blood of their martyrs, but were themselves torn with factions, some following the Jesuits in their bitter hatred of the Queen and her Court, others regarding the Jesuits as a curse on Christendom, and the fountain-head of all their persecutions.

Intelligent young men, too young almost to remember the great year '88, let alone the dark days before Queen Mary died, were cynical and contemptuous of everything which the older generation valued. To the few who realised the meaning of Copernicus's teaching, the new philosophy was corroding the foundations of old faith. Most of them had little faith in anything. In their eyes all statesmen were politic followers of Machiavelli, all churchmen foul with simony, all lawyers corrupt, all merchants caterpillars of the commonwealth, and as for soldiers—their faults were too patent even for comment.

A few erupted into satires, and taxed their superiors as boldly as they dared. Others found a reflection of their own disquiets in the new comedy of humours with its apparent zeal for reformation and its obvious delight in caricature. Somehow the world had become a pestilent congregation of vapours. Yet one man seemed to stand out conspicuous as a symbol of true nobility, the coming saviour of his country, perhaps even, if some hopes were fulfilled, their next King— Essex.

Men of all kinds felt this admiration, for in spite of his fortunes Essex never lost his early courtesy of manners to men of all ranks, and that kind of charm which wins and keeps devotion. The Puritans regarded him as one of themselves. Catholics noted that several of his best friends were of their faith, and hoped much from him. In the City he was universally popular; he was the soldiers' champion; and at Court many favoured him, if for no deeper reason than that the inner cabal in the Council were afraid of him. Now that their idol was crumbling, his admirers were utterly bewildered. A few recognised that they had been mistaken. Most, falling back on the simple and obvious explanation that there was villainy abroad, attributed Essex's failure to the jealousy and malice of lesser men. They waited with fear for the issue; so great a heart would not easily submit to his enemies.

CHAPTER XV

THE REBELLION

WHEN Cuffe returned to Essex's service, he began at once to work upon his master's feelings. In this he was well seconded by Sir Gelly Meyrick. Before long Essex House was open to all kinds of malcontents. Essex reacted to his company, and his mood of sorrow and penitence was soon changed into a blind fury at their insinuations that the Council and his enemies were poisoning the Queen's mind against him, and hoped soon to reduce him to poverty and beggary.

Being cut off from all access to Court, and feeding only on rumour and wild speculations, Essex was ready to believe the worst of his enemies, however fantastic the charge. They were traitors to their country. They were plotting to bring in the Infanta of Spain when the Queen should die. The proofs were obvious: Cecil and his friends for ever commending the Infanta's excellences to the Queen; and Cecil had said to a Councillor that he could prove the Infanta's title to be better than the title of any other competitor to the Crown; and Buckhurst had said on the report that the Archduke of Austria—her husband—was dangerously wounded or slain at the battle of Nieuport, that if he was dead the Queen had lost the best of her friends. Then there was the recent leniency shown to the Jesuits, a clear proof that the Spaniard was being favoured.

Moreover, they argued, everything was prepared for the Spaniard to make good his claim. Ralegh commanded in the West, and was Captain of Jersey, and was there ready to welcome them if they landed. Cobham was Lord Warden of the Cinque Ports, and Lord Lieutenant of Kent. The Treasury and the Navy were in the hands of Buckhurst and

Nottingham—both bosom creatures of the little Secretary; and besides, Cecil's elder brother, Lord Thomas Burghley, was Lord President of the North; and in Ireland Sir George Carew was Governor of Munster and would be Lord Deputy when Mountjoy came home. What further proofs of a plot in favour of the Infanta were needed ?

Such Popish intrigues could only be countered by opening the eyes of the King of Scots to this danger to his rights of succession. He must be warned. It was not easy for a messenger to reach Scotland, for Cecil's agents were watching closely. Nevertheless, Essex wrote a letter to King James pointing out his dangers, and asking that the Earl of Mar should be sent to the Queen to request that she should openly declare King James's right of succession to the English Crown, and so circumvent the machinations of those enemies of England who would prevent it. The letter was sent to Lord Willoughby, Governor of Berwick, who handed it to John Norton, a printer and bookseller who had business in Edinburgh; and by this devious means it reached the King.

An answer soon came from the King, a brief note of seven lines of writing, but so important that Essex laid it in a little black bag which he wore constantly about his neck. Talk at Essex House grew wilder and more desperate. The vague plan of forcing an entry into the Queen's presence was taking shape. Zealous Puritan ministers preached daily, and attracted large audiences of citizens. If anyone ventured to question the wisdom of these actions, he was immediately censured as an enemy to Essex's honour. Many of his old friends came to visit him. Some stayed to keep him company, but others, such as Sir John Harington, were so terrified by the things openly uttered that they fled away in alarm. One remark of Essex's was particularly noted; he said that now the Queen was an old woman, she was as crooked and distorted in mind as in body.

All these matters were duly reported in Court, and carried to the Queen's ears, especially by certain young ladies who had in former times yielded to Essex's importunities. Nor could she forget the contrast with his successor in Ireland. Late as the season was, Mountjoy still held the field, harrying the rebels. Mountjoy also was lonely, and felt that he was neglected at home, and maligned. He wrote, in a moment of bitterness, that he was treated like a scullion. The Queen had rarely been so well served and so competently, especially in these later days. She wrote to him with her own hand.

"Mistress Kitchenmaid," she began lightly; and then after keeping up the raillery for a few sentences, she continued "Comfort yourself therefore in this, that neither your careful endeavour, nor dangerous travails, nor heedful regards to our service, without your own by-respects, could ever have been bestowed upon a Prince that more esteems them, considers and regards them than she for whom chiefly I know all this hath been done, and who keeps this verdict ever in store for you; and no vainglory, nor popular fawning can ever advance you forward, but true vow of duty and reverence of Prince, which two afore your life I see you do prefer." This was the man whom Essex had lightly passed over as too bookish and inexperienced for the high command which only he was competent to hold.

After Christmas the resort to Essex House became greater than before and the words of the preachers even more indiscreet; they were boldly declaring the extreme Puritan doctrine that the superior magistrates of the realm had power to restrain even kings themselves.

At Court the Queen was busy entertaining the Duke of Brachiano, who had come over to England, after the marriage of Henri IV with Catherine de Medici, on a visit of compliment. The Queen discoursed with him long and often, and as usual was displaying her courtly accomplishments.

On January 9, 1601, as Southampton was riding in London, Lord Grey encountered and attacked him with drawn sword. The hatred between the two had existed for many months, and they had only been kept from mortal combat by the direct order of the Council. Although the Queen immediately committed Grey to the Fleet Prison, Essex interpreted the assault as an attempt to murder his friend.

The visitors at Essex House now included several noblemen, the Earls of Worcester, Sussex, Rutland, and Bedford, as well as Southampton, and many captains, gallants, and Puritans from the City, so that Essex appeared to be holding a rival and hostile court. It was generally felt that the Queen and her Secretary were afraid of him.

Essex had still many friends at Court, some of them better then he knew. The Lord Treasurer Buckhurst sent his son to visit him, with the message that he dealt effectively with the Queen on his behalf and hoped to have succeeded, but that Essex's behaviour was spoiling his chances. Three things especially were doing him no good. By admitting base and desperate men (such as Sir Edward Baynham, a notorious rakehell) the Queen might justly fear that he had no good intentions; by throwing his house open to all comers and by feasting some of the nobility and many others he was clearly affecting popularity; and the Queen could not but take ill that he had so many exercises of Puritan sermons, or rather conventicles, which attracted multitudes.

Essex replied haughtily that he knew no rascals who resorted to him, and since he was not prohibited from holding speech with any, he saw no reason to withdraw himself from such as came to visit him in good will. It was but civility to ask those who came to share such fare as he had: he invited and sent for none. As for the preachings, these were no conventicles but spiritual conferences which were his only consolation; and as for plurality of chaplains, he had but two. Some others came with their Lords and offered a sermon which he could not refuse, seeing the profit which he received thereby.

Such an answer did not quieten the suspicions of the Council, but as yet Essex had committed no open act which could be called in question.

Inevitably at such a crisis the name of Richard the Second

was again mentioned, and Coke made another attempt to sift out the truth about Hayward's book. Hayward was still in the Tower. On January 22, he was called before Coke and Sir John Peyton, and put through a most searching examination. Hayward affected entire innocence, but he made some curious admissions. He had read somewhere—in Boethius and others—that the subject is bound rather to the State than to the person of the King: he inserted the sentiment into the mouths of the Earls of Derby and Hereford to serve his turn: all good writers of history invent speeches and reasons. He had ready answers for the rest of the questions. When he was asked where he found the description of the Earl as not negligent to uncover the head, bow the body, stretch forth the neck, arm and so forth, he answered that he found in Hall's *Chronicle* and other authorities that the Earl was popular, but for the particulars, he took the liberty of the best writers: he gathered the description of the Earl out of his actions.

The scheme of forcing an entry into the palace at Whitehall and re-establishing his former position by arms was now maturing in Essex's mind. After discreet inquiries in the City a list of probable supporters was drawn up in addition to those sympathisers who openly visited Essex House. Essex compiled some suggestions on which he wished for the opinions of his intimate friends. After one preliminary meeting, there gathered at Drury House on Tuesday, February 3, a small committee consisting of Southampton, Sir Charles Danvers, Sir John Davies, John Littleton, and Sir Ferdinando Gorges.

Davies produced certain propositions, in Essex's handwriting, and a list of those whom he expected to support him, in all about a hundred and twenty. The propositions were three; first, to seize upon the Court; second, to seize the Tower; third, to seize the City. Alternatively, whether to seize the Court and Tower simultaneously, or first one and then the other.

Most were in favour of attempting Court and Tower simultaneously, but Gorges opposed, on the ground that their numbers were too few. The proposal to seize the Court was then debated. Davies's plan was that a number of the conspirators with their followers should enter Whitehall Palace dispersedly, and unostentatiously take up their places, some in the Hall, others in the Great Chamber, others in the Presence Chamber and the lobby, and others at the gate. Danvers was to be in the Presence Chamber, Davies in the Hall, Sir Christopher Blount at the gate, and Gorges at the gate of the preaching place. At a given signal they were to act. Danver's company was to seize the halberds of the Guard, and Blount to hold the gate. By this time Essex himself would be ready to enter the Court, and with the Earls and Barons who supported him, would pass in and present himself to the Queen. After this some should be sent into the City to justify their doings. It was agreed also to seize Ralegh, Captain of the Guard, and some of the Councillors. The plot having been successful, they would call a Parliament in which their adversaries should be tried.

The general feeling was that there would not be much resistance except from the Guard, but it was expected that many would be for them as they had been Essex's servants. Essex's own opinion was that he would come to Court in such peace that a dog would not wag his tongue against him.

Gorges again opposed the plan as impossible, which annoyed Southampton, who exclaimed angrily: " Then we shall resolve upon nothing, and it is now three months or more since we first undertook this." Gorges retorted that he knew nothing of that, but advised Southampton to try his friends in the City, by whom he had been promised help. This suggestion was so ill-received that nothing was decided except that each man should give his opinion in writing, and refer the decision to Essex himself.

Three days later, Sir Charles Percy, Sir Joscelyn Percy, Lord Mounteagle, and some others of Essex's friends went over the river to the Globe Playhouse and there interviewed some of the Lord Chamberlain's players. They asked the players to play

Richard the Second. The players were unwilling. They said that the play was so old and had not been played for so long that they would have little or no audience, but when the gentlemen offered to supplement their taking by forty shillings they consented. The next afternoon, which was Saturday, February 7, *Richard the Second* was accordingly acted before a large number of Essex's followers, including Lord Mounteagle, Gelly Meyrick, and Christopher Blount.

Meanwhile the movements about Essex House had been reported to the Council and the time now seemed ripe for action. The situation was not unlike that of thirty years before, when the Rebellion in the North broke out. Then, as now, the Queen knew that rebellion was imminent, and forestalled it by commanding to her presence the conspiring Lords, who were thus faced with the alternative of submitting, or of declaring themselves rebels before their plans had matured. The present threat was, in some ways, more serious. The Court was at Whitehall, and, except for the Guard and such gentlemen and servants as could be mustered, was unprotected. Essex, at Essex House, lay only a mile off, and between the Court and the City. No one knew whether the City would be loyal, and even in Court there were waverers who would desert if Essex's party seemed to be winning. If it came to the push, Essex might be able to collect the stronger force, and he was only twenty minutes' march from the Court Gates.

An emergency meeting of the Council was held at the house of the Lord Treasurer, for he had been sick and was taking physic and was too weak to stir out of doors. They decided to send for Essex.

By this time it was dark. The party from the Globe had returned and were supping, some at Essex House, Meyrick and others in the house of a friend by Temple Bar. The messenger from the Council arrived; but another and private message warned Essex not to go, for there was a plot laid to entice him to the Lord Treasurer's and then to take his life.

He was also warned that Ralegh and Cobham were intending to murder him in his bed that very night. Essex sent the messenger back with an excuse.

Again the Council sent, and this time Secretary Herbert. For the second time Essex refused, declaring that it would be too dangerous for him to venture abroad amongst his enemies. When Secretary Herbert had gone, Essex came into the withdrawing room and told those present of his warnings. All realised that the time had come when Essex must either submit or hazard. Danvers was for flight. He advised Essex not to resist, but with a hundred gentlemen to make for the sea, or to post off to Wales where he might command some port, and so to escape out of the country. Essex made no reply, but called a council of his friends. He said that he was resolved to defend himself from any more restraints. They considered immediate action. Should they attempt a night attack on the Court? There were three hundred men available at an hour's warning. Gorges again opposed the plan, and Essex himself felt more confident of success in the City. He was asked what assurance he had of his friends in the City. He answered that there was no question of it, for one among them, who held one of the greatest commands, was interested in the cause, and was colonel of a thousand men who were ready at all times. There were others equally sure, and able to raise as many. Some at this very moment, learning of the plot against him, had sent to know his pleasure.

To-morrow, then, they would venture.

All night messengers were going round to summon Essex's friends to Essex House in the morning, whilst in the house and garden a watch was kept against prowling assassins.

There were other communications from the Court. Gorges received a message from Ralegh asking for a meeting, and it was agreed that they should meet in boats on the Thames on the following morning. When Gorges mentioned the arrangement to Essex and Blount, Blount tried to persuade him to surprise Ralegh, or to kill him.

It was now the morning of Sunday, February 8. At daybreak Essex's followers began to arrive, and were cautiously admitted, but the stir and bustle at the gate of Essex House was causing much interest and excitement, and curious onlookers were gathering in the streets outside, whom Essex's followers took to be soldiers. Reports of these happenings were carried to Cecil. It was a very delicate situation. To act too soon was as dangerous as to act too late. But the Secretary made his preparations, and warned those about the Palace. At eight o'clock in the morning the Lord Mayor and the Aldermen would attend the sermon at Paul's Cross. A messenger was sent to tell him to be ready for emergencies.

Gorges kept his appointment with Ralegh. The boats drew alongside in midstream, and the two men had some conversation. Ralegh advised Gorges to go back to his charge at Plymouth, or he would find himself in the Fleet Prison. "Tush, Sir Walter," replied Gorges, "this is not a time to talk of going to the Fleet; get you back to Court, and that with speed, for my Lord of Essex hath put himself into a strong guard at Essex House, and you are like to have a bloody day of it." Ralegh begged him to leave his present company, but Gorges, who saw that a boat was putting off from Essex Stairs, with four musketeers, shoved Ralegh's boat away and bade him make haste. So Ralegh rowed back to Court to tell what he had heard, and Gorges returned to Essex House, where the bustle was continually increasing. As each man came in, the news that Ralegh and Cobham were plotting to murder Essex was passed on, and by ten o'clock the courtyard was full of excited gallants waiting for the next move. Essex was going round, greeting them with his news, but as yet had not announced any plan of action.

Suddenly there was a clamour at the outer gate. The Lord Keeper, the Earl of Worcester, Sir William Knollys, and Lord Chief Justice Popham, with their servants, were without, demanding entry in the Queen's name. The wicket gate was opened and the deputation admitted, but their servants were told to stay outside, except for the bearer of the Great Seal, which was inseparable from the Lord Keeper. They made their way through the noisy and hostile crowd. Essex, the Earls of Rutland and Southampton, Lord Sandys, Lord Mounteagle, Blount, Danvers, and many more crowded round them. Thereupon the Lord Keeper told Essex that they had been sent from the Queen to understand the cause of this assembly, and to let them know that if they had any particular cause of grief against any person whatsoever, it should be heard and they should have justice.

Essex, shouting out that everyone might hear him, cried that his life was sought; he would have been murdered in his bed. He had been perfidiously dealt with. His hand had been counterfeited and letters written in his name, and therefore they were assembled to defend their lives.

The Lord Keeper replied that if Essex had any such matter of grief, or if any such matter were attempted or purposed against him, he should declare it. It would be truly related to the Queen, and indifferently heard, and justice should be done.

Southampton mentioned the assault made on him by Lord Grey. The Lord Keeper answered that in his case justice had been done, and the offender imprisoned. He repeated his promise to deliver any grievance faithfully and honestly to the Queen; if Essex was unwilling to declare it openly, let him speak privately and he should be satisfied.

Upon this the crowd grew restive and broke into clamour. "Away, my Lord!" "They abuse you!" "They betray you!" "They undo you!" "You lose time!" The Lord Keeper, putting on his hat, in sign that he spoke as the Queen's representative, said in a loud voice, "My Lord, let us speak with you privately and understand your griefs"; and then turning to those crowding around him, he said, "I command you all, upon your allegiance, to lay down your weapons and depart, which you ought all to do being thus commanded, if you be good subjects and owe that duty to the Queen which you profess."

At this the crowd shouted back in derision, " All! All! All! "

Whilst he had been speaking, the Earl and most of his company contemptuously put on their hats again. Essex led the way into the house. The deputation followed, the crowd pushing in after them and shouting, " Kill them ! " " Kill them ! " " Nay, let us shop them up." All the while the Lord Keeper kept on asking Essex to speak to them privately. At length they reached the study, which they entered.

Essex had been taken by surprise at the unexpected coming of so important a deputation, and at this point completely lost his head. He had thought out no plan, but suddenly he resolved that he would make for the City, wildly imagining that at his appearance the Lord Mayor and Sheriffs would muster the train-bands to support him in a march on Whitehall.

" My Lords," he said, " be patient a while, and stay here, and I will go into London and take order with the Mayor and Sheriffs for the City, and be here again within this half hour."

He came out of the study, closing the door behind him, and leaving the prisoners under the care of Sir John Davies, whom he charged, as he loved him, to keep these Lords who had come from the Queen with all honour and courtesy until his return, and then he would go with them himself to the Queen. He also left Captain Owen Salisbury in charge of three musketeers and a caliver, standing with their matches ready, to guard the door.

Essex came back to his followers, and the whole mob poured out of the gate into the street. " To the Court. To the Court ! " they cried.

But Essex turned towards the City.

The company numbered in all about two hundred, but as none had received any detailed warning, they were unarmed except for their swords, rapiers, or daggers. As they moved forwards, others joined them, including the Earl of Bedford and Lord Cromwell. They passed down Fleet Street and under Ludgate. All the while Essex was crying out, " For the

Queen! For the Queen! A plot is laid for my life." The citizens crowded out of the houses to watch him pass, and some cheered, but none was armed. He begged them to arm themselves or they would be no use to him. No one stirred. Essex went on rapidly, past Paul's, where the people were coming out from the sermon, down the Poultry and Lombard Street, and so at length to Sheriff Smythe's house near Fenchurch. He, as it now appeared, was the high officer who was to produce a thousand armed men.

Lord Cromwell and some others had gone ahead. They went first to the Lord Mayor and then to the sheriff's, whom they found on the point of leaving. They told the sheriff that Essex was likely to have been murdered, and was coming to his house for safety. Smythe replied that if he were in danger, the Lord Mayor's house would be safer. At this moment Essex himself arrived, and pushing his way into the house declared that he would send for the Lord Mayor. The sheriff asked him not to bring all his company into the house; he would himself fetch the Lord Mayor. Essex was unwilling, and thereupon mounted the stairs with some of his company. The sheriff went out by the back gate and hurried away to join the Lord Mayor.

By this Essex realised that the event had passed beyond his control. He was utterly perplexed to know what to do next, and sweated so hard in his agitation that he had to change his shirt. For two hours he remained in the house, talking wildly, but determining nothing. At length dinner was brought him, and the party sat down to eat.

Three valuable hours had been wasted and nothing was done. Moreover, his enemies were now taking the offensive. Lord Burghley, with a herald and a dozen horsemen, had entered the City and at various points was proclaiming Essex a traitor and promising pardon to all who should leave him and depart. The report was brought to Essex whilst still at dinner. He sneered that a herald would do anything for two shillings, and that it was a trick of his enemies. Then, with a napkin still tucked round his neck, he ran down into the street, with the others following. He cried out to the bystanders that he was acting for the good of the Queen, the City, and the Crown, which certain atheists had betrayed to the Infanta of Spain.

It was now about two o'clock in the afternoon. Some horses had been procured. Essex mounted and rode into Gracechurch Street. Sheriff Smythe, also mounted, rode up to him, declaring that the Lord Mayor summoned him to yield and come to his house. Essex refused, and laying hold on Smythe's bridle, he said, " You shall go with me, and send for your company, and I will take the gates for the safety of the City." The sheriff replied that he had no company, only two or three apprentices. Essex looked at him wildly and cried out, " If you fear God, love the Queen, or care for religion, look to yourself."

At last Essex realised the ghastly truth that he had been living in a world of fantasy. The citizens of London would cheer him and throw up their caps, but not one would help him. There remained only the wild hope that if he could reach Essex House he might be able to effect some sort of bargain with the persons of the Councillors who were still in custody.

Much meanwhile had been happening at Whitehall. As soon as the news of Essex's eruption reached the Palace, messengers were sent out to call the men of Westminster and the neighbouring villages to arms. Weapons were collected, and a barricade of coaches was erected in the broad road leading from Charing Cross. As for the Queen, she remained unmoved, and continued the day's routine as if nothing out of the ordinary was happening. When she was at her dinner, the most alarming reports were brought in from the City. She observed merely that He that had placed her in that seat would preserve her in it, and so went on with undiminished appetite.

By three o'clock a little force consisting of three companies

MAP OF LONDON IN 1601

of foot and some sixty horse had been mustered. The Lord Admiral was made Lieutenant-General, with Lord Grey in command of the horse. The Queen could hardly be dissuaded from going with them to see if ever a rebel of them all durst show his face against her.

At Essex House the Councillors were still imprisoned in the study. The Lord Chief Justice at first tried to persuade Davies to let them go, but he replied that Essex had gone into the City and would be back in half an hour. The Lord Chief Justice said that the Earl would be deceived. Davies answered that Essex had great hopes of the City or he would never have gone there. "Then," observed the Lord Chief Justice, "if it be so, it will be an occasion of much effusion of English blood, and an occasion of spoiling the City by desperate persons, and it will be the worst for the Earl and his company in the end." Half an hour passed, and Essex did not return. Davies, to beguile the embarrassing tedium of the occasion, went out and brought down the Countess of Essex and Lady Rich to make such social conversation as was possible in the circumstances.

In the City the Lord Mayor was calling up the train-bands, and with his followers hovered in the neighbourhood to watch events. Around Ludgate the Earl of Cumberland and the Bishop of London were busy collecting men. Most of them were the Bishop's own servants, armed with his armour. They saw coming towards them under the gate Sir John Leveson, an old and very experienced commander. They asked him to put the company in some order. Leveson was at first reluctant, but at length consented, and seeing an old soldier named Waite, a tall man with a halberd, who obviously knew his business, he proceeded to marshal the soldiers. He had the chain from the posts set across the street. Behind he set the shot, and behind them the piles. While this was being done the Bishop rode up and down, clearing the street of idle gazers and exhorting the soldiers to stand to it like men.

About half an hour later Essex and his followers came down

from Paul's Churchyard intending to pass under Ludgate. Four pikes' length from the chain they halted. Essex asked who commanded there. "My Lord of Cumberland," they answered. Then Essex perceived Leveson, and sent Gorges to ask that he might be given peaceable passage to his house. Leveson replied that he was commanded that none should pass that way, and had so undertaken, and God willing would perform it. Essex then sent Captain Bushell, saying that he had parted with the Lord Mayor and the sheriffs in good terms, and they had given him liberty to pass to his own house, and he would offend none. Leveson answered that if the Lord Mayor or the sheriffs would affirm what he said, he would give place, but not otherwise. Again Essex sent Gorges asking that he might be allowed with but one gentleman to pass about a most grateful and acceptable message to the Queen and State. Leveson stoutly refused. Twice more Essex sent, and each time his messenger was rebuffed.

At last one of Essex's followers, losing all patience, cried out, "Shoot, shoot!" and they discharged their pistols within a three-quarter's pike length. The few shot with Leveson fired their pieces. A couple of bullets passed through Essex's hat; young Henry Tracy, his page, fell dead by his side; two citizens were mortally hit. Then Essex drew his sword and commanded Sir Christopher Blount to set on. Blount and a few others charged with sword and target, and coming close to the chain began hacking at the heads of the pikes. Waite engaged him, and was soon mortally wounded, but in the thrust of pike and halberd Blount was gored in his face, and felled by a blow on the head. Leveson's men levelled their pikes to advance. Essex called off his followers and retreated, leaving Blount in the hands of the enemy. They were not followed. As they went, Gorges asked that he might be sent on to release the Councillors and to go with them to the Queen. Essex answered that the Lord Chief Justice should be released, but none of the others. Gorges hurried on ahead.

They made their way down to the river to Queenhithe.

Essex's company was now much diminished, for his followers, seeing that the whole business was futile and hopeless, were slinking away to save themselves. When the few that were left reached the river, they took boats and were rowed to Essex House Stairs. Essex landed and went into the house to find that Gorges had arrived a quarter of an hour before and was gone off to Court by water with all the prisoners. He had told Meyrick and Davies that this was Essex's order.

There now remained surrender or defiance, and since there could be little hope either way, they hurriedly put the house in a state of defence, doors were shut and barricaded, and books piled in the windows. Essex had gone into the City wearing the black bag about his neck, and in his pocket a list of those who were to help him. He decided to protect his friends as far as he could. He therefore unlocked an iron chest containing various intimate papers, and a personal diary of his troubles during the last months. A small casket was broken open, and the private letters which it contained removed. Essex threw them all, with the black bag, on the fire. By this time the short afternoon had passed, and darkness was coming on.

The Lord Admiral and his army approached, a small but illustrious company. He assigned the leaders to their posts. Positions on the landward side of the house were occupied by the Earls of Cumberland and Lincoln, Lord Thomas Howard, Lord Grey, Lord Burghley, and Lord Compton. He himself, with Lord Effingham, Lord Cobham, Sir John Stanhope, Sir Robert Sidney, and Sir Fulke Greville, entered the garden by the river. Lord Burghley broke open the gate and entered the courtyard, where two of his soldiers were killed. Essex and some of the others appeared on the leads, waved their swords, and went back into the house. The cannon ordered from the Tower were approaching, and soon all would be ready for an assault. There was some desultory firing from the house, and from within could be heard the cries and shrieks of the terrified women.

Sir Robert Sidney was sent forward in the darkness to summon the rebels to surrender. Southampton appeared on the leads, and a long conversation followed. To whom should they yield? Southampton asked. To their adversaries? That were to run headlong to ruin. To the Queen? That were to confess themselves guilty. "But yet," he added, "if the Lord Admiral will give us hostages for our security, we will appear before the Queen; if not, we are every one of us fully resolved to lose our lives fighting."

Sidney reported these brave words to the Admiral, and came back with the message that conditions were not to be discussed with rebels, but yet for sparing the weaker sex he would allow the Countess, Lady Rich, and their women to come forth. Southampton thanked him for this consideration; but he added, they had fortified the doors with great labour; if they unfortified them to let the ladies out, they would make an open passage for the Admiral's forces to enter. Yet if the Lord Admiral would give them an hour to open the way, and another hour to refortify it, they would gladly accept the offer. This, too, was granted. The women came out of the house and were escorted away.

The rebels were thus left with an hour's respite in which to consider their position. Essex at first was for a heroic end. Since everything was lost, let them fight their way out. In this he was supported by Lord Sandys, who was now elderly. It was more honourable, he cried, to die fighting than by the hand of the executioner. The others were less eager for death, and Essex's courage also began to evaporate. With Southampton he reappeared on the leads and called to Sir Robert Sidney that he would yield upon conditions; that they might be dealt with civilly; that their cause should be fully and justly heard; and that Master Ashton, a minister of God's word, might be with him in prison for his soul's comfort. To the first, the Admiral agreed; to the second he said that there was no reason to doubt that it should be so; to the third, he promised to make intercession to the Queen.

When they heard the reply, they went down. The doors

were opened, and the noblemen came out from Essex House, and, falling on their knees, by the light of the torches each delivered his sword to the Lord Admiral. It was after ten o'clock, and a dark night, and the river being impassable under London Bridge it was too late to take the prisoners to the Tower. The Lord Admiral conducted Essex across the water to Lambeth Palace, where he was left in the charge of the Archbishop. The rest of the captives were led away to the various prisons of the City.

So ended Essex's last fight, in miserable failure. Had it been well planned and resolutely followed the rising might have succeeded. If he had attacked the Court at dawn his force would have been greatly superior to any that could be mustered at a moment's notice, and even if he had not immediately broken in, he would have cut off the Palace from the City. Essex had always regarded little Cecil as his enemy, often without any cause. On this Sunday, when at last it came to a trial of strength, the Secretary beat him, at all points, in a conflict of wits, intelligence, and resolution.

CHAPTER XVI

THE TRIAL

WHEN morning came, the Council were able to survey the situation. There were about ninety prisoners distributed amongst the City prisons or in the care of loyal subjects; among these were five Earls, three Lords, and sixteen Knights. It seemed incredible that such a disturbance could have been unpremeditated; and if so, then there must be confederates who would probably rise in open rebellion when they heard that Essex was a captive. The first step was to reassure the public. A proclamation was therefore issued which outlined the conspiracy, expressed the Queen's thanks for the loyalty of her people, and warned them against listening to or repeating seditious rumours.

On Wednesday, February 11, the most expert lawyers were summoned by commission to proceed to the examinations of the prisoners. There was so much to do that they were divided into groups. The work was pressed forward; confessions and examinations were collected and collated. In these labours Francis Bacon took a conspicuous part. It was quite hopeless for him to labour any more for Essex. Indeed, right up to the rebellion he had continued to press the Queen to restore Essex to favour, even when he saw that the advice was unpalatable. Bacon certainly owed much to Essex, but from the first he had shown clearly that if at any time he had to choose between the Queen and Essex, loyalty would come before gratitude.

Next day there was a further alarm. Amongst Essex's more reckless followers was a Captain Thomas Lee. He had served in Ireland, where he had a reputation as a desperate and dangerous person, who was known to be friendly with

Tyrone. On the day of the rising he approached Sir Robert Cecil and the Lord Admiral and offered to murder Essex; the offer was not accepted. About five in the afternoon of February 12, Lee came to Sir Henry Neville and Sir Robert Cross, and began to talk darkly of the events of the last few days. If, he added, half a dozen resolute men who had access to the Presence Chamber would go boldly to the Queen and refuse to leave till she signed a warrant for Essex and Southampton to be brought before her, it might be done. Neville and Cross reported the conversation to Cecil. That same evening Lee was seen to be lurking suspiciously about the door to the Queen's privy chamber. He was arrested, and then confessed that he had intended to break in to the Queen when she was at supper. Then he would have locked the doors and pinned her up till he had forced her to sign a warrant for Essex's release.

On Saturday, February 14, instructions were sent out to all the preachers in London that they should preach on the rebellion. They were to tell their congregations how Essex for the last six or seven years had tried to allure the hearts of the simple in order that he might himself become King. Let them stress his hypocrisy; how religiously he listened to two sermons a day, and all the time he was busy plotting treason. If he had not been prevented, this would have been the most desperate and dangerous rebellion since Richard the Second's time. At the same time special prayers of thanksgiving for the Queen's delivery were circulated for use in all churches. The sermons were not entirely to the Council's liking. Loyal preachers so zealously embroidered the story that it became ridiculous, while the preachers who favoured Essex left the impression with their hearers that they would themselves fetch him out of the Tower.

On Monday Captain Lee was brought up for trial at Newgate. It was a simple case. Sir Robert Cross swore to Lee's conversation. Lee could not deny his words, but he argued that they had been qualified with an "if"; he never meant any harm to the Queen. He was condemned to death and executed the next morning.

The examinations were still coming in, but as yet, though the commissioners for the trial of Essex and Southampton were already summoned for the 19th, the Council lacked decisive evidence that the rising was premeditated or that there had in fact been a treasonable conspiracy. On the 18th, however, all was revealed. One by one Essex's principal confidants, Gorges, Davies, Charles Danvers, and Christopher Blount, were brought before the Lord Keeper Egerton, the Lord Treasurer Buckhurst, the Lord Admiral, and Sir Robert Cecil. Then the whole story of the consultations at Drury House came out. The case was complete. Coke and his assistants worked desperately to have their papers in order for the morning.

On Thursday, February 19, Essex and Southampton were brought from the Tower to Westminster Hall for their trial. It was a ceremonious occasion, full of the pageantry of State. A special court had been prepared, in the form of a square. At the top side was set a chair and a footstool beneath a canopy of State for the Lord Treasurer Buckhurst, who presided as Lord High Steward. Immediately in front sat the Clerk of the Crown and his assistants, with their papers. On either side of the square were the benches for the Peers, and a lower seat for the judges summoned to advise on points of law: Sir John Popham, Lord Chief Justice of the King's Bench; Sir Edmund Anderson, Lord Chief Justice of the Common Pleas; Sir William Periam, Lord Chief Baron; Master Justices Gawdy, Fenner, Walmesley, and Kingsmill, and Master Baron Clarke. On the lower side, opposite the Lord High Steward, sat the Queen's Counsel: the Queen's Sergeant, Sergeant Yelverton; the Attorney-General, Sir Edward Coke; the Solicitor-General, Sir Thomas Fleming; the Recorder of London, Mr. John Croke; Mr. Francis Bacon, and Sergeants Heale and Harris.

When all were present and in their places, the Lord High

Steward entered, with seven sergeants-at-arms bearing maces before him. He proceeded up the Hall and took his seat. The maces were set down. The Sergeant-at-Arms thrice proclaimed silence, and the Clerk of the Court read out the commission. Then the Lieutenant of the Tower was commanded to bring forth his prisoners, and the second procession entered the Hall : Lord Thomas Howard, Constable of the Tower ; Sir John Peyton, Lieutenant of the Tower ; the Gentleman Porter carrying the axe before the two prisoners, who took their places at the bar immediately behind the Queen's Counsel. Here they kissed hands and embraced each other.

The roll of the peers was read out, and each answered to his name. When the Clerk read out the name of Thomas, Lord Grey, Essex jogged Southampton by the sleeve and laughed. Essex asked whether the privilege of challenge, which was permitted to every private person upon his trial, might be granted, not for his own part, yet the Earl who stood by him might perhaps make just challenge. The Lord Chief Justice Popham replied that the Law allowed no challenge of any of the peers, for such was the credit and estimation of the peers of England that they were neither compelled to an oath of arraignments nor subject to any exception. The Attorney also cited a precedent from Henry VIII's time. Essex answered that he was satisfied, and desired them to go on.

So the prisoners were called upon to hold up their hands, and the Clerk read the indictments, which were to the effect that on the 8th day of February last, at Essex House in the county of Middlesex, Robert Devereux Earl of Essex conspired with Henry Earl of Southampton, Roger Earl of Rutland, the Lord Sandys, and divers Knights and Gentlemen, to deprive and depose the Queen's Majesty from her royal state and dignity, and to procure her death and destruction; and also to cause a cruel slaughter of her Majesty's subjects; to alter the religion established, and change the Government of the Realm; and that for effecting thereof, they, the said earls, intended to go to her Majesty's house at Whitehall (her

Majesty then being in the said house), and by force of arms the person of her Majesty to seize and take into their custody; and that upon her Majesty sending unto the Earl of Essex divers of her Privy Councillors, with commandment upon his allegiance that he should disperse his disorderly company, he refused so to do, and imprisoned the said Councillors in the custody of Sir John Davies, Francis Tresham, and Owen Salisbury, with divers other persons; giving them commandment that, if any attack should be made by the Queen's forces upon Essex House, they should kill the said Councillors; that the said Earls of Essex and Southampton, with a number of armed men, issued into the City of London, with intent to persuade the citizens to join with them, and did there, after proclamation made, kill divers of her Majesty's subjects; that they afterwards returned to Essex House and fortified the same house against the Queen's forces, killing divers of her Majesty's subjects in the defence thereof.

Both earls pleaded not guilty, and for their trials put themselves upon God and their peers. Essex added, "I call God to witness, before Whom I hope shortly to appear, that I bear a true heart to her Majesty and my country, and have done nothing but that which the law of nature commanded me to do in my own defence, and which any reasonable man would have done in the like case."

The Lord High Steward having briefly charged the peers to their duty, Sergeant Yelverton rose to open the case for the Crown. He spoke briefly, likening the prisoners to Catiline, and reminding his hearers that the events of the rebellion were notorious, which made him wonder that the earls did not blush to stand upon their trials without confession, and to conjecture that there was some further matter than had yet appeared.

The Attorney-General rose next. His speech had been very carefully prepared, and he began by discoursing upon the law of treason. To resist the King's authority by force was treason. He cited recent examples: the case of the riotous apprentices in 1595, who proposed to whip the Lord Mayor; the cases of Bradshaw the miller and Burton the mason, in 1597; both these cases had been declared treason by learned judges. What, then, could be said of the present case, "when so many earls, barons, and knights, having assembled on a sudden three or four hundred persons, and expecting a multitude of followers, in a settled Government, do intend to take, not a slender fort, but the Tower of London; to invest, not a mean village, but this great City; to surprise, not the mansion of the Lord Mayor, but the sacred palace of the Queen? This must needs imply the death and destruction of the Queen, and is higher than the highest treason. How much the possession of the Tower of London by any subject doth concern her Majesty, your Lordships may judge; yet the possession of the City, which she hath more affectionately loved and respected than any of her progenitors, doth much more nearly concern her. And though the surprising of her Court, where her royal person is, in such manner as you shall hear, is of all these attempts the most dangerous, yet such is the godly care of her Majesty for the good of her subjects, that the change of her blessed Government by such a Catiline, popish, dissolute, and desperate company, that should have despoiled and dishonoured her good, loyal, and rich subjects, this should be more perilous to her than her own safety."

Coke was now warming up, and his rhetoric flowed on in an increasing stream, recapitulating and embroidering the well-known details of the rising, and working up to a climax of invective with, "This was not all; for the earl would call a Parliament, and himself decide all matters which did not make for his purpose; a bloody Parliament would that have been, where my Lord of Essex, that now stands all in black, would have worn a bloody robe; but now in God's just judgment, he of his earldom shall be Robert the Last, that of a kingdom thought to be Robert the First. Why should I stand upon further proofs? The treason is so evident, that my Lord himself will not deny it."

Essex at once began to reply.

"Will your Lordships," he said, "give us our turns to speak, for Master Attorney playeth the orator and abuseth your Lordships' ears with slanders against us? These are the fashions of orators in corrupt states, and such rhetoric is the trade and talent of those who value themselves upon their skill in pleading innocent men out of their lives, and who never think that they have sufficiently discharged their duty unless they aggravate all things against such as are charged by them. But, my Lords, our interest in this matter is greater than theirs, and considering some privileges which we might challenge, equal and indifferent hearing were but justice."

The Lord High Steward answered that it was fitting for the evidence first to be delivered, and then they should have liberty to speak what they would. But Essex pressed his request to answer each piece of evidence as it was produced, and the peers, thinking it very reasonable, desired the Lord High Steward to grant it.

The Clerk now began to read out the evidence, starting with the examination of Henry Widdrington, which described the events in Essex House on the morning of the 8th. Essex observed that the evidence was but hearsay, for Widdrington himself was not present, having been sent away into the country.

The Lord Chief Justice Popham was the next witness. He was sworn, and described, with graphic detail, the adventures of himself and those who entered Essex House with him, and how Essex led them into his book chamber and there left them guarded until released by Sir Ferdinando Gorges about four o'clock in the afternoon. The narrative was corroborated by the Earl of Worcester.

Essex replied that he had shut up his prisoners for their own safety.

The Attorney-General then asked why Essex did not dissolve his company when commanded upon his allegiance. Essex answered that the report that the house was surrounded by armed men had put his followers into such an ecstasy of fear that he could not suddenly dissolve them. Further questions followed, and the proceedings quickly degenerated into a wrangle between Southampton and Lord Grey until the Lord High Steward intervened to bring the Court back to the issue. After renewed altercation, between Essex and the Attorney, Sir Walter Ralegh was called.

" What booteth it to swear the fox ? " observed Essex as Ralegh took the oath.

Ralegh's testimony was that knowing Sir Ferdinando Gorges had come from his charge at Plymouth without leave, he had sent for him. They had met on the Thames on the Sunday morning and Ralegh desired him to depart the town immediately or he would be laid in the Fleet Prison. " Whereunto he replied," said Ralegh, " 'Tush, Sir Walter, this is not a time to talk of going to the Fleet; get you back to the Court, and that with speed, for my Lord of Essex hath put himself into a strong guard at Essex House, and you are like to have a bloody day of it.' Whereupon I advised him again to forsake that company, and he shoved off the boat that I was in, and bade me make haste, which I did. Then I saw a boat come off at Essex House Stairs, wherein were three or four of the Earl of Essex's servants with pieces."

Essex commented that Ralegh's evidence altogether differed from the version delivered by Gorges on his return.

The next testimony was the written confession of Gorges, detailing his version of the rising, and describing the plans which had been made for surprising the Court. When the confession had been read Essex desired that Gorges should be produced face to face. Gorges therefore again repeated his confession *viva voce*, adding that he had advised Essex on his return from the City to go and submit himself to the Queen. Essex disputed the testimony, and begged Gorges to speak openly whatever he remembered.

Gorges, who was confused and pale, quibbled that he had

delivered all that he remembered in his examination, and further he could not say.

"Sir Ferdinando," demanded Essex, "I wish you might speak anything that might do yourself good; but remember your reputation, and that you are a gentleman; I pray you answer me, did you advise me to leave my enterprise?"

"My Lord, I think I did," he answered.

"Nay," retorted Essex, "it is no time to answer now upon thinking; these are not things to be forgotten; did you indeed so counsel me?"

"I did," replied Gorges.

Essex cried out, "My Lords, look upon Sir Ferdinando, and see if he looks like himself. All the world shall see, by my death and his life, whose testimony is the truest."

Southampton now began to speak. He admitted that there had been consultations at Drury House about surprising the Court and Tower, but neither was attempted. He therefore desired the opinions of the Judges whether a thing consulted upon and not executed, and another executed and not spoken of, was treason. As for himself he knew nothing of Essex's intentions when he came that morning to Essex House; he heard nothing of the Proclamation; he never drew his sword all the day.

The Attorney-General interrupted to observe that it had been shown in evidence that he had a pistol when he was in the City.

"Mr. Attorney," Southampton retorted, "it is the uncivillest thing in the world to interrupt a man who is speaking for his life." As for the pistol, he took it from a man in the street, but it had no flint and could not hurt a fly. His behaviour during the rest of the day showed no signs of treason. "I beseech you, therefore, my Lords," he concluded, "not to judge of me according to the strict letter of the law, but as in your own consciences you are persuaded of me. If in this business I was too far carried away by the love I bore to my Lord of Essex, I confess I have offended; but that which I have before rehearsed was the whole end and scope of all my purposes."

Coke continued to wrangle for some time, and then the judges were required to deliver their opinions on the points raised by Southampton. Their conclusions were: First, that Essex in going with a troop from Essex House into the City and there calling upon the citizens to aid him in defending his life and forcing himself into the Queen's presence with power sufficient to remove certain of his enemies in attendance upon the Queen was guilty of high treason, inasmuch as the action threatened force and restraint to the person of the Queen. Secondly, that Essex's proceedings in the City amounted to actual rebellion, though he might intend no corporal harm to the Queen's person. Thirdly, that the adherence of Southampton to Essex in the City, although he might be ignorant of Essex's purpose, was high treason because the acts of Essex amounted to rebellion. Fourthly, that all persons who went with Essex into the City were traitors, but those who joined him suddenly in the City and dispersed as soon as Proclamation was made were within the terms of the Proclamation and entitled to a pardon.

The Court then returned to listen to the evidence, and two confessions of Sir Charles Danvers were read, wherein he detailed the conversations and plans discussed at Drury House. Then followed the confessions of Sir Christopher Blount, the Earl of Rutland, and Lord Sandys, who added to the others the detail that when Essex came back to Essex House he had burnt some of his papers, and how Essex had said that he had a black bag about his neck that should tell no tales. As to the contents of this bag, a portion of the examination of Edward Bushell was read, who had said that " the Earl said, that if a black purse he had about his neck were found, it should appear, by that he had in it, how he was betrayed in the City."

The Attorney-General took up the point of the black bag, and turning to Essex, he exclaimed, " You were confident in London, having been persuaded by your sycophants that all the City was on your part, and in the pride and overweening of their aid, you contemned the Queen's royal authority; her herald could not be hearkened unto."

Essex answered Coke, and then appealing to his peers, he said, " I do charge you all, my Lords, that notwithstanding all eloquence is used to make me a traitor, a Papist, a sectary, and an atheist, and to have aspired to the Crown, that you have a true regard to your consciences, and judge of me as a good Christian, and as one that never sought to exceed the degree of a subject; the which I doubt not by God's Grace to manifest, by going with courage and a cheerful heart to my death; howsoever I have been dealt withal, I had sought to appease all humours of revenge in me, and for confirmation thereof was resolved to receive the sacrament, until the attempt upon the Earl of Southampton by the Lord Grey. I thank God I am far from atheism; I doubt not but by His Grace to die a Christian, and as an Earl that have faithfully served my Prince and country, notwithstanding what others out of the weakness of their hearts have testified against me."

Lord Mounteagle's examination was next read, which agreed with the other accounts of the rising. Whereupon Coke commented on the miraculous way in which the truth had been revealed, coming from various witnesses of their own accord, without either rack or torture to any of them.

As to that, Essex retorted, the selfsame fear and the selfsame examiner might make the several examinations agree all in one, were they never so far distant. " God knows," he went on, " I was drawn into this hazard by those that have the Queen's ear, and abuse it, informing her of falsehoods against many of us; which, having felt a long time, I chose at last rather to hazard her Majesty's mercy than to abide the dangerous courses that they might work against me. My purpose was to have come unto her Majesty with eight or nine honourable persons, who had just cause of discontentment, though not equal with mine, and so prostrating ourselves at her Majesty's feet, to have put ourselves unto her mercy. And the effect of our desires should have been, that she would have been pleased to have severed some from her Majesty, who, by reason of their potency with her, abused her Majesty's ears with false informations; and they were Cobham, Cecil, and Ralegh. For we thought that my Lord Cobham carried himself in factious and dangerous courses, and told her Majesty many untruths; and he was a principal cause, as I think, of withdrawing her favour from us. And to have removed such a base informer from her Majesty, I would have bended my tongue, my brain, and my best endeavour with all diligence; but without purpose of harm to her Highness: for, I protest I do carry as reverent and as loyal duty to her Majesty, as any man in the world."

This outburst provoked another jar between Essex and his peers, and for the moment it seemed that the case for the Crown was being lost in irrelevant wranglings; but when the Lord High Steward had restored order to the proceedings, Francis Bacon, for the first time, rose. Turning to Essex, he said, " My Lord, I expected not that the matter of defence would have been excused this day; to defend is lawful, but to rebel in defence is not lawful; therefore what my Lord of Essex hath here delivered, in my conceit, seemeth to be *simile prodigio*. I speak not to simple men, but to prudent, grave, and wise peers, who can draw up out of the circumstances the things themselves. And this I needs must say, it is evident that my Lord of Essex had planted a pretence in his heart against the Government, and now, under colour of excuse, he layeth the cause upon his particular enemies.

" My Lord of Essex, I cannot resemble your proceedings more rightly than to one Pisistratus, in Athens, who, coming into the city with the purpose to procure the subversion of the kingdom, and wanting aid for the accomplishing his aspiring desires, and as the surest means to win the hearts of the citizens unto him, he entered the city, having cut his body with a knife, to the end they might conjecture he had been in danger of his life. Even so your Lordship gave out in the streets that your life was sought by the Lord Cobham and Sir Walter Ralegh, by this means persuading yourself, if the City had undertaken your cause, all would have gone well on your side. But the imprisoning the Queen's Councillors, what reference had that to my Lord Cobham, Sir Walter Ralegh, or the rest? You allege the matter to have been resolved on a sudden. No, you were three months in the deliberation thereof. Oh, my Lord, strive with yourself and strip off all excuses; the persons whom you aimed at, if you rightly understand it, are your best friends. All that you have said, or can say, in answer to these matters, are but shadows. It were your best course to confess, and not to justify."

To this deadly argument Essex retorted, " My Lord, I must here plead Mr. Bacon for my witness that I have just cause of exception against these men that before I have named; for when the course of private persecution by mine enemies was in hand, and most assailed me, then Mr. Bacon, who was a daily courtier and had free access to her Majesty, pretending to be my friend, and to be grieved at my misfortunes, undertook to go to the Queen in my behalf. And he drew for me a letter most artificially in my name, and another in his brother Mr. Anthony Bacon's name; which letters he purposed to show to the Queen, and he showed them both to me. And I saw by those letters that Mr. Bacon had pleaded for me as feelingly, and pointed out my enemies as directly and truly as might be. Which letters I know Mr. Secretary Cecil hath seen, and by them it will appear what conceit Mr. Bacon at that time had of those men and of me, though he here coloureth and pleadeth to the contrary."

The Attorney-General protested. " My Lord," he said to the Lord High Steward, " these criminations are not fitting, and would not be suffered but that the honour and patience of this assembly is so great."

Bacon replied, " This is no crimination; I confess I loved my Lord of Essex as long as he continued a dutiful subject; and I have spent more hours to make him a good subject to her

Majesty than ever I did about my own business. But since you have stirred up this matter, my Lord, I dare warrant you these letters of mine will not blush in the clearest light; for I did but perform the part of an honest man, and ever laboured to have done you good, if it might have been; for what I intended for your good was wished from my heart."

There was no relevant answer, but Essex now began to make other justifications: " As for that I spake in London that the Crown of England was sold to the Spaniard, I speak it not of myself, for it was told me that Mr. Secretary should say to one of his fellow Councillors, that the Infanta's title comparatively was as good in succession as any other's."

At this moment the little Secretary suddenly appeared from behind an arras where all the while he had been listening unseen. He knelt on one knee before the Lord High Steward and begged leave to answer so foul and false a report. The Lord High Steward and some of the peers made light of Essex's words, but Cecil was roused beyond control. For months he had patiently endured Essex's slanders without any chance of publicly defending his own name; now his indignation broke out.

" My Lord of Essex," he cried, " the difference between you and me is great. For wit I give you the pre-eminence, you have it abundantly; for nobility also I give you place— I am not noble, yet a gentleman; I am no swordsman—there also you have the odds; but I have innocence, conscience, truth and honesty, to defend me against the scandal and sting of slanderous tongues, and in this Court I stand as an upright man, and your Lordship as a delinquent. I protest, before God, I have loved your person and justified your virtues; and I appeal to God and the Queen, that I told her Majesty your afflictions would make you a fit servant for her, attending but a fit time to move her Majesty to call you to the Court again. And had not I seen your ambitious affections inclined to usurpation, I would have gone on my knees to her Majesty to have done you good; but you have a wolf's head in a sheep's garment, in appearance humble and religious, but in disposition ambitious and aspiring. God be thanked, we now know you; for indeed your religion appears by Blount, Davies, and Tresham, your chief counsellors, and by your promising liberty of conscience hereafter. Ah, my Lord, were it but your own case, the loss had been the less, but you have drawn a number of noble persons and gentlemen of birth and quality into your net of rebellion, and their bloods will cry vengeance against you. For my part, I vow to God, I wish my soul had been in heaven and my body at rest that this had not been."

"Ah, Master Secretary," Essex sneered, "I thank God for my humiliation, that you, in the ruff of all your bravery, have come hither to make your oration against me this day."

Cecil retorted, "My Lord, I humbly thank God that you did not take me for a fit companion for you and your humour; for if you had, you would have drawn me to betray my Sovereign as you have done others. But I challenge you to name the Councillor to whom I should speak these words. Name him if you dare. If you do not name him, it must be believed to be a fiction."

"Nay, my Lord," replied Essex, "it is no fiction, for here stands an honourable person, the Earl of Southampton, that knows I speak no fables, for he heard it as well as I."

Southampton was reluctant, but at last said that the Councillor in question was the Controller, Sir William Knollys.

Cecil again went down on his knee to beg that a gentleman of the Privy Chamber, or someone who had access to the Queen, should be sent at once to intreat her to command Sir William to give evidence. The Lord High Steward instructed Mr. Knivett to carry the Secretary's request to the Queen. To this Cecil, who was still very excited, added, "Master Knivett, I conjure you, as you are a gentleman and do tender your reputation, that you do not acquaint Mr. Controller with the cause why you come for him; and that you add this further from me to her Majesty, that if either for care of my credit or love of Mr. Controller, or for any other respect, she shall deny to send him, I do here vow, upon my salvation, that I will never again serve her in place of Council, while I live. I will live and die her true subject and servant, but will never more serve her as Councillor or Secretary."

When Knivett had left the Court, then the Queen's Counsel resumed their case, and sought to prove that Essex was a hypocrite in that though he had continual preaching in his house yet he kept Sir Christopher Blount, who was a notorious papist, and had promised toleration of religion. Essex denied the accusation.

By this time Knivett had returned with Sir William Knollys. The Lord High Steward repeated Essex's accusation to Knollys, and desired him to satisfy the Lords whether Cecil had ever used such speeches in his hearing or to his knowledge. It was a breathless moment, for upon the answer the whole issue depended—Essex's life and Cecil's fortune and honour as a statesman.

Knollys replied that he had never heard him speak any words to that effect, only that at the time when Doleman's book about the Succession was being discussed, the Secretary had remarked, "Is it not a strange impudence in that Doleman to give as equal right in the succession of the Crown to the Infanta of Spain as any other ? " This was the origin of the slanders on the Secretary, of which he was as clear as anyone present.

Essex was confounded, and could only say that the words had been reported to him in another sense.

Cecil pressed his advantage, "No, my Lord, your Lordship out of your malice towards me, desires to make me odious, having no other true ground than the breach between us about the peace with Spain, which I laboured for the profit and quiet of my country. But with you it hath ever been a maxim to prefer war before peace, in respect of the importance it gave to your Lordship and such as followed you. Hence was set forth your *Apology* against the peace, and hence was conceived a general hatred against those which were affected to the peace. Councillors of State have many conferences; I confess I have said that the King of Spain is a competitor of the Crown of England, and that the King of Scots is a competitor; and my Lord of Essex, I have said, is a competitor, for he would depose the Queen and call a Parliament, and so be King himself. But as to my affection to advance the Spanish title to England, I am so far from it that my mind is astonished to think of it; and I pray God to consume me where I stand if I hate not the Spaniard as much as any man living. I beseech God to forgive you for this open wrong done unto me, as I do openly pronounce that I forgive you from the bottom of my heart."

To which Essex replied, " And I, Mr. Secretary, do clearly and freely forgive you with all my soul; because I mean to die in charity with all men."

Then once more the Attorney returned to the evidence. He raised two points of law. The first was whether it was treason to offer by force to remove a Privy Councillor. The judges answered that it was treason. The second was whether it was treason for a subject to make a passage by force to the presence of the Prince. This too was declared to be treason. It was a plain case, commented the Attorney, that force was used, for some of the Queen's subjects were slain. And to prove this point Sir John Leveson was called and sworn to state that Essex had ordered Sir Christopher Blount to fight his way through, and had slain Waite.

Essex made another speech, explaining his motives and declaring that it was greatly against his mind that any blood had been shed.

Once again Coke began to spoil his case by trifling points. Why, he asked, if Essex had no sinister motive, did he cry out as he went that England was bought and sold to the Spaniard?

Southampton denied that any such words had been uttered.

Then Essex made a last appeal to the sentiment of his peers, that they should not be prejudiced by the oratory of the prosecution. His conscience was clear of any disloyal thought of harm to her Majesty. "If," he concluded, "in all my thoughts and purposes I did not ever desire the good estate of my Sovereign and country as of my own soul, I beseech Thee, O Lord, show some mark upon me and my soul in this place, for a testimony to all the world of Thy just vengeance for my untruth! And Thou, O God, Which knowest the secrets of all hearts, knowest that I never sought the Crown of England, nor ever wished to be of higher degree than a subject!"

For the second time Bacon rose. "My Lord," he observed, "I have never yet seen, in any case, such favour shown to any prisoner; so many digressions, such delivering of evidence by fractions, and so silly a defence of such great and notorious treasons. Your Lordships may see how weakly my Lord of Essex hath shadowed his purpose, and how slenderly he hath answered the objections against him. But admit the case that the Earl's intent were as he would have it, to go as a suppliant to her Majesty, shall petitioners be armed and guarded? Neither is it a mere point of law, as my Lord of Southampton would have it believed, that condemns them of treason, but it is apparent in common sense; to consult, to execute, to run together in numbers, in doublets and hose, armed with weapons, what colour of excuse can be alleged for this? And all this persisted in after being warned by messengers sent from her Majesty's own person. Will any man be so simple as to take this to be less than treason?

"But, my Lord, doubting that too much variety of matter may occasion forgetfulness, I will only trouble your Lordship's remembrance with this point, rightly comparing this rebellion of my Lord of Essex to the Duke of Guise's, that came upon the barricadoes at Paris in his doublet and hose, attended upon but with eight gentlemen; but his confidence in the city was even such as my Lord's was, and when he had delivered himself so far into the shallow of his own conceit, and could not accomplish what he expected, the King taking arms against him, he was glad to yield himself, thinking to colour his pretexts and his practices by alleging the occasion thereof to be a private quarrel." Again his parallel was apt and deadly.

Essex had little more to say, but to remind the peers of the conditions of his surrender.

Then the Lord High Steward directed the peers to consider their verdict, and ordered the Lieutenant of the Tower to withdraw his prisoners from the bar. The proceedings had been long, and the Lords refreshed themselves with beer, biscuits, and tobacco. They rose and withdrew into the temporary apartment prepared for them behind the canopy. Soon after, the two Lord Chief Justices and the Lord Chief Baron went in to them to deliver their opinions on the points of law. After half an hour the peers came back and took their seats. The sergeant-at-arms, beginning at the junior lord, called on Lord Thomas Howard, who stood up bareheaded.

"My Lord Thomas Howard," demanded the Lord High Steward, "whether is Robert, Earl of Essex, guilty of this treason whereupon he hath been indicted, as you take it upon your honour, or no?"

Lord Thomas Howard, bending his body, and laying his left hand upon his right side, replied "Guilty, my Lord, of high treason, upon mine honour." Each in turn, from the junior to the highest, likewise delivered his verdict. Then they were called upon again, and each delivered the same verdict upon Henry, Earl of Southampton.

The prisoners were brought back to the bar, and the Clerk of the Crown in due form demanded of Essex what he could say for himself why he should not have judgment of death. Essex spoke briefly. For himself, he was willing to die, but he asked their Lordships to intercede for Southampton. He would not speak to save his own life, yet howsoever he had been misled to transgress the law, he never had any treacherous or disloyal intentions towards her Majesty. He would not have them speak to the Queen of him as one who despised her clemency, but he would not be found to make any cringing submission to obtain it.

Southampton was next asked what he would say for himself. He pleaded for his life, praying the Lord Admiral and the Lord High Steward to intercede for him to the Queen. Since he was found guilty by the law he submitted himself to death, yet not despairing of her Majesty's mercy, which, if she were pleased to extend it, he would with all humility receive.

Then the Lord High Steward, after the usual exhortations to the prisoners to prepare themselves for God, proceeded to judgment, " Forasmuch as you, Robert, Earl of Essex, and Henry, Earl of Southampton, have been indicted of High Treason, and thereto have pleaded not guilty, and, for your trials, have put yourselves upon God and your Peers, who have found you guilty; and being demanded what you should say for yourselves why judgment should not be pronounced against you, you have alleged no sufficient reason, therefore the Court doth award that you both shall be led from hence to the place from whence you came, and there remain during her Majesty's pleasure; from thence to be drawn upon a hurdle through the midst of the City, and so to the place of execution, there to be hanged by the neck and taken down alive; your bodies to be opened, and your bowels taken out and burned before your face; your bodies to be quartered; your heads and quarters to be disposed of at her Majesty's pleasure, and so God have mercy on your souls."

Essex had one last request. " My Lord," he said, " I am not at all dismayed to receive this sentence, for death is far more welcome to me than life; and I shall die as cheerful a death as ever man did. And I think it fitting that my poor quarters, which have done her Majesty true service in divers parts of the world, should now at the last be sacrificed and disposed of at her Majesty's pleasure; whereunto with all willingness of heart I do submit myself. But one thing I beg of you, my Lords, that have free access to her Majesty's person humbly to beseech her Majesty to grant me that (during the short time I shall live) I may have the same preacher to comfort me that hath been with me since my troubles began; for as he that hath been long sick is most desirous of the physician that is best acquainted with the constitution of his body, so I most wish to have my comfort in spiritual medicine from him who hath been and is best acquainted with the inward griefs and secret afflictions of my soul. And my last request shall be this; that it will please her Highness that my Lord Thomas Howard and the Lieutenant of the Tower may be partakers with me in receiving the sacrament, to witness of me concerning what I have here protested for my loyalty, religion, and peace of conscience; and then, whensoever it shall please her Majesty to call me, I shall be ready to seal the same with my blood."

The Lords promised that they would move the Queen for his requests. The Sergeant-at-Arms stood up with the mace on his shoulder and proclaimed that the commission was dissolved. The peers rose to go home. Essex, as he was being led away, begged the pardon of Lord de la Ware and Lord Morley for involving their sons in his troubles.

It was now about seven o'clock in the evening, and news of the verdict soon spread through the City. As Essex was led back to the Tower, many left their suppers and ran into the streets to watch him pass. He walked with a quick pace, and lowered head, taking no heed of the spectators, though some spoke to him.

Connoisseurs of dramatic occasions were not dissatisfied with the trial. Essex had defended himself, they agreed, with great spirit, as if having lived popularly his chief care was to leave a good opinion in the people's mind at his departing. His protestations of loyalty certainly impressed many of his hearers, and there was considerable surprise that there should have been no mention at the arraignment of the charges that he had plotted with Tyrone, and with the Pope that he was to be King of England, about which his preachers had said much by commandment in their Sunday sermons. Southampton was very generally pitied, though it was felt that in pleading for his life he showed himself somewhat too submissive.

CHAPTER XVII

THE END

NEXT morning Essex was still excited by the events of the trial, and in the same mood, regarding himself as his country's saviour, pulled down by vicious enemies. They, not he, were in the wrong.

After a while, Dr. Thomas Dove, Dean of Norwich, was brought in to him. The Dean came primed with instructions from the Council, who were uneasy about the trial. They felt that there was too much sympathy for the condemned. Essex had been condemned quite legally and on good and sufficient evidence, but something more was needed to convince the public that, beyond any doubt, he deserved his fate.

Essex was not deceived. When the Dean began to urge him to acknowledge his offences, he replied that he was in no way guilty of offending Almighty God; and when the Dean was disposed to argue, he exclaimed, in passion, "If you knew how many motions have been made to me to do my best to remove such evils as the commonwealth is burdened with, you would greatly wonder."

The Dean withdrew to report his failure. A humbler instrument was more successful. The next visitor was the chaplain, the Reverend Abdy Ashton, by whose zeal for the Gospel Essex had been greatly fortified at Essex House and during these last days of waiting. Essex greeted his chaplain cheerfully. Here was a friend who would understand his heroic failure, but Ashton's message was very different from what he had expected.

Ashton, also, had received his instructions, subtly tempered with hints both of danger and of promotion. He knew from experience how to touch Essex's emotions, and launched at once into invective denunciation.

"My Lord," he exclaimed, "I am unfeignedly sorry to see no more sense in you of these and other fearful sins, into which you have fallen, whereby you have dishonoured God, shamed your profession, offended your Sovereign, and pulled upon yourself many notes of infamy. You have now manifested to the world, that all your show of religion was mere hypocrisy, that you are in your heart either an atheist or a papist, which doth plainly appear, in that all your instruments, followers and favourers, were of this quality; most of them men of no means, but either base persons, that you had raised, or such as lewdly consumed their own patrimony. And if there were any of better condition for their state, yet they were either recusants, or such as were discontented with the present Government; so as the badness of your cause and action doth herein show itself, that no one man but of the sort before-mentioned took your part, or liked your course. Besides, however you would colour it with other pretences, your end was an ambitious seeking of the Crown, the hope whereof for their own raising made these men to follow, animate and applaud you: so that if by a true confession and unfeigned repentance you do not unburden yourself of these sins, you shall carry out of the world a guilty soul before God, and leave upon your memorial an infamous name to posterity. Therefore I will say to you, as Joshua did to Achan (for you have dishonoured God more than ever he did), 'Give glory to God, and make confession of your fault.' For as Solomon saith, 'he that hides his sins shall not prosper.'"

Essex was amazed at this outburst, so unexpected and so bitter; but he defended himself vigorously, though admitting that his followers were indeed men of sundry qualities. He denied that he ever affected the Crown, and declared that he was moved by the misery of his country, oppressed by known atheists, papists, and pensioners of her mortal enemies. "The only means," he protested, "left to turn away these evils was to procure my access to her Majesty, with whom I assured myself to have had that gracious hearing, that might have tended to the infinite happiness of this state, both in removing evil instruments from about her person, and in settling a succession for the Crown, to the preventing of Spanish servitude, and saving of many thousand Englishmen's lives. No, no, Master Ashton, I never desired other condition than the state of a subject, but only to my Sovereign, and not to so base and unworthy vassals under her."

Ashton resumed in a more sombre, sorrowful tone. "My Lord, these are general speeches, and not much more believed of me now than they were of many then. You must remember, you are going out of the world; you know what it is to receive sentence of death here; but yet you know not what it is to stand before God's judgment seat, and to receive the sentence of eternal condemnation. Leave therefore all glorious pretences; free your conscience from the burthen of your grievous sins; for I protest I cannot believe that you had any other pretence than I have told you, or can name one man (other than such as I have mentioned) that was either adviser, persuader, or approver of your purposes. Neither see I any reason why that I, being watchman over your soul, should not as well have been advised withal, if these things had been so, as any other."

It was a cunning speech, and Essex fell into the trap. He knew that his enemies would naturally misconstrue his actions to the worst, but it had never entered his mind that his own respected chaplain could have so misunderstood his motives. He must justify himself by proofs. Thereupon he went on to relate the details, declaring that his whole aim had been to settle the succession by Act of Parliament on the King of Scots; and, besides, many great men, in Church and State, were with him. He named them.

Ashton now had what he wanted, but the circumstance was delicate, and the confession could hardly be made public.

" These be great matters your Lordship hath opened unto

me," he observed, " and the concealing them may touch my life. Also I hold myself bound in allegiance to reveal them. Besides the publishing of them may give satisfaction to many, that hold the same opinion of your courses, which I did. And farther, it may be dangerous to her Majesty's person in some practice hereafter by them or some of their instruments, the burthen whereof your soul must bear, if you can and do not prevent it, and I will be a witness against you, that you have spoken it."

Essex therefore repeated the confession, and Mr. Ashton went off to report the success of his mission.

When he was left to himself Essex was in black despair. Hitherto he had justified his whole action as a fine act, and himself as a martyr for his country. Ashton's words stripped away his confidence, and he saw himself now as his enemies saw him, an ambitious, self-seeking, self-cozened traitor, who had thrown away honour in this world and salvation in the world to come. But the sinner might still reach salvation up the ladder of confession. He sent for the Lord Thomas Howard, the Constable of the Tower, to beg him to move the Queen to send the Lord Keeper, the Lord Treasurer, the Lord Admiral, and Master Secretary Cecil that he might now clear his heavy conscience, confess his offences, and reconcile himself with his enemies.

The request was immediately forwarded to Court, and next morning—it was Saturday, February 21—the Lord Admiral and Cecil came hurriedly down to the Tower. When Essex appeared before them, he began, "I do humbly thank her Majesty that it hath pleased her to send you two unto me, and you are both most heartily welcome; and above all things I am bound unto her Majesty that it hath pleased her to let me have this little man, Mr. Ashton, my minister, with me for my soul. For this man in a few hours hath made me know my sins unto her Majesty, and to my God. And I must confess to you, that I am the greatest, the most vilest, and most unthankfullest traitor that ever was born in this kind. And therefore, if it shall please you, I will deliver now the truth, though at the bar, like a most sinful wretch, with countenance and words I maintained all falsehood." He confessed everything, with great penitence, revealing in full detail both the plot to seize the Queen, and the intention thereafter, that having her in possession they would have used the shadow of her authority for changing the government; and how they would then have summoned Parliament and condemned all their enemies.

Having thus relieved his conscience, he asked their forgiveness; first of the Lord Keeper that he and his had been put in fear of their lives. Then he asked forgiveness, in Christian charity, of all whom he had called his enemies.

The two Councillors asked a few questions. What of his accusation of Cecil at the trial? He vowed that in his own conscience he freely acquitted Cecil of it; he was ashamed that he had made it upon no better ground. He even professed that he bore no malice to Cobham or Ralegh; for aught he knew, they were true servants to the Queen and State. He had one request to make, that the Queen might grant him the favour to die privately in the Tower.

There was one other matter. Would he repeat his confession in writing? He took pen and covered four sheets of paper with his own handwriting. He spared no one, and accused especially Christopher Blount, and his two secretaries, Cuffe and Temple. He revealed the names of others privy to his designs, especially Lord Mountjoy and Sir Henry Neville the Ambassador to France, who had been invited to Drury House and there informed of the plan. " And now," he went on, " I must accuse one who is most nearest to me, my sister who did continually urge me on with telling me how all my friends and followers thought me a coward, and that I had lost all my valour. She must be looked to, for she hath a proud spirit." He even commented on Penelope's notorious love for Mountjoy.

Cuffe was sent for. When he came, Essex exhorted him to

call on God and the Queen for mercy, and to deserve it by speaking the truth, adding, " I that must now prepare for another world have resolved to deal clearly with God and the world, and must needs say this to you, you have been one of the chiefest instigators of me to all these my disloyal courses into which I have fallen." Cuffe was too astonished and disgusted to say more than to complain of Essex's inconstancy and betrayal of his most devoted friends.

In the meantime two other divines, Dr. Thomas Mountford and Dr. William Barlow, had been warned to attend to give spiritual assistance to the prisoner. They had heard nothing of Essex's interview with the Councillors or of the confession, and agreed together that they would first beat him to the ground with the dreadful judgments of God, and then raise him again with the comfortable promises of the Gospel. The prisoner, however, was in a very different frame of mind. He welcomed them eagerly, and his remorse was so feelingly expressed that Dr. Barlow was moved to remind him that Christ Jesus came into the world to save sinners.

Dr. Mountford was puzzled. He had been present at the arraignment, and the change in the prisoner was astonishing. " I wonder," he remarked, " that your Lordship, thus guilty to yourself, should be so confident at the bar. It offended many of your good friends."

" Yea," Essex replied, " but now I am become another man." He told them that he had already confessed to the Council, and though he implicated many by his revelation, " yet," said he, " I hold it my duty to God and the Realm to clear my conscience." He was still so eager to unburden himself to any one who would listen, that he repeated the confession to the embarrassed divines.

It would have caused much bloodshed, they observed.

Essex agreed, " God knows what danger and harm it had brought to the Realm." As for himself, he thanked God it had been prevented and that He had made him this example to be justly spewed out of the land. He wished that the time of his execution had come, for the Queen could not be safe so long as he lived upon the earth.

The conversation went on. He was willing and eager to answer every question. At length the divines turned the talk to the constancy of martyrs at their death, on which he remarked that they died in a good cause, but he should die in a bad cause.

Meanwhile the Queen was greatly agitated. She knew that Essex deserved death. His terrible words—" her mind as crooked as her carcase "—festered. The report of his confession and his latest conversations was brought to her. She was reminded of Lee's attempt, and how Essex himself said she could not be in safety so long as he lived, until he had been spewed out of the land. But yet he was the only man in these last years for whom she really cared. She waited to see if he would write to her or ask for his life. No message came from the Tower. She signed the writ for his execution.

On Tuesday, February 24—it was Shrove Tuesday—the preparations were begun for the execution. By the Council's orders, two executioners were secretly conveyed into the Tower, lest one by himself might falter at the last moment. Exact instructions were sent to the Constable and the Lieutenant. Two divines, Drs. Mountford and Barlow, were to accompany Essex to give him all comforts for his soul, and at the same time to make sure that he confined his speeches at the execution within discreet limits. He might very profitably confess his great treasons and sins towards God, and express hearty repentance and earnest and incessant prayers to God for pardon; but if he should attempt to make any particular declaration of his treasons, or accusation of his adherents, or any justification of himself, as that he had no ill meaning but against his private enemies, then the Constable and the divines, with becoming moderation, but quite firmly, should prevent him. The useful Master Ashton was also to persuade Essex privately to use few words and patience, and to go with him to the end.

The writs of execution were despatched to the Tower

Then the Queen countermanded the order, and sent Sir Edward Carey to the Tower to say that the execution should be stayed. In the evening there was the customary Shrovetide feasting at Court, and a play was performed by the Lord Chamberlain's players. After the play, the Queen retired to her private apartments. Nothing had come from the Tower. She gave orders that she would have the execution proceed. Mr. Darcy was sent off to the Tower with the message.

Essex was in bed when the Lieutenant of the Tower, with the three divines Mountford, Barlow, and Ashton, came to him with the message that he must prepare for death. He rose, and opening the window of his chamber, spoke a few words to the guard, asking them to pray for him. The rest of the night he spent in prayer and confession, and listening to the exhortation of the divines.

At dawn, the spectators who had been summoned to witness the execution were assembling. By the Queen's order the Earl of Cumberland, the Earl of Hertford, Viscount Bindon, Lord Darcy, Lord Compton, Lord Morley, and Lord Thomas Howard, the Constable of the Tower, were present. A bench had been provided for them, and they took their places facing the scaffold, which was enclosed with a railing and covered with straw. Behind the noblemen stood about a hundred others, knights, gentlemen, and aldermen of the City. Ralegh also came, to answer—so he said—if Essex should object anything against him; but some, suspecting that he wished rather to gloat, murmured. So Ralegh betook himself to the Armoury, and looked on unseen from a window.

The little procession approached; Essex and the three divines, escorted by Sir John Peyton, and a section of partizans of the Guard. As he came, Essex murmured a prayer for strength and patience to the end. He was seen to be dressed all in black, with a gown of wrought velvet, a suit of satin, and a black hat. He mounted the scaffold. He turned to the divines, and said, "O God, be merciful unto me, the most wretched creature on the earth."

He faced the Lords, and, taking off his hat, bowed to them, and with face upturned, began to speak.

"My Lords, and you my Christian brethren, who are to be witnesses of this my just punishment, I confess to the glory of God that I am a most wretched sinner, and that my sins are more in number than the hairs of my head; that I have bestowed my youth in pride, lust, uncleanness, vain glory, and divers other sins, according to the fashion of this world, wherein I have offended most grievously my God, and notwithstanding divers good motions inspired unto me from the Spirit of God, the good which I would, I have not done, and the evil which I would not, I have done; for which I humbly beseech our Saviour Christ to be Mediator unto the Eternal Majesty for my pardon; especially for this my last sin, this great, this bloody, this crying, and this infectious sin, whereby so many, for love of me, have ventured their lives and souls and have been drawn to offend God, to offend their Sovereign, and to offend the world, which is as great a grief unto me as may be. Lord Jesus, forgive it us, and forgive it me, the most wretched of all; and I beseech her Majesty, the State, and Ministers thereof, to forgive it us. The Lord grant her Majesty a prosperous reign, and a long one, if it be His will. O Lord, bless her and the nobles and ministers of the Church and State. And I beseech you and the world to have a charitable opinion of me for my intention towards her Majesty, whose death, upon my salvation and before God, I protest I never meant, nor violence to her person; yet I confess I have received an honourable trial, and am justly condemned. And I desire all the world to forgive me, even as I do freely and from my heart forgive all the world.

"And whereas I have been condemned for my religion, I was never, I thank God, atheist nor papist, for I never denied the power of my God, not believing the word and scriptures, neither did I ever trust to be justified by my own words or merits, but hope, as a true Christian, for my salvation from God only, by the mercy and merits of my Saviour Jesus Christ, crucified for my sins. This faith I was brought up in, and therein am now ready to die; beseeching you all to join yourselves with me in prayer, not with eyes and lips only, but with lifted up hearts and minds, to the Lord for me, that my soul may be lifted up above all earthly things, for now I will give myself to my private prayer; yet for that I beseech you all to join with me, I will speak that you may hear."

He took off his gown and ruff. One of the chaplains whispered to him not to be afraid. He answered that he had been divers times in places of danger where death was never so present nor certain, and he had felt the weakness of his flesh, and therefore he desired God to strengthen him in this great conflict and not to suffer his flesh to have any rule over him. He asked for the executioner, who came forward and knelt for forgiveness.

" Thou art welcome to me," he said, " I forgive thee. Thou art the minister of justice."

So he knelt in the straw before the block, and with hands clasped, and with long and passionate pauses, he began to pray. " O God, Creator of all things and Judge of all men, Thou hast let me know by warrant of Thy Word, that Satan is then most busy when our end is nearest, and that Satan being resisted, will fly. I humbly beseech Thee to assist me in this my last combat, and since Thou acceptest even of our desires as of our acts, accept of my desire to resist him, as with true resistance and perfect grace; what Thou seest of my flesh to be frail, strengthen, and give me patience to be as becometh me, in this just punishment inflicted upon me by so honourable a trial. Grant me the inward comfort of Thy Spirit; let Thy Spirit seal unto my soul an assurance of Thy mercies; lift my soul above all earthly cogitations, and when my life and body shall part, send Thy blessed angels to be near unto me, which may convey it to the joys in Heaven."

Then he repeated after the chaplain the Lord's Prayer, in which the spectators joined, sobbing, and when he came to the petition " as we forgive them that trespass against us," he repeated it, " as we forgive all them that trespass against us." One of the divines reminded him to say over his belief and whispered it quietly clause by clause before him. He was also reminded to forgive and pray for his enemies. He asked God to forgive them as freely as he did, because, he added, " they bear the image of God as well as myself."

Then he took off his doublet, and stood before them in a scarlet waistcoat. He bowed to the block, and said, " O God, give me true humility and patience to endure to the end, and I pray you all to pray with me and for me, that when you shall see me stretch out my arms and my neck on the block, and the stroke ready to be given, it would please the Everlasting God to send down His angels to carry my soul before His Mercy Seat "; and then, with eyes uplifted, " Lord God, as unto Thine Altar do I come, offering up my body and soul for a sacrifice, in humility and obedience to Thy commandment, to Thy ordinance, and to Thy good pleasure. O God, I prostrate myself to my deserved punishment."

He lay flat in the straw, and fitted his head to the block. One of the divines asked him to say the beginning of the Fifty-first Psalm: " Have mercy upon me, O God, according to Thy loving kindness, according to the multitude of Thy compassions, put away mine iniquities. Wash me thoroughly from mine iniquity, and cleanse me from my sin." Then he stretched out his arms and cried, " Executioner, strike home. Come, Lord Jesus, come, Lord Jesus, and receive my soul: O Lord, into Thy hands I commend my spirit."

Essex was still speaking when the headsman struck. There was no sound or movement. He struck again; and again.

The spectators lingered a while, gazing on the headless carcase sprawled in the straw. Then they made their way numbly to the Tower Gate, and passed out through the silent crowds, each man to his own affairs.

THE COMMENTARY

Sources

A COMPLETE bibliography of materials for the life of Essex would include almost every major source for the last twenty years of the reign of Queen Elizabeth. There is so much material that between 1591 and 1601 it is possible to trace Essex's whereabouts almost for every day of his life. The most important sources are :—

I. The papers of the Marquis of Salisbury at Hatfield House. [HATFIELD.] These include not only a number of letters to the Cecils but a vast collection of letters to Essex. It is clear that after the rebellion of 1601 most of Essex's own papers passed into the hands of Sir Robert Cecil, and are included in the Hatfield collection.

II. The various collections of State Papers, especially Domestic and Ireland, in the Public Record Office.
It seemed more convenient to refer to the page of the relevant volume of the Calendars of I and II.

III. The papers of Anthony Bacon, now in Lambeth Palace Library, were digested and largely reprinted in Thomas Birch's *Memoirs of the Reign of Queen Elizabeth*, 2 volumes, 1754. [BIRCH.]

IV. W. B. Devereux, in *Lives and Letters of the Devereux, Earls of Essex*, 2 vols., 1853, printed a large collection of letters to and from Essex, many from private sources, but none from Hatfield. [DEVEREUX.]

V. Accounts of the principal events in Essex's life are to be found in the contemporary historians, chroniclers and commentators, especially in:

William Camden's History of the *Most Renowned and Victorious Princess Elizabeth, late Queen of England*. [CAMDEN.]
John Stow's *Annals, or a General Chronicle of England*. [STOW.]
Letters written by John Chamberlain during the Reign of Elizabeth, edited by Sarah Williams, 1861.
The letters of Rowland Whyte from the Court to Sir Robert Sidney, printed in *Letters and Memorials of State . . . from the originals at*

Penshurst Place, edited by Arthur Collins, 2 vols., 1746. [SIDNEY PAPERS.]

Sir Henry Wotton's *Of Robert Devereux, Earl of Essex, and George Villiers, Duke of Buckingham : some observations by way of parallel in the time of their estates of favour* [printed in RELIQUIÆ WOTTONIANÆ]. Sir Robert Naunton's sketch of Essex in FRAGMENTA REGALIA.

VI. *The Life and Letters of Francis Bacon*, by James Spedding, 7 vols., 1861, is the principal source for all matters concerning Bacon and Essex. [SPEDDING.]

VII. The background of the period and its contemporary gossip from 1591–1603 are recorded in the three volumes of my *Elizabethan Journals*. As those volumes are fully documented, I have not burdened the present book by repeating all sources for casual incidents.

These sources have been used throughout. Additional sources of importance for particular events are recorded in their places.

In reprinting letters and other documents spellings have been modernised and abbreviations expanded.

THE PORTRAITS OF ESSEX

IT seems likely that only one portrait of Essex (painting or drawing) was made during his lifetime, and that many versions of varying size and quality were afterwards made from it. They differ in costume and pose, but the facial characteristics are similar. Costume and pose were conventional, and, without precise records, of little importance in determining originals; it is the composition of the face that matters.

Of the extant portraits generally known, one at Trinity College, Cambridge (which is reproduced as frontispiece), has the greatest claim to be considered an original or near original.

The engraving (reproduced, facing page 240) came out in the winter of 1599–1600, and its sale was forbidden by the Council, but apparently without success, for in August 1600 they issued an order that the practice of selling engraved portraits of noblemen and others should cease, and that only portraits of the Queen (if well done) should be engraved and sold publicly. (*Last Elizabethan Journal*, pp. 67, 113.)

The engraving has the same facial characteristics as the Trinity portrait; it is likely therefore that this portrait, or its original, was painted during Essex's life.

NOTES

Page 1 line 18   *They had four children.*   Devereux, i, 8.

page 1 line 20   *Robert, born on November 10, 1567.*   There is some doubt about the year of Essex's birth. The date November 10th, 1567, is given in Thomas Milles' *Catalogue of Honour*, 1610, p. 863. This book is a lavish collection of the coats-of-arms of the nobility, and an early specimen of " Complete Peerage." Milles was an officer in the Excise and author of some interesting works on economics.

Later writers, including Thomas Fuller, in the *Worthies,* and Devereux follow Milles. The year 1567 is supported by Camden, who states that Essex died in the thirty-fourth year of his age. The date was accepted in the earlier editions of the *Dictionary of National Biography* in the article on Essex written by the late Sir Sidney Lee, but in the re-issue of 1908 it was silently altered to November 19th, 1566, on the authority of *Sloane MSS.,* 1697 f. 54*b*. This manuscript is one of several astrological treatises bound together, which I asked Mr. D. C. Collins to examine. He comments as follows: " The MS. is obviously an astrological notebook of the early seventeenth century in which various horoscopes are cast by way of exercise ; among them, for example, is one of Philip II of Spain. The opening at f. 54*b*–f. 55*a* gives four parallel horoscopes—Robert Devereux, 2nd Earl of Essex; his son, the son of the Earl of Dorset [Thomas Sackville, Lord Buckhurst, created Earl of Dorset 1604], presumably the second Earl, who died in 1609; Henry Brooke, Lord Cobham. Dates of birth are given or can be calculated from all the horoscopes, but though in the re-issue of the *Dictionary of National Biography* the altered date of Essex's birth is based on the horoscope, no alterations were made in the articles on the other three, though in each case the horoscope gives exact dates which were otherwise unknown, viz. Robert Devereux, third Earl of Essex, born January 11th, 1591; Robert Sackville, second Earl of Dorset, born September 20th, 1561; Henry Brooke, Lord Cobham, born November 21st, 1564.

" But the matter does not end here. The date November 19th, 1566, is NOT the date indicated in the horoscope, as can be seen by reference to contemporary astrological tables, e.g. George Hartgyll's *General Calendars or Most Easy Astrological Tables,* 1594. In the horoscope the sun is shown as being in Scorpion in the Eleventh House succeeding, whereas Hartgyll's tables show that on November 19th the sun was in Sagittarius, which it had entered on November 13th. Hartgyll's tables further show that the sun would be in Scorpio on November 10th, which is the usually accepted date for Essex's birth. As a rough test I checked the position of the stars in the First House, the Seventh House, and the Eighth House with the following result:

	Horoscope.	Hartgyll.	
		November 10th	November 19th
1st House.	Sagittarius ascending.	Sagittarius ascending.	Capricorn.
7th House.	Gemini descending.	Gemini descending.	Cancer.
8th House.	Virgo descending.	Virgo descending.	Libra.

" It follows that the horoscope was cast for the date November 10th, and that the date November 19th in the *Dictionary of National Biography* is wrong.

" The positions of the stars noted in the horoscope are no indication of the year, because between 1566 and 1567 the changes were so slight as to be hardly noticeable. Indeed, Hartgyll's table was intended to serve for forty years."

As for the year 1566, it should be noted that the horoscope was not cast at Essex's nativity, but forty years or so later. Either Milles or the astrologer has confused the year—an easy mistake at a time when a man's age was indifferently recorded as " 30 years " or in " his 31st year," and especially when the birthday fell so late in the year. Thus Stow says, that when Essex succeeded to the title [September 1576] he was ten years old; when he went into Flanders [December 1585] he was nineteen; when he returned [December 1586] he was twenty-one; one at least of these ages must be wrong, if not all three.

In such a conflict of statements I prefer the evidence of Milles, corroborated by Camden, and have therefore assumed that Essex was born on November 10th, 1567. Readers who consider the horoscope of greater validity should add one to Essex's age whenever mentioned.

page 2   line 28   *express his mind in Latin* . . . Devereux, i, 166.

page 3   line 4   Letter to Lord Burghley. Devereux, i, 166. Reproduced in facsimile, facing p. 2, from Lansdowne MSS. 22, f. 86.

page 3   line 34   Latin letter to Lord Burghley. Devereux, i, 167.

page 4   line 9   *Very modestly at Cambridge.* Devereux [ii, 487] prints some accounts of Essex's expenses at this period.

page 4   line 19   *a son, Robert Dudley.* The question of Robert Dudley's legitimacy, which affected a number of noble persons, was fought out in the Star Chamber in 1606, and the Court decided against him. As often happens in English Law, the issue was not a direct inquiry but arose out of a charge of tampering with witnesses.

page 4   line 28   *another secret marriage.* See Collins' Peerage, iv, 462.

page 5   line 19   Letter to Lord Burghley. Devereux, i, 171.

page 6   line 5   *She became his star.* For details of Sidney's love for Penelope Devereux, see Miss Mona Wilson's *Sir Philip Sidney,* 1931,

Chapter X. After some years of unhappy married life with Lord Rich, Penelope left him to become openly the mistress of Charles Blount, Lord Mountjoy.

page 6   line 8   *Dorothy Devereux also made a marriage.*   See *The Life . . . of John Aylmer*, by John Strype, edition of 1821, p. 217.

page 7   line 6   *Leicester's motives.*   See *Reliquiæ Wottonianæ*, and *Fragmenta Regalia*.

page 8 and following.   The chief authorities for Leicester's sojourn in the Low Countries are Stow; Hatfield Papers; *Correspondence of Robert Dudley, Earl of Leicester, during his Government of the Low Countries*, 1585-6, edited by J. Bruce, 1844; Sidney Papers; *Sir Philip Sidney*, by Mona Wilson; C.S.P. Foreign.

page 9   line 27   Letter from Sir Francis Knollys. Devereux, i, 178.

page 15   line 23   *a personal letter to Leicester.*   Printed in full in *Letters of Queen Elizabeth*, edited by G. B. Harrison, 1935, p. 174.

page 16   line 19   Letter from the Queen to Heneage. Printed in full in *Letters of Queen Elizabeth*, p. 175.

page 19   line 3   *likely to have a disastrous sequel.*   C.S.P. Foreign, vol. xxi, part ii, p. 117; Leicester Correspondence, p. 391.

page 21   line 36   *no relic could have been holier.*   Sidney's will is printed in Sidney Papers, i, 109. It was a disaster for Essex that his first introduction to the service of the State should have been in a campaign which was more spectacular than active. In his most impressionable years he was infected with the romance of war, for to some the soldier's profession is a religion, older than the oldest, with its own code, ritual and ecstasies. Hereafter Essex regarded himself, as above all things, a soldier.

page 25   line 28   *made notes on the details.*   See Hatfield MSS. iii, 216-9.

page 26   line 19   *his burial in Paul's.*   A magnificent engraving of the procession was published by Thomas Lant, one of the heralds, in 1588.

page 29   line 10   *constantly in her presence.*   See Devereux, i, 186.

page 30   line 29   *at Theobalds.*   C.S.P. Dom. p. 420.

page 30   line 31   *Essex was troubled.*   The details of this incident are taken from a letter which Essex wrote to Edward Dyer, dated July 21, printed in Devereux, i, 186. In the letter he does not name the sister; either Penelope or Dorothy might have been out of the Queen's favour at the time.

page 32 line 4 *amongst them Charles Blount.* The source of these two well-known stories is Naunton's *Fragmenta Regalia.* Naunton gives no date for either.

page 34 line 3 *Essex's own contingent.* C.S.P. Spanish, p. 419.

page 34 line 32 Leicester's will is printed in full in Sidney Papers, i, 145.

page 35 line 4 *Christopher Blount.* The D.N.B. suggests that he was a younger brother of Charles, afterwards Lord Mountjoy; and if so, born about 1565. He was thus about the same age as his stepson. Essex's family life was complicated, for his mother's brother-in-law was his sister's lover. The women of the family—his mother and two sisters—were devoted to him.

page 36 and following A long account of the Portugal Voyage is given in *Hakluyt's Voyages* (Everyman edition), iv, 306.

page 37 line 14 Letter to Sir Francis Knollys. Devereux, i, 206.

page 43 line 19 Letter from the Queen. Devereux, i, 204.

page 45 line 7 *letters with the King of Scots.* Hatfield, iii, 435.

page 46 line 6 Essex's marriage. There is some mystery about the date and circumstances of Essex's marriage. The account here given is from *The Court of King James the First,* by Bishop Godfrey Goodman (edited by J. S. Brewer, 2 volumes, 1839, vol. i, 149). Goodman knew many of Essex's contemporaries, but he wrote many years after the event and is not necessarily reliable. He does, however, give as his authority Dr. Overall, afterwards Bishop of Norwich, who received the story from Essex himself in 1599. The story is reasonable enough, but there is no external evidence of the exact date of the marriage. The first child, Robert (afterwards third Earl of Essex, victim of the notorious nullity suit and leader of the Parliamentary forces in the Great Rebellion), was baptised on 22nd January, 1591, which gives April 1590 as the latest date. There is little suggestion in any of the surviving records that it was a romantic marriage; nor was Essex a faithful husband. The Queen was always hysterical when her favourites married, but her annoyance was not unreasonable. According to the accepted notions of the time, it was the duty of a nobleman to enhance the fortunes of his House, name and position by marrying a lady of suitable wealth and family, and especially since Essex's own estate was so decayed.

Of Frances Sidney, the new Countess, very little is known. She seems to have been a good wife after Xenophon's pattern, placid, faithful, and a little simple. During the last months of Essex's troubles she was blackmailed by a servant called Daniel, who was very properly punished in the Star

Chamber. Although she shared in Essex's troubles, she did not incur the same suspicion as her more vigorous sisters-in-law. There is no known portrait of her and she remains in history a "gracious silence." She bore Essex five children, Robert (baptised 22nd January, 1591); Walter (baptised 21st January, 1592) and Henry (baptised 14th April, 1595), who both died young; Frances (born 20th September, 1599) and Dorothy (born about 20th December, 1600) [Devereux, ii, 196]. Essex's children seemed to have played very little part in his life; indeed, I do not remember to have come across any mention of them in his letters or other records.

Professor Conyers Read (in *Mr. Secretary Walsingham*, vol. iii, p. 170), basing his observations on a letter written by a Dr. William Gifford in June 1587, remarks: " It has been generally assumed that this marriage [i.e. Essex to Lady Sidney] did not take place until after Walsingham's death, the assumption being based upon the fact that the first child of the marriage was not born until April [sic] of 1591. But Dr. Gifford's letter is positive evidence to the contrary, and it may be that a marriage was performed in the spring of 1587, but was kept secret from fear of the royal wrath, until the coming of the child made further concealment impossible. If this was indeed the case, it is not unlikely that the marriage did provoke Leicester's hostility, since his antipathy to his step-son was notorious."
This statement Professor Read qualifies in a footnote: " It ought to be pointed out that Dr. Gifford's letter is a little obscure on this point. In enumerating the differences between Leicester and Walsingham he wrote: ' Secondly because Walsingham has married his daughter my Lady Sidney to . . .' The last part of the sentence I have been unable to decipher, but it can hardly refer to any other marriage than that with the Earl of Essex."

Conclusions based on a manuscript which cannot be deciphered must always be haphazard and uncritical. Actually the sentence in Gifford's letter reads " Secondly, because Walsingham hath married his daughter my Lady Sidney to Cecil's son's son." There is no trace in the Hatfield records of such a marriage. Moreover, the child was not born in April but in January.

page 48 line 1 the Queen changed her mind. See *Acts of the Privy Council*, edited by J. R. Dasent, xxi, 220, 289, 292.

page 48 line 29 Letter to the Queen. Devereux, i, 222.

page 49 line 23 The expedition to Normandy. Important particular sources are *The Correspondence of Sir Henry Unton*, edited by Rev. Joseph Stevenson, 1847; *A Journal of the Siege of Rouen by Sir Thomas Coningsby*, edited by J. G. Nichols, in vol. i. of the Camden Miscellany, 1847; *Memoirs of Robert Carey, Earl of Monmouth*, edited by G. H. Powell, 1905.

page 51 line 4 Letter to the Council. Devereux, i, 225.

page 53   line 7   *Newhaven,* the Elizabethan name for Le Havre.

page 54   line 8   *a very violent attack of fever.* This fever was probably malaria. Henceforward Essex was subject to sudden and severe fevers at all times, but particularly after violent exertion or emotional disturbances. Though some of his disappearances from Court were due to offended dignity, he was often acutely ill. His depression and melancholia probably had a physical origin. Bishop Goodman in the passage embodied in p. 82, line 9, hints that he may have suffered from venereal disease. If so, it would partly account for the obvious degeneration in his mental powers after 1596.

page 55   line 7   *complained to Sir Robert Cecil.* Devereux, i, 233.

page 55   line 10   *he wrote to the Queen.* Devereux, i, 237.

page 55   line 26   Letter to Burghley. Devereux, 1, 238.

page 57   line 17   The capture of Gournay. *Unton Correspondence,* pp. 96–97. A very attractive, contemporary, pictorial map of the siege is reproduced in my first *Elizabethan Journal,* pp. 58–9.

page 58   line 4   *Essex sent Robert Carey.* Carey's *Memoirs,* p. 17.

page 60   line 15   Letter to the Queen. Devereux, i, 244.

page 61   line 5   Letter to the Queen. Devereux, i, 249.

page 62   line 5   *gallantries on both sides.* For Essex's challenges to Villars, see *Coningsby's Journal,* p. 76, and Hatfield, iv, 161.

page 63   line 20   *a most noble brave King.* Unton *Correspondence,* pp. 117, 129.

page 63   line 32   *stood by him covered.* The etiquette of wearing the hat was exact. The inferior removed his hat when in the presence of his superior, who remained covered; but Essex kept his hat on because he represented the Queen. See later, pp. 250, 285, 286, for similar niceties.

page 64   line 3   *a body made of iron.* They were mistaken; Essex was not naturally strong, but he was filled with a kind of dæmonic energy, which drove him at times far beyond his strength, and then, in the reaction, left him exhausted and utterly melancholic.

page 65   line 12   Letter to Cecil. Hatfield, iv, 165.

page 66   line 23   Letter to Cecil. Devereux, i, 272.

page 67   lines 6 and 34.   Letters from the Queen. Devereux, i, 267, and Hatfield, iv, 166.

NOTES

page 70   line 13   *At rare intervals there is born a man.*   In our own times two Englishmen have left this kind of impression on those who knew them: Rupert Brooke and T. E. Lawrence. One who was an intimate friend of Rupert Brooke confirms the aptness of the parallel in a private letter: " it came into my mind once more (I often used to feel it in earlier days) that Sidney is the only person I have read or heard of who must have had the same effect on his friends as Rupert had. Certainly I can say that I never knew anyone whose death made such a difference. And that is true, I believe, not only of everyone who knew him well or pretty well but even of a good many who were only acquainted with him. Not one of his friends but would agree, that friendship with him was one of the greatest things that could happen. Impossible to say just how or why it seemed to differ *in kind* from other friendships."

page 72   line 9   Francis Bacon's letter to Lord Burghley. Spedding, i, 109.

page 74   line 17   *his collar of S's.*   Spedding, i, 120.

page 75   line 6   *a member of her Privy Council.*   A.P.C. xxiv, 78.

page 77   line 7   Letter to Bacon. Spedding, i, 254.

page 79   line 33   Anthony Standen. See Birch, i, 66.

page 80   line 24   For Antonio Perez (not to be confused with Don Antonio, ex-king of Portugal) see Birch, i, 153.

page 81   line 28   Dr. Roderigo Lopez. This account of Essex's first dealings with Lopez is from Goodman [i, 150], and reproduces therefore the gossip of a later generation.

page 83   line 20   *When Essex came next to the Queen.*   See Birch, i, 150-2.

page 84   line 26   *returned together in a coach.*   See Birch, i, 153.

page 85   line 21   Lopez' trial. The whole story is very complex, and the full truth still not quite certain. The best account is that by Martin Hume in *Treason and Plot*. Hume had access to Spanish Papers which show that Lopez was less guilty than he was generally supposed. He was, however, a knave, and had been engaged in spy work for years. He was also credited with supplying Leicester with poisons. Probably his story at the trial was true—that he had taken the reward from the Spanish King but never intended to harm the Queen, though he may have been prepared to poison Don Antonio.

page 86   line 12   *again broached the subject.*   Spedding, i, 289.

page 87   line 15   Letter from Southampton to Essex. Hatfield, iv, 96. The letter is dated in the Calender " 2nd March, 1590-1." If the date is correct, Southampton visited France in 1591; and his friendship with Essex dates from this time. The letter might, however, have been written when Southampton went to France in Sir Robert Cecil's mission in 1598. For Southampton, see *The Third Earl of Southampton*, by Mrs. C. C. Stopes, 1922.

page 88 line 4   *to break the news.* Spedding, i, 371.

page 90 line 13   *a copy of the Conference was given to the Queen.* For this and most other items of Court gossip, see Rowland Whyte's letters in Sidney Papers, i, 347 and following.

page 90 line 20   *a pretty device for Accession day celebrations.* Spedding, i, 386.

page 93 line 14   *secret instructions for the French King.* Birch, i, 153.

page 96 line 6   *relief expedition.* For the correspondence concerning the capture of Calais, see C.S.P. Dom. p. 196 and following, and Hatfield, vi, 132 and following.

page 97 line 19   *attended a meeting of the Council.* A.P.C., xxv, 331.

page 98 line 30, and page 99 line 11   Howard's letters to Sir Robert Cecil and the Queen. Hatfield, vi, 144. C.S.P. Dom. p. 204.

page 99 line 26   Letter to Lord Burghley. Devereux, i, 336.

page 100 line 17   Letter from the Queen. C.S.P. Dom. p. 205, printed in full in *Letters of Queen Elizabeth*, p. 245.

page 101 line 21   To issue a proclamation. C.S.P. Dom. p. 211.

page 101 line 25   Letter to Ralegh. Hatfield, vi, 169.

page 102 line 15   Letter to Cecil. Hatfield, vi, 172.

page 103 line 4   Letter to Cecil. Hatfield, vi, 174.

page 104 line 9   Letter to the Council. Birch, ii, 8.

page 107 line 4   Letter from the Queen. *Letters of Queen Elizabeth*, p. 245.

page 108 and following   The more important particular authorities for the Cadiz voyage are *A Relation of the Voyage to Cadiz*, 1596, by Sir William Slyngsbie (*Naval Miscellany*, i, Navy Records Society); *The Naval Tracts of Sir William Monson*, edited with a long commentary by M. Oppenheim, for the Navy Records Society, 1902, vol. i, p. 344 and following; and authorities therein cited.

NOTES

page 108   line 6   Letter to the Council. Devereux, i, 349.

page 123   line 12   *a library of books.* These Essex afterwards gave to Thomas Bodley for his library at Oxford, where they yet survive.

page 125   line 4   Letter to Burghley. Reproduced in facsimile, facing p. 124 from Lansdowne 82, f. 12. " Cales " is the usual Elizabethan form of Cadiz (as " Calis " or " Callice " is for Calais), as in the rude rhyme made upon the Cadiz Knights which ran:

> A Gentleman of Wales,
> With a Knight of Cales,
> And a Lord of the North Countree,
> A Yeoman of Kent,
> Upon a rack'd rent,
> Will buy them out all three.

page 125   line 21   Letter to Reynolds. Birch, ii, 45.

page 126   line 15   *account of the Cadiz action.* Birch, ii, 81 and following.

page 128   line 14   *Reynolds felt hurt.* Birch, ii, 108.

page 129   line 25   *the expedition would leave her with a debit balance.* It is usual to denounce the Queen's meanness in demanding some financial return from the Cadiz voyage, but her difficulties are seldom appreciated. For the true explanation, see Professor J. E. Neale's *Queen Elizabeth, passim,* and especially pp. 284-90, 333. " For all its drabness and difficulty, finance is the essence of Elizabeth's story. Her ordinary revenue —from crown lands, customs, etc.—amounted in the first twelve years of her reign to about £200,000 per annum, and in the last decade to about £300,000—a sum, after making allowance for the difference in the value of money, ridiculously small, and nothing approaching the revenue of her rivals, France and Spain. Financially, England was not a great power. Out of the ordinary revenue Elizabeth had to maintain herself, her Court and the whole system of government. In a separate category fell what was called extraordinary expenditure, the chief items in which were fortifications and war. Here the Crown was entitled to call on parliament to come to its aid with taxation; but here only, for the normal cost of government was regarded as the private concern of the sovereign, just as much as the financing of a nobleman's household and estate was the nobleman's concern. Taxation was not a normal but an abnormal incidence on the country; and any sovereign, who like Elizabeth, looked to popularity as the source of her strength, had to bear this in mind. Over the whole reign parliamentary taxation averaged rather less than £80,000 per annum; for the first thirty years it averaged little more than £50,000. Thus, until 1588 Elizabeth had a total average income, ordinary and parliamentary, of not much more than £250,000 a year, out of which to uphold her royal magnificence, run her government, fight her few battles and play paymaster to Protestant Europe."

page 130   line 1   *a very humble letter to Essex.*   Birch, ii, 146, 153.

page 130   line 26   *Essex House was almost a European Court in miniature.*   The Hatfield Papers include many original letters written to Essex from abroad. At this time, and until his departure for Ireland in 1599, Essex was receiving fuller and more accurate information of foreign affairs than the Cecils. In the four years 1596–9 the letters to Essex average about 150 a year, to the Cecils about twenty-five. In addition there was the voluminous correspondence of Anthony Bacon.

page 130   line 29   *a new fashion.*   For the Cadiz beard see *Second Elizabethan Journal*, p. 128. The description of Essex's manner is from *Reliquiæ Wottonianæ*.

page 132   line 1   *The relationship between these two.*   From this time Essex's fortunes began to decline. His psychological relations with the Queen were bound to cause disaster. When he succeeded, she was jealous; if he failed, she would be angry. Neither could face the third possibility—that he should retire altogether from public life. The Queen was harassed by conflicting emotions. When Essex was with her, she was fascinated by him; but when he was absent, she felt intense irritation with herself for giving way to a man whose weaknesses she knew too well, and she vented on him her annoyance with herself. Moreover, the personal relationship was complicated by a variety of political issues. Those in great place, even more than common men and women, need the services of the psychoanalyst.

page 132   line 14   Bacon's letter of advice.   Spedding, ii, 40.

page 135   line 18   *Burgh's advice.*   C.S.P. Dom. p. 299.

page 136   line 8   Letter from Lady Bacon.   Birch, ii, 218.

page 136   line 32   Letter to Lady Bacon.   Birch ii, 219.

page 137   line 33   *wrote down both proposals.*   C.S.P. Dom. p. 350.

page 138   line 5   Rowland Whyte is the authority for the Court gossip of these weeks.

page 139   line 35   *taking physic without leave.*   The periodical purging which physicians inflicted on their patients was a drastic and formidable affair, and incapacitated the victim for several days.

page 142 and following   The most important accounts of the Islands Voyage are those by Sir Arthur Gorges, captain of the *Warspite* (printed in *Purchas His Pilgrims,* Maclehose edition, 1907, vol. xx); by Sir Francis Vere in his *Commentaries* (printed in Arber's *English Garner*, vol. viii); and by Sir William Monson, who was Essex's captain (printed

NOTES 339

and edited with the valuable commentary of M. Oppenheim, for The Navy Records Society, 1902, vol. xxiii). Gorges was a partisan of Ralegh; Vere was contemptuous both of Essex and of Ralegh; Monson on the whole favoured Essex but admitted that the muddles were to be attributed " to the want of experience in my Lord, and his flexible nature to be ruled." The various accounts can hardly be reconciled.

page 142 line 1   *Essex's instructions.* C.S.P. Dom. p. 439.

page 143 line 16   *Vere was chagrined.* This, on a larger scale, is the situation at the beginning of *Othello,* when the experienced soldier Iago is superseded by the courtier Cassio, also a mere book soldier. Young noblemen and courtiers, who were given commands for which they had no training, were liable to be a nuisance and to cause trouble. The Queen usually forbade noblemen to take much part in military operations.

page 143 line 24   Letter to the Queen. Devereux, 1, 413.

page 145 line 18   Letter from Ralegh to Cecil. C.S.P. Dom. p. 466.

page 145 line 30   Letter from Howard, Burghley and Cecil. C.S.P. Dom. p. 470.

page 146 line 21   Letter from Burghley. C.S.P. Dom. p. 469.

page 147 line 32   *a long account of the incident.* C.S.P. Dom. p. 473.

page 148 line 15   *Sir Anthony Shirley.* This famous swashbuckler had only just returned from a filibustering expedition to raid Spanish towns in South America. He left England for his journey to Persia soon after returning from the Islands Voyage. For his life, see *Sir Anthony Sherley and his Persian Adventure,* by Sir E. Denison Ross, 1933.

page 148 line 36   *posted to Court.* C.S.P. Dom. pp. 486, 487.

page 149 line 9   Letter to the Council. Hatfield, vii, 352.

page 151 line 2   *The St. Matthew . . . obliged to make for home.* Her loss to the expedition was most unfortunate, for she carried the heavy guns.

page 151 line 18   Instructions for Robert Knollys. Hatfield, vii, 368.

page 154 line 1   Letter to Cecil. Hatfield, vii, 386.

page 168 line 8   Instructions for Sir Thomas Jermyn. Hatfield, vii, 439.

page 169 line 4   Letter to Cecil. Hatfield, vii, 445. This letter is endorsed with the times of receipt at the various stages of the post service.

" At Plymouth the 26 of October about 10 of the clock in the morning. For life, for life, ESSEX "; Ashburton 4.30 p.m.; Exeter " past 8 of the clock in the night "; Honiton, 10.30 p.m.; Crewkerne, 1.30 a.m.; Sherborne, 4.30 a.m.; Shafton, 7 a.m.; Salisbury, 9 a.m ; Andover, noon; Basingstoke, 3.30 p.m.

page 169 line 18   Letter to Cecil. Hatfield, vii, 445.

page 169 line 33   Letter to the Council. Hatfield, vii, 446.

page 170 line 14   *The Queen wrote.* Hatfield, vii, 449.

page 171 line 15   *in no mood to meet criticism.* Some research student should write a thesis on *Some aspects of the effect of physical fatigue on the course of history ;* but unfortunately one does not learn about such matters from books. Nothing is so upsetting to the nerves, temper and judgment as a long, tedious and interminable journey on foot or horseback. As one goes on, mile after mile, one becomes more and more irritable, peevish and unreasonable. Essex had not ridden for months, and he must have arrived at Court stiff and saddle sore, and ready to quarrel with his own shadow.

page 171 line 24   *the old Lord Admiral.* Howard was now sixty and his services deserved reward, but as a newly created Earl he would normally be junior to Essex. In virtue of his office, however, he took precedence of all but the Earl Marshal. Precedence was punctiliously observed in the numerous ceremonials of the Court.

page 171 line 35   *suffered from ague.* Hatfield, vii, 479.

page 172 line 21   *an anonymous letter.* S.P. Dom. p. 532.

page 174 line 28   *De Maisse kept a careful journal.* De Maisse's Journal (translated and edited by G. B. Harrison and R. A. Jones, 1931) gives a vivid day by day account of his mission and of the English Court at this time: De Maisse and Rowland Whyte (Sidney Papers) are the chief authorities for events during these weeks.

page 175 line 23   *at last he came to Court. Vere's Commentaries,* Arber's English Garner, vol. viii.

page 176 line 30   *strangely attired.* De Maisse's Journal, p. 25.

page 178 line 2   *in that condition.* The Queen had postponed De Maisse's audience on the ground that she had a sore throat and received him *en deshabillé.*

page 178 line 31   Letter to Cecil. Hatfield, vii, 520.

page 181 line 31   *his private affairs.* Essex was chronically in debt, but his creditors were pressing. Earlier in the year Reynolds had drawn up a list of his debts immediately due which Cecil had laid before the Queen.

NOTES 341

page 182 line 2   *de Maisse noted of Essex.* De Maisse's Journal, p. 116. He also remarked, "I have always found the Earl of Essex very open."

page 183 line 2   *many new problems.* C.S.P. Dom. p. 1.

page 183 line 23   *an active part in the work of the House.* For details see *A Compleat Journal of . . . the House of Lords and the House of Commons throughout the whole reign of Queen Elizabeth*. By Sir Simonds D'Ewes, 1693.

page 184 line 16   *Southampton was in disgrace.* Sidney Papers, ii, 82, 83.

page 185 line 1   Letter to Cecil. Hatfield, viii, 42.

page 185 line 13   Letter from Cecil. C.S.P. Dom. p. 29. Twelve miles' row in an open boat over a choppy sea was a bad start for a long journey. Wilkes died of the effects of his tossing on 2nd March.

page 188 line 10   *appalling corruption of the British officials.* See State Papers, Ireland, *passim*.

page 188 line 33   Letter from Bacon. Spedding, ii, 95

page 189 lines 22, 23   *aged dignity . . . my dear kinsman*, i.e. Bacon's uncle Lord Burghley and cousin Robert Cecil.

page 190 line 13   *the Garter feast.* The Journal of Sir Roger Wilbraham, Camden Miscellany, vol. x, p. 15.

page 191 line 10   Letter from Cecil. C.S.P. Dom. p. 44.

page 192 line 5   *the health of his old father.* Hatfield, viii, 102.

page 192 line 24   *taking out his prayer book.* This incident is related by Camden.

page 192 line 32   *one young satirist.* Everard Guilpin in *Skialetheia*, Satire i, reprinted in Shakespeare Association Facsimiles, vol. 2, entered for publication 15th September, but written in the previous months.

page 193 line 19   *an Apology.* Contemporary manuscript copies are not uncommon. The *Apology* was openly printed in 1603 after the Queen's death.

page 194 line 12   *He protested that it was never his intention.* Hatfield, viii, 545.

page 194 line 22   *On July 1st.* For evidence for this date see note on the incident in *Last Elizabethan Journal*. Although there is plenty of evidence of a violent and sensational quarrel between the Queen and Essex, only Camden has recorded the details of the affair.

page 195   line 28   Letter from Knollys. Birch, ii, 389.

page 196   line 6 ⎱   Letter from Buckhurst, and Essex's
page 198   line 26 ⎰   reply. Birch, ii, 385 and following. A
number of contemporary copies of these two famous letters exist, for they
were circulated amongst Essex's friends. They are usually dated 15th and
18th October. Unless there was another violent quarrel in October, after
the reconciliation in September, the date is too late. There is no evidence
of such a quarrel, which would hardly have escaped the notice of John
Chamberlain and his gossips. Chamberlain, on October 3, writes that
Essex " is at Court in as good terms (they say) as ever he was "; and on
October 20 he records Essex's activities over the Court of Wards and the
Irish Command. Speed, however, dates the letters 15th and 18th *July*,
which is a far more probable date. Essex's letter was afterwards used
against him: see p. 263.

page 197   line 34   *God Himself requireth it as a principal
bond of service to Himself.* To rebel against the Sovereign, who was
God's Vicegerent on Earth, was to rebel against God. This notion was so
strongly ingrained that even in the Great Rebellion, the Parliamentary
party at first mobilised troops for the King's " protection " from his
enemies. At this time the sentiment was not uncommon. Thus in the
of *Sir Thomas More*, probably written after Essex's rebellion, More,
addressing the London rioters, says—
   " What do you then,
      Rising 'gainst him that God himself installs,
      But rise 'gainst God ? "

page 201   line 23   Letter to the Queen. Devereux, i, 493.

page 202   line 20   *He spoke to Lord Grey.* Hatfield, viii, 269.

page 203   line 17   Letter from Knollys. Birch, ii, 390.

page 204 line 17   *important source of foreign news.* Amongst
the papers at Hatfield written during the four months May to August
1598, there are about fifty letters to Essex from abroad. His correspondents
included the French King; the Duc de Biron; Gilpin, the Queen's Agent at
the Hague; the Count of Nassau; the States General; Sir Francis Vere;
Sir Edward Norris, Governor of Ostend. For the same period only five
letters to Cecil from correspondents abroad are preserved.

page 205   line 1   Letter to the Queen. Hatfield, viii, 318.

page 206   line 11   *the funeral of Lord Burghley.* Chamberlain's Letters, p. 15, C.S.P. Dom. p. 83.

page 206   line 31   Letter from Cecil to Southampton. C.S.P.
Dom. p. 90.

page 207   line 14   *Lee wrote to him.* C.S.P. Dom. p. 88.

page 208 line 13   Letter to the Queen. Hatfield, viii, 332.

page 209 line 13   Letter to the Queen. Hatfield, viii, 416.

page 211 and following   The particular sources include the State Papers, Ireland; the Calendar of Carew MSS.; Sir John Harington's Letters and Journal, printed in *Nugæ Antiquæ*; and the *Itinerary* of Fynes Moryson (Maclehose edition, 4 vols., 1907). Moryson was Mountjoy's secretary.

page 211 line 7   *the two Danvers brothers.* Henry and Charles Danvers were friends of Southampton. On October 4, 1594, they murdered a neighbour, Henry Long, gentleman, brother of Sir Walter Long. The murder arose out of an ancient family feud. The brothers fled to Titchfield House. Southampton hid them until they could escape to France, where they remained until 1598, when they received a pardon.

page 211 line 12   *If he performed in the field.* Nugæ Antiquæ, i, 240.

page 212 line 2   Letter to Fulke Greville. Hatfield, ix, 4.

page 212 line 16   Letter to Lord Willoughby. Hatfield, ix, 9.

page 214 line 32   *not only precepts but lively patterns.* At a time when the free discussion of State matters was high treason, readers and playgoers looked to history for a reflection of their own times and problems. In June following it was decreed that no English Histories should be printed unless allowed by members of the Council.

page 215 line 4   *the play of Richard the Second.* For the significance of Shakespeare's *Richard the Second*, see my *Shakespeare at Work*, p. 127, etc. Compare Guilpin's similar description of "great Felix," on p. 193.

page 215 line 29   *And who was this A. P.?* It was very generally believed by Essex's enemies, and the Queen herself, that the book was seditious propaganda. According to the evidence of Wolfe [see p. 267], only one edition was published, from which the epistle was cut out after 500-600 copies were sold. Actually four editions have been identified, two printed by Alde, and two others, probably printed in the seventeenth century; all are dated 1599 and include the epistle. The book is still not uncommon in booksellers' catalogues. The Council were naturally suspicious of " A. P." Ben Jonson told Drummond that Essex was the author of the epistle signed " A. B. " " before the translation of the last part of Tacitus." If Hayward was innocent of all seditious intent, he was simpler than his contemporaries thought possible.

page 215 line 30   *Essex's instructions.* Carew Papers, p. 292.

page 216 line 15   *a licence that he might return.* Carew Papers, p. 295.

page 216   line 19   *a triumphal departure.*   Stow's Annals.

page 217   line 4   Letter to the Council.   C.S.P. Ireland, p. 1.

page 217   line 24   *reached Chester.*   Great preparation was made for Essex's worthy reception. Mr. S. H. Atkins sends me the following extract from the Assembly Books in Chester Town Hall— p. 256. At an Assembly in the Pentice, March 1st, 1599, before the mayor, Richard Rathburne (or Rathbone):
"At wch assembly Mr Maior declareth that he is credible informed that the Right Ho: the Erle Marshall of England will speedely repaire to this citie to take shippinge for Ireland And moueth that some such order may be taken for the receipt and entertaynemt of the saied Erle as may be both befittinge soe honorable a personage and tend to the credite of the citie vppon whose motion it is by the same Assembly agreed and ordered that there shallbe prepared at the ousight and appointmt of Mr Dauid lloyd and Mr William Aldersay Ald for the said Erle a good banquett vppon the cities Chardges and that a siluer cupp of x^{li} or xx^{ty} marks price shalbe bought and fortie Angells of gould alsoe prouided vppon the cities chardges and putt into the saied cupp and soe be psented vnto his Ho: And at the same Assembly Rauff Rathburne Thomas Harvy John Lea George Boyes and John Lyniall are appointed Harbingers to prouide Lodginge for the souldiers appointed to come to this citie and to see them shipped vidz Thomas Heruie for Liuerpoole and Wallezey John Lea for Burton head and the other three as Mr Maior shall at his pleasure Appoynte."

page 217   line 25   Letter to the Council.   C.S.P. Ireland, p. 1.

page 218   line 12   Letter to Cecil.   C.S.P. Ireland, p. 6.

page 222   line 2   *a journal of his journey.*   *Nugæ Antiquæ,* i, 260–275.   C.S.P. Ireland, 37.

page 222   line 4   Letter to the Council.   C.S.P. Ireland, p. 36.

page 223   line 23   *a regrettable reverse.*   C.S.P. Ireland, pp. 58–60, 69, 81–91. This kind of warfare, where organised troops are opposed by nimble, lightly armed natives, fighting in their own country, needs a far higher standard of discipline and training than " civilised " warfare, especially in rearguard actions. The clumsy musket was little use against a scattered enemy, and Essex's soldiers were ill-trained, and lacked all enthusiasm.

page 226   line 33   Letter to the Council.   C.S.P. Ireland, p. 36.

page 227   line 23   Letter to the Council.   C.S.P. Ireland, p. 91.

page 228   line 18   Letter to the Council.   C.S.P. Ireland, p. 95.

page 229   line 30   Letter from the Queen.   C.S.P. Ireland, p. 98.

page 234   line 32   Letter from the Queen.   C.S.P. Ireland, p. 105.

NOTES 345

page 237 line 7 *another lamentable disaster.* C.S.P. Ireland, p. 113. Moryson, iii, 245.

page 238 line 11 *noted as a strange thing.* Chamberlain's Letters, p. 63. Thomas Wilson (in *The State of England*, 1601, Camden Miscellany, vol. xvi, p. 23) notes " There are accounted to be in England about the number of 500 Knights. . . . I reckon not among these my Lord of Essex's Knights (whose father living or many of them hardly good gentlemen and which for a difference of their Knighthood are scornfully called Cales, Roan, or Irish Knights) but such as are chief men in their countries." Essex was thus actually responsible for about a quarter of all the Knights in England.

page 238 line 21 *the resolution to be recorded in writing.* C.S.P. Ireland 126.

page 240 line 13 Letter to the Council. C.S.P. Ireland, p. 136. This letter was delivered at Court on September 5th, but Cuffe apparently did not arrive for another eight or nine days.

page 243 line 12 Letter from the Queen. C.S.P. Ireland, p. 150. This and the previous letters were written, or at least dictated by the Queen herself. The Council also wrote to Essex on September 14th, noting that they need not reiterate the contents of the Queen's letter " having found it her Majesty's pleasure of all particulars by her own hand " [*ibid.* p. 149].

page 248 line 1 *Friday September 28th.* For this event and the Court news and gossip of this chapter Rowland Whyte is the main authority. [Sidney Papers, ii, 127 and following.]

page 251 line 34 *blank and hopeless melancholy.* For the first few days Essex supposed that the Queen would send him back. He made several memoranda on the situation, in one of which he proposed to reduce the army to 9,000 foot and 800 horse. When he returned to Dublin, he said, he would conclude the treaty with Tyrone, lull him with security, and then find a pretext for a sudden and overwhelming attack. [Carew, pp. 336–7.]

page 253 line 4 *Essex's friends were anxious.* For the intrigues of Essex, Danvers, Cuffe, Mountjoy and Southampton see the confessions and other papers published as an Appendix to *Correspondence of King James VI of Scotland with Sir Robert Cecil and others.* . . . Edited by John Bruce, 1861 [p. 101, BRUCE].

page 255 line 4 *Dr. John Overall.* Goodman, i, 145.

page 255 line 16 *Farewell to Southampton.* There is a manuscript copy in the British Museum. It was printed in 1642.

page 256 line 35 *his malice . . . less than was usually supposed* It is usual to denounce Cecil as a subtle schemer who by delicate Machiavellian ways engineered Essex's downfall. Thus Lytton

Strachey, in one of the most notable character sketches in *Elizabeth and Essex*:

"He sat at his table writing; and his presence was sweet and grave. There was an urbanity upon his features, some kind of explanatory gentleness, which, when he spoke, was given life and meaning by his exquisite elocution. He was all mild reasonableness—or so it appeared, until he left his chair, stood up, and unexpectedly revealed the stunted discomfort of deformity. Then another impression came upon one—the uneasiness produced by an enigma: what could the combination of that beautifully explicit countenance with that shameful, crooked posture really betoken? He returned to the table, and once more took up his quill; all, once more, was perspicuous serenity." ... "He inspected the career of Essex with serious concern. Yet, perhaps, in some quite different manner, something, sometimes—very rarely—almost never—might be done. At a moment of crisis, a faint, a hardly perceptible impulsion might be given. It would be nothing but a touch, unbetrayed by the flutter of an eyelid, as one sat at table, not from one's hand, which would continue writing, but from one's foot. One might hardly be aware of its existence oneself, and yet was it not, after all, by such minute, invisible movements that the world was governed for its good, and great men came into their own? That might be, in outline, the clue to the enigma; but the detailed working-out of the solution must remain, from its very nature, almost entirely unknown to us". ... "We can, with luck, catch a few glimpses now and then; but, in the main, we can only obscurely conjecture at what happened under the table." [p. 106.]

W. B. Devereux even went so far as to insinuate that, had he been allowed access to the Hatfield Papers, the full truth of Cecil's schemings would have been revealed.

In fact, Cecil showed remarkable patience and was genuinely desirous of working with Essex. It was not until Essex insisted that no one but his enemy could be reasonably civil to Cecil, that Cecil became Essex's opponent. Cecil's position was very difficult. He was not a nobleman, and if ever the Queen's support should be withdrawn he had no powerful following to defend him. He was always a little conscious of a sense of social inferiority.

page 257 line 1   *Dr. Hayward's book.* C.S.P. Dom. p. 404.

page 257 line 34   *very anxious for Essex.* Bruce, p. 103.

page 258 line 15   *Mountjoy took up his duties with enthusiasm.*
For a remarkable character sketch see Fynes Moryson, ii, 260. Moryson was his secretary in Ireland.

page 259 line 29   *Henry Cuffe . . . Essex's evil genius.*
See *Reliquiæ Wottonianæ.* Birch, ii, 82.

page 260 line 32   Letter to the Queen. C.S.P. Dom. p. 435.

page 262   line 3   *York House to receive his official censure.*
This description of the proceedings is taken mainly from Moryson, ii, 311.

page 266   line 20   *Dr. Hayward was summoned to Court.*
The examinations of Hayward, Wolfe and Harsnett are in S.P. Dom. [pp. 449 and following].

page 268   line 2   Letter from Bacon. Spedding, ii, 190.

page 268   line 25   Letter to Bacon. Spedding, ii, 192.

page 269   lines 13, 14   *imped.* To "imp" is "to insert a new feather into the wing or tail of a hawk with a broken one." Mue (or "mew"), "a place in which falcons were kept; also, metaphorically, any close place. Probably because birds were confined in them while moulting." (Nares' Glossary.)

page 270   line 11   *Cuffe renewed his sneers.* There is discrepancy between Camden and Wotton about the date when Cuffe was dismissed. Camden implies that it was in the late summer, Wotton very shortly before the rising.

page 270   line 22   *The crisis was at hand.* It was part of Essex's trouble that he was absolutely dependent on the Queen for his income, for the properties left him by his father were all mortgaged. Wotton says that the sum which he received from the Queen, "besides the fees of his offices, and the disposition of great sums of money in her armies, was (about the time of his arraignment, when faults used to be aggravated with precedent benefits) valued at £300,000 sterling in pure gift for his only use by the Earl of Dorset [i.e. Lord Buckhurst], then Lord Treasurer, who was a wise man, and a strict computist, and not well affected towards him." Of this money, Wotton declares Anthony Bacon to have extracted a generous picking, by subtle hints of blackmail—£4,000 in cash, and at least £1,000 a year in annual pension.

page 271   line 12   Letter to the Queen. C.S.P. Dom. p. 468.

page 272   line 28   Letter to the Queen. C.S.P. Dom. p. 479.

page 274   line 11   *Essex's rise and decline.* The passage which follows is based on my reading of the period. Reflections of the anxieties and disillusion of these years can be seen in many contemporary books and plays. No one, for instance, at the time could have failed to notice the striking parallels between Essex's story and much of Shakespeare's *Troilus and Cressida* [worked out in *Shakespeare at Work,* pp. 217 and following].

If any confirmation of the upheaval caused by Essex's downfall is needed, Stow's words will suffice: "Such and so great was the hearty love and deep affections of the people towards him, by reason of his bounty, liberality, affability, and mild behaviour, that as well scholars, soldiers, citizens, sailors, etc., Protestants, Papists, Sectaries, and atheists, yea, women and children which never saw him, that it was held in them a happiness to follow the worst of his fortunes."

page 276 and following   Of the usual sources Camden and Stow are particularly important for the rebellion and the events leading up to it. Most of the confessions, examinations and contemporary accounts are in S.P. Dom. D. Jardine's account of the trial is most valuable. See also Sloan MSS. 718; and Mrs. Stope's *Southampton*.

page 276   line 9   *feeding only on rumour and wild speculation.* See Cuffe's confession. Bruce, pp. 81-4.

page 276   line 18   *The Archduke of Austria.* In 1598 he had renounced his ecclesiastical orders and returned his Cardinal's hat to the Pope as a preliminary to marrying the Infanta of Spain.

page 278   line 9   *"Mistress Kitchenmaid."* The whole letter is printed in *Letters of Queen Elizabeth*, p. 279.

page 278   line 12   For Buckhurst's message and Essex's reply see *Records of the English Province of the Society of Jesus*, by H. Foley, S.J., i, 7.

page 280   line 2   *the truth about Hayward's book.* C.S.P. Dom. p. 539.

page 280   line 25   *gathered at Drury House.* See the two examinations of Sir Ferdinando Gorges in Hatfield, xi, 69, and C.S.P. Dom. p. 577. There is considerable discrepancy between the two versions.

page 288   line 1   *napkin still tacked round his neck.* Speed in *The History of Great Britain*, third edition, 1633, p. 1213.

page 289   line 26   *Sir John Leveson.* Hatfield, xi, 59. A pike was 16 feet long.

page 294   line 18   *Francis Bacon . . . loyalty would come before gratitude.* Bacon has suffered unnecessary calumny for his part in the trial. He was genuinely horrified at the rebellion, for it sinned against his most sacred principles. His attitude towards Essex had been entirely consistent; from the beginning he warned Essex that the Queen must come first. [See p. 88.] He had risked much for Essex's sake, and if there is any question of desertion, then it was rather Essex that deserted his adviser. In fact, however, Bacon was far less important in Essex's life than is usually supposed.

page 294   line 27   *Captain Thomas Lee.* C.S.P. Dom. pp. 562, 563, 584. Lee's action is extraordinary. On the day of his arrest he had written to his kinsman Sir Henry Lee, sending a list of the prisoners, and adding " my hopes are well strengthened that my true declaring myself in this time hath (if anything may) well confirmed Mr. Secretary and the Lords of me, which with your good notice to him I doubt not but will much prevail for me." [Hatfield, xi, 44.] Cecil, writing to Sir George Carew, said that Lee's " bloody practise " hastened Essex's death.

NOTES 349

page 295 line 17 *instructions were sent out to all the preachers.*
C.S.P. Dom. pp. 565, 584. At Paul's Cross the sermon was a great success. The preacher, as the Bishop of London reported to Cecil, " delivered to the people the whole matter of the arch traitor. The auditory was great (though the Lord Mayor and his brethren were absent), and the applause for her Majesty's deliverance from the mischiefs intended exceeding great, loud and joyous. The traitor is now laid out well in colours to every man's satisfaction that heard the sermon, as I suppose or could judge by men's countenances." Hatfield, xi, 55.

page 296 line 17 *to Westminster Hall for their trial.* There are several accounts of the trial, printed and manuscript, of which the completest is that by D. Jardine, who combined a number of sources into one narrative. Spedding analysed the proceedings in detail in vol. ii, chapter ix.

page 300 line 25 *The Lord Chief Justice Popham was the next witness.* It caused no astonishment that two of the judges in the case should have stepped down from the bench to give evidence against the accused; nor did the accused themselves protest. Unfair as the procedure may appear nowadays, it must be remembered that Essex's contemporaries had different conceptions of a trial of treason. Essex's actions were so open and notorious that there could be no argument. Even in cases where there was a doubt, the real trial was at the examination of the prisoners. If it was then decided to prosecute, the trial was rather a public demonstration of guilt than a weighing of the evidence.

page 309 line 10 *toleration of religion.* At a time when religious and political creeds were inseparable, freedom of speech and doctrine seemed as impossible as to-day in a Fascist, Nazi or Communist state.

page 315 and following *Dr. Thomas Dove.* Birch, ii, 475 and following.

page 318 line 27 *When Essex appeared before them.* Accounts of this interview by Cecil and Nottingham are to be found in Goodman, ii, 16, 17, and Winwood's Memorials, i, 300.

page 319 line 36 *Cuffe was sent for.* Birch, ii, 478. C.S.P. Dom. p. 588.

page 321 line 22 *instructions were sent.* C.S.P. Dom. p. 591.

page 322 line 1 *the Queen countermanded the order.* As often, there is some discrepancy in the sources, particularly in the details of the time when Essex was warned to prepare for death. In the letter sent by the Council, dated " Tuesday night," the Constable and Lieutenant of the Tower were instructed to visit Essex within half an hour after he had supped [C.S.P. Dom. p. 591]; in one account of the execution [*ibid.*, p. 592] Essex is reported to have spoken to the guard between 10 and 12 o'clock; in another account [ibid., p. 595] he was warned at 1 a.m. Camden says that the Queen countermanded the execution once. If so, the countermand was probably given in the early evening, and the order to proceed shortly before midnight.

page 322 line 6 *Nothing had come from the Tower.* There is, unfortunately, no contemporary account of Essex's last hours between the departure of Cecil and Nottingham on the Saturday and the coming of the divines at midnight on the Tuesday. He may have expected a reprieve, and so have been surprised by the summons; but there is no hint of it. Apparently, unless the romantic story of the Ring has some foundation in fact, he made no appeal to the Queen. Nor did he ask for his wife or children, or send any message to them, or to his mother or sisters; nor did he make any kind of will. I think it more likely that in these last days he lived in a state of religious torpor, entirely absorbed in himself; and that, with the aid of Master Ashton's fervid evangelical ministrations, he was persuaded to long for death. This religious strain in Essex was deep and powerful, and at other times during the last eighteen months he had been similarly affected by acute religious melancholia. Ashton had certainly a great influence over his emotions.

page 322 line 16 *to witness the execution.* There are accounts of the execution, appended to the descriptions of the trial, and in S.P. Dom. The official eyewitness's account was by Dr. Barlow, one of the divines; it was printed as an appendix to his sermon on the conspiracy.

The Sequel. The crowd fell on the headsman as he came out of the Tower, and he would have been killed had not the sheriffs rescued him. Those who delight in grim coincidence may note that Essex died eight years, to a day, after he was made a Councillor, and that he was buried near the body of Anne Boleyn, the Queen's mother.

Of the other conspirators, Southampton remained a prisoner in the Tower till after the Queen's death. Blount, Danvers, Davies, Meyrick and Cuffe were arraigned on 5th March, and condemned to death, the most telling evidence against them, if any was needed, being Essex's own written confession. Meyrick and Cuffe were executed at Tyburn on 13th March, Danvers and Blount were beheaded in the Tower on 18th March. The rest were spared, though heavy fines were laid on them, which, for the most part, were unpaid.

Essex's widow was married again, in 1603, to the Earl of Clanrickard. Penelope was divorced from Lord Rich in 1605 and married Charles Blount, now Earl of Devonshire; but he died in 1606, and she in 1607. Essex's old mother survived them all, lively to the last. She died in 1634 at the age of ninety-four.

INDEX

Albert, Cardinal Archduke of Austria, 95
Alva, Duke of, 36
Anderson, Sir Edmund, 296
Andrada, Emanuel, 82
Antonio, Don, 14, 26, 36, 40, 42, 44, 82
Arklow, 224-6
Armagh, 204
Ashley, Sir Anthony, 103, 110, 117, 120, 122, 125-6, 128
Ashton, Rev. Abdy, 292, 313, 315-18, 321-2
Athlone, 237
Audley, Lord, 11, 21
Aumont, Marshal d', 51
Axel, 18
Azores, 30, 123; expedition to, 142, 152 et seq., 171, 175

Babington's Plot, 24
Bacon, Anthony, 70-1, 269, 306; his services for Essex, 73, 80, 84, 127-8, 193-4
Bacon, Francis, 70-3; in service of Essex, 73-4; displeases Queen, 74, 76; seeks office, 76-8, 84-8; gift of land to, 88; advises Essex, 131-4, 188-9, 211, 249-50; on Hayward's book, 257; presents case against Essex, 263-4; seeks to help Essex, 268-9, 272, 294; at trial of Essex, 296, 305-6, 311
Bacon, Lady, 70-1, 81, 136
Bagnal, Sir Henry, 187, 204
Barlow, Dr. William, 127, 320-2
Baynham, Sir Edward, 279
Bedford, Earl of, 71, 279, 286
Berck, 18-20
Berkley, Sir Richard, 258
Biron, Marshal, 50-2, 55-7, 59, 63, 65

Blackwater Fort, 187-8, 204
Blount, Sir Charles, see Mountjoy, Lord
Blount, Sir Christopher, 95, 186, 282, 309; marriage of, 35; and Cadiz expedition, 110, 115, 123; and Azores expedition, 153, 155, 157, 166; an ill-counsellor, 164; in Ireland, 211, 217-18; and rebellion, 247, 281, 283, 285, 290, 296, 310, 319; confession of, 303
Bodley, Thomas, 125-7
Bouillon, Duc de, 102
Brachiano, Duke of, 279
Brett, Captain, 223
Bridges, Mistress, 139, 184
Brille, 8, 10
Brittany, 46-7, 51
Brooke, Sir Calisthenes, 216
Buckhurst, Thomas Sackville, Baron (Lord Treasurer), 65, 75, 129, 138, 180, 190, 276, 282; and disgrace of Essex, 251, 254, 269, 271, 279; and trial of Essex, 296-7, 300, 312-13
Burgh, Lord, 126, 135, 187-8, 239
Burghley, Lady, 70
Burghley, Lord, 16, 30, 34, 55, 69, 75, 79, 137, 140; and the young Essex, 2-3, 5; Essex's letters to, 3, 99, 125; and death of Mary of Scots, 25-7; wife of, 70-1; and Francis Bacon, 71-3; favours Coke, 78, 85; and the Queen, 86, 97, 129; letters of, to Essex, 130, 145, 146; desires peace, 174, 180-1, 183, 192; illness of, 192; death of, 202-3; funeral of, 206
Burghley, Lord Thomas, 10, 277, 287, 291
Bushell, Captain Edward, 290, 303
Butler, Sir Philip, 37

Cadiz, 29, 109–21, 127–9
Cahir Castle, 222–3, 230
Calais, 96–100, 183
Cambrai, 93
Carew, Sir George, 103, 142, 151, 194; and Cadiz expedition, 110, 113; in Ireland, 224, 247, 277
Carey, Henry, 229
Carey, Robert, 32, 58, 60
Carey, Sir Edward, 322
Cascaes, 42–3
Cashel, Pass of, 221
Cecil, Sir Robert, 55, 68, 69, 71, 75, 145, 171, 180, 194, 266–70; Essex's letters to, 65–6, 102, 103, 153–4, 169, 178, 218; appearance of, 79; and Lopez's plot, 82–3, 85; and Attorney-Generalship, 84–5; Howard's letter to, 98; appointed Secretary, 126; reconciliation of, with Essex, 138, 140, 144, 183, 185, 252; letters of, to Essex, 147, 185, 191; leads Commission to France, 182, 183–6, 189–92; letter of, to Southampton, 206; assists Essex, 207, 256, 307; and Essex's return from Ireland, 149–52, 254; rumoured to favour Infanta of Spain, 276–7, 307; and Essex's rebellion, 284, 293, 295–6; and Essex's slanders, 305–10, 319; Essex confesses to, 318–9
Chamberlain, Captain, 223
Cinque Ports, Wardenship of, 138–9, 141
Clifford, Captain Alexander, 111
Clifford, Sir Conyers, 54, 95–6, 128; and Cadiz expedition, 106, 110, 115, 119; in Ireland, 187, 237
Cobham, Henry Brooke, Lord, 202, 249, 291, 305, 319; and Wardenship of Cinque Ports, 138–9, 141, 276; rumoured to be plotting Essex's death, 283–4, 306

Cobham, William Brooke, Lord, 75, 138
Coke, Edward, 75–6, 85, 296; and Attorney-Generalship, 76, 78, 86; and Hayward's *Henry the Fourth*, 257, 266–7, 280; presents case against Essex, 262–3; and trial of Essex, 296, 298–300, 302–4, 310
Compton, Lord, 291, 322
Conference About the Next Succession to the Crown of England, 88–90, 309
Constable, Sir William, 226, 242
Conway, Sir Edward, 119, 123
Cromwell, Lord, 286–7
Cross, Sir Robert, 295
Cuffe, Henry, 125–8, 240, 243, 259–60; evil influence of, 259, 276, 319–20; dismissal of, 270, 272
Cumberland, Earl of, 137, 289–90, 291, 322

Danvers, Sir Charles, 211; plans to rescue Essex, 253, 257, 259–60, 272; part of, in rebellion, 280–1, 283, 285, 296; confession of, 303
Danvers, Sir Henry, 60, 211, 240, 242
Darcy, Sir Francis, 57–9, 240
Davies, Sir John, 280–1, 286, 289, 296
Davison, Secretary, 13–15, 24–5, 27
Delft, 11
Derby, Earl of, 75
Devereux, Dorothy, see Perrot, Lady
Devereux, Penelope, see Rich, Lady
Devereux, Walter, 1, 37, 40, 48, 54
Dieppe, 47–8, 60
Doesburg, 19–20
Doleman, R., book of, on Succession, 88–90, 309
Dombes, Prince de, 47, 51
Dort, 11
Douglas, Richard, 45
Dove, Dr. Thomas, 315

INDEX

Drake, Sir Francis, 29–30, 36, 40, 42–4, 92
Drumconragh, 241–2
Dublin, 2, 209, 257–8; Essex in, 218, 227; declaration of Captains at, 238–40, 246
Dudley, Robert, 4
Duyvenvoord, Sir Jan van, 110, 113, 124

Edmondes, Thomas, 87
Effingham, Lord, 291
Egerton, Lord Keeper, 251, 254, 256, 262, 265–6, 269, 296; letter of advice of, 196; Essex's letter to, 198, 263; in Essex House, 284–6, 289–91
Elizabeth, Queen, 27; and Essex's father, 1–2; and Leicester, 4–5, 34; Essex presented to, 7; vacillations of, 8, 24–5, 48, 96–8, 103–4, 131, 138–40, 179; and Leicester's Governorship, 13–16; and death of Mary of Scots, 24–7; Essex the favourite of, 28–9, 45, 147, 149; quarrels of, with Essex, 30–1, 137–9, 171–6, 178–9, 194–208; at Tilbury, 35; orders Essex to return to England, 38–9, 43–4, 57–9, 68; letters of, to Essex, 43, 67, 100, 107, 229, 234; helps Henri IV, 46–8, 54–5, 60, 63, 93, 96–100; Essex's letters to, 48, 55, 60–1, 143, 201, 204–5, 208, 256, 260, 270, 271, 272; angry with Essex, 54–5, 58; Privy Council of, 75; and Bacon, 76–8, 86; plots against, 83–6; difficulties of dealing with, 86; and siege of Calais, 96–100; critical of Essex, 102–3, 127, 171; dissatisfied with results of expeditions, 127–9, 171; Essex's relationship with, 131–4; receives Raleigh, 141; and Polish ambassador, 147; desires peace, 174, 181; French ambassador on,

176–8; yields to Essex, 178–9, 209; receives Essex's mother, 186; and Irish expedition, 210–11, 216–17, 219; Essex complains of treatment of, 217–18; Essex disobeys, 219, 233, 238; censures Essex, 229–36, 243–6; forbids Essex's return, 236; Essex surprises, 249–50; imprisons Essex, 251 *et seq.*; and illness of Essex, 255–6; cancels trial, 256, 263; and Irish knights, 265–6; signs warrant of execution, 321–2
Escovedo, John de, 80
Essex, Countess of (Lady Sidney), 21, 45, 253, 255–6, 258, 289, 292
Essex, Countess of, *see* Leicester, Countess of
Essex, Robert Devereux, Earl of, parentage and childhood of, 1–5; letters of, 3, 5, 37, 55, 65–6, 77, 99, 101, 104, 125, 136, 149, 151, 169, 198, 212, 217–18, 222, 226, 228, 255, 263, 268; comes to Court, 7; charm of, 7, 28, 179, 275; in Low Countries, 9–11, 13–14, 16–22; Sidney's bequest to, 21; communications of, with King of Scotland, 27, 45, 86, 277; the Queen's favourite, 28–9, 45, 130–2, 134, 147, 149; Master of Queen's Horse, 30; his dislike of Ralegh, 30–1; quarrels of, with Queen, 30–1, 137–9, 171–6, 178–9, 194–208; rivals of, 32–3, 79; and Armada, 33–5; joins Portuguese expedition, 36 *et seq.*; incurs Queen's anger, 38, 54–5, 58, 229–36, 243–6; Queen's letters to, 43, 67, 100, 107, 229, 234; and farm of sweet wines, 45, 260, 270–2, 274; marriage of, 45–6; commands French expedition, 47 *et seq.*; letters of, to Queen, 48, 55, 60–1, 143, 201, 204–5, 208, 256, 260, 270–2; bestows knighthoods,

23

60, 120, 238, 265-6; challenges Villars, 62; examples before, 69-70, 133; and Francis Bacon, 73-4, 87; intelligence service of, 73-4, 79-84, 130; as courtier, 74, 90-1; Privy Councillor, 75; seeks place for Bacon, 76-8, 84-8, and Lopez's plot, 83-5; growing power of, 87, 130; dangerous dedications to, 89-90, 214-15, 264, 267; secret instructions of, to Henri IV, 93-5; and relief of Calais, 96-100; prepares for voyages, 101 et seq., 142-9; and Cadiz voyage, 108 et seq., 126-9; his account of expedition, 125-9; enemies of, 127, 199, 211, 228; fits of depression of, 131, 251, 255; advised as to his behaviour to Queen, 131-4, 172-4, 196-8, 203-4; popularity of, 132, 134, 180, 192, 275; amours of, 136-7, 139, 184; is reconciled with Ralegh and Cecil, 138, 140, 144, 183, 185; Master of the Ordnance, 139; commands Azores expedition, 142 et seq.; fails to tell Ralegh of changed plans, 155, 163; weakness of, as commander, 163-4; prepares against Spanish invasion, 169-70; retires from Court, 171-4; illness of, 171, 208, 217, 252-6; refuses to sit in Council, 174, 176, 178, 204-5; opposed to peace, 174, 181, 192-4, 309; created Earl Marshal, 178-80; degeneration in character of, 179-80; de Maisse and, 181-2; allowed to purchase booty, 184; and Garter Feast, 190-1, 258-9; accused of courting popularity, 192-3, 215, 295; *Apology* of, 193-4, 259, 309; justifies his anger, 198-201; arrogance of, 209, 213; appointed to command in Ireland, 209-10, 211-13; compared to Bolingbroke, 215; instructions of, 215-16; complains of ill-treatment, 217-18, 228-9, 232, 236; in Ireland, 218 et seq.; disobedience of, 219, 233, 238, 247, 250, 254, 262, 265; asks for reinforcements, 219-20, 228, 234, 236-8, 243; Queen censures proceedings of, 229-36, 243-6; makes truce with Tyrone, 241-3, 254; plans rebellion, 247, 280-3; returns to England, 247, 248-9; disgrace of, 251 et seq., 274; accused of aiming at Crown, 253, 295, 307, 310; plans for rescue of, 253, 257-60; religious solace of, 255, 277-9, 313-4; cancelled trial of, 256, 263; a prisoner in Essex House, 258-9; official censure of, 262-5; released, 270; believes in Popish plots, 276-7; " plots to murder," 282-5, 306; summoned by Council, 282-3; seeks support in City, 283, 286-8; rebellion of, 284 et seq.; surrender of, 292-3; trial of, 296 et seq.; verdict against, 312-14; confessions of, 315-21; execution of, 321 et seq.

Essex, Walter Devereux, Earl of, 1-2

Essex House, Essex a prisoner in, 258-9; rebellious talk in, 277-82; Counsellors detained in, 284-6, 288, 290-1; in state of siege, 291-3

Falmouth, 168, 171
Faro, 122-3
Fayal, 153, 155-60
Ferrol, 137, 142, 150-2
Fleming, Sir Thomas, Solicitor-General, 87, 263, 296
Flores, 153-4
Flushing, 8, 10-11, 104
Fontaine, M. de la, 125, 127

Fortescue, Sir John, 75, 85, 129, 139
France, campaign in, 46 *et seq.*; and war with Spain, 93, 105, 174, 190; commissioners sent to, 180, 182, 183-6, 189-92
Fuentes, Count de, 40, 83, 85

Gama, Ferrara de, 82, 85
Garter Feast, 190, 258-9
Gerrard, Sir Thomas, 95, 110, 115, 248
Gifford, Gilbert, 23-4
Gilpin, George, 130
Goodyere, Sir Henry, 21
Gorges, Sir Ferdinando, 60, 66, 150; and Azores expedition, 142, 148; and rebellion, 280-1, 283-4, 290-1, 296, 300-1; confession of, 301-2
Gournay, 55-8
Gratiosa, 153, 160
Grave, surrender of, 17
Greville, Fulke, 32, 126, 208, 212, 291
Grey, Lord, 202, 248-9, 297; in Ireland, 220, 224; and Southampton, 278-9, 285, 301; and Essex's rebellion, 289, 291
Groin, the, 38-9, 123

Hagan, Henry, 241
Hague, the, 12
Harington, Sir Henry, 223, 226-7
Harington, Sir John, 277
Harsnett, Rev. Samuel, 267
Harvey, Sir William, 210
Hatton, Sir Christopher, 65
Hawkins, Admiral, 92
Hawkins, Dr. Henry, 130
Hayward, John, *King Henry IV* of, 214-15, 257, 264; examination of, 266-7, 280
Heneage, Sir Thomas, 15-16, 75, 85
Henri IV, King of France, 60-1, 93; seeks help of Elizabeth, 46-7, 93-6, 102; Essex and, 46, 50, 93, 130; and siege of Rouen, 51-4, 63-5, 67-8; secret instructions to, 93-5; and peace with Spain, 174, 180-1, 189-90; marriage of, 278
Henry the Fourth, Hayward's book on, 214-15, 257, 264, 266-7, 280
Herbert, Dr. John, 184
Hoby, Edward, 120
Hoby, Sir Thomas Posthumas, 71
Hollock, Count, 17-19
Howard, Lord Charles (Lord Admiral), 33, 75, 84-5, 92, 95-6, 144-5, 179-80, 190, 194, 210, 249, 251, 254, 266, 277; anger of, 98-9, 101, 106; and Cadiz expedition, 104, 108-9, 111-12, 114-15, 117-24, 126, 128-9, 163, 171; created Earl of Nottingham, 171, 178; and rebellion of Essex, 289, 291-3, 295-6; Essex confesses to, 318-19
Howard, Lord Henry, 208, 249
Howard, Lord Thomas, 140, 171, 190, 249, 291, 314, 318, 322; and Cadiz expedition, 95, 103, 110, 113, 117-18, 121-2; and Azores expedition, 142-3, 145, 148, 153, 157, 161; at trial of Essex, 297, 312
Hunsdon, Lord Henry (Lord Chamberlain), 75, 138, 172, 180-1, 190, 249
Huntingdon, Countess of, 253
Huntingdon, Earl of, 26, 38, 92

Ibarra, Stephen de, 83
Indian treasure fleet, 129, 142, 152, 154-5, 160-1
Ireland, Spanish help for, 105, 137, 142, 170, 227; rebellion in, 187-8, 194, 204, 209, 257; corruption of officials in, 188; Essex appointed to command in, 210, 211-13, 215-16; Essex's campaigns in,

219 et seq.; making of knights in, 238, 265–6; Mountjoy in, 257–9, 273; proposal to bring army from, 258–60

James VI, King of Scotland, 27, 45, 86, 253, 258–9, 277
Jermyn, Sir Thomas, 168, 240

Kilkenny, 221–2
Killigrew, Mr., 195, 207–8
Killigrew, Sir Henry, 48, 56
Knollys, Sir Francis, 1, 4, 9, 25, 37–8, 75
Knollys, Sir Robert, 151, 153–4
Knollys, Sir William (Controller), 194, 208, 214, 249, 266, 270; appeals to Essex, 195, 203; detained in Essex House, 284–6, 289–91; at trial of Essex, 308–9

Lee, Captain Thomas, 294–6
Lee, Henry, 253, 258–9
Lee, Sir Henry, 190, 207
Leicester, Countess of, 2, 4–5, 14, 31, 35, 186, 258
Leicester, Earl of, 2, 4–5, 7, 8 et seq., 25, 27, 30, 33–5, 69, 265–6
Leighton, Sir Thomas, 48, 56–7, 67
Leinster, 219
Leveson, Sir John, 289–90, 310
Leyden, 13
Lincoln, Earl of, 291
Lisbon, 39, 41–2, 129, 147
Littleton, John, 280
Loftus, Lord Chancellor, 247
Lopez, Dr. Roderigo, 81–6
Lord Mayor, raises men and ships, 33, 97–8; and Essex's rebellion, 284, 287, 289
Lovelace, Sir William, 240, 243
Low Countries, 183; Leicester in, 8–22, 30; Squadron from, with English fleet, 104–5, 143, 153–4;

send commissioners to France, 180

MacPhelim, Brian, 2
McFeaghe, Phelim, 226
Maise, Hurault de, 174–82
Markham, Sir Griffin, 60
Mary, Queen of Scots, 1, 9, 23–7, 80
Maryborough, 220–1
Matthew, Toby, 90
Maurice, Count, 14, 18
Mayne, Duke of, 51, 62
Medina Sidonia, Duke of, 119, 121
Meyrick, Sir Gelby, 83, 120, 128, 164, 270, 276, 282; and Azores expedition, 155–6, 158–9
Monson, Captain, 114, 117
Montpensier, Duke of, 52
Morgan, Sir Matthew, 110, 116, 240
Mounteagle, Lord, 281–2, 285, 304
Mountford, Dr. Thomas, 320–2
Mountjoy, Lord (Charles Blount), 6, 32, 120, 171, 190–1, 249, 319; Essex's duel with, 33; and Azores expedition, 142–3, 153; and Ireland, 209, 257–9, 273, 278; and plans to rescue Essex, 253, 257–60, 272; Queen's letter to, 278
Munster, 187, 224, 229, 235

Nevers, Duke of, 51
Neville, Sir Henry, 295
Nieuport, 273, 276
Nimeguen, 18
Normandy, 47, 60
Norris, Edward, 19
Norris, Sir John, in Low Countries, 8, 17–21; and Portuguese expedition, 36, 38–40, 42–4; in France, 47; in Ireland, 187, 239
Norris, Sir Thomas, 209
North, Lord, 11, 18, 21, 27, 249
North, Sir Robert, 21
Nottingham, Earl of, see Howard, Lord Charles

INDEX

Noyon, 48-50, 52
Nuys, 18

O, Monsieur D', 50
Offaly, 232, 244
O'Neill, Con, 242
Ormonde, Earl of, 34, 170, 188, 220, 230-1
Overall, Dr. John, 255
Oxford University, 65

Parma, Duke of, 9, 23, 33; in Low Countries, 17-20, 30; in France, 46, 52, 56, 65, 67
Parsons, Robert, 89
Paulet, Sir Amyas, 23, 71
Pelham, Sir William, 18-20
Peniche, 39-40
Penzance, 92
Percy, Sir Charles, 60, 223, 281
Percy, Sir Joscelyn, 281
Perez, Antonio, 80-2, 93
Periam, Sir William, 296
Perrot, Lady (Dorothy Devereux), 1, 6, 256, 258
Perrot, Sir Thomas, 6, 20
Peyton, Sir John, 280, 297, 322
Phellippes, Thomas, 23-4
Philip II, King of Spain, 29, 36, 74, 80, 134, 209
Picard, Chevalier, 62
Pico, 153
Plymouth, 101, 106, 135, 144-5, 148, 168, 170
Polish Ambassador, 147
Popham, Sir John, Lord Chief Justice, 257, 284-6, 289-91, 296-7, 300
Port Royal, 112-15, 117-19
Portugal, 36 *et seq.*
Preston, Sir Amyas, 119
Puckering, Lord Keeper, 74-5

Ralegh, Sir Walter, 7, 171, 178, 186, 249, 276, 281, 305, 319; Essex's rivalry with, 30-1, 69; sent to the Tower, 74; Essex's letter to, 101; and expedition to Cadiz, 95, 103, 106, 110, 112-15, 119, 121, 127-9; reconciliation of, with Essex, 138, 140, 183; restored to Captaincy of Guard, 140-1; and Azores expedition, 142, 145, 151-65, 168, 171; letter of, to Cecil, 145, 147-8; at Fayal, 155-60; rumoured to be plotting Essex's death, 283-4, 306; meets with Gorges, 283-4, 301; at execution of Essex, 322
Ratcliffe, Sir Alexander, 237
Reynolds (secretary), 125-6, 128
Rich, Lady (Penelope Devereux), 1, 5-6, 45, 256, 258, 289, 292, 319
Rich, Lord, 6, 37-8, 45, 249
Richard the Second, The Tragedy of, 215, 282
Robsart, Amy, 4
Rotterdam, 11
Rouen, siege of, 51-7, 59, 62-8
Russell, Lord John, 71
Russell, Sir William, 11, 20, 187, 239
Rutland, Roger Manners, Earl of, 87, 211, 249, 279, 285, 297, 303

St. Lawrence, Sir Christopher, 223, 248
St. Michael's, 153, 160-5
St. Pol, Count, 99-100
Salisbury, Captain Owen, 286

Sancy, M. de, 98
Sandys, Lord, 285, 292, 297, 303
Santa Cruz, Marquis of, 30
Schenck, Colonel Martin, *see* Skink, Colonel
Scrope, Lady, 270-1
Sentleger, Sir Warham, 242
Sheffield, Lady Douglas, 4
Shirley, Sir Anthony, 148-9, 155
Shrewsbury, Earl of, 190, 249

Sidney, Lady, *see* Essex, Countess of
Sidney, Sir Philip, 5–6, 10, 13, 18–21, 26, 45, 70
Sidney, Sir Robert, 21, 26, 130, 138–9, 184, 291–2
Skink, Colonel, 16–19
Sligo, O'Connor, 237
Sluys, 30
Smythe, Sheriff, 287–8
Southampton, Countess of (Elizabeth Vernon), 184, 206–7, 210, 258
Southampton, Henry Wriothesley, Earl of, 164, 166, 260, 272; enters Essex's service, 87; in disgrace at Court, 184, 206–7, 210; marriage of, 206–7; and Mastership of Horse, 210, 219, 233–4; in Ireland, 211, 220, 225–6, 240, 241–2, 259; part of, in rebellion, 247, 280–1, 285, 292; plans rescue of Essex, 253, 257; Essex's farewell to, 255; and Grey, 278–9, 285, 301; trial of, 296 *et seq*; pleads for his life, 313–14
Southwell, Sir Robert, 113–14
Spain, and the Low Countries, 8, 95, 183; war with, 29–30, 33, 92, 183, 192; expeditions against, 92, 95, 101 *et seq.*, 108 *et seq.*, 137, 140; expeditions of, against England, 29, 33–4, 134–7, 142, 168–71, 234; makes peace with France, 190
Spain, Infanta of, and succession, 276–7, 288, 307
Spanish Armada, 29, 33–4
Stafford, Sir Edward, 4
Standen, Anthony, 79–80, 83
Stanhope, Sir John, 291
Stanley, Sir William, 30
Star Chamber, Court of, 27, 75; Essex censured by, 253–5
Sussex, Earl of, 110, 122, 279

Tercera, 153–4, 161
Tinoco, Emanuel Louis, 82, 85–6

Turenne, Viscount, 46
Tyrone, Hugh O'Neill, Earl of, rebellion of, 187–9, 204, 231, 240; Essex's instructions regarding, 216; plan to attack, 219, 234–5, 245, 263; Essex makes truce with, 241–3, 250, 254

Ulster, colonisation of, 1–2; rebellion in, 187; campaigning, 219, 227, 234–5, 237–46
Unton, Sir Henry, 48, 56, 63, 68, 93–5
Utrecht, 17

Vere, Sir Francis, 95, 97, 130, 213–14; and Cadiz expedition, 101, 103, 106, 110, 113, 115–17, 123, 163; and Azores expedition, 142–3, 155, 164, 166; justifies Essex, 175
Vernon, Elizabeth, *see* Southampton, Countess of
Villa Franca, 162–3, 165–7
Villars, Marquis of, 50, 54, 62, 64–5

Walshe, Lieutenant Peter, 223, 227
Walsingham, Sir Francis, 9, 16, 23, 25, 27, 34, 45–6, 70–1, 80
Wanstead, 171, 174, 206, 208
Warwick, Ambrose Dudley, Earl of, 27
Warwick, Countess of, 30–1
Waterford, 222–4
Whitgift, John, Archbishop of Canterbury, 3, 75, 79, 126–7, 259, 262, 264, 267, 293
Wicklow, 223–4, 226–7
Wilford, Sir Thomas, 97
Wilkes, Sir Thomas, 184, 186
Williams, Sir Roger, 19–20, 30, 37–42, 47–9, 63, 68, 91, 93, 163

Willoughby, Lord, 18, 21, 26, 212, 277
Wingfield, Sir Edward, 37, 110, 240
Wingfield, Sir John, 21, 95, 110, 113, 116, 118, 120
Wingfield, Sir Richard, 110
Wolfe, John, 267
Wolley, Sir John, 75
Woodhouse, Sir William, 110

Worcester, Earl of, 190, 249, 251, 279, 284, 300
Wotton, Henry, 128, 242
Wotton, John, 54
Wotton, Sir Edward, 138

Yelverton, Sergeant, 262, 296, 298

Zutphen, battle of, 20–1